T0354837

PANDEMONIUM

MIKE LAUTERBORN

authorHOUSE

AuthorHouse™
1663 Liberty Drive
Bloomington, IN 47403
www.authorhouse.com
Phone: 833-262-8899

Published by AuthorHouse 07/15/2020

ISBN: 978-1-7283-6640-1 (sc)
ISBN: 978-1-7283-6639-5 (e)

Library of Congress Control Number: 2020912546

Print information available on the last page.

This book is printed on acid-free paper.

DEDICATION

To my late Mom, who passed in May 2013 and was spared the misery of the Covid-19 crisis, though she endured her own pain in battling pancreatic cancer. A nurse in her early career and general do-it-yourselfer, she would have risen to the occasion during the pandemic.

To my Dad, who marked his 84th birthday in the midst of the outbreak, and dealt with isolation and the strangeness of the situation like a champion, preparing lavish meals to dine on his deck, walking around his neighborhood for miles every week and always looking ahead and eager to get back to traveling and exploring more of the world.

The Roaring 20s. That's what we labeled the decade that lay ahead. We readied ourselves to greet it with a confident, celebratory and forward-looking attitude.

As the final hours of 2019 ticked away, many voiced their New Year's intentions and hopes. Ironically, one social media poster wished for "a cure for the common cold" along with trivial things like "gum that doesn't lose its flavor" and "Ziploc bag closures in every cereal box".

For my part, and buoyed by my 55th birthday celebration in New York City the day before, I paced from my beach area neighborhood to the local theatre company in our cheery, shoreline Fairfield, Connecticut downtown to enjoy a New Year's Eve rock 'n roll show. It was a fantastic, wild performance with a joyous midnight toast.

Meanwhile, on the other side of the world, China reported a cluster of cases of pneumonia in people that had visited the Huanan Seafood Wholesale Market in Wuhan, Hubei Province. The seeds of the tsunami had been planted.

CHAPTER 1

HAPPY NEW YEAR?

New Years Day, 2020. With no awareness of what was transpiring across the globe, my 20-year-old son, Phil, and I welcomed the new year at home with homemade raisin and cinnamon waffles with bacon and coffee. He was on a month-long break from school and we ate together, admiring a bright red cardinal in the hedge at the back of our house. Our mood was peaceful and hopeful. A local personality, Ira Joe Fisher, sighed about the fading holidays in a Facebook post, remarking about "stepping into a new now. With the happy hope that this year will be different by being better than last year. The year will do as the year will do. It's up to you and up to me to provide the better part. By BEING better. By DOING better. Rising from the calm and stepping into 2020… better."

Another post reminded us of the encouraging words of Ralph Waldo Emerson: "He is rich who owns the day, and no one owns the day who allows it to be invaded with fret and anxiety." A thought that we would circle back to for comfort before much passage of time.

In the day's news, we read about soldiers from the 82nd Airborne Division out of Fort Bragg, NC deploying to Iraq, where an attack initiated by Iran-supported militiamen had taken place at our U.S. Embassy. We wished our boys well, promising to keep them in our prayers and thanking them for their service.

My 83-year-old Dad checked in by text from southern California. Mid-December, he had flown from his home state of North Carolina out to San Francisco and boarded the Carnival Grand Princess cruise liner to sail down to Mexico. The liner returned him to SF on Dec. 28 and he set off

1

by car headed south down the California coast, to visit friends all along the way. His check-in came from Burbank in SoCal. Three days later, he was back home.

Later that first week of January, our community mourned the closing of a local pizzeria after "50 years of slices", the shutdown of a cinema that had offered wonderful offbeat films and the passing of an iconic steakhouse. At the same time, we looked forward to a year of celestial events that included 13 full moons, and we mused about the charming towns we might visit around our state when the weather warmed.

Jan. 5. With an ache, we followed the terrible reports of widespread brushfires across Australia. To date, 24 people and over 500 million animals had died while an area the size of Belgium burned.

That evening, a Sunday, I went to my local brewery in adjacent Black Rock for a beer or two, bumping into a couple of longtime friends I hadn't seen in ages. We caught up, and had a burger as well at an eatery next door, running into more friends there. We hugged and sat close to each other and clinked glasses and shared food.

The following morning, I woke with a sore throat, chills, a fever, headache, pink eye and body aches, and my lower lip had swelled up. I assumed it was the flu, though its presentation was strange — the side effects in particular. I had never been vaccinated for the flu, choosing instead to treat it like I would any cold, with natural foods, tea with honey and lemon, rest, over-the-counter medications and throat lozenges, to build up my natural antibodies. My quick attention to it mitigated its impact I think and the bout passed in a few days, during which time I kept mostly to myself.

Jan. 7. Chinese health authorities confirmed that the "cluster" of pneumonia cases they had reported a week ago was associated with a novel coronavirus, which they labeled 2019-nCoV. We barely noted the report, instead marveling at new luxury car releases, celebrating the rise in the bald eagle population across Connecticut and frowning about new reports from Australia that animal losses had mounted to over 1.25 billion. Announcements of fundraisers, pledges and relief concerts related to the latter dominated the news.

Jan. 9. Our attention was drawn to the downing of a Ukrainian airliner, with 176 people on board, by a surface-to-air missile fired by Iran. The aircraft was thought to have been mistaken as a threat — a U.S. response to Iran firing missiles just hours earlier at two Iraqi bases where Americans were stationed.

Puerto Rico was rattled by a series of earthquakes the following day, knocking out power, damaging structures and driving people to shelters. Here in New England, our weather had gone haywire, with temperatures tickling the 60-degree mark, certainly not usual for our winter. Days later, volcanoes erupted in Japan, the Philippines and Mexico. Our planet seemed restless and agitated.

Mid-January, we cheered on the Australian Navy, which made an unprecedented beer run down under, delivering 800 gallons of brew to stranded residents. We were glad, too, of rain that also arrived there, to help put out the ruthless brushfires.

The month bore on, bringing news of the U.K.'s Prince Harry and Meghan Markle departing the royal family, a setback in Australia in which rainfall had created flash flooding, and "prayers" for Floridians as the temps across their state dropped into the 20s, causing iguanas to drop out of trees. Meanwhile, our local community busied itself with art openings, food festivals, chili competitions and, in Asian households, celebrations of the Lunar New Year. Life seemed to be playing out more or less as usual.

Jan. 19. A 35-year-old man, with a four-day history of cough and fever, visited an urgent care clinic in Snohomish County, Washington. He shared that he had recently visited family in Wuhan, China. Subsequent tests confirmed that he was positive for 2019-nCoV. It was the first identified case in the United States.

That confirmation wasn't at all on my radar though and I busied myself that day shuttling my sophomore son Phil and a backseat full of his belongings to his UConn dormitory apartment in Stamford, CT. It was to be his first experience living away from home.

Jan. 23. My world traveler Dad was wheels up again flying to Myanmar to help build a house in Thanatpin with a Habitat for Humanity team. His flight route was North Carolina to New York to Hong Kong and finally to Yangon (formerly known as Rangoon and the largest city in Myanmar). On a three-hour layover in Hong Kong, he messaged us, "Lots of people are wearing masks, even the stewardesses, because of the new China flu epidemic. Wish me luck!" It was the first time the "coronavirus" really entered my thoughts, though from initial photos he later relayed, of his team huddled together and close encounters with villagers, there seemed to be no related local concern, and no cases had been identified there. However, China's cases now numbered 571, according to WHO, which had begun issuing daily situation reports.

Jan. 26. Our hearts stopped when we learned about the loss of L.A. Lakers basketball legend Kobe Bryant, his 13-year-old daughter and fellow passengers killed in a helicopter crash in California. USA Today ran a front page story about the tragedy the following day. In a sidebar was an article headlined, "Rush is on to develop vaccine for coronavirus", relating that drugmakers were "hustling to make a vaccine to counter the rapidly spreading respiratory virus that has sickened at least 1,975 people in China and five in the United States."

Jan. 31. My concerns about the virus heightened when my Dad let me know his return travel plans were being adjusted because of the increasing outbreak. There were now 9,720 confirmed cases in China, including 12 cases in Hong Kong, and the infection had spread to 19 countries. Dad's original ticketed route home called for him to fly first to Hong Kong and then to New York and on down to North Carolina. He messaged, "It's possible that Cathay Pacific will cancel our flights through Hong Kong or that U.S. airports will close to flights from Mainland China and Hong Kong. Habitat is trying to book us flights from Yangon to Dubai to JFK. Tentatively they've got me on an Emirates flight leaving early Sunday morning. I'll keep you posted. Many flights are already sold out, going anywhere away from Southeast Asia. The medical supply stores are also sold out of masks. I had one home from my days in China; I wish I'd thought to bring it."

That evening, I attended an art show opening at our local library. I noticed one guest wearing a face mask, but didn't give it too much thought. When I emerged from the gathering and walked across the street to my car, I saw that the left side passenger door had been significantly dented. Footage from a library security camera later determined that someone had come down the road and executed a horrendous three-point turn, backing into my car in the process. The footage didn't capture the license plate of the offender. Another example of a disturbance in the Force.

Feb. 1. My Dad reported that his group was successful in booking flights home that would avoid coronavirus hot spots. He detailed that he would leave Yangon, Myanmar early morning tomorrow and fly to Hamad International Airport in Doha, Qatar. He would spend more than half a day there on layover before boarding a second flight in the middle of the night to NYC, arriving early the next day. From there, it would be a hop to Raleigh Durham, NC. I wished him safe travels, advised lots of hand washing and suggested he secure a mask if he was able to.

Feb. 2. WHO reported over 14,411 confirmed cases now in China along with 146 cases outside of the country, mostly confined to Western Pacific and Southeast Asian areas. A photo in my social media feed that day showed a mass of Chinese citizens, all wearing face masks, walking through a public thoroughfare.

Here at home, Groundhog Day took place with the usual rodent humor and, later, families and friends gathered together to watch Super Bowl LIV, pitting the San Francisco 49ers against the Kansas City Chiefs. The Chiefs won the day 31-20 but it was the halftime show, featuring Jennifer Lopez and Shakira shaking their Latina booties, that captured the most attention and buzz.

A social media post encouraged "Within four weeks, the maple sap will be flowing. Within six weeks, the earliest migrating birds will begin to arrive in numbers. Within eight weeks, the early spring wildflowers will emerge from the earth. You will feel the warm sun on your face again." Tired of winter, we were hopeful for the brighter days ahead.

Feb. 3. Dad arrived safely back in the U.S., checking in from JFK, reporting, "Loooooooonnnnngggg day's flights! Left the hotel in Yangon at 5AM Sunday, Burma time, flew 7 hours to Doha, Qatar, then had a 13-hour layover in Doha, then a 14-hour flight from Doha to JFK that arrived an hour late, which meant that by the time I got through the TSA line I missed the flight to RDU. I'm in the AA Flagship Lounge now 'til I board a flight to Reagan National and finally RDU. I haven't added all that up yet but I will when I get home. Door to door I'll bet it'll be close to forty elapsed hours!"

Feb. 4. President Trump delivered his State of the Union address, highlighting his administration's successes before a sharply party-divided House of Representatives. Speaker of the House Nancy Pelosi, his bitter foe, tore up her copy of his speech as he concluded his presentation. The following day, the President avoided impeachment when he was acquitted by the U.S. Senate on charges that he had withheld aid to Ukraine in return for investigating Democratic presidential candidate Sen. Joe Biden's son's business affairs in that country. The expected "not guilty" judgement was decided almost exclusively along party lines, 52-48.

Feb. 8. Another report from China: "The Wuhan coronavirus outbreak is now deadlier than SARS", Bloomberg News noted. In fact, 34,598 cases and 723 deaths had been confirmed there, according to WHO. We paused for a second, no longer, continuing to flit about to restaurants, movies, galleries, theaters and breweries. Valentine's Day transpired with expected romantic outings. We laughed to see a photo of a couple that won an exclusive Valentine's dinner in the middle of NYC's Grand Central Station, scheduled at 2am when the Station was emptiest so that they wouldn't be interrupted by the usual crush of commuters.

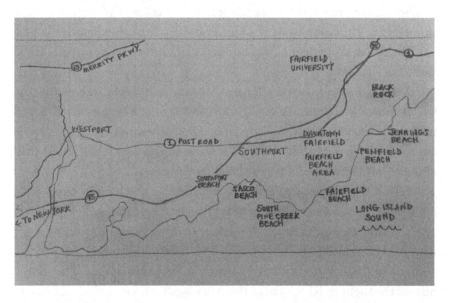

The week of **February 17**, we jammed at local Mardi Gras celebrations and live music shows, pressed together munching on boiled crawfish and tipping back beers. It was the last time we would feel so carefree. A wave of unimaginable grief was quickly building.

February 26. WHO confirmed 78,191 confirmed cases and 2,718 deaths in China along with 2,918 infections and 44 deaths across 37 other countries. As a precautionary measure, several Connecticut universities started cancelling certain study abroad programs (eg. in Italy) and recalling students back to the U.S. For the first time, we felt impacted in our state and parents worried about their children overseas, anxious for their safe return.

February 27. With 186 cases and three deaths, Japan took the bold step of closing its schools nationwide to control the spread of the virus. We wondered if other countries would follow suit.

That evening, I attended a local fundraiser held in a downtown restaurant. It was the first time I felt nervous around a crowd of people, in light of the virus. I was very conscious of where I placed my drink, carefully selected bites from a passed around food tray and elbow bumped people in greeting.

Phil had come home from school in Stamford last night and awoke saying he wasn't feeling well. His symptoms, as the illness dug in, included a fever, sore throat that felt like shards of glass when he swallowed, body aches, fatigue, dizziness, a nagging cough, heaviness in his chest and chills. It seemed like the flu, and yet more severe. For a solid week, I offered every aid I knew: throat lozenges; decongestant; gargling with hot salt water; green tea with honey, real lemon juice and slivers of ginger; severe cold gel caps both day and night; chicken noodle soup; hot showers; plenty of rest. I washed his clothes and bedding often and continually wiped everything down. He skipped several days of school but thankfully and gradually healed, though the cough hung around for another week. Had he had a bout with the coronavirus? We wouldn't ever know but, in reflection, suspected he likely did.

February 28. With 59 cases now in the United States, my Town of Fairfield issued a statement on the coronavirus, offering prevention tips and response guidance.

February 29. Fairfield issued another statement, this time with regard to coronavirus preparedness planning townwide. I took that in stride and, that evening, ducked out to attend an outdoor "ice bar bash" at a local restaurant. I looked on with a bit of concern as people danced closely together and lined up to press their mouths against an ice luge through which vodka shots were poured.

Meanwhile, the Centers for Disease Control and Prevention (CDC) reported America's first death from the virus — a male in his 50s at a hospital in Washington state.

March 2. At this point, the U.S. had only 62 confirmed cases, and they were concentrated on the West coast. Seemingly safe here in the East, we laughed about a social media image of a wreath of garlic on a door labeled "Italian vaccine against coronavirus" and grumbled about a plastic bag ban that had gone into effect in our state and how that would present challenges shopping.

March 3. Tornadoes struck Nashville, TN, killing over 20 people and causing widespread damage. It was a cruel blow as our anxieties about the virus grew. Our hearts went out to the folks there.

March 5. U.S. cases doubled to 129 but the outbreak still seemed remote to us in the Northeast. I giggled watching a YouTube video post by Vic DiBitetto, known for his frantic "I gotta get the bread and milk" post that became a go-to amusement every time there was a snowstorm. Now dressed up to his neck in a trash bag, he had switched it up with a new phrase, "I gotta get the gloves and soap!", referring to protective gear to shield him from the coronavirus.

Later that day, we learned that at least 200 people in our state were being monitored for the coronavirus and had been told to self-quarantine. And yet we still joked with memes like a picture of the band The Cure slugged, "I'm no expert on Covid-19, but this is The Cure". Covid-19 had become the new handle for the virus, standing for Coronavirus Disease 2019.

March 6. Late afternoon, I attended the opening of a relaunched bar and restaurant in town. Fairfield's First Selectwoman was there along with other town officials. I offered elbow greetings and winced when someone preferred to shake hands. I cleaned my fingers with hand sanitizer that I kept in my car and drove east to a brewery for a cask beer festival. The event was sold out and the younger oriented attendees didn't seem to be at all concerned about the coronavirus. I felt a bit anti-social when I offered elbow bumps there and again hand sanitized upon departure.

March 7. New York Gov. Andrew Cuomo declared a state of emergency after confirming 76 cases of coronavirus in his state. While a bit concerned about that news, I attended another very busy brewery event in the afternoon then an annual party at Fairfield's nature center. Again, I was careful about selecting food off trays and placed a napkin over my drinking glass when I set it down, but otherwise joked with fellow attendees about new ways to greet each other as handshakes and kisses hello were discouraged with a notice at the check-in table. With humor, we bumped elbows, did "jazz hands", offered Spock greetings and tapped feet.

March 8. With 5,883 cases, Italy announced that it would be quarantining 16 million of its countrymen and closed everything from gyms and pools to museums and ski resorts to contain the virus spread. Again, concerning but distant. Mid-afternoon, I took in a classical concert and visited another brewery to celebrate International Women's Day, photographing friends and staff in celebratory mode. I didn't know it then, but these were the last public gatherings I would attend in March.

Later, I read that the State Dept. was urging Americans not to travel on cruise ships at this time and that NYC had issued new commuter guidelines for its transit systems.

March 9. I welcomed the day with my girlfriend, Jenny, a classical pianist, at her home in Westport. We didn't know it then, but it was the last day I would see her in person for weeks to come as we soon decided to self-isolate at our own houses in fear of giving each other or family members the virus. FaceTime, text messages and email became our new norm. We were officially in an "isolationship".

Later that morning, I brought my cat to the vet for her biannual exam. I toted her in a carrier and was concerned that the tech there, who was bare-handed, touched the handle. Hand sanitizing followed.

In the news, U.S. cases nearly doubled again, to 213, and we learned that the Port Authority of New York and New Jersey chief had tested positive for the coronavirus. Therapists noted an increase in new patients suffering anxiety. Bill and Melinda Gates pledged $100 million to the virus response. Local businesses began posting signs asking people to stay home if they were experiencing respiratory infection symptoms. Experts opined that the virus could live on your cell phone for nine days and advised on how to clean it. Rhode Island's governor declared a State of Emergency.

March 10. With 24 cases, Ireland canceled all of its St. Patrick's Day parades. Meanwhile, U.S. cases more than doubled again, to 472, and the NCAA wrestled with what do about about upcoming college basketball tournament games and March Madness, given the large crowds they attract. Boston followed Ireland's cue and canceled its own St. Patrick's Day Parade out of an "abundance of caution", a phrase that gained sudden popularity.

Local dominoes started tumbling. Norwalk, CT's mayor announced that schools would close March 12 and all city gatherings had been put on hold. Westport and Weston schools went on adjusted schedules to allow teachers to prep for potential extended closings and a move to online instruction. Hartford, CT postponed its St. Pat's Parade. Quinnipiac University went online with classes for the rest of its Spring semester. Gas prices were cited as likely to fall below $2 per gallon in coming weeks. The situation was becoming increasingly nerve wracking.

March 11. More local hits. Fairfield Theatre Company postponed its annual St. Patrick's Day show. Westport, CT public schools suddenly closed. Milford, CT's Lauralton Hall closed for the balance of the week due to the possibility of a parent of a student being exposed to the coronavirus. Weston, CT schools announced closure until further notice. Greenwich, CT schools closed through next week. NYC's St. Pat's Day Parade was canceled for the first time in more than 250 years. Pres. Trump initiated a month-long suspension of flights from Europe, excluding the UK. Italy, with 10,149 cases and 631 deaths, closed all stores except for groceries, pharmacies and those selling essentials.

The "bombs" were falling all around us now. And yet, there were normal pursuits still to be savored, like the TV viewing that evening of an ACC Men's Basketball tournament game between the UNC Tar Heels and Syracuse Orangemen. My dad, who lives specifically in Chapel Hill, NC and had taught for 20+ years at UNC, and I had adopted the ritual of watching these UNC match-ups from our respective home areas and commenting on them via text during the games. We didn't realize then that this would be the last NCAA game of the year, as the organizing body shut the whole thing down the next day.

CHAPTER 2

THE PANIC BEGINS

March 12. The shit really hit the fan — a day I define as Quarantine Day 1. First, Darien, CT public schools announced closure through March 26. Fairfield University's Quick Center canceled its March 13 jazz trio show, then all subsequent events. Stratford, CT public schools closed after a person connected to an elementary school contracted the virus. Fairfield Parks & Recreation canceled all its March and April programs. CT's Mohegan Sun casino postponed its events through the end of the month. A Dayton, Ohio college canceled classes and over 1,000 students gathered in the street to jump on cars and throw objects at cops. Norway, with 489 cases, shut itself down for two weeks. Late night TV programs were suspended.

Most significantly from my perspective, Fairfield, CT public schools closed indefinitely. This triggered in me the sudden urge to head to our local Stop & Shop grocery store. The panic was officially on, with a couple hundred people there on the same bender, snatching up supplies and leaving shelving bare. Eggs, toilet paper, paper towels, cleaning products, pasta, lemons, bread, meat and more were all in the initial cross hairs. It was the first feeling of actual dread that I experienced about the situation.

March 13. All bets were off. We were suddenly in a different world. Much like the day after 9/11 or Hurricane Sandy, we were waking up to a new reality. Pres. Trump officially declared a National Emergency, giving certain powers to the Secretary of Health and Human Services and freeing up billions of dollars to facilitate virus testing across the country. Following the lead of regional CT public schools, UConn ordered students residing

11

in the dorm in Stamford, CT to collect their belongings, bring them home and prepare for online classes, commencing on March 23 after their week-long break. My son Phil's brief residency there had come to an abrupt halt. So now he was home, and public school kids were home, and stores were in chaos, and folks were just trying to stay upright with all the punches.

The situation called for a drink. "The Quarantini" and "EmerGINc" cocktail became the go-to's as more local upcoming events got cancelled and cultural venues closed. As an alternative, venues began to offer virtual tours of their facilities and collections. The stock market started to tank, ending a decade-long bull market. A local hardware store promoted a first-come first-serve supplies-while-they-last offer of N95 masks, isopropyl alcohol, antibacterial hand soap and wipes. Two Greenwich, CT residents tested positive. NYC's largest Chinese restaurant, Jing Fong, went dark. The Czech Republic, Denmark and Hungary all closed their borders. Japan confirmed the first case of RE-infection. New social media emojis, all with masks, were introduced.

A homemade dinner and a pour of Guinness capped the day's reports. It would be the first of many homebound dinners.

March 14. Today began Phil's nine-day Spring Break, normally a period he would spend with his elder brother and my ex-wife, Marlene, in Miami, Florida. But our new situation made that a no-go. Although Miami's mayor had contracted the virus, a State of Emergency had been issued in Palm Beach County and all state schools were ordered closed through March 30, there were apparently "car loads of kids driving around partying" and people out "sunning, walking and drinking", according to Marlene. The following day, all public beaches in Miami and Fort Lauderdale were ordered closed, though Spring Breakers continued to congregate in defiance.

The first forward looking projections were made suggesting how this current challenge might change how we conduct ourselves and do business in the future. The Westport Weston Health District warned about social gatherings, saying, "This is not a time for partying." Meanwhile, we marveled at Taiwan's ability to limit their cases to 50 in a country of 23 million. Videochatting became more focal as we were encouraged to practice "social distancing", the new term of the day. Local food drives aimed to collect goods for neighbors in need. More online-only diversions, education and entertainments were advanced. The U.S. cruise industry suspended operations. Twenty confirmed virus cases were announced for Connecticut as our Fairfield First Selectwoman made the first of her subsequent daily official briefings. Movie theaters closed in PA and NJ. Westport closed its playgrounds and beaches to prevent social gatherings.

March 15. It was a beautiful day and with fewer and fewer places to go and little else to do, Fairfield folks flocked to our beaches in droves, strolling, walking dogs, climbing on playground equipment and picnicking, assuming they were doing something healthy and positive. Most were not aware that the virus could be spread through the air or by surface contact.

Our Stop & Shop revised its hours to allow more time for workers to unload deliveries and stock shelves. It also announced its pick-up services were suspended and home delivery would be delayed. Johns Hopkins began to offer a comprehensive online virus tracking dashboard so regular folks could monitor cases worldwide. A National Day of Prayer was conducted. A Portland, Oregon distillery began turning their alcohol waste into hand sanitizer, setting off a new line of output amongst distilleries nationwide. Local chambers of commerce encouraged buying local to support suddenly struggling small businesses. Brazen young people ignored calls for social distancing and continued to flock to bars. NYC Mayor de Blasio reluctantly announced schools there would close March 16 through April 20. The Federal Reserve cut rates to zero and launched a massive $700 billion quantitative easing program. Our CT Gov. Lamont issued an Executive Order to close all state schools starting March 16. Major retailers began shutting down. CA, OH, IL and MA closed their bars and restaurants.

March 16. I decided to get out ahead of the herd today and take another stab at grocery shopping, heading to my local Stop & Shop. Shoppers had apparently already massed outside the store before it even opened and had streamed in like locusts, picking many shelves clean. A cashier reported that the toilet paper, which had been replenished last night, was gone in 10 minutes. Other depletions included bread, orange juice, frozen vegetables, detergent, fresh and boxed pasta, chicken, soup, bottled water, many frozen foods, pineapples, spinach, shredded cheese, butter, tissues, milk products and orange juice. Regarding replenishment, another staffer said the store's delivery schedule was uncertain — there might be a delivery tomorrow. As to shoppers, there were four types: self-focused (towing two overflowing carts, kids coughing), cautious (wearing gloves, being selective, securing basic needs), hyper-cautious (wiping down each item as they placed it in their cart) and distressed (often elderly, staring at empty shelves). This was no time to be brand conscious, that was apparent. You basically had to settle for whatever was available.

The Statue of Liberty and Ellis Island closed, following the lead of other tourist venues like Disney World and Disneyland. Experts strongly advised against children having playdates and emphasized the effectiveness of soap and hand washing. Per order of CT's governor, restaurants, bars, casinos, gyms and movie theaters closed across the state, though restaurants were still allowed to offer takeout and delivery services. Gatherings of over 50 people were also squashed in CT. In places like Culver City, CA, people lined up around the block at gun shops to stock up on weapons and ammo. In contrast, encouraging messaging — urging kindness, empathy, patience and understanding — became increasingly abundant on social media. New Jersey also closed its restaurants, bars, casinos and movie theaters and imposed a statewide curfew. D.C.'s Health & Human Services dept. reported a cyberattack attempt aimed at slowing down its system.

The European Union (EU) closed its borders to non-essential entry of all foreign nationals. Our Town of Fairfield made a "local declaration of emergency and ordered the closure of all parks, playgrounds, public golf courses, beaches and other public recreation spaces where people had been congregating; town offices were also temporarily closed. Fairfield officials urged people to stay in their homes and limit non-essential travel. Photos of barren parts of NYC, eg. Times Square, popped up on social media. Westport, CT announced 20 identified cases of the virus and went into emergency mode. Alerts went out about people posing as personnel from the Centers for Disease Control and Prevention (CDC) to gain access to homes. A social media influencer was shamed for posting a video of herself licking a toilet seat as a "coronavirus challenge". CT's Beardsley Zoo, in Bridgeport, announced closure. Canada closed its borders to most foreign travelers. One day before its most celebratory day of the year, Fairfield's Gaelic-American Club closed indefinitely. San Francisco went on 24-hour lockdown for three weeks. The first human trial of a coronavirus vaccine was scheduled. The Kentucky Derby was postponed for the first time since 1945. Social distancing memes ruled the internet.

March 17. St. Patrick's Day. Favorite Irish bars all closed. No parades to attend. I decided to turn the frown upside down and forge ahead with homebound festivities to celebrate my part-Irish heritage. It was Irish coffee to start followed by a homemade Irish breakfast of fried eggs, whiskey flavored beans, thick bacon, maple smoked sausage, fried tomatoes, muffins with jam and a pint of Guinness. To bring the family members into the picture, we took selfies of ourselves and shared toasts by email. I FaceTime chatted with my Dad as well, conducting as live a toast as we could manage. I tuned into Irish songs located on the Internet and streamed those from my computer throughout the day. Dinner was equally thoughtful, consisting of corned beef, steamed carrots, mashed potatoes, steamed cabbage and buttered soda bread.

The news continued to spill forth of course. Panic buying was putting both grocery workers and shoppers at risk of infection. Photos showed the empty streets in front of the Temple Bar in Dublin, Ireland. More photos surfaced of empty NYC areas. Stop & Shop set aside hours for elderly and vulnerable customers to shop. New England Patriots Quarterback Tom Brady announced his departure from the team, sticking a knife in Boston fans at an already low moment. Amazon *suspended all warehouse shipments except medical supplies and high-demand products. The U.S. Small Business Administration announced low-interest federal disaster loans. Coronavirus cases passed the 5,000 mark in the U.S. My little town of Fairfield began to look like a ghost town, with the exception of cars at Rite-Aid pharmacy and people picking up food from restaurants. A couple left a $9,400 tip at a Houston restaurant to help staff get through their shutdown going forward. A national blood shortage was emerging as people feared infection at donation sites. A finding suggested that people with blood type A might be more susceptible to the virus. Police in Spain were using drones to enforce new rules meant to contain the virus spread. Uber continued to operate though ride usage was down 50%. "Flatten the curve" became the new cry, referring to how people could prevent a climb in new cases. A story emerged about a group that went off the grid on a rafting trip for 25 days and came back to a changed world. An L.A. taco eatery began offering emergency kits complete with taco fixings, toilet paper and eggs. Major hotel chains began shutting down due to unprecedented low occupancy. A report suggested that CT public schools may remain closed for the remainder of the school year.*

March 18. New day, the "hump" of the week. I decided to be productive and rake out my yard, given that my pre-paid lawn service would be visiting to fertilize sometime soon. I admired some sprouting daffodils and my cat, which had found a sunny spot in which to bask.

The news pounded away. Nearly 1 in 5 households had already lost work because of the "pandemic", the term being popularly used for the worldwide public health crisis. Memes helped people deal with their reality, ranging from depictions of "types of people stuck at home" and at-home diversions to homeschooling failures. The CT Audubon urged socially responsible and distanced walking on its trails, where people had now migrated. Trader Joe's began limiting the number of shoppers in its stores at once to 20. A 5.7-magnitude earthquake in Utah knocked out power to thousands and disrupted health lab work. People half-heartedly joked about hunting for food should grocery stores close. The U.S. Navy said it would deploy its hospital ship USNS Comfort to NYC to offer more beds to treat the sick. Parents were finessing their homeschooling regimens. Italy recorded 475 coronavirus deaths in one day. Connecticut unemployment rates reached 30,000 in a week. A Ridgefield, CT man became the first Covid-19 death in the state. Malls, bowling alleys and amusement parks were ordered to close in NY, NJ and CT. Ninety-nine percent of craft brewery businesses were being impacted. People began putting their Christmas lights back up to help spread cheer. Fairfield announced its first two confirmed cases, counted among statewide CT cases numbering 96. A photo of Los Angeles' 405 highway showed it devoid of traffic, a shock to those that know it and drive it. A CDC analysis suggested that the virus poses a serious risk for younger people. Letter carriers shared that the postal service pressured them to deliver mail despite having virus symptoms.

March 19. It was the first day of Spring, arriving like a rabid lion, with blizzards in the Midwest, heavy rain in the north and the nation singing the blues. Feeling cabin feverish, I headed out in the car to tour our little Fairfield downtown and beach area, finding streets empty but essential businesses doing the best they could muster with curbside delivery.

The day's news crested like an incoming tide. Bridgeport, CT announced its first three cases of the virus. The Olympic committee was weighing the fate of the Summer Games in Tokyo. Horse racing continued across America but without any live audiences. The Stop & Shop plan to accommodate elderly shoppers went afoul, putting the group more at risk being massed together with each other. A New Canaan, CT man became the state's second virus death. Italy reported 427 new virus deaths, overtaking China's toll. The U.S. passed the 10,000 mark for confirmed virus cases. Our Town of Fairfield confirmed three cases to date and more strongly urged staying at home and not congregating, while cases topped 150 in the state, with 42 cases in Westport alone.

March 20. The day was deceivingly pleasant given all the worldwide chaos and again I turned my attention outdoors to yard projects, weeding a path and raking some more. When I took my yard waste to our town dump, I noticed the clerks there were wearing latex gloves. I was nervous about handling cash and again liberally used hand sanitizer.

The news remained unavoidable, a daily damage report you might say. Futurists mused about how the world will be different when we emerge from our current challenges. Carnival offered its idle cruise ships as temporary hospital spaces. A much hoped for new Harbor Yard Amphitheater in Bridgeport, CT delayed its Fall opening to 2021. NYC apartment dwellers united to sing "Hey Jude" from their apartment windows. Our town continued to stress social distancing. The TJX family of stores, which included our local Marshalls, announced it would close. Folks wondered if the universe was sending us a message to slow down and take a step back and realize how we really impact Earth and one another. People expressed living with a strange mixture of normalcy and emergency. The U.S. filing deadline for taxes was moved to July 15. Tom Brady announced he had signed with the Tampa Bay Buccaneers. Eighteen thousand pounds of toilet paper was found in a stolen tractor trailer in North Carolina. NY Gov. Cuomo ordered the state to lock down, shutting all non-essential businesses. Internet users joked about conducting pub crawls in their homes and changing from day pajamas to night pajamas. WHO reported almost 210,000 infections and nearly 8,800 deaths worldwide. CT's Gov. Lamont ordered all non-essential businesses to shut as cases rose to 194, with four dead. Drive-through virus testing sites began to operate in certain locales in CT. Italy announced 627 more deaths in 24 hours. Reports began surfacing of animals invading empty cities where quarantines had been enacted. NYC, with cases at 5,151, became the epicenter for the virus in the U.S.

March 21. I awoke to news of singer Kenny Rogers' death. He knew "when to fold them (his cards)" folks remarked. As the day was pleasant, I enjoyed it snacking and social distancing on the back steps and made a fine spaghetti-and-meatballs dinner.

In the news, forward thinkers suggested there wouldn't be a defined all-clear signal at the end of our crisis. It was suggested that idle college campuses may be used as care facilities. L.A. County had given up on containing the virus, telling doctors to skip testing of some patients. The virus was killing more than one person an hour in NYC. People tried to maintain a sense of humor online, vowing, "When this is all over, we are throwing the biggest St. Patrick's Easter de Mayo of July party anyone's ever seen." In CT, over 72,000 residents applied for unemployment in the past week. EarthCam webcams showed deserted city scenes all over the world. Our local Fifth State Distillery began offering ethanol-based hand wash. Virus cases in New York state rocketed to 10,000, with 6,000 cases in NYC alone. Flights were temporarily halted at NY and Philadelphia airports after virus exposure concerns. The military entered NYC, rolling in with columns of Humvees. Fairfield announced five cases in town and reassured residents there was no food shortage. The U.S. had over 25,000 confirmed cases, in third place behind Italy at over 53,000 cases and China with over 81,000 cases. Guidance emerged about how to protect yourself when interacting with touchscreens and gas pump handles.

March 22. I decided to make another foray out for groceries at the local Stop & Shop, a run that I hoped would keep us amply stocked for a while.

My shopping strategy had taken on an air of military rigor. I described the process to my Dad in an email:

"For me, the goal is minimizing risk. Here's MY strategy… When I go for groceries, I plan on getting a two-week supply to minimize my risk of exposure. I take a list with me so that I'm getting only those specific items, to minimize my time in the store — get in and get out as quickly as I can. I wipe my cart handle down with wipes provided at the store entrance and only touch the very edge of my cart handle, and only with my palms. As far as shopping, I take a wide pass by any other shoppers and go the other way if I notice anyone coughing or obviously ill. I don't touch any shelving and use a cloth to touch door handles and any other high-contact areas. As I select my products, I'm being more conscious now of anything that is air exposed, like fruit and vegetables. When possible, I get a bag of apples instead of loose apples, or bag of oranges instead of loose oranges, package of lettuce vs. an open head of lettuce, lemon juice instead of whole lemons, packaged bananas instead of a loose bunch. It's tricky and sometimes I just pass altogether on a certain item. Then I head to the register, which is the last tricky leg. There, I try to maintain space between the shopper in front of me and the person behind. And I don't let anyone bag my groceries — the less handling the better. (Self-checkout may be the ideal way to go.) I bring paper bags with handles (Trader Joes) as they are less likely to retain the virus on the surface than the vinyl bags, and bag myself. As to paying, I bring a cloth with me and wrap it around my finger to type on the keypad then throw out the cloth. And I pay with a card versus cash, as cash can be a virus carrier, using the chip method so I'm the only one handling my card. When I get to my car, I'm careful not to touch the car handles and interior until I've cleaned my hands with hand sanitizer that I keep in the car. Once home, I put everything away and again wash my hands at the sink. As far as the consumption end of things, we wash all fruit and vegetables before eating and, just in general, wash our hands several times a day as items may still be contaminated. And we try to remember not to touch our face in general."

My grocery store visit this day was much like the two previous outings, though less crowded. It quickly became apparent why: dwindling supplies and aisle after aisle of depletions. Store management cited panic buying as the reason but it seemed to us that the store was not getting its usual deliveries. There were big empty spaces for juice, eggs, toilet paper, canned pet food, coffee, meat (big time), soup, pasta and more. Encouraging was that a majority of shoppers were now wearing gloves and/or masks as well as many of the cashiers and staff. People took wide passes around each other as they shopped and staff was overall respectful and helpful and asked about your well being, as we did about theirs given that they were on the front lines putting their own health in jeopardy. Wipes were available at store entrances to wipe down carts and hands. Signs had been placed limiting purchase on many items, noting price increases due to distribution restraints and apologizing for lack of inventory.

In the news, theorists suggested social distancing might lead to a "social recession". Airports began to resemble aircraft graveyards, with planes lined up in rows on the tarmac. Domino's Pizza announced it was hiring 10,000 delivery people nationwide as demand soared. Chicagoans under stay-at-home orders conducted a city-wide sing-along of Bon Jovi's "Livin' On A Prayer". China, at the mature end of the virus outbreak and recovering in large part, scrambled to curb a rise in imported virus cases. There were local calls to CT residents and businesses for the donation of protective gear for hospital staff and health workers. NYC looked to build field hospitals as cases there topped 10,300. Worldwide, cases numbered over 310,000. Italy reported 793 dead in a single day. People wondered if going to the beach and hiking was ok and safe, as well as if they might contract the virus from food. A post about a DIY mask made out of a bra garnered a lot of views. Another post referenced "hooking up" in this time: "Corona free man seeks corona free lady with toilet paper. Send pictures of toilet paper!" Comparisons of this time were made to the 1918 worldwide Influenza pandemic and World War II conditions at home with respect to rationing, home gardening and conserving. As Americans continued to dig in at home, they posted about drinking, home activities, keeping fit and managing their children. CT announced 327 cases and eight deaths statewide.

March 23. Snow was the weather prediction for tomorrow. In New England, we call this the "third winter", which is preceded by the "spring of deception" and followed by the "mud season". I decided to prep for it with a big pot of homemade chili.

The news droned on, becoming a non-sensical buzz at this point. Thousands of stolen coronavirus respirator masks were found in Oregon and donated to hospitals as an arrest was made. A Portland strip club was forced to close, so now the dancers do food deliveries, operating as BooberEats. CT's Gov. Lamont outlined his "Stay Safe Stay Home" business closure exemptions and said he was keeping schools in the state closed until at least April 20. Total U.S. cases surpassed 35,000 while the death toll hit 414. Quarantined families joked about overdrinking, overeating, rewarding themselves for getting dressed, the challenges of working from home and accomplishing cleaning tasks. Cases in NY state swelled to over 15,000, more than either France or South Korea. The 2020 Tokyo Olympics were officially postponed. NY Gov. Cuomo ordered all hospitals to add beds. An asteroid whizzed by Earth at a distance of 90,000 miles. CT cases totaled 415, with 74 of those in Westport and ten deaths across the state.

March 24. The anticipated snow arrived, but delivered just flurries along our southwestern CT shoreline. We labeled the weather "corona-crazy" and carried on. Dinner was a "Quarantuna" Corona Casserole.

Cases in Italy neared 64,000, with a death toll at 6,820. The faces of healthcare workers and praise for them dominated social media. Local caterers, in the absence of events, started offering family meals for delivery. Drivers in Toronto were using emptier roads and highways to street race. Westport Country Playhouse delayed its season opening to July. To combat depression, Fairfield Social Services set up a Friendly Caller Program with nurses and library staff making calls to people feeling isolated. U.S. cases hit 46,400, with deaths over 500. People worried about contracting the virus from mail, packages and mail/package delivery crews. The Spanish army found dead abandoned residents in nursing homes. Star Trek's Patrick Stewart read Shakespeare online to entertain homebound fans. One hundred and twenty-nine members of the NYPD tested positive. CT cases hit 618, with 12 deaths. CT Gov. Lamont now expected schools to be closed until the fall. Looking ahead to Easter and summer, we imagined wearing hazmat suits while conducting our usual seasonal activities. The White House urged people who fled New York to self quarantine for two weeks. The U.S. Postal Service was at risk of shutting down by summer.

March 25. Our lives as we knew them just a month before had screeched to a halt. The majority of us Americans were now homebound and newly imagining ourselves as cooks, teachers, gardeners, therapists, exercise instructors, policy experts and bartenders. The case and death numbers mounted numbingly and with such surreal effect as to be white noise.

My eldest son, 24-year-old Evan, received a "public safety alert" by text to his phone. He lives in Columbia Heights, D.C. The region had over 1,000 confirmed coronavirus cases and three deaths. He'd been working for his company SmartBrief, Inc. from his apartment for the past two weeks, per their mandate. I expected that would continue to be the case until further notice. He'd stocked up with food and supplies and was riding it out with his girlfriend, Cat, who was also working remotely. Both were healthy and safe, thank goodness. The alert read as follows:

"STAY HOME. You have a critical role to play in stopping the spread of COVID-19 in DC. Effective at 10pm tonight (Wednesday, March 25), the District of Columbia will close all non-essential businesses through Friday, April 24. We are depending on you - be a good neighbor, STAY HOME. For the latest information, visit coronavirus.dc.gov/wea"

The day's news shot at us like darts. The government agreed on a $2-trillion stimulus bill, the largest in U.S. history — good news for many, but no help for some. Workers in eight Amazon warehouses tested positive. Hollywood's box office recorded zero revenue for the first time ever. Singer Jackson Browne and Britain's Prince Charles tested positive. We found more ways to amuse ourselves at home, with art and streaming music and movies, while corona-cationing in "Las Kitchenas", "Costa Del Balconia" and "La Rotonda De Sofa". Deaths in Spain overtook those in China while India put 1.3 billion people into lockdown. The Justice Dept. said that coronavirus crimes can be charged as acts of terrorism. Beloved Actress Betty White read "Harry the Dirty Dog" online. Fairfield announced a weekly bell ringing initiative, from residents' porches every Wednesday at 7pm. Our Town of Fairfield also noted nine residents positive out of 875 cases in the state and 19 deaths.

March 26. My son Phil, while online schooling, had been working on a gas-powered scooter and was able to get it running for the season. I looked on as he tuned it in the back yard, and adopted an early afternoon happy hour, lounging in an outdoor Adirondack chair.

The news gong pounded away. America had its deadliest day yet, with 223 deaths, making 928 to date and over 65,000 cases. The global death toll topped 20,000, with over 487,000 worldwide cases. Memes grew in abundance as we learned that the virus can survive on the soles of our shoes for up to five days. More than three million Americans filed for unemployment claims last week, quadruple the previous one-week record. New Orleans became a virus hotspot, with 1,800 cases and counting, thought to have been spurred by Mardi Gras celebrations back in February. NYC topped 21,000 cases, with 100 dead in the past 24 hours. Beloved Harlem Globetrotter Fred "Curly" Neal passed, along with actor Mark Blum. An Oxford study suggested millions of people may have already built up a coronavirus immunity. By day's end, America had moved into the first slot for most world cases, with over 82,000. We moaned about news that the 2020 hurricane season was expected to have above-normal activity.

On a side note, two passengers who traveled on the Grand Princess cruise ship, from San Francisco to the Hawaiian islands and back, Feb. 21 to March 4, died from the virus. They were among 103 passengers who had tested positive. The ship was the same vessel my Dad had traveled on and disembarked from just two months before, out of the same port and terminal. His trip timing, and that of his Myanmar excursion, were remarkable, bringing him home safely and just under the wire in both cases.

March 27. The day was warm, drawing people out to the streets to walk and ride and garden. Phil remarked how, during this strange time, he had never seen more people outside and interacting together.

NYC's cases rose to over 23,000, with another 84 deaths recorded. Our Gov. Lamont set new physical distancing measures for the state. A post about social distancing pickup lines made the rounds — "If Covid-19 doesn't take you out, can I?" On a bright note, koalas rescued from Australia's brushfires were being released back into the wild. U.K. Prime Minister Boris Johnson tested positive, causing more worry across Britain. U.S. cases passed 85,000. On the upside, Los Angeles reported its third week of clear skies due to an absence of smog. Italy's death toll topped 9,000, with more than 969 deaths in one day. Our Town cases hit 18 out of 1,291 in Connecticut, while the U.S. broke the 100K case mark.

March 28. The day was gray and lousy with rain and temps that didn't get above 45. It matched our moods and kept us indoors, to make chicken noodle soup and watch movies on Hulu.

My Dad shared an email exchange he'd had with his sister, the deputy mayor of a city with a population of around 32,000 in southeastern New Hampshire. She admitted to feeling "stir crazy" under a stay-at-home order and detailed, "Restaurants and theaters and such had already been shut down a while ago, but now all non-essential businesses in the state must shut down. This is a nightmare. It is very difficult to live like this. ALL city buildings are closed to the public (including the elected officials). Staff are still working in the buildings in some cases and remotely at home if possible. Obviously police, fire, public works, water, sewer and many others like welfare and City Clerk staff must still be there. We have transitioned to all necessary meetings being held remotely. The IT staff has been very busy making all this work. As Deputy Mayor, I already had two of those this week. Being technologically challenged, this is very awkward for me, but doable. One of our city councilors tested positive and was hospitalized in Boston last week. He is recovering. I have passed the 14-day period since my last in-person contact with him." She added that, in her limited downtime, she had been reading John Barry's The Great Influenza about the 1918 pandemic, noting that the parallels between our current circumstance and those times were "intriguing".

As ever, the news from all around kept pounding away. Commercial airlines began operating cargo-only flights in the absence of passengers. More than 500 members of the NYPD had the virus now. With some hope, a CT-based healthcare leader predicted the virus would peak in the state the second week of April; other models weren't as optimistic. Abbott Labs announced the launch of a five-minute Covid-19 test that could be used almost anywhere. Meanwhile, the virus was killing people in NYC at the rate of one every 17 minutes. In reaction to New Yorkers fleeing their state, other states began setting up checkpoints at their borders and points of entry, with police collecting personal and destination information and requesting two-week self-quarantines. Technology company X-Mode had tracked the heat signatures of students that had clustered for Spring Break in Fort Lauderdale, Florida and released a map that showed how and where they had migrated since — a frightening sprawl across the Eastern half of the country, where they were potentially bringing cases of the highly contagious virus with them. A report showed that virus cases, once concentrated on America's coasts, were now popping up in the middle of the country. Spain's misery continued, announcing a record 832 new deaths. Italy surpassed China for infections as the global total reached 600K. Russia, until now largely unaffected by the virus, said it would be closing its borders. Plastic bags, banned for environmental reasons but now shown to be less likely to carry the virus, were reintroduced to the public. CT rejoiced about Chris Tillett, the state's first confirmed case, who had emerged from a medically induced coma and was beginning his recovery. CT's Better Business Bureau warned of scams related to the government's promised relief checks. Fairfield, with cases rising to 20, announced its first death from the virus — an 85-year-old male with underlying health issues. The White House began considering a short-term quarantine for virus "hot spots" in NY, NJ and CT. NYC's Javits Center, normally busy with conferences and trade shows, completed its transformation into a hospital with partitioned rooms. More than 9,000 retired Army medical personnel responded to a call for assistance. Photos posted by a New Yorker showed a refrigeration truck staged to accommodate corpses parked behind Lennox Hill Hospital. Norwalk, CT's Mayor confirmed 139 cases and four deaths, stats positioning the city as the state's hot spot. The MyPillow company said it had begun making face masks for hospitals. Cases in Florida topped 4,000.

March 29. It was another gray day, with buckets of rain coming down, occasional crashes of thunder and temps in the mid-40s. It seemed clear that the universe was mad with us, or was it just driving us indoors to be safe? I spent the morning comforting myself with a large cup of coffee and tuning into live and recorded music sessions posted on Facebook by several musician friends. Continued rain in the afternoon called for the making of a beef-and-sausage-based pot of chili, wolfed down while reaching out by text and email to friends and family to check on their well being. The replies were positive — "doing well" and "ok" or "trapped inside but not too bad". One connection was with my longtime friend, Cam, who worked for a cargo airline. His business was in flux with regard to shifting workloads and demand, though he felt fairly confident it would weather the storm.

The news drummed away. Paramedics in NYC expressed terror as the 911 system began to grow overwhelmed. Empire State Building managers announced a new nightly light show to raise New Yorkers' spirits. Dr. Anthony Fauci, the longtime director of the National Institute of Allergy and Infectious Diseases, warned that between 100K and 200K Americans could die from the virus, an outcome that averaged forecast models. Thailand's King Maha Vajiralongkorn was reported to be self-isolating in a luxury hotel with a harem of 20 women. A posted video showed New Yorkers collectively clapping from their apartment buildings to show appreciation of the city's healthcare teams, hospital workers, the NYPD, the FDNY, truck drivers, essential workers and delivery and sanitation crews. In NJ, 700 police officers had tested positive for the virus. CT Gov. Lamont's request for a Major Disaster Declaration for the state was approved by the Federal Emergency Management Agency (FEMA). Norwalk, CT's Mayor shut down the city's parks and beaches to vehicular traffic, reduced occupancy rates to 50% for stores and businesses, and limited to one person the number of people from a household that were permitted to shop. The

Amish in Lancaster County, PA busied themselves sewing protective masks for surrounding communities. Cases in CT rose to 1,993 with the majority (1,245) in Fairfield County, where there had also been 21 deaths. Worldwide identified cases since the start of the pandemic topped 720K, with over 535K currently infected; the balance had been discharged or died. Top pop stars and musicians held an online live concert conducted from their own homes, with pneumonia-stricken Elton John emcee'ing.

March 30. Monday. The beginning of a new "work" week, whatever that meant these days. It was gray and uninspiring, with more rain in the forecast. Mid-morning, Phil and I decided to make the weekly anxiety-producing grocery run to our Stop & Shop, expecting the worst though we had heard that the panic shopping had subsided. We were pleasantly surprised to find that was mostly true. Staples like bread, meat and orange juice were back on the shelves, as were most other items. Absent or in very short supply were items like eggs, Kleenex, toilet paper and paper towels. The deli counter was indefinitely closed, with sliced meats packaged and placed on shelves for pick-up. Shoppers, most of whom wore gloves and/or masks, were very conscious of each other, steering wide or waiting six feet behind one another as grocery selections were made. Plexiglass shields had been placed at all the registers manned by cashiers, who wore latex gloves and frequently disinfected belts, bagging areas and touch pads. Disturbingly, we noted that thoughtless shoppers had dropped their used latex gloves in the parking lot in several spots.

On the way back home, we made a wide loop through our Fairfield downtown and beach area to see what we could see. Scenes that popped on our radar included a few motorists getting McDonald's takeout, a line of a dozen cars doing pick-ups at Doughnut Inn, an almost completely empty parking lot at Marshalls/CVS, a couple of people outside Mo's wine/spirits, a completely shuttered and closed 7-Eleven on Reef Road and good old Bud's Deli open and doing brisk business. There was little traffic everywhere and many pedestrians walking about wore latex gloves and masks.

My aunt Elaine checked in by email, noting, "the hardest part for me is being isolated." At the same time, Phil received an alert from his school that it would be testing the emergency sirens on its Storrs campus. The sirens are part of UConn's emergency notification system, UConnALERT, and meant to notify students when business operations are impacted by weather closings and significant class schedule alterations. It seemed more like they were testing the system so they could announce a Purge.

In the never-ending news, the President extended the nation's social distancing policy through April 30. We learned about a choir practice that took place in early March in Washington state that resulted in 45 members out of 60 becoming ill. NYC losses mounted as 98 people died from the virus in less than seven hours — a death every 9.5 minutes — and total cases pushed past 33K. The Navy's USN Comfort sped to NYC, drawing throngs of attention from shore as it passed and arrived. A temporary field hospital was erected in NYC's Central Park. Global cases reached 775K, of which 160K were recovering, 36K dead. In the U.S., there were 160K cases and over 2,800 dead. More evidence indicated the virus could be transmitted by air, particularly in confined spaces. Brooks Brothers announced it would make 150,000 masks a day to support the virus fight. Vermont closed all its hotels, vacation rentals and campgrounds. Fairfield, CT cases were up to 35, among 2,571 cases and 36 deaths in CT. Norwalk, CT's cases had alarmingly risen to 271, to lead the state.

March 31. Another gray, dull day, and so quiet for a Tuesday. More like a Sunday. No one walking by the house. No traffic, with the exception of a sanitation truck doing pick-ups, its crew masked and gloved. I was itching to take a drive, just to break out of isolation, and so took a big loop around Fairfield, Black Rock and Westport, CT to get a pulse reading and see how we were all faring. Our towns were quieter to be sure, but still percolating here and there as businesses conducted curbside and takeout operations. As for the highway, due to the lack of traffic, vehicles were zipping along at a very hurried pace. I called Hansen's Flower Shop to order a spring bouquet, collecting it from a worker who came out to my car. I drove the flowers to my girlfriend Jen's house in Westport, rang her bell and held them up as she appeared at and looked through the door. She was pleasantly surprised to see me and let me inside with some hesitation. We awkwardly circled about each other without breaking our pact of physical distancing, and chatted about how weird the world had gotten as she put the flowers in a vase. Then I wished her a good rest of the day, which she would spend conducting virtual lessons with her piano students via FaceTime and Skype.

Later, I combed through some old photo albums, screenshooting select ones to share by email, text and Facebook. The shots recalled joyous, simpler times and were a good distraction from our current situation.

With regard to the news, the numbers were getting numbing and I focused less on those and more on general developments. After all, we recognized that both cases and deaths were going to climb. That said, one story shared that the virus would be peaking at different times across America, which would present challenges as those states peaking earliest began recovery while others were still in the throes of the outbreak. U.S. dead topped 3,000. A curious symptom popping up amongst virus patients was a temporary loss of sense of taste and smell. In NYC, cases rose to over 38,000 with 914 dead — in the latest stretch, a death occurred there every 2.9 minutes. Fairfield, CT cases inched up to 40, among 3,128 cases and 69 deaths in the state. The U.S. Open's home site in Queens, NY had been converted to a temporary emergency facility to support Elmhurst Hospital.

April 1. The morning was bright and inspiring, though nippy. I poured a big cup of coffee and stood on the front porch watching a lawn service crew — masked and gloved — raking out and mowing a neighbor's yard down the street. Another day in pandemic paradise.

Notably, the date marked April Fool's Day. A popular meme proclaimed it had been "canceled this year as no made-up prank could match the unbelievable shit going on in the real world right now." Still, a number of parents pranked their kids by waking them up early, telling them school was back in session and hustling them to their bus stops. A local business, Redline Restorations, fooled us all with a very convincing Facebook post noting it had gone out of business.

Phil received an email from his school, officially letting him know that his dorm had been taken over by the state, to be repurposed as an overflow medical/health care dedicated facility. The email stated, "We hope everyone has been well and being safe in their new environments. We wanted to send a quick email to inform all of you that, as of yesterday, 3/31/2020, the 900 Washington Blvd building will be used by the State of Connecticut as the Covid-19 crisis grows. This being said, the Residential Life department at UConn Stamford has been temporarily moved and packages/mail will **no longer** be retrieved by our department. We are sending this as a courtesy to make sure you change your address for all billing statements, tax forms, packages, monthly subscriptions, Amazon orders, and any other packages/mail you would receive. As we no longer have access to the building, all packages/mail that will continue being sent to 900 Washington Blvd will be either tossed or returned to sender. Residential Life is not responsible for any mail or packages misplaced or lost moving forward. **We highly encourage you to take a few minutes to change your address for all future mail/packages."**

Mid-afternoon, I took a drive through our beach area, neighboring Black Rock, and Fairfield's Post Road commercial district to take a community pulse reading. Our beach was completely deserted, which was a shock given that on any other pleasant day, it would have been clogged with people strolling up and down. It was an indication that our First Selectwoman's urgent tone and action was working. I *did* notice three women sitting on the deck of the Jacky Durrell Pavilion but they were keeping at least six feet apart from each other to effect physical distancing. As far as businesses along the Post Road, I noticed takeout and curbside pick-up signs all along.

At 7pm, I heard a sustained clattering coming from outside and remembered it was Wednesday and that our Town had encouraged residents to stand on their front steps and ring bells. I joined three other adjacent neighbors in unity, banging away on a skillet with a metal serving spoon. We heard a similar clatter from the next street. We laughed and waved and called to each other, glad to see that we were all well and keeping in good spirits.

The day's news didn't seem to beat me over the head like it had every day before for the past couple of weeks, though there were still some low points. The CDC said it was weighing the wider usage of masks by citizens as the U.S. death toll topped 4,000. China was apparently trying to restart itself with a reported 63K people recovered, but with mixed results. Farmers' livelihoods may be threatened by the slump in restaurant food sales. Spain registered an overnight death toll of 849, its highest one-day count so far. Southern Connecticut State University's fieldhouse had been repurposed for hospital patient overflow as state cases surged over 3,000. Norwalk, CT stores had been ordered to limit shopper counts inside as that city's cases pushed over 300. Global cases topped 876K as of 9am. Yale researchers had found a way to sterilize and recycle thousands of respirator masks. Palm Sunday and Easter masses would be broadcast live from St. Patrick's Cathedral. Fourteen hundred members of the NYPD had tested positive for the virus. Booze sales were booming as people stockpile alcohol. Local police warned of a scam linked to the 2020 Census that had been issued to all U.S. citizens in the past couple of weeks. Our CT Gov. Lamont reached an agreement with over 50 credit unions and banks in the state to offer mortgage relief to residents and businesses. Our Fairfield First Selectwoman noted that our case count was up to 48 and that we had a second death.

April 2. The sun streaming through my bedroom curtains around 6am stirred me to rise, shower and make coffee. I stood for a bit on the front porch, just listening to the wind, which had replaced the sound of cars that would normally be shooting by along the adjacent main road, rushing to a work destination and trying to beat highway congestion. I'd read that the Earth had become so still in light of greatly reduced human activity that seismologists' equipment was picking up on the slightest of ground vibrations, even at the surface level. It was an upside to our current condition.

I reached out to and connected by text with my son Evan in D.C. after reading an article about the challenge of social distancing when you have roommates like he does. I asked him if they had adopted a system, to which he replied, "We're doing the best we can. The only person allowed in the house is Cat (his girlfriend). We disinfect surfaces and work in different parts of the house during the day. But, ultimately, if one of us gets it, we're probably all going to get it. So we're trying to limit leaving the house as much as possible, unless it's for exercise."

Mid-morning, as the wind really began to kick up, with gusts up to 30mph, there arose a cacophony of car horns beeping at the front of the house. With some alarm, we rushed out to the street to look and, lo and behold, a convoy of cars came rolling through, with motorists and their passengers waving signs and shouting hello. It was a parade of teachers from our beach area's Sherman Elementary School saying hello to their homebound students, but also served as a bright moment to raise *all* of our spirits, drive hope and unite our town citizenry in this very trying time of isolation. #fairfieldstrong.

Our Gov. Lamont issued an executive order effective April 3 with new guidelines for retailers (primarily grocery stores), including occupancy capped at 50% of store capacity (customers to be counted as they enter), markings on the floor at checkout to encourage six-foot spacing, aisle traffic flowing one-way, Plexiglass shields at the registers (as we had already seen), one member per household only shopping, discontinuation of all self-serve foods and product sampling, touchless credit card transactions, cart-and-basket sanitizing by staff, and staff required to wear gloves and masks.

The global number of coronavirus cases ticked over one million, with over 51,000 dead. Two hundred and ten thousand people had recovered out of the total — staggering numbers as the roller coaster continued to climb up the track. I distracted myself with Facebook challenges like "I Spy" wherein you are given a color and asked to post a picture from your camera roll that reflects that color, and a Then-and-Now photo challenge of pics of one's self. I knew I must have reached a new level of boredom as I never participated in these challenges. At the same time, it was fun and engaging to see responses.

I reached out to Dad by FaceTime and found that my brother, Dave, had arrived at his house, to stay for a couple of days. Earlier in the week, Dave and I had debated about whether his visit was a good idea or not given that Dad's been safe and germ-free in self-isolation in his home and that

Dave had the potential of introducing the virus to him. But Dave said he and his wife, Jill, had been exercising caution in their West Virginia home and whenever they had to make a run for anything. Humorously, he wore a vintage WWII gas mask to my Dad's and brought medicinal supplies: two four-packs of Boddington's Pub Ale.

I had adopted the routine of watching TV in the evenings, binging through my Hulu on-demand service on a variety of series and the occasional movie (often apocalyptic-themed). I was currently enjoying the series "Californication" (2007-2014), about a down-in-the-dumps writer (David Duchovny) who had moved from NYC to L.A. to be with his "baby mama". His trouble getting inspired to write disrupts their union sending him in pursuit of many female flavors of the moment while maintaining a dysfunctional relationship with his family. Another enjoyable (and a little too reality based) series I had favored was "The Last Ship", about a U.S. Navy guided missile destroyer, the fictional USS Nathan James, on patrol in Antartica when a global viral pandemic erupts and wipes out over 80% of the world's population. Unaffected, the ship and its crew must try to find a cure, stop the virus and save humanity. Another winner was the series "Blindspot", about a mysterious tattooed woman found naked by the FBI inside a travel bag in Times Square. She has no recall of her past or identity. The FBI discovers that her tattoos contain clues to crimes they set out to solve. Dubbed "Jane Doe", she becomes part of the team in that endeavor.

In the news, brought to us by the letters W, T and F, a leading virologist suggested that people disinfect their grocery items (and launder their reusable shopping bags) when you bring them home and before putting them away, even those going in the refrigerator. Forty-four of a group of 70 students who ignored warnings and traveled two weeks ago from Texas to Florida for Spring Break returned home with the virus. Stop & Shop supermarkets donated $1M to support regional food banks. Massachusetts' governor used the New England Patriots' plane to transport a million N95 masks from China. Virus deaths in Spain rose past 10K, with 950 new victims. On the job front, 6.6 million Americans filed for unemployment benefits last week, double that of the previous week. New Mexico's governor warned that tribal nations could be "wiped out" by the virus. Our local Trader Joe's temporarily shut down after an employee tested positive. A train engineer purposely crashed his train just 250 yards short of the USNS Mercy in the Port of Los Angeles, in an attempt to put a spotlight on an alleged conspiracy. A report noted that 3.4 million travelers poured into the U.S. as the coronavirus pandemic erupted, likely bringing the infection with them. Fairfield's cases inched up to 50, with a third death announced. Sacred Heart University offered its currently empty dorms to first responders. A Facebook group was formed to match idle RVs with health care workers needing a place to isolate after long hospital shifts.

April 3. Today was my Dad's 84th birthday. I called him through FaceTime, unintentionally waking him up. My brother, who was still there visiting, joined the session and, together, we sang my Dad the Happy Birthday song. Dad mentioned that Dave was his first real human interaction in three weeks given that he lives in an already isolated area. Usually busy with adult education classes and cultural pursuits, Dad added that it felt weird that he had nowhere to go and nothing to attend these days. As to their day agenda, the two planned breakfast and, later, wine and beer sampling. Dave had also brought a curious large box that demanded attention. The latter turned out to be a cake. They took and shared a photo of themselves seated around it, with my Dad wearing a dust mask and holding a large knife in one hand and a glass of wine in the other, and Dave wearing his gas mask. These were strange times indeed.

It being a Friday, I mused about the oft-used acronym T.G.I.F. (Thank God It's Friday). What did that even mean these days? Usually a celebratory day signaling the end of the usual work week for most and a time to break out the wine, Friday had been muted as a standout. *Every* day had become Friday, *every* day was a day to break out the wine. Memes echoed this: "Today's forecast: 99% chance of wine."

Certain conservative groups began to advance the idea of "a clear and indisputable liability case to be made against China, which should include remuneration of the economic costs to our nation." One party suggested that Pres. Trump actually send communist dictator Xi Jinping a bill for "the damage caused by the CCP's abject and willful negligence", claiming that, for two months beginning in Nov. 2019, China "actively concealed evidence of the emerging threat and likely pandemic, systematically covering up the viral outbreak" in its country that resulted in the spread of Covid-19 worldwide. This questioning of the validity of China's relatively modest infection and fatality reports among the country's 1.4 billion people had been countered by folks on the other side of the aisle defending that China had acted early on and that it was its draconian measures that had limited the spread in its country, and prevented a greater impact on the world. This debate was likely to continue.

Not to be trite, but it seemed like the day's cold rain was falling like the collective tears of the hundreds of thousands of threatened, sick and devastated families at home and across the world who were hurting in so many ways. I turned to a steaming bowl of scrambled eggs and bacon as a momentary retreat and comfort from the misery.

I noticed an FB post asking, "Anyone else's car getting 3 weeks to the gallon at the moment?" and realized that I hadn't filled up my car since March 12, an extraordinary fact given the usual driving around that I do. Not only that, but my tank was still 3/4 full.

I achieved — well, partly achieved — another first today: going to the post office to mail a book to a friend. Because of the recommendation now to wear a face mask out in public, I dug out a bandana (red and imprinted with Jose Cuervo logos) from a bag of Halloween accessories in my attic to use as my protective gear, and grabbed a pair of winter gloves. Pulling up near the post office, I wrapped the bandana around the lower half of my face, tied it tight at the back, donned a cap and the gloves, and walked over to the facility, feeling much like I was aiming to rob a bank. There was just one other person inside — a middle-aged woman who pulled up a winter scarf over her nose and mouth as I walked in — and no clerk. The customer service room was locked shut and a sign was affixed to the door noting that the clerk had taken a one-hour lunch break. I had arrived halfway into that break and wasn't about to wait for a half hour to carry out my task. Mission aborted.

In the ever-present news, Microsoft Founder Bill Gates urged that we temporarily shut down the ENTIRE country to help contain the virus spread. An exposé focused on NYC's wet markets of live animals, tagging them as a "ticking time bomb". Vaping was said to increase the virus risk, which presented a particular threat to young people. Several FB pics showed that New Yorkers were still unsafely crowding subway cars. A set of twins born during this pandemic were named Corona and Covid. Our Fairfield, CT's cases rose to 62, with four deaths. America had a single-day death toll of over 1K, to over 6,900 deaths, while cases topped 260K. CT's Lime Rock Park race track postponed its season-opening races that had been scheduled in May. The Fed launched the Paycheck Protection Program offering loans to small businesses nationwide.

April 4. My girlfriend, Jen, and I started the day on FaceTime, an interaction that she referred to as our "virtual escapades". It was a brilliant term worth noting. With the morning shaping up to be another gray one, I went the comfort food route again, preparing my bacon and scrambled eggs breakfast special.

Mid-morning, I mustered up the courage to make another stab at the post office, donning my "Halloween" gear as I stepped from my car. The service counter was, fortunately, open this time, manned with not just one, but two clerks. On what would have been a busy service Saturday, there was only one other customer inside — an elderly woman without a mask or gloves who seemed to cower in a corner as I entered. Both clerks wore blue latex gloves but were, surprisingly, not masked. A distance line had been marked with red tape on the floor several feet from the counter. A payment touchpad, that normally would have been *on* the counter, had been placed on a stool near the line, allowing for physically distanced credit card transactions (I didn't ask if they were accepting cash or not). I passed off my package, paid and scooted out, the whole process completed in less than two minutes — certainly an all-time record for any post office visit I'd ever made in my entire life. As I quick-stepped from the facility to my car, that "bank robber" thought occurred to me again, like I had just made a heist and was fleeing the scene. My anxiety and adrenaline was at Level 11. I imagined policemen were even more amped with all of us running around with masks and gloves, making it hard to determine the bad guys from the good guys.

The day brightened weather-wise by afternoon and became mild and pleasant enough, in fact, to slip into shorts (for the first time this year), spray on some sunscreen and sit in a lounge chair on my back porch. The palatable conditions brought the neighbors out of their foxholes, too, to navigate safely around each other and chat at a distance out on the street. Others poked around in their gardens, getting them season ready.

I noticed online that many of my Facebook friends had followed my lead and adopted bandanas as simple cloth facemasks to wear in environments where physical distancing was a challenge. It inspired me to revisit my Halloween supplies and dig out three more bandanas — one paisley, another Jose Cuervo version and stars-and-stripes. I pulled two more — one from

Bulleit Bourbon and the other from Tito's Handmade Vodka — from my garden shed that I had stapled up to the inside of the doors. I had suddenly established a Spring Fashion Collection, photographed myself wearing each one and posted the pics online.

As I was preparing dinner, I got a call from Phil's mom, checking in from Miami. She spoke about the overnight curfew there, how she was keeping indoors mostly and studying for a real estate broker exam, disinfecting everything constantly and watching people in the street below from her balcony. She said only half of our state's social distancing measures had been implemented there and that local stores were way too crowded to be safe — she bailed out of one the other day.

In the day's news, Wisconsin leaders faced a dilemma with regard to successfully conducting primary voting set for April 7. An article related that abused partners are in greater danger being homebound and that domestic violence incidents had surged. Idle runway models were shown on social media conducting their own fashion shows at home. A woman flying to see her dying mother was the only passenger on an American Airlines flight and received personalized treatment with an upgrade to first class and announcements that referred to her by name. Worldwide virus cases raced past 1.1 million, with over 60K deaths. The U.S. State Dept. temporarily halted the issuance of passports. A funny video clip showed how one flight attendant was working from home — dressed in her flight outfit, serving a drink to her significant other and checking his boarding pass. Disney donated 150K rain ponchos to hospitals and medical professionals. An image of a bottle of Jameson Irish Whiskey with a spray nozzle attached to the spout offered it as a throat spray. Total virus cases reached 120,000 in Italy. A hopeful forecast model suggested that CT would see the virus outbreak peak by April 16 and potentially be over by June 1. Unemployment filings reached 220K in CT. New Orleans was reported to have the highest virus death rate (32 per 100K people) of any area in the nation. New Jersey's cases totaled 34K with 846 deaths. Popular Mechanics suggested that airships might make a comeback as planes are grounded and environmental concerns rise. NY state suffered its hardest day so far, with 630 dead and over 10K new cases.

April 5. The date marked Palm Sunday, observed by Christians the world over and particularly meaningful at this challenging time. Social media was dotted with posts of crosses made of palm leaves and with live feeds of church services, conducted by pastors from empty churches.

An old college friend from Lexington, Mass. phoned mid-morning. His son had been accepted to UConn and he was seeking some insight about the school. He mentioned that his girlfriend was ill and likely had the virus, but had been advised by her doctor to ride it out at home though to report any deterioration in condition. She was in the midst of the fever. My friend's business typically produces I.D. tags for conventions and such but had switched gears to produce health staff identification badges as well as updatable wristbands for virus patients that indicated their infection status.

I connected by text with my Dad. My brother left him yesterday and, given the absence of usual traffic congestion, took a scenic route back to his home in West Virginia. He reported to my Dad that traffic was really whipping along, with "some drivers acting as if they believed that the troopers were on lockdown, too."

At noontime, my cellphone sparked to life with an incoming Code Red message from our Town of Fairfield. It was our First Selectwoman with a message to residents, in which she stressed that people stay away from the beaches and parks and that Fairfield police will be enforcing the ban (and imposing $92 fines to anyone trespassing). She recommended the use of cloth face coverings when out in confined public spaces, per the CDC. She also noted we now have 70 confirmed cases in town and that we have entered a period of outbreak "acceleration" and to expect the next few weeks to be increasingly challenging. She concluded her message with the clever phrase, "We can get through this together, if we stay apart."

Mid-afternoon, Phil and I kicked back to watch F1 eSports' presentation of the Virtual Grand Prix, featuring a combination of retired drivers (eg. Jenson Button), test drivers, content creators and the like sitting in their own homes at simulators and competing against each other, in lieu of actual Formula 1 racing, which had been suspended for the season due to the coronavirus. The race this weekend was to have been in Vietnam, but F1 eSports didn't have a virtual representation of that track so they simulated it on the Albert Park track in Melbourne, Australia. There were 20 "drivers" in all, paired two to a team, driving for the usual teams like McLaren, Renault and Ferrari, and supported by the usual sponsors like Rolex and Pirelli. The "event" began with an 18-minute qualifying round, then transitioned right into an abbreviated 29-lap race. The graphics and sound effects were so realistic that we felt like we were watching an actual race. Ultimately, the match was won by Charles LeClerc.

My Dad shared an email from a relative of ours in South Wales. He's a teacher who said he's been home for the past three weeks and had become well versed in a menagerie of virtual meeting programs like Microsoft Teams, Collaborate, Zoom and Skype, through which he was teaching his students. He noted that his campus was closed until July 31 and had no idea how the Fall semester was going to work at this point. He described the overall situation as "surreal" and was "sad to see what is happening" in major cities across the world. As to personal restrictions, officials allow him to go out for food shopping and one hour of exercise only, which had to be solo. He assumed it would be his regimen for the next few months at least. He had just returned from a walk along a canal, saying it was a beautiful and sunny afternoon but "amazingly eerie and quiet".

My Dad posted to his FB page a similar observation. He remarked that while sipping coffee on his sunny deck this morning, he couldn't determine which was louder — "the rush of the little waterfall 40' below my house or the tweeting of the birds in the trees 40' above" in the absence of any mechanical sounds whatsoever. "No cars, no leaf blowers, no airplanes, not even helicopters heading up Morgan Creek to the hospital. Eerie." He compared the silence, as I have, with 9/11, when he and my Mom drove 2,304 miles across the country from Phoenix to get back home. He vowed, "We got through that. We'll get through this. Stay safe."

Britain's Queen Elizabeth II addressed her nation in a rare broadcast aimed at thanking those on the front lines and reassuring and inspiring the country's citizens. She spoke of how history would reflect on this time, noting "those that come after us will say the Britons of this generation were as strong as any." She encouraged a collective effort, saying, "Together we are tackling this disease. If we remain united and resolute, then we will overcome it." She concluded, "Better days will return. We will be with our friends again, we will be with our families again, we will meet again." It was Churchillian in its power.

My evening entertainment was the classic comedy flick "Zombieland", starring Jesse Eisenberg (Columbus), Emma Stone (Wichita), Woody Harrelson (Tallahassee) and Abigail Breslin (Little Rock) as survivors of a zombie apocalypse. It was narrated by Eisenberg, playing an introverted, mostly isolated college kid who finds himself suddenly in a world infested by raging, blood-thirsty zombies. He falls in with three strangers for an extended road trip battling the undead while heading west across the Southwestern United States. The film was relevant to our current crisis in many ways. Though we weren't battling zombies, we *were* fighting a virus that continually ambushed us. The scenes showed empty roads, empty cities, empty stores and a deserted amusement park. One of Columbus' rules is "Enjoy the little things", a reminder of how precious all of life's elements are, especially when you become deprived of them. "I miss people", said Columbus. We sure did, too, in the sense of being able to interact with them as we traditionally had.

In the news, NYC reported more burglaries of businesses closed due to the pandemic. Film star and former California Governor Arnold Schwarzenegger personally delivered 50K masks to doctors on the front lines. Worldwide virus cases passed 1.2 million with 65K+ deaths. State of CT projections moved the virus peak date from April 16 to April 26 with the "curve" finally flattening out through June into the first week of July. Our Town of Fairfield announced it will fine people $92 if they are found trespassing in areas that have been ordered closed. An article recalled that, in 2005, Pres. George W. Bush had the foresight to think about the possibility of a pandemic and initiated some of the groundwork prep that has helped us now. Ridgefield, CT-based restaurant Hoodoo Brown delivered 300 chicken dinners to the night shift "warriors" at Danbury Hospital, which had been particularly burdened with virus cases. A tiger at NYC's Bronx Zoo tested positive for the virus after coming into contact with an infected employee — it was the first documentation of an animal contracting the virus in the U.S.

April 6. To quote a tune from The Bangles, "It's just another manic Monday". Unlike the tune, I wasn't sure I wished it was Sunday, which for them was their "fun day", their "I don't have to run day." Honestly, every day had become an "I don't have to run day." Sunday drifts into Monday which tumbles into Tuesday and rolls over to Wednesday and so on.

I got up the courage again to make an angst producing run to my Stop & Shop grocery store, donning my makeshift stars-and-stripes bandana facemask. I found prices up all across the board; continued shortages on eggs, juice, frozen vegetables, toilet paper and paper towels; shelf stocking staff not wearing gloves or masks; and shoppers not adhering to new one-way only aisle arrows or taped down markings delineating safe physical distancing at the registers. Because of the absence of paper products, I went down the road to CVS, popping my head in to inquire — no luck. I continued my search, stopping at The Pantry mini-grocery and, surprisingly, found the "white gold" I sought. Purchase was limited to four rolls of t.p. and two rolls of p.t., for $10 in all, or about $1.60 per item. Talk about a gouge! The store, by the way, had limited the number of shoppers in-store to ten and was in the process of transitioning to curbside service, with employees or police officers stationed at the front or rear of the shop to enforce the policy.

Early afternoon, I received a text from my half-sister Nancy, who lives near my Dad in North Carolina. She let us know that her brother was in Crouse Hospital in Syracuse, NY with pneumonia and positive for Covid-19. He'd been there for 3-4 days with fever and his breathing had been getting harder. He hadn't gone on a ventilator or been moved to ICU yet, though may be moved there today. He was on meds and being evaluated for plasma transfusion from recovered patients. His wife had already had a bout with the virus and been recovering at home. She was awaiting a scheduled plasma pheresis to be done at Upstate Medical Center, which was running this protocol. "One donor can actually donate for several patients," Nancy said.

I realized today marked one month since I last saw my girlfriend, Jen. She had been keeping busy online teaching her piano students, getting her trees trimmed, checking on her sister in Norwalk, CT (who has asthma which puts her at greater risk for contracting the virus), connecting via FaceTime with her parents (Dad in Malaysia and Mom sheltering with Jen's other sister in Australia), Zoom chatting with friends and colleagues, and recording and putting online a classical song dedication every day. As for relating to each other, we'd texted and FaceTime'd each other throughout the day every day, providing emotional support, sharing memes and links to articles, and minimizing our sense of detachment and isolation.

The afternoon turned out to be very pleasant, bright and nearing 60 degrees. It brought neighbors out on their porches to sun, stroll the street and ride bikes and scooters. Between online classes, Phil took his Suzuki motorcycle out for a spin.

The evening's TV entertainment was again apocalyptic themed:

"The Last Warrior", released in 2000, starring Dolph Lundgren. It was no Academy Award winner but did have "current situation" parallels that I found notable. The plot sum-up was that a powerful earthquake splits California into an island and a band of survivors come together in a war equipment junkyard. They search for food, fuel and fellow survivors, while also dodging a violent plague that causes the skin to boil. It was the dialogue snippets though that really connected with me.

"I thought it couldn't get any worse, then it did," narrated Lundgren, suggesting to me how Covid-19 rushed over us as we stood looking.

"The old way of life is gone, and the new order has begun," he continued, making me wonder how things will be different after the pandemic has passed.

They marked time from the day of the quake, eg. Day 30, A.E. (after earthquake). I'd been marking time since our CT schools shut down — today signaled Quarantine Day 26 (Q.D. 26?). Perhaps we will mark time with the assignment A.P. (after pandemic) when our crisis has passed?

"Don't leave me here with these sick people," said a character named Candy as a team set off to find an antibiotic, illustrating the fear many of us have now while first responders devote themselves to the fight.

"We're going to have something different if I have to barf it up and call it a casserole," said one character with regard to the tedious process of meal making when you start to run out of fresh ideas or have limited ingredient resources.

One soldier told another that he had been delivering supplies when the quake hit, adding that the supplies were toilet paper, which had become a luxury as it had these days.

"I don't think it's there (America) anymore," says Lundgren, wondering what lay beyond their isolated environment. "What do you mean? America's still gotta be there," replied a group member. "Not the America we knew," Lundgren says. Certainly we should expect our country to be different after this health crisis, but hopefully in a positive way.

"Many will come, many will go. I just didn't think I'd lose three in a matter of hours," says Lundgren, saddened that several team members had left the camp. I thought that line could easily have been said by one of our front lines health workers as patients die at an incredible rate.

"Things aren't like they used to be before the Big One, but we found a place, ours. We made contact between us. In the best of times, it's what we cherish. In the worst, it's all we hang onto," Lundgren concluded about his group's reality. The reference made me think how we had hunkered down with our families, and in our neighborhoods, and re-connected collectively to share in the hardship and hope of our time.

In the news, an article related the tale of a couple who traveled to the Maldives March 22 for a six-day honeymoon and had been unable to return home — the staff has been at their full disposal and they have been wiling the days away sunning and snorkeling. Texas police were searching for an 18-year-old woman who claimed on social media that she would purposely spread the virus, an act now considered a terroristic threat. U.S. cases mounted to over 337K and over 10K dead and climbing, hinting at the difficult weeks yet to come. Dozens of squirrels had openly reclaimed a park in Santa Monica, CA as residents there are on lockdown. Worldwide virus cases neared 1.3 million and over 70K deaths. Tesla electric car company had created a hospital ventilator prototype largely fashioned out of its car parts and was in the process of mass producing it. Ridgefield, CT's First Selectman Rudy Marconi tested positive for the virus. It was reported that AMC movie houses may not recover and will shut down for good. The White House advised Americans to avoid grocery stores if they are able to over the next few weeks. Heart damage and cardiac arrest were observed as new troubles befalling virus patients. Auto insurer Allstate announced it would return $600M in premiums as the pandemic cut driving. British Prime Minister Boris Johnson was moved to intensive care after his condition worsened.

April 7. I had the most adventurous extended outing of the past month this morning. It began with another trip to the post office — geared up, transacting via the physically distanced paypad, hand sanitizing back at the car, all as before. The clerk was masked and gloved; one other customer was masked. Then I headed west through Fairfield's empty downtown and Southport's quiet village to a Starbucks on the Post Road in Westport. Though the cafe was closed, the drive-thru was open and about a dozen cars were in line for orders. I picked up a Venti latte from the clerk who was gloveless and unmasked and handled my credit card with the very tips of his fingers. I took a loop along Westport's desolate Main Street and then banked south to my girlfriend Jen's house, to deliver the latte. Dressed in pajamas and pink fuzzy slippers, she greeted me through the door, was happy about the gesture and poured it into two of her own cups for us to enjoy at a distance on her patio, with Kleenex and a large pump bottle of hand sanitizer centered on her patio table. Inspired by the java, she decided to sit at her Steinway piano in her glass-enclosed lounge area to entertain me with a private concert. I sat in a chair on her lawn just outside opened sliding doors to hear her play. Her song selection was Elton John's appropriately titled "Someone Saved My Life Tonight". One line really rang true: "We've all gone crazy lately." Then, as the sun decided to peek out, we hatched a plan to take a walk around her area. I pulled up my bandana over my nose and mouth and walked six feet behind her as we strolled, admiring homes, budding trees and blossoming flowers. Quite accidentally, a couple that I knew came strolling by in the opposite direction, complimenting our physical distancing strategy. It was a pleasant visit overall. Later on, Jen texted, "It will be nice to head out again when all this is over, to get dressed up and be able to enjoy the little things like eating out with you. Maybe late summer I anticipate. Strange times. Now more than ever we need scientists and epidemiologists to find a vaccine and cure. Our whole existence will change."

On the return home traveling east along the Post Road, I stopped at Hemlock Hardware after noticing stacks of bagged-up mulch, remembering that it was something I had wanted to get to. The transaction — a wallet-punching $69 for 10 bags of Scott's Triple Shed Extra Fine mulch — was conducted without contact between customer and proprietor by holding one's credit card up to the window so that the clerk could punch the credit card number into his payment processor. It was self-help from there, with me loading the bags into the trunk to tote home.

Mid-afternoon, I was inspired to spread the mulch around. I made quick work of it while enjoying mild temperatures and a light breeze. Rain was in the forecast so I felt good that I was getting it down before it arrived.

Dad checked in by email late afternoon, reporting his travels on foot and sightings in his Chapel Hill, NC area. "Walked six miles this afternoon after doing Stephanie's class (yoga) via Zoom for an hour this morning. (I feel so virtuous!) Critter count: one camel, three llamas (including two white ones I'd never seen before), four donkeys, and ten horses (including two tall long-legged guys I'd bet on if they were wearing numbers). One of the good things about this enforced stay-at-home business is that with no other commitments and nothing else I have to do, I can enjoy this beautiful area where I live. With so many plants in bloom, the air is positively perfumed. Too often over the past few decades I've been somewhere else, China or wherever, at this most perfect time of the year here. Not so this year and I'm taking advantage of it."

Early evening, I heard from a longtime friend in Panama, which had over 2K cases and 59 deaths thus far. She said that a quarantine was imposed and alcohol sales had been banned since mid-March. "People got crazy on the first weekend," she said. "Lots of car accidents, social BBQs, traffic jammed in the countryside and crowded beaches." Now the norm is masks, gloves and some exaggerated protective clothing.

Dinner was a homemade pizza and a pour of Guinness, to mark National Beer Day, which celebrates the day in 1933 that the Cullen-Harrison act was signed into law, reversing the prohibition on selling beer in the United States.

As the sky dimmed, I remembered tonight was the occasion of the Pink Moon, the largest supermoon of the year. It looked big and bold and mysterious, behind a shroud of clouds. I admired it standing in the middle of my street.

The evening flick was a French film with English subtitles called "A Breath Away" (2018). It told the story of an immense toxic gas cloud released by an earthquake that envelops Paris, and a couple trying to protect their daughter, who has an auto-immune syndrome that confines her to an oxygen-fed chamber in the family's apartment. While the gas kills everyone in the street, it is heavier than air, and the couple finds refuge above the mist in their elderly neighbors' top-floor apartment. The girl is still in her chamber in the family's now fog-filled flat, with only limited battery power to keep her air filtration system operating. With the mist still slowly rising, food in short supply, and all power and communication cut, the couple must brave the fog and the corpse-strewn streets to find equipment that will enable their daughter to escape with them from the city. Again, there were parallels with our current situation, eg. the lethal fog rushing through like this virus has enveloped us. People fleeing Paris like people fled NY to Long Island, New Jersey and Connecticut. The rising mist was like the marching daily case count that we had all been watching with concern. One poignant quote: "I think we've crossed the line. It won't get better. It'll only get worse. There must be a tolerable number of dead, a mortality threshold

45

to stay under. Beyond it, society won't recover." The quote reflected our fear that the virus would grow too overwhelming to control, affecting the very structure and societal machinery that keeps order.

The news: NYC's Mayor de Blasio was considering temporary mass burials in Central Park should local morgues become overwhelmed. A new study showed that the virus can live in your respiratory tract for up to 37 days. Actress Honor Blackman, who played Pussy Galore in the James Bond film "Goldfinger" (1964), died of natural causes at age 94. A couple that gave up having a home to travel full time, were now stuck in place by the pandemic. Lime Rock Park in Lakeville, CT announced the postponement of its Trans Am Memorial Day Weekend racing event. Worldwide, virus cases spilled over 1.4 million, with over 81K deaths. U.S. cases reached over 400K and 12,854 dead. Israel had begun using McDonald's drive-thrus for speedy virus testing. A scientist warned that the virus was particularly dangerous near the ocean and beach as the particles are thought to carry and drift much farther than initially imagined. New York State logged its deadliest single-day virus death total, with 731 fatalities. Our town of Fairfield's case count rose to 94 and a fifth person died.

April 8. It had rained overnight, as expected, and now the morning was gray. I watched a pair of sparrows across the road, involved in a mating dance, thrashing and tumbling around each other. Another trio pecked at seeds my neighbor had newly spread in bare patches in his front yard. I heard the sad coos of a mourning dove. Nature marched on, oblivious to our crisis.

I shared with Jen by FaceTime about seeing the mating birds. She was enjoying a cup of tea and watching squirrels chase each other in her yard. Our animal chat migrated to talk about black widow spiders and how the females kill the smaller males after mating, baby spiders that eat their mothers alive, and baby sharks that cannibalize their siblings in the womb. Nature, we decided, can be as harsh as human existence at its most trying times.

Phil shared that his mom and fellow Miami residents had begun the tradition every evening at 8pm of banging on pots and pans, as we were doing here every Wednesday evening. My eldest son Evan let me know that things were pretty much unchanged in D.C. He had been running on foot over to his girlfriend's place as he didn't feel comfortable anymore taking the Metro or an Uber. They had been wearing makeshift masks whenever they go outside now. He said she was going to sew him a proper one later this week. Though his company, SmartBrief, was doing well, he was afraid of an imminent recession.

Late morning, I made pancakes — something I hadn't done in ages — using overripe bananas, chocolate shavings and thawed frozen berries, with a side of bacon. My initial intention was to make banana bread but the recipe I found online was too involved. I had enjoyed cooking during this time, as a pursuit and a distraction from reality.

I had been thinking of my Mom lately. She passed on Memorial Day 2013 at the age of 74 from pancreatic cancer. She was gone less than three months after her diagnosis. I'm glad she was spared our current world misery, though she endured her own. A nurse early on and general do-it-yourselfer who was inclined to help anyone and everyone and was reusing, recycling and repurposing before it became trendy, Mom would have risen to the occasion during this time. She would have been sewing and distributing fabric facemasks, volunteering at soup kitchens, conducting food drives, donating blood, checking on neighbors, making nutritious home cooked meals, doing house and garden projects, and more. "Waste not, want not," that was her motto.

Midday, I went on another gasp-inducing outing, to the local Home Depot, to buy grass seed and top soil to patch my back yard. The parking lot was fairly full when I arrived and shoppers in masks and latex gloves were going to and fro pushing carts piled mostly with gardening items. I had hoped to enter the open-air, fenced-in garden department but found the gate locked and blocked. Then I noticed that all would-be shoppers were being steered to one entrance on the far left. Up a ramp and along a corridor marked with arrows I went, hooking a left past a staffer with a clicker counting heads, and into the store. Most shoppers I whooshed by were masked and gloved and there were safe distance markings on the floor at the registers. I went straight through to the garden department, collected my haul and circled back to pay. Back along another lane and out into the parking lot I went, pretty painless all in all actually.

I spent half of the afternoon breaking up the soil in bare patches, sprinkling seed, dropping a soil top layer and then watering down all the treated areas. It was an enjoyable labor and another distracting pursuit.

At 7pm, we migrated to our front porch for the Wednesday evening community bell ringing and pot pounding. Neighbors up and down the street grinned and waved as we clanged away.

Nursing aching hands from the yard work, I kicked back in the living room for my evening apocalyptic visual fare, this time choosing "Contracted: Phase II". Released in 2015, the film stars Matt Mercer as Riley, one of the last people to come in contact with a woman named Samantha, who suffers from a mysterious and deadly disease that begins to threaten the world. But I grew restless and distracted as I watched this selection and reached out by FaceTime to Jen. We thought we would engage in another round of "virtual escapades" but really wanted to see each other in person.

Swallowing hard and crossing myself for luck, and against our better judgement, I broke out of quarantine to drive to her place. It was late evening at this point and I didn't want to stand out on the road. After all, an 8pm curfew had just been imposed for all residents in neighboring Bridgeport. So I went along back roads to Southport and jumped on I-95 southbound there, making the short ride to Westport. As I went along, I looked for signs from the universe that what I was doing was ok. But the still-full moon seemed to coldly and disapprovingly glare down at me and make my passage obvious. A police SUV that went by in the fast lane didn't reassure me either. But then a traffic signal that's always red when I come to it shone green like a thumbs-up, which led me to Jen's house and a single light shining like a beacon welcoming me to shore. There followed a nerve-wracking but glorious reunion, ending 32 days of true physical distancing. We hoped we would not regret our decision.

The news this day: NYC suffered its worst 24 hours, pushing its death toll over 4K. Fifty-one recovered virus patients tested positive again in South Korea. The virus peak for Connecticut was projected to be April 22, with an expectation on that date of a peak high of 192 daily deaths; the ultimate cumulative death toll for CT was projected to be 5,474. Instructors at Bridgeport's Housatonic Community College had been building with 3D printers face shields for local hospital staff. The suspension of all Broadway shows was extended through June 7. Democratic presidential candidate Bernie Sanders suspended his campaign, leaving Joe Biden as the party's lone nominee. Virus cases in the U.S. topped 420K with over 14K deaths. Worldwide, cases moved past the 1.5 million mark with nearly 88K deaths. The Himalayas became visible for the first time in 30 years as pollution levels in India dropped. Similarly, emissions of toxic fumes from London traffic fell to the lowest level since the 1950s.

April 9. The morning was a sad gray as I rolled along the Post Road from Westport to Fairfield, at a time that would normally be peak Thursday rush-hour, with oncoming traffic bumper to bumper moving in the opposite direction towards Stamford. But in the five-mile span I traveled, I noted just a dozen vehicles, primarily contractor vans. And the lots in front of normally busy businesses were completely empty.

Rain began falling mid-morning and grew heavier as the day progressed. High winds added intensity and drama, as if we weren't already surrounded by enough stimulation. I passed the time listening to music, which came from many different sources. Classical music streaming from a local radio station. Rock and pop streaming from regional rock stations, with its deejays working their shifts *from their respective homes*, often with their kids joining in. More streaming music of all types from a Bridgeport-based indie station. Live streaming performances on Facebook from musician friends like Glenn Roth, Benny Mikula, Brian Dolzani, Rick Torres, Tracy Recalde, Anna Urbanska, Beto Petrillo, Tommy Weeks and Chris Cavaliere, all of whom responded to posted comments in real-time and asked how our homebound days were going. Other musician friends, like the Merwin Mountain Band, steered our attention to their pre-recorded YouTube performances. Of course, I had to include my gf, Jen, in this group, who was playing and posting one song every day reflecting her mood, the day or an occasion. Even bellydancers like Melina Bello were getting in on the virtual performance act. To boot, ticket brokers like Live Nation Concerts had converted to promoting virtual music. Live Nation, for instance, rebranded itself as Live From Home, offering shows like "Meghan Trainor: The Live From Home Tour", set for April 13, from her couch.

Late afternoon, the sun peeked out finally, which inspired me to start cooking dinner — penne pasta with ground beef, vegetables and peeled tomatoes. As I prepared the meal, a military helicopter flew over heading west then u-turned and came back east. I imagined it was assessing ground situations but then thought it might be doing a coastal patrol after reading that two Russian spy planes that neared Alaska today were intercepted and turned back by U.S. fighter jets in what officials called a test of our reaction timing during this public health crisis.

Typically late day, I had made a habit of tuning in to live briefings from various government teams. At the federal level, it was the White House Coronavirus Task Force team consisting of Pres. Trump, Vice Pres. Mike Pence, Dr. Anthony Fauci and Dr. Deborah Birx, the latter an American physician and diplomat who specializes in HIV/AIDS immunology, vaccine research and global health, now serving as Coronavirus Response Coordinator for the task force team. At the Connecticut state level, it was Gov. Lamont with changeable team members and remote Q & A from local media. Finally, at the local level, our First Selectwoman Brenda Kupchick, Fire Chief Denis McCarthy, Health Director Sands Cleary and Police Chief Chris Lyddy.

The living room cinema attraction this evening was "The Host", a 2006 South Korean monster film that kicks off with scofflaw American military personnel pouring dozens of bottles of formaldehyde down a drain that empties into South Korea's Han River. Several years later, a huge ravenous mutated creature emerges from the water and begins wreaking havoc on local residents. It carries off several people, including a young girl, to deposit in a deep sewer as "snacks for later". The military is called in to evacuate the riverside area, restrict access and detain anyone who may have had contact with the creature, as it has been found to be the host of and to transmit a virus. Those detained are sprayed and quarantined, including the girl's family. When the family learns that the girl is still alive, they break out of containment to go rescue her. To me, the parallels of the film and our modern day crisis were obvious: the beast being symbolic of the virus; the virus being transmitted from a live animal to a human; and the scenes of hazmat suits, military presence, quarantine and containment.

News of the day: Another 6.6 million Americans filed for unemployment benefits in the past week. A report indicated that the virus landed in NYC in mid-February, with the seeds planted mostly by visitors from Europe. New Jersey mandated that face masks be worn by everyone in grocery stores. New York had the dubious distinction of having more virus cases (nearly 152K) than any country; at the same time, Connecticut claimed the highest virus hospitalization rate. A field hospital opened outside Bridgeport Hospital as an overflow space to treat moderately ill Covid-19 patients who needed care, like oxygen or IV fluids. The owner of a Georgia Bar, Tybee Island's Sand Bar, removed $3,714 worth of bills that had been stapled to the venue's walls to give to her unemployed staff.

CT state police warned of a stimulus check scam wherein a person claiming to be from the IRS would call, email or text you to verify your personal/banking information. In a bright spot during this dark time, 70,000 endangered sea turtles worked on increasing their numbers, laying eggs on empty beaches in India as people were quarantined. Unrelated to the virus, MAD Magazine cartoonist Mort Drucker passed at age 91. A Belgian-Dutch study found that runners, walkers and other outdoor exercisers are particularly susceptible to transferring the virus when they are close to each other. Our CT Gov. Lamont ordered our schools and non-essential businesses to stay shut until at least May 20. The IRS said that 50 million Americans would be receiving stimulus payments of $1,200 or more via direct deposit by tomorrow. NYC had begun to bury virus victims in a potter's field on Hart Island near City Island in the Bronx. A Belfast bar launched a "fresh Guinness to your door" delivery service. Worldwide, virus cases pushed over 1.6 million cases, with nearly 96K deaths; of these, the U.S. had 466K cases and 15,572 deaths.

CHAPTER 3

THIRTY DAYS IN

April 10. While having my morning coffee on what was starting off as a bright but blustery day, I had a FB Messenger exchange with a Swedish friend. I had shared a news story link with him regarding how Sweden was handling the crisis. The country was mostly sharing guidance with its people about how to stay safe by social distancing but not doing broad shutdowns like we had done. Instead, it was urging those at higher risk — people over 70 and with underlying conditions — to remain home. Its virus cases and deaths were on par with most other countries though it was faring much better economically. "According to my friends and family, everyone is pretty much self-sequestering unless they need to go out. Funny how that works when you have a responsible populace," my friend said, adding, "My cousin is opening a new restaurant April 30 with nothing holding him back, so that's good for the economy."

Today marked Good Friday, the Christian holiday commemorating the crucifixion of Jesus and his death at Calvary, observed during Holy Week on this Friday preceding Easter Sunday. For the faithful, it is a day for somber reflection, honoring the way Jesus suffered and died for their sins. As terrible as the day was for Jesus, it marked the dramatic culmination of God's plan to save his people from their sins. I wished prayers for the world, encouraging that we treasure in our memory those who have passed and to think good thoughts for all people struggling, hug our families tight and look ahead with hope to brighter, happier days.

Our Gov. Lamont held a mid-morning online briefing acknowledging the holiday and its meaning to him, as a period of hope and renewal. He said we've been fighting a war and that its end may come soon. At the same time, he cautioned, "This silent enemy doesn't just surrender" and continued to urge strict social distancing, ramped-up testing and vaccine development. He continued, "This is a war that is never won. It's a war that we have to figure out how we wind it down in the safest way possible for people. I know the urgency many of you feel to get back to your everyday lives, but I've got to urge you one more time: Now is no time to take your foot off the accelerator. Now is no time to relax the social distancing."

Indeed, here in Fairfield, our First Selectwoman announced that Connecticut now had 9,784 positive cases, 380 deaths and 1,464 hospitalizations. Our Town itself had 144 cases and now seven deaths. On the upside, 34 had fully recovered. We were still in the thick of the battle.

Today also marked my Quarantine Day 30 — thirty days since March 12, when everything suddenly and dramatically shut down around us and people raced to the stores to panic shop and stock up. When the "shit hit the fan" as I noted in my day planner. As of that day, the U.S. had just 987 cases and 29 deaths. To appreciate the magnitude of how our situation had changed, as of this morning, the U.S. had identified over 475K cases and logged over 17K deaths. Similarly, globally, 30 days ago there were 125K cases and over 4,600 deaths; now there were over 1.6 million cases and over 100K deaths. Seemingly unimaginable and altogether surreal.

Early afternoon, I headed out to do the weekly shopping — bandana in place, gloves on, paper bags in hand. For a change, I was actually reassured, finding fewer items out of stock, people mostly adhering to proper distancing and aisle directions, and garbage bins set out throughout the parking lot for the disposal of used latex gloves. I even found toilet paper, limited to two single rolls per shopper. Depletions/low stock items included fabric softener, dishwashing liquid, disinfectant wipes, napkins, paper towels, hand soap, pasta, shredded cheese and hand sanitizer. Otherwise, there was plenty of bread, eggs, milk, vegetables, beer, water and like essentials.

In the evening, I curled up with a bowl of scrambled eggs I'd cooked up and caught a prime time feature, an action flick from 2011 titled "Sucker Punch", at "Mike's Home Theater". It was about a young woman who had created a fantastic alternate world to help her escape the mental institute where she was trapped. I only got through a third of it before my eyes grew heavy and I retired to bed.

In the news, a store in California announced a grocery giveaway that drew a mile-long line of cars and hundreds of other people on foot. A group of U.S. senators composed a letter to China calling on the country to close its wet markets. As they struggle to stay afloat, restaurants and sommeliers have been selling their rarest and most prized wines and spirits from their collections. The popular Faxon Law Fairfield Road Races, held annually in my area in June and one of the top races in the country, was postponed to September and was going to be led by a new director. Sacred Heart University announced a virtual career and internship fair in lieu of having a live, in-person event. It was suggested that "normal" travel may not resume for two years after the pandemic had been deemed brought under control and that lighter, efficient aircraft will be the preferred mode of transport going forward. NASA reported a 30% air pollution drop in the northeastern U.S. The passenger ferry that runs back and forth between neighboring Bridgeport, CT and Port Jefferson, NY had begun focusing on carrying freight in the absence of passengers. Virologists have begun looking at how this virus could jump to another species and re-infect us down the line.

April 11. The day started brightly, with the sun streaming through the budding branches of the Bradford Pear tree and bright yellow Forsythia bush in my front yard, and lighting up the daffodils along the southern side of my house. It was a hopeful start to Easter weekend and yet I knew the world story was still a sad one.

Connecting by FaceTime, Jen told me of a strange dream she had in which her feet had grown roots that required pruning. I provided the interpretation that she was feeling mired being homebound and eager for an outing. Though by no means the grand excursion she had imagined, a trip she took later to her local Trader Joe's to buy toilet paper served to quell her wanderlust for the moment!

In our call, we also spoke of wet markets and how viruses in general had sprung from animals to humans, including the tiger at the Bronx Zoo that had been spotlighted in the news. We wondered if my cat, Stormy, could be susceptible and decided, yes, she could be but not in a way that would be harmful to anyone. What a morning discussion!

On a daily basis, Facebook notifies you of your friends' birthdays as they occur and it had been my habit to wish every one of my friends — over 4,500 — a Happy Birthday. Among today's celebrants was an artist friend who I had last seen at the opening of her work in mid-February at

54

Southport Galleries. It was a grand time, with hugging, drinking, eating and lively conversation — the good old days, seemingly ages ago. And now that gallery had closed, a victim of stalled business, and the space had a "For Lease" sign in front of it. Another celebrant was an area mom whose children had gone to school with mine and who was also a UNC Tar Heels fan. I last saw her Feb. 21, with her husband, at Aspetuck Brew Lab in neighboring Black Rock, where we clinked glasses, chattered about the team and our kids, and generally soaked up the joyous atmosphere, with not a care about the coronavirus.

As I wouldn't be seeing my Dad in person this Easter, I took advantage of a free e-card offer from 123Greetings, customizing a text message that paired with a graphic of three chicks hatching one by one from eggs, each with an instrument in hand on which they offered a musical note then jammed collectively.

Mid-morning, I turned my attention to the yard, finishing the rest of the bare patch clawing, seeding and watering, which occupied both my body and mind. I noticed my adjacent neighbors engaged in a similar manner, mowing, pruning, raking, etc. The labor earned me a Corona and sandwich on my back steps, which was being well favored by the midday sun.

Late afternoon, I made an Asian meal of chicken diced up in rice with green peppers, onions, broccoli, garlic, cabbage and soy sauce. As I finished up, I described the dish to Jen and she thought it was more "Amer-Asian", as it lacked typical Asian ingredients, like black bean sauce and bok choy. But it still got a passing grade.

Dad checked in by email to indicate that the pandemic wasn't slowing him down any. He shared a selfie and reported on his exercise regimen, "I took yesterday off, so today I fast-walked 10 miles at just under a 14-min./mile pace. I kept the turnover steady even on the toughest uphills. I don't know when I've felt so strong. I'm bummed that the Senior Games got canceled — I might've kicked some serious butt!"

Queen Elizabeth II rose to the occasion again, offering a heartfelt Easter weekend message suited to us all. "This year, Easter will be different for many of us, but by keeping apart, we keep others safe. But Easter isn't cancelled. Indeed, we need Easter as much as ever," the Queen said in her address. "We know that coronavirus will not overcome us. As dark as death can be, particularly for those suffering with grief, light and life are greater.

May the living flame of the Easter hope be a steady guide as we face the future."

It was all the inspiration I needed that early evening. As the last light of the day was slowly being extinguished, I hopped in the car and headed to Jen's. I moved quickly, as if I was racing to beat a curfew, though none had been imposed on us. My timing was perfect as the sun was just setting, lighting everything up in a warm glow, and yet, a digital sign on I-95 glared "Stay Home, Stay Safe". I tried to ignore the warning and joined the slipstream of cars whooshing along, then quickly navigated the backroads to Jen. When I arrived at her Westport home, she was reclined in her living room engrossed in watching on her laptop a makeup application tutorial. I poured myself a vodka and cranberry cocktail and sat beside her, joking about the "before" and "after" looks of the tutorial model — so radically different that the cosmetics surely fostered false advertising.

In a short while, we moved upstairs to her TV area, where she did some ironing as we watched a Chinese-produced film, "The Farewell", about a family coming to terms with their matriarch's lung cancer diagnosis. Then we migrated to listening to, of all things, acoustic Christmas songs provided by her Alexa smart speaker. We needed a little Christmas cheer and why not in our world turned upside down? We enjoyed songs by Willie Nelson, Dolly Parton and renditions of "Frosty the Snowman", "Joy to the World", "Jingle Bells", "Silent Night" and "I'll Be Home For Christmas". It was a perfectly ridiculous and beautiful moment. For us, Easter Eve had become the new Christmas Eve, with the streets and neighborhoods hushed, and families huddled together enjoying meals and togetherness and looking forward to the holiday.

On the heels of that, we pulled up Hulu Live on her laptop to watch a historic "Saturday Night Live" remote presentation, dubbed "SNL at Home". Prior to this, the last new episode of SNL was March 7, when Actor Daniel Craig hosted with musical guest The Weeknd. It seemed like a lifetime ago. Now, with the cast and crew engaged in social distancing, SNL's aim was to air monologues and segments made at home and without a live audience. This was an unprecedented experiment for the show, which hadn't canceled an episode since 1986, when the World Series between the New York Mets and Boston Red Sox entered extra innings, and the show was broadcast two weeks later.

Sharing a pint of Ben & Jerry's Cherry Garcia ice cream (again, why not?), Jen and I looked on as Actor Tom Hanks, who had survived his bout with the virus, kicked off the SNL presentation, vigorously thanking all the first responders and health care workers everywhere. Then the segments unfurled: Pete Davidson singing a Drake song from his mom's basement, SNL cast members posing as fellow office employees having a Zoom meeting, Coldplay's Chris Martin singing "Shelter from the Storm", a Weekend Update Home Edition, and "Bob Tisdale" of Sky Sports offering play-by-play about mundane happenings in his home, among the clips. Commercial breaks were PSAs from NYC's Health Director, reminding folks to stay home, and the Red Cross, seeking blood donations. There was also a tribute to the show's Music Producer Hal Willner, who had passed April 7. The show closed with credits scrolling in front of an empty stage set.

News of the day: Worldwide virus cases had increased by another 100K in the past 24 hours, to 1.7 million (includes 382K recovered), with over 103K deaths; U.S. total cases tipped over 500K (incl. 28K recovered), with over 20K deaths. An article discussed the sounds or lack thereof that we were now hearing in the absence of human congestion and bustle. Research showed that this virus was mutating to overcome people's immune systems; Australia, for example, was contending with two strains of the virus, and there were actually three strains affecting the world. Educators suggested that plans needed to be made now for continued student instruction from home in the increasingly likely event that schools will not be ready to reopen in the Fall. It was announced that Pope Francis would be live-streaming his Easter Sunday service. Hundreds of U.S. meat plant workers had tested positive for the virus, raising questions about America's food supply chain. NYC Mayor de Blasio said city schools will remain closed through the rest of the 2019-2020 academic year. CT Gov. Lamont said food trucks could operate at rest stops to feed truckers and essential workers. A lab in Iceland proposed that 50% of virus cases have no symptoms, which could spell big trouble going forward. A band of billionaires and their posse of young women defied lockdown measures and flew a private jet from the U.K. to France, where they got into a scuffle with authorities on the tarmac. With the addition of Wyoming, a Disaster Declaration had now been issued in all 50 states, the first time in American history. Shuttered theaters had begun taking archived show footage and offering viewing online for the cost of a ticket. Indigenous

Amazonian tribes, at risk of genocide, were being impacted by the virus. Delta Air Lines adopted new "back to front" and "boarding by row" passenger loading procedures. Americans were boozing it up while working from home, throwing back alcohol between Zoom meetings. Sidewalk art was popping up all over.

April 12. Easter morning. Sun filtered through the trees in a completely hushed Westport setting, with the exception of a lone Canadian goose that flew over honking a greeting.

Pope Francis had already delivered his noon live-streaming service from St. Peter's Basilica in Rome, sharing many thoughtful observations and hopeful wishes. He acknowledged first responders and others on the "front lines", saying, "Look at the real heroes who come to light in these days: they are not famous, rich and successful people; rather they are those who are giving themselves in order to serve others." He noted our dark days: "For weeks now it has been evening. Thick darkness has gathered over our squares, our streets and our cities; it has taken over our lives, filling everything with a deafening silence and a distressing void, that stops everything as it passes by; we feel it in the air, we notice it in people's gestures, their glances give them away." He spotlighted our superficial ways, saying the storm exposes "our vulnerability and uncovers those false and superfluous certainties around which we have constructed our daily schedules" and lays bare "all those attempts to anesthetize ourselves." He chastised, "We have all gone ahead 'at breakneck speed', ignoring the wars, injustice, and cries of the poor and our ailing planet. We carried on regardless, thinking we would stay healthy in a world that was sick." He concluded, "In the midst of isolation when we are suffering from a lack of tenderness and chances to meet up, and we experience the loss of so many things, let us once again listen to the proclamation that saves us: He is risen and is living by our side."

Weaving my way east back to Fairfield, I noticed the sun playing on the buds and new flowers, and took in Easter signs: waves glinting at Southport's Mill Tide basin, an oversized upright rabbit holding a spotted Easter egg and standing by the door of an auto repair shop, colorful hearts arranged in the shape of a bigger heart in a dentist's office window, a message at St. Thomas Aquinas R.C. Church: "Risen, Lord Jesus heal our world, Blessed & Safe Easter", and a banner in front of Saugatuck Sweets ice cream parlor similarly exclaiming "He is Risen! Happy Easter!" I spotted a neighbor couple strolling, and stopped to say hello to another who was planning on making a ham for Easter dinner.

Back at home, I caught a live Easter greeting on Facebook from NY Gov. Cuomo. He had flown upstate and was standing in front of Pathways Nursing & Rehabilitation Center in Niskayuna, outside Albany, and shared, "We're going through a difficult time here as everybody knows, seeing a lot of pain, a lot of loss. Again last night we lost hundreds of New Yorkers to this terrible disease. It's been disorienting, everybody is suffering on a lot of levels. People are afraid, people are anxious. They're under stress everywhere they turn... A lot of pain, a lot of suffering. But also when things are at their worst, sometimes people are at their best. And sometimes just when you need it, people can really show you how great they can be." His reference was to the fact that the Center had offered 35 ventilators to downstate hospitals, which inspired Cuomo's visit, to thank the facility for its gesture and generosity.

After enjoying our family-famous Eggs Lauterborn — an Eggs Benedict adaptation — as brunch, I stepped outside to hose down areas of the lawn that I had newly seeded. People passed as I handled the task, including a dad and his daughter on bikes, and his wife trailing on foot. I called out to the man, "How are you?" He replied, "Trying to keep optimistic."

I noticed on Facebook that a former neighbor had put up a photo late last night of dyed Easter eggs and the caption, "Happy Easter to all, and to all a good night." Another posted a photo of her mom's Easter tree — a white needled evergreen tree aglow with white lights and dotted with plastic pastel-colored Easter eggs. More folks making the Easter-Christmas connection.

While baking a ham for Easter dinner, I FaceTime'd Dad to check in on him. He was bundled up in a blanket and watching the movie "The Heist" on Netflix. He was feeling kind of low and bored without company, so I did my best to cheer him up, including suggesting he join me in a virtual pour of Guinness.

The evening film feature was "The Homesman", a 2014 historical drama set in the 1850s Midwest, directed by and starring Tommy Lee Jones as a claim jumper saved from hanging by Mary Bee Cuddy, a frontier farmer played by Hilary Swank, who persuades him to help her escort three women who have suffered breakdowns to a safe haven in Iowa. I zero'ed in on how isolation can toy with mental health, driving people to normally uncharacteristic behavior. CT mental health experts, in fact, said isolation due to the virus crisis is causing "a perfect storm of psychological trauma" rarely seen, if ever.

News: More than a dozen tornadoes struck the South, from Texas to Louisiana, leaving many structures damaged and nearly two-dozen people dead. That same storm system was expected to hit CT tomorrow, with a combo of heavy rain, flooding, lightning and wind gusts up to 60mph. Global virus cases increased by another 100K in the past 24 hours, to 1.8 million (412K recovered) with over 110K deaths. In the U.S., cases topped 535K (over 30K recovered) with over 20,600 deaths, indicating that we were still headed up the slope. A firefighter in Rio de Janeiro went up into the air in a cherry picker to play his trumpet high above the city and cheer citizens in isolation. German police trying to enforce social distancing were attacked by a group of young people with iron bars and stones. The Dept. of Environmental Protection closed several of CT's state parks citing that the public was not adhering to social distancing guidelines. Our Fairfield First Selectwoman said our Town now had 173 cases (including 54 recoveries) and eight deaths; overall, CT now had over 11.5K cases and 494 deaths. Indonesia's Krakatoa volcano erupted, another illustration of how completely pissed off Mother Nature was at us. NYC's Mayor de Blasio decided to move 6,000 homeless with the virus (or at risk for it) to hotels. If we didn't have enough on our plate already, a high pathogenic bird flu was detected on a turkey farm in South Carolina — it killed over 1,500 turkeys before being identified April 6; the balance of birds (32K) were euthanized and the farm contained before any entered the marketplace. Firefighters struggled to control wildfires that ignited near Ukraine's Chernobyl nuclear site and have been burning for the past week, stirring up radiation and threatening surrounding areas.

April 13. The start of a new week. The predicted storm had rushed in overnight, drumming us with rain, flooding local roads and whipping tree branches around all morning. As I sipped on a cup of coffee, I listened to the wind howl, rain spatter on the windows and a cacophony of sirens on fire engines headed to a local calamity.

I tended to my left eye, which had sprouted a stye on the upper eyelid, swelled up and reddened. My Dad, coincidentally, had grown a similar node, same spot. We suspected it was due to disrupted sleep patterns of late and agreed that hot compresses would counter the attack. These days, any little health issue could potentially be a greater crisis though. At all costs, one wanted to avoid a clinic or hospital visit for fear of unintentionally contracting the virus.

I thought about the mental inventory I had been making on a daily basis as I roamed the house, almost as if I was a military supply officer. Toilet paper, five rolls, check. Paper towels, two rolls, check. Eggs, two cartons, check. Disinfectant wipes, two containers, check. The home bunker was secure for now.

Browsing Facebook, I noticed all the new member groups that had sprung up to support one mission or another. "Bells of Unity" allowed folks from all over to post general concerns. "Healthy Cooking During Corona" was a repository for recipes. "Fairfield County Local Curbside, Takeout & Delivery" offered menus, restaurant pickup hours and the like. Another, "203 Rainbow Hunt", encouraged CT followers to post pics of drawings or depictions of rainbows. "Faith, Hope & Peace" promoted general positivity.

The local PTA president announced that her group would pay for the cost of producing signs congratulating seniors on graduating (in lieu of a live graduation ceremony) and would also handle posting these in the front yards at the students' homes. A great gesture, but what a muted end to years of schooling. As other Facebook friends had done, I posted a photo of myself from my high school senior year as a shoutout to the Class of 2020.

I read a Facebook friend's sad and frustrated post announcing the death of her family's matriarch: "I can't express what a horrible time in life we are in. My grandmother passed away this morning and my family and I can NOT go and see her because she's in a nursing home that has been locked down because of Covid-19. We are waiting to find out her cause of death. This virus has kept us all hostage, prisoners. Strips us of simple hellos and goodbyes. Strips us from physical touch and natural human energy we feel from being around our loved ones. She couldn't even have us by her side for a last goodbye."

Mid-afternoon, as the wind really kicked up, knocking out power to 700 customers in our local service area and 17,000 customers in all across the state, the power here at the house flickered, shutting everything off for a flash and knocking the internet offline. I crossed my fingers that it wasn't a sign that we would soon have a bigger problem. Fire engine sirens continued at intervals throughout the balance of the afternoon.

Along with an occasional beer on a sunny afternoon or with a sit-down dinner, I had incorporated the habit of having a daily shot of Jack Daniels Bourbon. In fact, I would actually gargle my first sip, figuring that, at 80 proof, it would kill any bacteria or virus scout trying to creep in. Then, today, I read that a German virologist confirmed that drinking alcohol can protect against the virus — that it's susceptible to alcohol because of its fatty coating. That was good enough for me. God bless Dr. Juergen Rissland.

Dinner was leftover ziti, followed by a FaceTime with Dad, who had gone on walkabout during the day again, pausing for a glass of wine at a safe distance with a widow down the road from him. The evening feature was the 1968 classic "The Night of the Living Dead", in which the radiation from a fallen probe to Venus causes the recently deceased in one region of the U.S. to rise from the grave and seek the living as food. There were a slew of parallels to our current dilemma that poured forth. The White House calling emergency meetings about the "epidemic". Citizens ordered to go home and lock down. Tracking the spread of the outbreak. National emergency declaration. News sources urging people to stay tuned for survival instructions. Disagreement among a group of people that take refuge in a rural home on how to protect themselves — one set barricading in the basement; another set boarding up windows and doors on the main level. The diversity of the people that take refuge: the do-ers; the armchair quarterbacks; the self-appointed leaders; those who collapse and wilt under stress; the diplomats. The recommendation to carry bodies to the street and burn them ("The bereaved will have to forego the dubious comforts that funeral service will give.") Rescue stations set up (like the field hospitals we've needed). The conclusion by those taking refuge, "This isn't a passing thing."

In the ever-present news: The virus was having a huge impact on the NYPD - nearly 20% of the force had been affected; aligned with that, over 50 NYC education employees were dead from the virus, including 21 teachers. Our local community mourned the passing from the virus of a "perfectly healthy" 30-year-old physical trainer, proving that there was no denying the seriousness of this disease. A Georgia TV station showed a photo of a house sitting in the middle of a road where it had been dropped by yesterday's tornadoes that tore up the South. Global virus cases climbed to over 1.9 million with 118K deaths, 440K recovered; of these numbers, the U.S. claimed over 577K cases and over

23K deaths, with nearly 34K recovered. Women had begun panic-buying hair coloring kits and grooming supplies as they looked ahead to society reopening. A report opined that large music concerts wouldn't return until Fall 2021 at the earliest. In like manner, a financial official suggested that America could be shut down in part for a good 18 months, with likely virus flare-ups, until a vaccine is ready. Our Town of Fairfield was up to 197 cases, but with no additional deaths; CT as a whole topped 13K cases, with 262 deaths. Greenwich, CT residents were encouraged to go out on their front porches and make some noise as a thank you to front line responders. The governors of NY, NJ, CT, PA, DE and RI joined forces to design a post-pandemic reopening plan. America's meat supply chain was becoming threatened by large plant closures.

April 14. On this date in 1935, the "Black Sunday" Dust Bowl storm struck the American Midwest. It was one of the most devastating events of the 1930s dustbowl era that wreaked ecological havoc in that region. Crops had died and, with nothing to hold down the soil, the region had become plagued by continual and catastrophic dust storms. The ruin drove thousands of farmers to move west to seek work. The subject matter was the inspiration for Author John Steinbeck's novel "The Grapes of Wrath", published in 1939. The book won the National Book Award and Pulitzer Prize for fiction, and it was cited prominently when Steinbeck was awarded the Nobel Prize in 1962. The crisis at that time had threads of connection to modern challenges I observed, as farmers and cattle ranchers today struggled with decreased demand for food because of virus-induced restaurant closures, food plant workers getting sick and food plants closing.

The morning started dry but cool, keeping us indoors. I boiled some water in which to dip a washcloth and press to my eyelid, which was still swollen with an engorged stye. With my "good" eye, I paused to read a news alert on my phone that NY Yankees Co-Owner Hank Steinbrenner had died at age 63 after a long illness. A photo of a 93-year-old woman holding an "I Need More Beer!!" sign to a front window in her home caught my attention, too — the accompanying story reported that people responded, sending her CASES of beer.

I'd noticed online many instances of at-home face mask making, a real "wartime"-like pursuit to ensure that family members, neighbors and front-line workers have the virus protection they needed. There was some real home assembly line production going on, as well as an integration of creativity, not only in construction but fabric and design choices.

In a midday briefing, NY Gov. Cuomo said there had been "flattening" with regard to the number of daily lives lost in his state, though that was still in the hundreds and now totaled 10,834. He also made reference to NASA's famous Apollo 13 mission launched 50 years ago. On this date, the oxygen tank on its service module exploded, which canceled the mission's aim to make a landing on the Moon and sent the three astronauts aboard into a mad scramble with Mission Control to save their lives. "Somehow they figured out how to get a spaceship back 220,000 miles, *50 years ago*. That's America," Cuomo said. He referenced that event with regard to collaborating as a nation to strategically plan how we go forward, saying, "OK, figure out how to do testing, figure out how to use technology to do tracing. And that we have to do together."

Early afternoon, I tuned into a live Facebook performance by local musician/singer Tracy Jo Recalde, of Tracy Jo & The Toads, aired through our Fairfield Theatre Company's page in a new series they were titling "FTC's Stay Home". Tracy and her crew were performing from the porch of her home in Black Rock, CT and accepting tips through Venmo and PayPal.

I killed the last of my 1.75-liter bottle of Jack Daniels and switched gears to a decorative bottle of Tres Generaciones 100% Puro de Agave Triple Destilacion Plata Premium Tequila, Bottle #6816503, throwing back a mid-afternoon shot.

I read about a New York man who embarked on a three-day road trip to New Mexico after his stepfather passed. It was remarkable in that there were barely any cars on the road, and gas stations and hotels and such along the way were desolate and empty. He was truly traveling through an apocalyptic landscape.

A National Geographic post noted that Anthropologist Jane Goodall was currently idled and reflecting that we are living in "a dark time now, but perhaps the silver lining is that many people are rethinking their relationship with nature and the future." She expanded, "Some people will never have known a world without pollution, but now they are experiencing clean air. I just hope enough people, having discovered what life COULD be like, will get together and be strong enough a force to insist that their governments introduce legislation to keep the air clean. That enough people realize the danger of the way we abuse the natural world and the cruelty we inflict on animals. Because now, with COVID-19, the result of our sometimes thoughtless, sometimes greedy behavior is hurting US."

The sun peeked out late afternoon inspiring me to service my lawnmower for the season and give my lawn its first mow. I stood back and admired the closely cropped grass — looking lush and green. My reward was some reheated leftovers and a sit for a spell on my back porch. I took a moment to scroll through some news stories on my phone and one in particular popped out: "11 surprising industries the coronavirus downturn is affecting". I'm not quite sure what I was expecting but it was NOT a list that included private investigators, impersonators, sex doll companies and matchmakers. Less surprising occupations that *were* hurting included tattoo artists, sports equipment manufacturers, notaries, pet sitters, auto mechanics, check cashers and buskers.

As the sun dropped down out of the sky, I tuned into a live feed of Pres. Trump giving his daily White House Task Force briefing. He offered, "The United States is continuing to make substantial progress in our war against the virus. We grieve at every precious life that has been lost to the invisible enemy. But through the darkness, we can see the rays of light. We see that tunnel. And at the end of that tunnel, we see light. We're starting to see it more than ever before. We've held our rate, the numbers, everything we've done. We've been very strong on it and very powerful on it… I salute the American people for following our guidelines on social distancing… Their devotion, *your* devotion, is saving lives."

The News at 11: The CDC Director called for antibody testing to determine who is and who isn't immune to the virus and the extent of the infection as we move forward, while urging that we "stay firm" until the virus has not just slowed but stopped. CT's Lime Rock Park canceled an early May event, its Touring Car Fest. Seed sellers were seeing a huge surge in demand as Americans began planting their own food gardens. A health advisory cautioned that the virus lasts on surgical-type face masks for a week, guiding how to clean them with antibacterial sprays or switch up to a different type of mask. An emergency was declared in Japan as a second wave of virus infections emerged — a situation America would be well advised to monitor. Stargazers were alerted to a rare upcoming event: Mars, Saturn, Jupiter and the Moon lining up now through April 16. Our local Westport Country Playhouse postponed its entire 2020 season to next year; likewise, *The Palace Danbury Theater postponed all of its shows that had been scheduled through May 31. An update from our Fairfield First Selectwoman noted 197 cases to date, and four more deaths, bringing our total to 12; CT overall had 13,381 cases, 602 deaths. A second round of layoffs nationwide had begun, targeting white collar jobs now. CA Gov. Newsom shared a six-point plan for reopening his state, which presented a solid model for all the states.*

April 15. In any other year in America, today would have been Tax Day. Instead, millions of people were waiting for stop-gap stimulus checks from the IRS.

In the overnight, global Covid-19 cases pushed over the two million mark with almost 127K deaths; U.S. cases topped 614K, with over 26K deaths. Covid-19 had become deadlier than *nine* other major viruses since 1967, COMBINED, including Marberg (1967), Ebola (first identified in 1976 and still ongoing but only in small increments), Hendra (1994), H5N1 Bird Flu (1997), Nipah (1998), SARS (2002), MERS (first identified in 2012, still ongoing but in small numbers) and H7N9 Bird Flu (2013). The only virus it had not outpaced *as yet* was H1N1, which ran its course in 2009 and 2010, numbering over 762 million cases across 214 countries and killing about 284,500 people. "Our" Covid-19 had already killed nearly half the H1N1 number amongst woefully far fewer cases, in as many countries, making it on track to become the deadliest of them all. Notably, these zoonotic diseases all jumped from animals (fruit bats, poultry, pigs) to humans. Eric Toner, a senior scientist at the Johns Hopkins Centre for Health Security, commented about these viruses, "Infectious diseases will continue to emerge and re-emerge. I think it's part of the world we live in now. We're in an age of epidemics because of globalization, because of encroachment on wild environments."

Late yesterday, the President announced the halt of funding to the World Health Organization, while a review is conducted. He said the group had severely mismanaged and covered up the spread of the Coronavirus. The annual funding totals $400-500 million. "Had the WHO done its job to get medical experts into China to objectively assess the situation on the ground and to call out China's lack of transparency, the outbreak could have been contained at its source with very little death," he said. Ever-contentious House Democrats took immediate issue with the halt, likening it to the

President's Ukraine aid freeze, and promised to swiftly challenge it, though they cited no specifics.

I wished a happy birthday online to a disc jockey friend, John, who goes by the name DjGroove Seven, who would spin at many local parties. I had a distinct memory of him at what was then known as the Westport Arts Center, providing the tunes from his turntable set-up on an outdoor deck during summer, with long views of the Saugatuck River and people cheerfully floating about with glasses of wine in hand.

A song came on mid-morning, Twenty One Pilots' "Level of Concern", which offered timely lyrics: "Panic on the brain, world has gone insane, things are starting to get heavy" and the chorus "wonderin' would you be my little Quarantine, or is this the way it ends?"

It wasn't the only song out there penned around this pandemic panic. U2's Bono crafted a song titled "Let Your Love Be Known", which he said was a St. Patrick's Day gift from Ireland to quarantined Italians singing to each other from balconies. A snippet of lyrics: "Yes there is isolation, You and me we're still here, Yes when we open our eyes we will stare down the fear."

An online culture site called SLATE said the "race to write the Coronavirus anthem is on", noting on March 24 that more than 470 related songs had already been posted to music sharing service Spotify. SLATE noted that "for the most part, sickness has never been so inspiring to songwriters as, say, calamities at sea. Maybe disease is too grindingly depressing to lend itself to romanticizing or moralizing, compared with war, crime or heartsickness." However, virus songs had indeed managed to get past the "cultural gatekeepers" to spread to the planet's listening devices — the sounds of "humanity freaking out and goofing around in the face of global threat and social disruption." And, apparently, many of these songs had adopted a fake cough as the song starter. So popular had this "pandemic pop" category become that Spotify dedicated a playlist to it dubbed "The Sound of the Virus", with songs ranked by popularity that had the effect of pushing the more listenable tracks to the top. Overall, though, the bucket was a floating mess of throat clearing, faux panic, t.p. digs, hints of Chinese slander and even hand-washing ballads.

I received in my email inbox a plea to sign a petition to "Save the USPS", citing that it "employs around 600,000 workers, including numerous veterans, but it could be shut down in September" after the President rejected a bill that would save it from running out of money. While I felt bad about the workers, it seemed ludicrous to try and save a "prize institution" that would need financial transfusions to survive. What purpose did the service really fulfill at this point? The only mail I received these days was the occasional catalog, junk fliers, financial statements and bills, all of which could be accessed in an online format. And, now with the virus circulating, I had become anxious about even fetching the mail from the mailbox and handling it. It was time for the USPS to park its trucks — sell them off to food purveyors and turn their buildings into farmers' markets; re-direct the employees to big shippers like Amazon.

Late morning, I got inspired to repair a birdhouse that had sat disused at the back of my shed for a year or more. The wooden birdhouse "box" itself was attached to a six-foot tall post, with the cutout, ironically, of a gray cat attached to the front of it at the top. My late Mom had purchased it some 15 years ago or more for my family when my boys were small and I was still married. She bought it from an old man one summer at a craft fair that was a regular event on our Town's Sherman Green, walking distance from my home. She thought it would be great fun for the boys to watch birds visiting it.

Recalling Mom's intention, I decided to rescue the birdhouse from abandonment, restore it for the use of a couple of finches I had seen milling about recently and enjoy their visits myself. Of course, big old Phil was welcome to enjoy the visits, too, though I thought he would have little interest at this stage. I called this my Urban Redevelopment project and the spot in which the birdhouse resided Downtown East, Tribeca perhaps.

The wood panel at the back of the "box" had deteriorated from weathering. At first I tried to nail it back together but then pried it off and cut a new wooden panel, which I nailed on. Then, to give the little home more protection, I cut to size, crimped and fitted a sheet of copper as a "roof", nailing it in place. Next, I created a hole in a garden bed, set the pole and house into the hole and pounded shims around each side at the bottom for extra stability. Stepping back to admire the job, I thought Mom would be proud of the work and hoped that the finches would find it appealing. A benefit to the structure was that the copper would be a good heat conductor serving to make the little house a cozy incubator for baby birds.

Early afternoon, I tuned into NY Gov. Cuomo's daily virus update, which began with a stats report. Hospitalizations, flat. Net change in hospitalizations, down. Net change in hospitalizations 3-day, down. ICU admissions, down. Intubations (ventilator usage), down. All good news showing a continued flattening and, yet, 2,000 people a day in the state were still being diagnosed with the virus and, on average, about 700 a day had been dying since April 9. However, the conclusion was that the "infection spread is down to a manageable level."

That said, Cuomo addressed the hot topic of reopening, something folks everywhere were eager about. "We're not going to open what was," he began. "We're going to a different place, and we *should* go to a different place, and we should go to a *better* place. If we don't learn the lessons from this situation, then all of this will have been in vain… We're going to a different place which is a new normal… This is the way of the world… When is this over?… It's over when we have a vaccine… 12 to 18 months."

While toying with the topic of reopening, Cuomo also ordered that anyone outside in public in the state of New York wear a mask or some kind of face covering in situations where you can't be physically distant from other people, like riding public transit. He gave a three-day window before the order took effect to make sure everyone could get into compliance. Meanwhile, over in neighboring New Jersey, cases had climbed to over 71K and the death toll pushed over 3K.

China took a spotlight in my thoughts, in part because of an email exchange with my sister-in-law, Jill, who suggested that the CCP may be trying to deflect blame for the virus crisis at the same time as others are trying to assign it to them. She mentioned a Chinese friend and neighbor who had just become a citizen last year and who, she said, has been growing "uncomfortable with new revelations about the CCP's role in the pandemic and fears a backlash, being associated with China." I mentioned about my girlfriend, Jen, who is Malaysian-Chinese, who had expressed concern about the backlash, too, given the report of a number of recent anti-Asian attacks.

Proud of her ancestral Chinese ancestry, Jen had poo-pooed the conspiracy theories about China, though she really didn't have anything to gain by adopting that stance. As she explained it, she is Malaysia born but pure Chinese, with roots in Xiamen, a seaside area in Fujian Province in southeastern China on the South China Sea across from Taiwan. Her Fujianese great-grandparents were sea merchants and traveled southwest from Xiamen (then called Amoy) to Malaysia to escape social injustice and for better economic and career prospects. They settled in Kelantan, where Jen was born and where her paternal grandfather became a well-off land owner and her maternal grandfather was a sundry shop owner.

I read that virtual nightlife had become a thing, with live-streaming Paid Zoom Clubs. The clubs consist of networked rooms, each with different themes and activities that a subscriber can join. Participants can "share" drinks, dance to dj sets, even "jump" in a hot tub wearing swimming attire. Clubbing under quarantine, what a thing. An emergency support system for the virus-sacked entertainment industry.

In line with my mention yesterday about the Dust Bowl and difficult 1930s, an article emerged saying the pandemic was very likely to cause the worst recession since the Great Depression, with the global economy expected to contract by 3% this year, according to the closely watched International Monetary Funds' latest World Economic Outlook forecast.

Leading up to the dinner hour, I cleaned our grill and fired it up for the first time this season, slapping two fatty chicken breasts, coated in teriyaki marinade, onto it. They made a great accompaniment to a steaming scoop of Mac 'n cheese. As I was cleaning off the grill surface afterwards, I heard voices and looked to my neighbor's lot diagonal from mine. The home was for sale and the agent and a prospective buyer, both with surgical masks on, were standing on the deck surveying the back yard. These were strange times indeed.

I read about Tom Von Essen, former NYC Fire Commissioner who led the fire dept. during the Sept. 11, 2001 terror attacks and who was now FEMA's regional administrator in charge of the federal response to the coronavirus in NY and NJ. He compared 9/11 to the pandemic, noting, "There were people who left it all. Left it all on the table that day for strangers. And that's happening now. There're people in the emergency rooms. There're people in the ambulances. They're leaving it all. They're leaving it all out there for total strangers." The battle against Covid-19 has been the biggest event FEMA has faced because of its effect on all 50 states, six territories in the commonwealth and hundreds of tribal nations.

Von Essen gave a nod of gratitude to other front line people, too, those working everyday ordinary jobs. "They're taking a chance and making minimum wage. When you think of some of the people in the supermarkets, cash registers, people stacking shelves, and someone walking by and coughs, they must be scared."

Phil had hoped to visit his Mom in Miami during his Spring Break period. Maybe he would get the chance this Fall: American Airlines was offering round-trip passage from NYC to Miami for $89, with no change fees. It was just one of dozens of extraordinary deals listed in a daily TravelZoo email I receive.

I noticed a benefit coming up this Saturday night, titled "One World: Together at Home". The usual late night talk show suspects would be emcees of the two-hour musical special while the star lineup would include biggies like Elton John, Paul McCartney, Stevie Wonder, Lady Gaga and newcomer Billie Eilish, to name a few. A six-hour streaming event leading up to the special was also planned, with no less than 80 stars taking part.

Sports had become a wonky thing these days. In the pro baseball world, now into what would have been its regular season, you could tune in to watch a classic game from years' past. It was quite a treat actually to see sports heroes of yore at their athletic best accomplishing the feats that made them legendary.

A disturbing upside of this crisis and the schools being shut down everywhere: March 2020 was the first March without a school shooting since 2002.

In April 1912, the great Titanic oceangoing vessel hit an iceberg and sank on its maiden voyage. Many Americans have been feeling like passengers on the ship and that our iceberg is Covid-19. Who will hang on and live, and who will slip beneath the cold waves?

As the sun started settling down for the night, I hopped in the car aiming for Jen's, still an anxious flight, for some momentary freedom and normalcy. A "get out of jail free card" played for a night. Jen was glad to see me though wondered why I hadn't brought a roll of toilet paper, which she considered justly admission to her domicile! She let it go though and soon I was munching on a home-baked apple tart and sipping at a decaf coffee. We retired to her TV room and locked onto the evening entertainment: "The Spy Who Came In from the Cold", a 1965 British Cold War spy film, shot in black and white and starring Richard Burton. The movie depicted British agent Alec Leamas' mission as a faux defector to East Germany who must plant damaging misinformation about a powerful East German intelligence officer. As part of the masquerade, Leamas pretends to quit British intelligence and live as a surly alcoholic. The grayness of the film quality and the isolation and distancing Burton's character engaged in, combined with his bent for the drink, threw lines to our modern circumstances.

Nightly news recap: Georgia brewery Wild Heaven had produced a pale ale called Fauci Spring, named after White House Task Force member Dr. Fauci. Colleges were thinking of dropping SAT and ACT requirements as admission criteria for next year's student applicants. Our regional Delamar Hotels announced its availability to accommodate first responders and healthcare workers as needed. An Indiana firefighter awaiting his stimulus check found $8.2 million in his bank account by mistake. Retail sales fell 8.7% in March, the largest ever decline on record. State budgets were beginning to strain as tax revenues dried up and virus-related spending climbed. Our Town of Fairfield reported 220 cases now, with 18 total deaths. A Harvard study suggested that social distancing might be necessary into 2022, given likely flare-ups of this virus over the next year and a half until a vaccine is available. Research indicated that people are having more vivid, unusual dreams during this dark time as they process their turbulent emotions. A 107-year-old man quarantined in Florida shared his thoughts on living through the 1918 influenza pandemic.

CHAPTER 4

OPENING UP AMERICA AGAIN

April 16. The morning started as gray as last night's film. Rolling back to Fairfield was quick, with just a handful of cars on the Post Road, though it would normally be rush hour. Just over our town line and standing out amidst the quiet, I began to notice the trumpeting appearances of patriotism. First, an oversized inflatable eagle in a red, white & blue vest with wings upraised in front of Fairfield Automotive Service. Then flag banners attached to street lamps the length of the main road through Downtown. About a dozen American flag banners posted on Sherman Green. The giant flag draped across the front of Saugatuck Sweets ice cream shop. The statue of a fireman, with a surgical mask around its mouth and nose, next to a flagpole by the firehouse. And a large American flag flapping in the breeze in front of the American Legion post.

The flag sightings made me think about the phrase "United We Stand, Divided We Fall", which had taken on more importance than ever as our country faced one of its greatest challenges and bordered on fractioning into territories as some urban areas rebelled against Federal directives and citizens felt that their freedoms were being slowly eroded, perhaps permanently. We desperately needed to get on the same page — a place of national unity and collaboration. This was no time for single-minded alliances that betrayed the collective effort.

The phrase, notably, was birthed in another time of great upheaval in this country, the Revolutionary War. Founding Father John Dickinson coined it in a tune, "The Liberty Song", writing, "Then join hand in hand, brave Americans all! By uniting we stand, by dividing we fall!" Patrick Henry cemented the phrase in 1799 when Kentucky and Virginia legislatures took a stand against the federal government. Henry urged, "United we stand, divided we fall. Let us not split into factions which must destroy that union upon which our existence hangs."

Mid-morning, my friends Kwong and Becky stopped by, to pick up a book. They were my first visitors in quite a while. We socialized at a distance on my front walkway. She was eight months pregnant and they had just come from a checkup at Yale New Haven Hospital. She described the process of being there: calling them when you arrive, them calling you back in the car when they were ready to receive you, mask and gloves for mom, no other family permitted. We spoke about how strange these times were — our having a pleasant visit and yet all around us misery. We discussed increasing anti-Asian sentiment, in light of Kwong's Chinese background, his family's local Oriental market and a conflict a family member had at an area Walmart. Becky shared the difficulties her employer, Earthplace Nature Discovery Center in Westport, CT, was having being shut and the online activities they had launched.

Late morning, "the face of New York", Gov. Cuomo, gave his daily briefing. He shared that there had been more flattening in rates and yet, yesterday in his state, another 2,000 people were diagnosed with the virus and 606 people died, "still a tragic rate" he noted.

A local intimate apparel store, In the Mood Intimates, shuttered for now but still surviving online, launched an initiative called "The Comfort Project", a donation program to bring comfort to the frontline nurses and doctors at hospitals around the U.S. The way it worked is that you purchased a gift card or clothing (robes, socks, sweaters, PJs, loungewear) for these healthcare workers and the store delivers these items to the hospital, in this case Bridgeport Hospital, for which they had over 80 bags ready to go.

Early afternoon, with the thought of flags fluttering around in my head, I pulled an American flag out from my basement, attached it to a pole and secured it in a flag holder affixed to a column on my front porch. It immediately began flapping in the breeze, standing out in a sky that was now bright and light blue with ragtag clouds.

Dinner planning started happening late afternoon, with steak, baked potatoes and broccoli on the menu at Chez Mike. My meal making skills had really kicked into high gear these days, with varied dishes and a penchant for breaking out of the traditional box. The challenge would be seeing if I could go the distance with creativity.

At the very moment a Chef's Warehouse truck pulled up across the street and its driver began removing several boxes from the back via a hand truck and carting them to a neighbor's house, I happened to be reading a piece about food delivery services on an online site called Medium. Though people had already been using them, these services were expected to attract even more folks, making it the "new normal" and potentially spurring people to never look back at grocery store environments. Other predicted soon-to-be "in" things: eSports, famous musicians live-streaming instead of touring, everyone wearing masks at hospitals, and cities banning cars more often. Essentially, what we were looking at was a big shift in how we live. The future may never have looked more interesting.

After the dinner hour, Pres. Trump provided his daily Task Force briefing, a significant one focused on the process of getting America back to work. He recapped the battle to date, noting, "We've marshaled every instrument of American power and we've unleashed our most potent weapon of all: the courage of the American people." He stated current findings, offering, "Our experts say the curve has flattened and the peak in new cases is behind us." He took a going-forward stance: "Based on the latest data, our team of experts now agrees that we can begin the next front in our war, which we are calling Opening Up America Again. And that's what we're doing, we're opening up our country. And we have to do that. America wants to be open, and Americans want to be open… A national shutdown is not a sustainable long-term solution. To preserve the health of our citizens, we must also preserve the health and functioning of our economy." That said, he declared: "My administration is issuing new federal guidelines that will allow governors to take a phased and deliberate approach to opening their individual states." And he provided the plan: "Our approach outlines three phases of restoring our economic life. We are not opening all at once, but one careful step at a time. Some states will be able to open up sooner than others. Some states are not in the kind of trouble that others are in."

The President's plan specifically called for protecting senior citizens and other vulnerable populations, getting healthy Americans back to work, establishing benchmarks on testing and easing restrictions as cases declined. Instrumental in all of that, he said, was Americans' vigilance in continuing to practice vigorous hygiene, teleworking when possible, staying at home when you felt sick, sanitizing commonly used surfaces and being highly conscious of one's surroundings.

The phases? The first part keeps vulnerable people at home, prohibits visits to nursing homes and hospitals, and allows a gradual return to work. Phase Two allows resumption of nonessential travel, opening of bars with some restrictions, and reopening of schools and youth activities. In Phase Three, there would be no restrictions on workplaces and vulnerable people can resume social interactions but at proper social distance. Visits to hospitals and nursing homes can resume.

Pres. Trump emphasized that governors will be empowered to tailor an approach that meets the diverse circumstances of their own states, going ahead with each phase as appropriate. He encouraged states to work together to harmonize their efforts.

The News: The Small Business Administration said funding had been exhausted for its $350 billion Paycheck Protection program after approving 1.6 million loans through almost 5,000 participating lenders. NASA discovered an exoplanet called Kepler-1649c 300 light years from here that's remarkably like a "second Earth". Global virus cases ticked up to 2.1 million, with over 136K deaths (523K+ recoveries); in the U.S., cases were at 644K+ with 28K+ deaths (nearly 49K recoveries). Another 5.2 million Americans filed for unemployment benefits last week, bringing total claims to 22 million over the past four weeks. Bridgeport, CT Mayor Ganim issued a mandatory face mask requirement for the entire city. Actor Brian Dennehy passed at age 81. NYC Mayor de Blasio announced that public outdoor pools would be closed this summer, and beaches would likely be off limits as well. LEGO had been making 13,000 visors a day for medical workers. Our Sustainable Fairfield Task Force invited town residents to participate in a week-long virtual 50th Annual Earth Day celebration. NY Gov. Cuomo extended his state's shutdown to May 15. Fairfield's cases grew to 246 with 21 deaths; CT overall had 15,884 cases and 971 deaths. A man broke into a New Haven, CT restaurant and ate and drank there for days before being discovered and arrested. Wade's Dairy said it would be reintroducing home milk delivery service. A Walmart in Louisiana had the smart idea of pre-making "essential item carts" for the elderly. An article debated the ethical dilemma of making food at home versus getting takeout. A study showed that the virus appeared to travel in "stealth" mode as testing of U.S. Navy sailors showed — spreading mostly among young, healthy people who are asymptomatic. Dry conditions in the American West over the past two decades may hint at a catastrophic mega-drought to come. Police warned the public about a text message scam that alerts "Someone who came in contact with you tested positive or has shown symptoms for COVID-19 & recommends you self-isolate/get tested", with an official looking link that draws you into the "dark web".

April 17. It was that panic-producing time again: grocery shopping. I donned all my protective gear and headed out, on the heels of the senior citizen shoppers-only timeframe when I figured Stop & Shop would still be relatively clean and there would be ample enough inventory. En route along the few long blocks to the store, I saw on the side of the road a few tables of items that had been plucked from the adjacent home and placed there with a big FREE sign. The elder homeowner was Fairfield's unofficial town historian and I learned from two helpers there that she was selling her house. I wondered if the move was motivated by the virus or part of a downsize plan that had already been in motion.

Pulling into the store lot, for the first time I saw the cart boy with a protective plexiglass shield covering his face, paired with his bird's egg blue latex gloves. It was a new look for him.

I wiped down my cart handle as prescribed and set off around the store to do my business. All but one or two shoppers were gloved and masked — such a weird, accepted new normal — and most were being compliant about aisle direction and distancing. Inventory was better than it had been over the past month, but there were still depletions: juice was spotty, toilet paper & paper towels were non existent, dishwashing liquid and disinfectant wipes were "clean" out, the pizza dough container was empty, and flour and brownie mixes had both taken huge hits.

At the register, I announced to the cashier that I would be handling all the bagging, to minimize touchpoints, and had to shoo another staffer that didn't hear my announcement who came over to help. I felt badly about that but this was about survival.

Because of the lack of paper goods, I had to make a second town stop, as I had before, at The Pantry. Along with two rolls of paper towels, customers were now allowed *four* rolls of toilet paper, and now the price for all was half of what it had been the previous visit. Supply and demand pricing tactics I assumed.

The unload process back home was just that, a process, with strategic removing of potentially tainted gloves and my pullover for deposit straight in the wash. I didn't remove my bandana at first, as a contractor was just across the street spraying for mosquitos and the wind was blowing my way. As the serviceman had a respirator on, I thought it was wise to keep protected myself, at least until I was indoors. It was like biohazard bingo out here.

After much hand washing and surface disinfecting, I settled down to check email, sparking to one inbox insertion in particular, from a company called Inside Weather. The subject line was, "Forecast: High chance of cabin fever". The humor made it a must review. There was an offer of Frank Lloyd Wright-inspired furniture. A PPE Open Source resource tab for doctors, nurses and loved ones. A DIY guide to creating protective gear with materials on hand. An adaptable WFH (work from home and not to be confused with WTF) desk set-up. "Quarantine Creations" — furnishings designed to inject some spark in your "same four walls" cell. The sign-off? "See you inside!"

With much trepidation, I made another foray out into the local apocalyptic landscape, to Southport Veterinary Hospital. On my last visit, a month ago, the techs there had detected a potential kidney issue with my cat, Stormy, and wanted to wait a little bit and check things again. The visitation process had completely changed since that initial visit. Now, one was required to pull up in the parking lot and call the facility, which would send out a masked tech to collect your pet from your car. Once service was performed, they bring your pet back out and let you know they will follow up by phone and/or email.

On my return home, I swung wide, once again on a flag appreciation mission. Truly we have a patriotic town, with flags everywhere — at gas stations, churches, banks, the post office, town circle, car wash, funeral homes, town hall, historical landmarks, the YMCA and more. The sightings inspired me to pull up at town hall, in fact, and ring the Town Clerk, Betsy Browne Miller. I relayed to her the sightings and how they made me feel and wondered if the town might create a dedicated field of flags like they erect for Veterans Day, to offer as a display of unity. I thought that families might sponsor flags and the funds could go to first responders or as a fund to help families who have lost loved ones to Covid-19. She said she would look into it — there were logistical and equipment considerations that had be considered. In the same breath, she mentioned that our Town's Memorial Day Parade, one of the largest in the state, had been canceled. Given that, perhaps there was even more of a role a flag display might serve?

The daily constant, NY Gov. Cuomo, got on the horn again midday.

Cases in his state were still coming in around 2,000 a day and the number of deaths was "refusing to come down dramatically", with another 630 the total yesterday, which Cuomo called "still breathtaking in its pain and grief and tragedy." While that number was generally a flat one, there would be no rush to normalcy. Cuomo said the going-forward process would be "incremental between today and tomorrow" and we had gone from "fire through dry grass" and "response to crisis" mode, to "controlling the beast" and now transitioning to "un-pausing" and "re-opening" while being cognizant of the public health crisis we were all still in.

Late afternoon, I made a "throwback to growing up" batch of Teriyaki burgers, sandwiched between English muffins to enjoy with a local beer. As I sat down, a friend appeared at the door to pick up a book. She was masked and gloved, the first person to come to my door like that. She apologized for the accessories, though it wasn't a problem for me at all, just a little startling.

CT Gov. Lamont stepped to the mic to report cases in the state were nearing 17K, with over 1K deaths and nearly 2K hospitalizations. The numbers still indicated an upward climb though hinted at some arcing. To try to push the curve down, Lamont ordered masks be worn by all state citizens in circumstances wherein you aren't able to maintain a safe physical distance.

Afterwards, I tuned in the President's White House Task Force briefing. The highlight for me was his announcement of a $19 billion relief program for farmers and ranchers and the mass purchase from them of dairy, meat and agricultural produce to get food to people in need and to community and faith-based organizations. Pres. Trump said another $14 billion would be provided in July that would continue to help farmers and ranchers.

Early evening, I received an email from Music for Youth, which promotes music amongst children and young people. The email presented MFY's Digital Friday Night Cafe, a selection of pre-recorded music video performances by families and friends of the group. There was little Isabella Mariani (9) and her pal Mia Jung-Pitkin (8) playing a concerto for two violins, with Mia's dad Joel on piano. And 12-year-old Andrei Orasanu and his father Serban playing an acoustic guitar version of Luis de Narvaez' Fantasia del Quarto Tono. The very talented Alex Beyer and George Li on piano playing Mozart's Sonata for Piano, four hands, in D Major. And 4th grader Leo Calejesan and his dad Edward performing a guitar duet. Really quite a treat overall — the upside to being homebound.

The Creature Feature in Mike's Walk-In Theatre: 1987's "Empire of the Sun", set in 1941 before Pearl Harbor and starring a young Christian Bale as the son of a British textile plant owner living in a community of Westerners in Shanghai, China. The family is well to do, with servants and all, but their lives get upturned and they become separated by an attacking Japanese occupation force. As the posh community evacuates to places like India and Australia, Bale first tries to make a go of it at home on his own. He essentially finds himself in a state of isolation as many of us were now in, going through the stock of canned food, eating chocolates, riding his bike around the house as an amusement, walking in the basin of a drained pool. Deciding his parents were not coming back for him, he heads to town and, unsuccessful in trying to surrender, he takes to scrounging food while all around him those that didn't get out are dying in medical facilities of fever or barely surviving in camps. Ultimately, the Americans come to the rescue, he is reunited with his parents and there are great get-togethers and celebrations and satisfying long hugs. The nightmare was over. I hoped our bad dream would be over soon, too.

The Nightly News: Stargazers were encouraged to look up to catch the Lyrid Meteor Shower peaking April 22. Providing a look at the likely new norm of air travel, Emirates had instituted a slew of safety measures, including quick blood tests before boarding, barriers at check-in desks, all passengers wearing masks in the airport and on the plane, no reading materials on board and no large carry-ons. Globally, new virus cases surged past 2.2 million, with over 150K deaths; this included U.S. total cases at over 685K and deaths at over 35K. Florida said it would start reopening its beaches in a move that seemed premature. Busch said it would give a year of free beer to couples whose weddings were postponed due to the virus. In the week of April 6 to April 12, Covid-19 killed more people than any other cause of death except heart disease. China admitted that its virus death toll in Wuhan was 50% higher than reported, but denied it had intentionally covered up the figures — it said there were 1,290 more deaths, to a total of 3,869, and 325 more cases, to total 50,333, in Wuhan. The U.S. said it would launch its first astronauts into space since 2011, pandemic or no. A report said "shockingly lethal outbreaks" of the virus were killing far more people at nursing homes than previously known. Discarded face masks and gloves were becoming a rising threat to ocean life, conservationists warned. On the other hand, bald eagles were found nesting in an Arizona cactus for the first time in decades.

April 18. I was up with the first light, which was dreary and filtered by rain that had been with us all through the night and would continue all through the morning. I watched it streak down the window and peered out at how lush the mid-Spring landscape had become. Reporting to the bathroom to shower, I noticed in the mirror that I was looking a little rounder and hopped on the scale for grins. I was perturbed to find I was 11 pounds over my usual weight, though I attributed at least a pound or two of that to last night's rich dinner and the bowl of ice cream that followed. Dad had been eating "well", too, remarking on one recent meal he'd enjoyed with a fine wine on his deck, "I've paid a lot of money for meals not this good! Someone suggested that when this was over, many of us will have to join either AA or WeightWatchers or both. Ohhhhkay!"

Phil's school, UConn Stamford, posted to its Instagram last night, "Proud to work with @cityofstamfordct to support Stamford's efforts to fight COVID-19. Connecticut residents recovering from coronavirus could start moving as soon as this weekend into our main residence hall at 900 Washington Blvd. The City of Stamford will operate the building as a place where recovering coronavirus patients can rest after their hospitalizations. The occupants will be people who have been treated and discharged, but who still test positive for COVID-19 and need places in which they can recover in isolation without potentially exposing family or others to the illness. Thank you to Mayor Martin and his administration for leading our city through this challenging time." UConn exhibited big heart to do this; at the same time, we wondered where Phil's belongings had been stored and had they been exposed to the virus, either through handling or in their current environment, wherever that was? And what would be required to disinfect the whole building once the crisis had passed and these patients moved back out? Phil and I were both kind of relieved that he wouldn't be living there again, though we weren't even sure he would be living at Storrs in the Fall either, depending on how things went going forward.

While my bandana face masks seemed to be doing the trick protection-wise, I was finding that they often slipped down my face, became loose at the back and also became hot on my face underneath, to the extent that I was perspiring a bit — which I was doing more of given the intensity of the situations in which I was using them. I happened to connect with Kerri Tanner, the owner of a Westport, CT-based e-commerce start-up company called AnytownUSA, which offers only American made products, like face masks, across nine categories. Through her, I ordered what I thought would be an excellent new solution: a proper moisture-wicking, reversible face mask with nose wire.

I expressed birthday wishes online to several friends and missed the situations in which we last saw each other. My friend Maura whom I last saw last year on St. Patrick's Day at our local Irish club. And Carrie at a community gathering at the town farm she co-runs in Westport. And Chelite who I last saw at a huge Caribbean street fest in Brooklyn. All sites that were jammed with people but were now quiet as all get-out.

On the topic of gatherings, Facebook maintains a page called Events, which chronologically organizes happenings in which you have expressed interest. I got an alert that noted I had six events coming up today, which I thought was peculiar during this time of shutdown. It turned out that, of the six, one was a piano factory tour that was marked "postponed". Another was for a tech-oriented Maker Faire this weekend which had also been postponed, though was not marked as such. A third was a Milford Arts Expo and concert, which had also been pushed. The fourth was a chocolate and wine cruise down the Connecticut River, postponed until late July. In fact, the only two events that were still a "go" were a livestream by a young musician named G. Rockwell and a Virtual Hologram Show being offered through an Ansonia, CT-based bar & grill, both set for tonight and both hoping for virtual tips through online pay services.

The rain that was falling here along the southwestern coast was coming down as snow in the northern parts of Connecticut. Some people were none too pleased with it, being nearly May and just making their already challenging lives harder. Said one, "These seasons really need to stay in their own damn lane!!" Others commented, "Let it snow, let it snow. Winter wonderland."

A news item noted that every resident of my town of Fairfield that had died after contracting the virus was over 50 years old — 13 were nursing home residents. Not that this made it any safer for us to be out and about, but it was a notable observation.

Mid-morning, I had to make one of those anxiety producing trips, to the post office. Hopping into the car with all my protective gear in hand and a pre-addressed book package, I happened to look over and see my neighbor, Lorenzo, in mask and gloves, taking groceries out of his car. I asked how he was faring and he told me he had just come from Yale New Haven Hospital, where he had begun working as a physical therapist with people recovering from Covid-19. He said these people were so out of it, in kind of a stupor. One of the biggest challenges for him was just getting them to focus, much less trying to get them to stand up. He said there was a whole process involved with being there and there were two floors dedicated to PT. Workers like him accessed the floors in a dedicated elevator and changed gear (mask, gloves, protective face shield, scrubs) after every patient/room visit. Lorenzo had previously worked in a nursing home in Greenwich, facilities that have been decimated by the virus. He commented, "All it takes is for just one infected NHA to go from one patient to another to spread it."

I pulled up curbside by the post office, near Unity Pharmacy, in our little downtown. There were masked and gloved customers standing at a distance from each other outside the pharmacy, being called in one at a time — one comes out, one goes in. It was like Thunderdome 2020.

The post office had two other customers when I walked in, both masked and gloved. The lone clerk was in the back at that moment apparently. Another customer, masked, entered and stood six feet behind me. We looked at each other and remarked how weird life was. I told her I was there to mail a book and that I was a writer and she commented that her husband was, too, of children's books, though he also had a full-time occupation. He was working on one new book called "Odd Fish". As to her occupation, she owned a children's swimwear business and was a mom of two children, ages 3 and 20 months. She said she was doing some real juggling with everything during this crisis, including grocery shopping, which she elected to do herself, about every 10 days. "My husband always forgets something, so it's just easier for me to do it," she smiled, sharing that the stores seemed chaotic to her, with people all over the place and not following rules.

Over some lunch — bologna had become my go-to — I read a "poem" by a writer named Jessica Salfia, in which she had taken the first line of a number of emails she'd received and organized them into stanzas, with each stanza concluding "As you know, many people are struggling." Some chosen lines meshed with that endpoint, like "Count your blessings. Share your blessings." Others did not: "You're invited to shop all jeans for 50% off!" It was an interesting approach to capturing these "not normal" times.

Midday, NY's Gov. Cuomo gave his daily briefing. Total hospitalizations, down. Net change in total hospitalizations, flat. ICU admissions, down. Intubations, down. All good news, BUT, as he said, "Happy days are not here again" as there were about 2K new cases reported yesterday ("still an overwhelming number" and the same rate as late March when infections were taking off) and 540 new deaths. Of that death toll, 504 were in hospitals, 36 in nursing homes. He called the latter environments "the feeding frenzy for this virus". With regard to pushing ahead, he said "testing is the single most important topic" and, basically, that it needed to be done in a very widespread manner.

An email brought me news that Novo Fogo Organic Cachaça, nine other spirit brands and Chilled Magazine had organized a cocktail competition challenging bartenders across the USA to submit their most imaginative drink recipes over a four-week period, with weekly winners. Also in the alcohol category, local liquor store Harry's offered the sale of a bourbon on top of which they would throw in a $20 gift certificate from one of Fairfield's businesses, to help keep the local economy chugging along.

I read on FB about the passing of a friend's mom. As a teen in Westchester County, NY, I had delivered newspapers to the family's house and would speak with her once a month when I collected for the service. My friend regretted, "We are not able to have any service for mom at this time. We will when the time is right and gather to celebrate her wonderful life."

An article on the History Channel site discussed the 1918 Spanish Flu, which had its first wave in March then returned with a fury for a second wave in August. The virus was believed to have mutated and was also carried by soldiers over to and all through Europe. The piece heightened my fears of a second wave here, particularly since there had been confirmation that *this* virus had mutated as well.

I had long participated in a San Francisco, CA-based lending program called Kiva that profiles small mom-and-pop businesses around the world and allows you to donate money to them to help them achieve their goals. Today, I helped a woman named Nelisa in Cordova, Cebu, Philippines buy items to sell, including lotion, shampoo and other supplies through her sundry store. It seemed like a good deed and karma during this dark time.

Early afternoon, a feeling of tiredness crashed over me like a big wave, tumbling me into unconsciousness in my living room. I awoke groggily aware that I had a visitor and looked outside to check, noticing a car that was unfamiliar. It turned out to be my friend Stacey, who had come earlier than expected to collect a book. She was sporting a surgical mask, so I put one of my bandanas on, to be socially amenable but also so we could chat safely on my porch. She was wearing a Patriots hat and said she would remain a fan of the team, though she would be tuning into Buccaneers games, too, since her favorite QB Tom Brady joined them.

Stacey had come down from Waterbury, CT to visit her mom and sister in neighboring Bridgeport. All were well in her family she said, including those in her native Cambodia. And all were well at her job, too, as the manager of the bakery department at the BJs big box store in Waterbury. There were few restrictions at that store due to its size — there could be 600 shoppers in there at once, she said. Of course, they were masked and gloved and staying clear of each other. And before employees entered the store, their temperatures were taken with forehead sensors to be sure they were fever free, a first indicator of the presence of the virus.

Stacey and I had last seen each other at a pizza restaurant called Two Boots in Bridgeport, which closed in May 2017 after being open less than a year, but we had stayed connected through Facebook. We were celebrating Mardi Gras when last we met up, with beads around our necks and big plastic goblets containing cocktails. We hoped it wouldn't be long before we could be doing that again. She promised to make egg rolls for the occasion.

Late afternoon, I noticed a FB friend's post of a photo of her "quarantent", a tent she had placed in her living room to practice "campentine", a spin on quarantining. It housed a sleeping bag, blankets and pillows and sat across from a glowlight in a steel fire pit, simulating a campfire. It was brilliant, honestly. And apparently not an isolated thought, as I saw a photo of a family from Plano, Texas having similar backyard camping fun.

Another post showed a projection of the American flag on the peak of the 14,690-foot-tall Matterhorn mountain in the Swiss Alps offering hope and strength to America during our virus battle.

I read about a luxury world cruise that began 15 weeks ago when the virus was in its infancy that was just now returning to port and a ravaged world.

I noticed an "Act Now" petition being circulated by a group called Stand For Health Freedom, which encouraged people to ask their respective mayors and governors to reopen their towns, cities and states. While I was all for getting back to the idea of living, it seemed like a barrel-ahead move that didn't take into consideration the real risks involved with doing that, particularly in our hard hit tri-state area. Another petition was being circulated, directed at CT Gov. Lamont, asking that professional barbers, hairdressers and cosmetologists be allowed to perform their designated services, one client at a time and with all sanitation protocols met, in their place of business starting April 28. That one seemed more reasonable to me.

For dinner, I enjoyed a ham steak, mashed potatoes and broccoli — rehashed leftovers essentially — computer-side so that I could tune into Pres. Trump's daily briefing. He noted many "positive trends for winning", citing that "on a per capita basis, our mortality rate is far better than other nations of Europe, with the lone exception of Germany." He continued, "Since we released the guidelines to open up America... a number of states… have announced concrete steps to begin a safe, gradual and phased opening", among those Texas, Vermont, Montana, North Dakota, Idaho, Ohio and North Carolina. He went on to talk about testing, saying units were being mobilized all over and should be set to render the results needed.

I adopted a plan to go to Jen's, an action that had become less of a daring flight but still required planning. I decided to bring to her "tidings of comfort and joy", in the form of a roll of toilet paper with a fancy red frilly bow mounted on top of it and two plump oranges tucked in a Ziploc bag.

As I warmed up the car, I put the radio on to NY news station 1010 WINS, which started its 7pm report with a live audio capture of New Yorkers in Brooklyn cheering from their windows in tribute to the city's health care workers. This tribute had become a nightly ritual.

I decided to take the Post Road, versus the highway, to Jen's, electing to stop at our town's Dairy Queen to order two small Oreo Blizzards at the counter, to add to the bounty I was bringing her. Though I was one of only three customers, there were lines of pink tape on the ground showing proper distancing for waiting, which we three obeyed. The servers, who were masked and gloved, posed for a photo at the pickup window. Then off I continued to Jen's as the sun slid down out of the sky and filtered its rays through the budding trees.

Jen laughed and smiled at my presentation and even got on a video chat with a girlfriend in NYC to show her what I had brought. Her friend, who was tucked in bed, laughed with us and was glad for the interaction.

As Jen played and attempted to video record a Mendelsohn piece on her piano, I poked through my social media sites. In my FB inbox, I found a video a friend had shared, in a hush-hush wanting-to-be-anonymous manner. It was of a woman providing information about what she thought would be an excellent drug to treat the coronavirus and her wonderment about why there wasn't wider news about it. A couple of years back, a doctor had made a mistake applying an epidural in her neck and created a cerebral spinal fluid leak, which resulted thereafter in frequent high pressure headaches. She was prescribed a drug brand called Diamox, which is acetazolamide, which is also used to treat the symptoms of high altitude sickness: fluid build-up, dizziness, labored breathing, fever, headaches and the like. Recently, she was listening to a doctor talking about how the coronavirus presents itself and comparing it to the symptoms of high altitude sickness. He added that ventilators seemed to be aggravating treatment — patients were able to breathe when they came in then were put on ventilators that forced air into them, actually making it more difficult for them to breathe. The ventilators were hurting, not helping, it appeared. This woman immediately made the connection to Diamox and began to do some research to see if it was being used as a treatment for the virus. Her search was fruitless but then she connected with a FB member group of people taking Diamox. Through the group's administrator, she was able to ask its members if any had had the virus and if Diamox had helped. One of the members had and, yes, it had been helpful, preventing her from having to seek any hospital attention. Further research turned up that a pharmaceutical company called CureUS was exploring Diamox as a countermeasure to treatment of the coronavirus. This revelation really stunned me and I immediately rang up my brother and his wife, excellent researchers, and put them on the case to look into it.

At 8pm, the much anticipated "One World: Together At Home" concert aired, through multiple streaming formats — Jen and I tuned in on Prime Video. As aforementioned, this concert featured leading musicians performing from their homes, late night talk show emcees and other noted celebs coming together in tribute to health care workers. It was a historic show, on par with the Live Aid concert on July 13, 1985, which attracted 72,000 people at Wembley Stadium in London and over 89,000 people at JFK Stadium in Philadelphia — a worldwide rock concert organized to raise money for the relief of famine-stricken Africans. "We Are The World" was that event's theme — tonight's theme tracked with that.

With some awe, we enjoyed a wobbly voiced, 77-year-old Paul McCartney playing and singing "Lady Madonna" on his organ at home; the septuagenarian Rolling Stones in split-screen mode performing "You Can't Always Get What You Want"; Jennifer Lopez ("JLo") singing Barbra Streisand's "People"; John Legend and Sam Smith performing "Stand By Me"; Green Day lead singer Billie Joe Armstrong strumming and singing the band's "Wake Me Up When September Ends"; Billie Eilish singing the late Bobby Hebb's 1963 soulful hit "Sunny", with her brother Finneas on an organ (he threw in a four-note James Bond "No Time To Die" integration); and Andrea Bocelli, Lady Gaga, Celine Dion and Lang Lang teaming up for Bocelli's "The Prayer". Matthew McConaughey chimed in with some thoughtful words, too: "This is a virus that knows no lines and respects no boundaries and that none of us are immune to. So what can we do? We've got to take care of our health care workers on the front line but buy them time by taking care of ourselves. We've got to take care of our elders, the most susceptible of all of us. We've got to keep their spirits high, keep them quarantined and safe until this is over. If we take care of ourselves, we take care of each other."

For grins, Jen and I kept the tube on to watch 1953's "Roman Holiday" starring perky Audrey Hepburn as Princess Ann visiting Rome and Gregory Peck as American reporter Joe Bradley, sent to interview her. Exhausted from her touring schedule, the princess, fuzzy from a sleep aid, sneaks away from her palatial accommodations during the night and ends up being taken in by Joe, who is initially unaware that she's the princess. When he realizes her true identity, he supports her wish to just be an anonymous version of herself for a day, to see Rome as other regular people see it — the same kind of breakout we all wished for ourselves during this time of quarantine.

Versions of Eddie Cantor's 1929 "Makin' Whoopee!" song, performed first by Frank Sinatra then Ella Fitzgerald and Louis Armstrong, played by Alexa, were the sounds that made our current life seem a little more cheery for a moment and lulled us to sleep.

Saturday Night News: A travel site shared recipes for 11 cocktails that promised to take you around the world while you were stuck at home. It had been a year since a fire at Notre Dame Cathedral devastated the landmark — its stubborn presence was a testament to the resilience of the French people; at the same time, the site is quiet as repair work had been stopped due to the virus (France had over 147K cases and nearly 19K deaths, as of today). Fairfield's Sacred Heart University announced that it had to furlough a number of employees whose workload had significantly decreased due to virus shutdowns. Floridians flocked to a reopened Jacksonville Beach and were shown in mass numbers walking along the shore, no masks, not properly social distanced — all of which seemed to spell future trouble. Fairfield's numbers today: 253 cases, 26 deaths, 91 recoveries, new case rate seeming to slow. Over 160 South Koreans who had Covid-19 once again tested positive for it, suggesting the virus goes dormant, which presents new challenges to the testing process. A husband-and-wife team figured out a way to decontaminate tens of thousands of face masks simultaneously, thereby making them reusable and eliminating one-time use waste. Globally, there were now well over 2.3 million cases, with nearly 160K deaths; this included U.S. cases at over 735K and deaths nearing 39K. NY, NJ and CT announced the reopening of its marinas, some good news for boaters. Today marked the 25th anniversary of the Oklahoma City bombing, when two men blew up a truck outside the Alfred P. Murrah Fed Building, killing 168 and injuring 680+.

April 19. Sun streamed through the slats of Jen's window blinds and stirred me to return home. I passed a string of safely distanced shoppers waiting outside Trader Joe's and all the empty store lots along the Post Road, then spotted The Tasty Yolk food truck parked roadside and doing business near Dairy Queen. Joy of joys! Some normalcy! A real breakfast sandwich, on a glorious, bright Sunday morning! For a moment, it seemed liked pre-virus days, with the exception of the counter girl wearing latex gloves and encouraging touchless credit card payment, and two other customers waiting more than six feet apart from me and each other.

My brother Dave reported back that the Diamox drug I had asked him to look into was not a new discovery, but certainly not an amplified one either. He shared that the National Institutes of Health had been exploring the use of it for the past month as both a treatment and preventative for the virus — an aid to removing fluid from the lungs. Dave couldn't confirm if it was in trials or had been approved. But he did find a study reporting that Covid-19 damages the lungs, while HAPE (high altitude pulmonary edema) impairs the lungs' function, therefore the treatments should differ. That said, it could still be a possible treatment in concert with other drugs.

Midday, NY Gov. Cuomo gave his daily briefing, noting that the hospital-oriented rates were down and New York was "seemingly past the apex" and, yet, 1,300 new cases were identified yesterday ("still a lot of people") and 507 more New Yorkers died (down, though still a lot). In general, he said the state had been good about controlling outbursts of the virus but that nursing homes were still the #1 concern (an "optimum feeding ground for the virus").

Early afternoon, I browsed an US Magazine emailed newsletter, rolling my eyes at learning Dwayne "The Rock" Johnson and his wife Lauren were "practicing making babies again" in quarantine and that the infamous Kardashian family conducted a car parade to celebrate family member Kourtney's 41st birthday.

Mid-afternoon, I made a sandwich and sat on my back porch in the sun. As I enjoyed this peace, I scrolled on my phone through lists of songs of hope and inspiration, hunting for a song to suggest to Jen. Based on last night's One World concert, we thought she could do her own gig, "Hope From Home", offering a song a day like she does but have it connect with a charitable cause — a local charity or the hospital she and her family send money to back in Malaysia. We settled on the song "Bridge Over Troubled Water" by Simon & Garfunkel to be her lead-off presentation, in support of the CT Chapter of the American Parkinson Disease Association.

Back on FB later, I giggled at a photo a friend had posted of a ground hog spotted in his backyard, remarking, "I think it saw its shadow. Guessing that means 6 more weeks of quarantine?" Well played, JG.

I noticed that our town's annual in-person Dogwood Festival had been cancelled but turned into an *online* fundraiser. Held for the past 100+ years, the event typically offered dozens of vendors, live music, crafts, food, a garage sale, clothing, art and more, with proceeds assisting state charities. It was sad to see it get nix'ed, at least as a live affair.

Dinner was spaghetti with diced pepper, onions, garlic and Italian sausage, immediately followed by a tune-in to some live instrumental guitar jams on FB by New Haven, CT-based Tim Palmieri.

The Multi-Mega Cineplex with its larger-than-life screen, BOSE sound system and awesome comfy lounge chairs and loveseat… in the next room… called to me mid-evening. My attention was snagged by a live airing: "The Last Dance", about pro basketball legend Michael Jordan, focused on his last championship year (1997-1998) with the Chicago Bulls. I was hoping to see a lot of great footage of him playing and an illustration of the phenomenal talent he was, but instead it was an airing of dirty laundry — squabbles with management, inferiority complexes, blah blah blah.

I switched to more appetizing (?) fare, "What We Become", a Danish film with English subtitles released in 2015, offering a story about members of a family fighting for survival when a mysterious plague unleashes flesh-eating zombies in their small town. Zombies aside, there were a lot of modern day parallels, which is what I'd been heightened to look for lately. First, they are alerted via media of an infectious disease that struck a nursing home, like Covid-19 did at first in Washington. An elder neighbor then dies and disappears, and later returns and kills his wife. Other strange things start happening in the neighborhood, which brings police, who set up a control zone around their area, like the National Guard isolated New Rochelle. Citizens were advised to not go to the hospital, but to call a hotline in case of illness. As the epidemic fueled up, town sirens were sounded and soldiers appeared in total biohazard gear, ordering people inside. More government guidance followed, about proper hand washing (sound familiar?). Anyone who tried to leave was turned back. Men in orange suits and a big truck showed up, spraying everything with disinfectant. Temporary field hospitals were set up, with capacity to receive hundreds of patients, like those established in NYC. Researchers worked feverishly to find a treatment. Citizens were then sealed in their homes with huge plastic sheeting. Water and food was delivered to them by soldiers; empty jugs and trash was exchanged. The isolation zone was expanded as quarantined people began to get anxious and quarrelsome inside. Meanwhile, dead bodies were being processed at a local school, dumped in dumpsters and piled up in truck trailers, the latter like NYC. The featured family hatches a plan to see what's going on outside, sending two men out with weapons. They encounter trash at the school, abandoned cars, bodies in the street and are even fired upon. While they are gone, things break down at home as a neighbor mom dies and comes back to life, and a little girl goes missing looking for her pet. The walking dead grow in number and, ultimately, everyone is overwhelmed. I have to say it was weird watching a pandemic while being in the middle of a real-life one.

I had let out our cat for a run-around earlier in the evening and she didn't heed my calls as I headed to bed. I asked Phil, who planned to be up late, to try and get her in. Then, given the absolute stillness of our neighborhood, we heard her and another cat wailing at each other. It was almost haunting and particularly pronounced in its shrillness and decibel level. Phil went outside to retrieve her, brushing a bush in the process that disturbed a mourning dove nestled inside it which burst out practically at Phil's face. Though startled, he managed to corral our cat and herd her inside, apparently unharmed. Quite the Wild Kingdom experience.

In the News: Singapore had gone from a model of how to handle the virus to having nearly 6,600 cases (as of today) as it overlooked a cluster of infected migrant workers. Germany was in the process of reopening its stores as its country began its recovery process. VP Mike Pence spoke at the U.S. Air Force Academy graduation, a ceremony that featured just the nearly 1,000 graduates and staff — no friends or families. *The Navajo Nation had lost more people to the virus than 13 states. EasyJet Air was considering flying without the middle seat occupied. Lyft was offering thousands of free rides to help those in need. A 99-year-old British man had raised $17 million for UK health workers by walking laps around his garden. People had been recreating travel photos at home. China imposed new lockdown measures as fears grew of a second wave. DEEP closed more state parks in southwestern and western CT due to overcapacity. A Florida drive-in was reportedly the only theater in the U.S. showing new movies. A German newspaper printed in its pages a mock invoice directed to China — a bill for $162.4 billion for coronavirus damages. Hospitals reported a sub-epidemic of people who needed hospital care but dared not visit facilities during this pandemic. Retail clothing stores, like Neiman-Marcus, had begun to file for bankruptcy as stores were shut and no one was buying clothes. Global virus cases topped 2.4 million with over 165K deaths (615K recoveries); included in those numbers were U.S. cases at over 762K, with over 40K deaths (almost 70K recoveries). A terrible mass shooting took place in Nova Scotia, in which 16 people were killed, including the gunman, motive unknown.*

April 20. The start of a new week. Gray. Dreary. Chilly. Coffee injection needed for motivation.

I got an errant event alert from the University of Bridgeport's Arnold Bernhard Center for the Arts & Humanities, about a spring play, "The Seussification of Romeo & Juliet", that had been scheduled for today. It would have been a wonderful performance but the university had closed the campus for the remainder of the semester, therein canceling the play.

Jen shared a video clip by text which noted that China had approved three Covid-19 vaccine candidates for clinical trials. The first vaccine, an adenovirus vector vaccine, developed by a team led by an academician, Chen Wei, with the Chinese Academy of Engineering, was the first to be approved to enter clinical trials. The first phase of the clinical trial was completed at the end of March; the second phase started April 12. An 84-year-old man in Wuhan was among the first volunteers to be vaccinated, on April 13. The vaccine carries the gene of the coronavirus spike protein, the major surface protein used by the virus to bind to a receptor to invade cells, so that the subject's body will produce the immunological memory of the protein. When the real virus attacks, the body will identify its spike protein and stop its invasion, according to Chen. The 108 volunteers who completed the first phase of the trial on March 27 had ended centralized medical observation and were reportedly in good condition. The second phase recruited 500 volunteers and introduced the placebo control group to further evaluate the immunogenicity and safety of the vaccine. As of 5pm on April 13, 273 volunteers had been vaccinated. The other two vaccine candidates included an inactivated vaccine developed by the Wuhan Institute of Biological Products under the China National Pharmaceutical Group (Sinopharm) and the Wuhan Institute of Virology under the Chinese Academy of Sciences, that was approved for clinical trials on April 12; and another inactivated vaccine developed by Sinovac Research & Development, a company based in Beijing, that was approved for trials on April 13.

Through FB, I wished a happy birthday to a music producer/composer/pianist friend who has been recovering from Covid-19. Back in early March, he began experiencing a simple, nagging cough but didn't think much of it — "every year I have a season of flu and coughing, usually brought on by stress." A week passed with no improvement, "then some unusual things happened: I started getting chills all over my body though the house was warm, and my cough was getting progressively worse. Oh, and I started losing my sense of taste and smell." His wife started calling around about testing as things went from bad to worse, with intense pain. He spoke to a doctor at Yale Hospital, who recommended him for testing. An opening allowed him to get tested in Bridgeport.

He described the visit: "After going through some security clearances, I drove up to a well organized set of doctors. After confirming that I was the patient, the doctor said, 'Roll your window down, look at the blue light in front of you, and tilt your head back, don't move.' The doctor produced this very long Q-tip and before I knew it, she stuck it in my left nostril. 'Oh it was not so bad' I thought to myself thinking this was a piece of cake. That was when the doctor said, 'It did not work, we will have to do the other nostril…. and she stuck this Q-tip in my right nostril all the way to the back of my head and started swabbing!!! Oh it was extremely uncomfortable and a little painful but 10 seconds later the procedure was done, and the doctor told me to go home."

Back at his house, while waiting on the test results, he began taking an old prescription of antibiotics, drinking hot liquids and sleeping, warding off waves of chills and gradually getting some taste sense back. On April

3, his test results confirmed he had the coronavirus, one of 3,854 people that had tested positive in Connecticut at that time. He continued his home regimen, experiencing periodic setbacks of spiking fever, for which he applied cold compresses and took Tylenol, showered a lot and stayed near a humidifier. He went through a period of bloating, then weight loss (over 12 pounds) and emotional outpouring, finally declaring on April 8, "Today I am proud to say that I am a survivor of Covid 19," though a few trace symptoms lingered — a light cough, post nasal drip, loss of appetite and weakness. It all sounded like a horrific experience and he was truly thankful to have gotten to the other side intact.

I connected with my son Evan by text late morning, for a "situation" update. With regard to work, he said, "We may be trying to head back into the office next month, but on a rolling basis. No more than 30% occupancy." As to how he had been keeping himself busy, he shared, "Playing guitar, watching movies, running a lot, cooking elaborate meals, video games, etc."

Midday, the voice of measured reason, NY Gov. Cuomo, conducted his daily briefing, starting with a general status — new cases flat, though 478 more lives lost yesterday, "still horrifically high." Going forward, he said, "Assuming we're off the plateau and we're seeing a descent... how long is the descent and how steep is the descent?... and that's what we're trying to figure out." He was looking for a certain level of confidence, which he suggested might come in a week to a month. In the meantime, he said, "The question shouldn't be *when* do we reopen and *what* do we reopen. The question should be let's use this situation, this crisis, this time, to actually *learn the lessons*, value from the reflection and reimagine what we want society to be." He suggested we apply our eye to a variety of categories — public transportation, housing, public safety, health systems, social equality and use of technology. He cited the formation of a multi-state coalition involving NY, NJ, CT, PA, DE, RI and MA.

At the same time, he offered caution. "The weather's going to warm, people are a little more relaxed because they see the numbers coming down and we know human behavior," he said. "They want to get out of the house. They want to be more active... When that activity level increases, you can very well see that infection rate spread." He said that he would be watching "the dial" until we have a medical treatment or vaccine. In the meantime, beaches, public facilities, schools, parades and concerts had to remain shuttered as they would all be magnets to people — that an event in one state would draw people from another.

To break up his studying, Phil took a motorcycle ride out and, notably, reported seeing "burnout" marks on rural roads and in parking lots, from joyriders blowing off steam in their cars. Really, the quiet roads had become a new frontier for speed enthusiasts.

Early afternoon, I FaceTime'd with my Dad after receiving an email from him with a photo attached of a "beer bread" that he had baked. He said it looked good and smelled fantastic, but was a little heavy, and would be best as a breakfast side with butter or jelly. More regularly, he had been baking muffins, taking a cue from my late Mom's recipe. Dad was wearing a bathrobe and a t-shirt from the Pequot Turkey Trot from 2002, a race we might well have run together. He pointed his phone camera outside to show me how lush the surroundings had gotten. "The ro-ro's (rhododendrums) have popped out and everything is growing like mad," he shared.

Meanwhile, Jen was putting together her daily inspirational FB post, leveraging the classic 1939 song "Somewhere Over the Rainbow". Her effort spurred me to make a donation to her APDA group for $100. We also discussed song choices for tomorrow's post, so she could rehearse, landing on Elton John's "Circle of Life", featured in "The Lion King".

Another event notice popped up on FB, of the Litchfield Distillery's Bourbon, BBQ & Bluegrass event, that had been set for May 1. It, too, had been canceled due to Covid-19.

I read that the Los Angeles Tourism & Convention Board had been live-streaming the sunset from Venice Beach each evening via its social media channels, calling it the "Magic Hour", which viewers could watch while tuning into interactive injections from the city's chefs, musicians, artists and even magicians.

I was fascinated to learn that, during the American Revolution, there was a smallpox outbreak that threatened to wipe out the Continental Army. Despite political opposition, George Washington, the army's commander in chief, embraced science-based medicine to battle it and, in the process, ushered in our new country's first public health policy. His strategy involved immediately isolating anyone suspected of infection and limiting outside contact. In conflict with the Continental Congress, he also ordered all troops to be inoculated against the virus via a procedure called variolation, which entailed making a small incision in the patient's arm and inserting a dose of the live virus — great enough to trigger immunity but minor enough to prevent severe illness or death. Infection rates dropped from 20% to one percent. As infection rates dropped, colonies lifted their bans on the inoculations.

I read that Hart's Island, where unclaimed bodies from this virus pandemic were being buried, had a storied history. At various times in its past, it served as a training ground for soldiers of color, a prison for Confederate soldiers, an asylum for TB patients, a reformatory for wayward boys, and a burial ground for people felled by AIDS.

While dining computer-side again, I tapped into the President's daily press briefing. One update was particularly interesting and that was about oil, given the price per barrel had closed the day at -13.1, which was a historic drop — the first time ever in negative territory, signaling that there was virtually *no* market for oil and sellers must pay up to store crude supplies. Pres. Trump said, "Based on the record low price of oil... we're filling up our national strategic petroleum reserves, looking to put as many as 75 million barrels into the reserves themselves, that would top it out. That would be the first time in a long time it's been topped out and we'd get it for the right price."

I took a post-dinner nap in the living room, awaking facing the front windows of the house and looking up at a sky turning the slightest bit rosy as the sun was setting. I snapped a photo with my phone and posted it to Instagram, with the caption: "Seen from post-homebound dinner napping vantage point" with the hashtags: #homebound #lockedup #doingtime #fairfieldprisonblues #wheresmyharmonica #inthepokey #propiedaddelacarceldefairfield #bunkview #wheresmybunkmate #jailed #uptheriver #staringoutthewindow #whowillpostmybail. Clearly I was having a case of cabin fever. And where *was* my bunkmate, anyhow?

I rang Jen finding her at her piano running through "I'm Still Standing" as an alternate to "Circle of Life", which she had decided was too Disney-ish. As we chatted, I opened up an email from my sister-in-law, who shared a montage of currently running TV commercials. Amusingly, they all used a somber piano background and many of them even used the same word/phrase drops: family, for x number of years, always been there for you, people, especially now, today more than ever, during these trying/

challenging/uncertain/unprecedented times, even though we are apart, home, here to help, here for you, you can trust us, together, clapping.

I could sense Jen wanted company, so spontaneously adopted the plan to head over to her place. As it was 9:30 and long ago dark, I took the back roads to 95, eerily encountering not a single other car on the way to the on ramp. As before, the highway ride was like being on a NASCAR track, with the speed at an 80mph minimum. I hopped off in Westport and navigated another back road route, passing only three other cars... and a surprised deer... who literally was a "deer in the headlights".

Jen had messaged me while I was en route to say she was going to take a quick shower and to let myself in and stay in the kitchen. She had set out a plate of food for me: a block of cheese, an orange, a pot of fig jam and a container of chocolate covered cherries. I soon found out it was a gentle bribe to get my help in constructing a letter to a renter of an apartment her mom co-owns in Malaysia. The renter was seeking a reduction in the monthly rental rate due to the uncertain business climate caused by Covid-19. However, he was already receiving a generous discount and was over 20 days late with his monthly payment. It seemed like a ploy on his part to take advantage of the worldwide situation. And Jen's mom depended on the income.

The News: The Skechers company raised over $5 million to help shelter animals across the U.S. affected by the pandemic. Researchers warned of a wave to come of neurological illnesses caused by the virus. A local restaurant, Martel, announced that one of its employees tested positive for the virus, which forced them to temporarily shut down until further notice. Two astronauts that left for the International Space Station in October, long before the virus began, and who had watched the world's crisis unfold remotely in their own isolated way, were just returning to Earth. Vermont began easing some of its restrictions in very gradual measures; in a like manner, so did GA, TN and SC. CDC-adjusted definitions for virus count inclusion pushed up CT's number of cases to 19,815, with 1,331 deaths. The Brewers Association said diminishing supplies of CO_2 due to a drop in ethanol production may threaten beer, soda and seltzer supplies. The Town of Fairfield's cases bumped up to 300, with 33 deaths. The IRS was hitting bumps in the road, given employee shortages, closed assistance offices and piled up unopened tax refund requests as it worked with antiquated systems and to process stimulus checks. The Atlantic Hurricane season was just six weeks away, *but may kick off earlier than June 1, as it had for the past five years. Westport announced it had canceled its Memorial Day and July 4th celebrations.*

April 21. It was Ruby Tuesday, though there was nothing glowing about it. The morning was gray and a crazy salvo of weather was forecast: showers, thunderstorms, hail and gusty winds up to 33mph for the daytime; and even gustier winds up to 43mph, more showers and plummeting temps with wind chill values between 20 and 25 degrees for the evening. Joy of joys.

Today also marked three months since the first coronavirus case was confirmed in the United States. Now over 800K cases had been confirmed and over 45K people had died. Of course, there was all the economic and mental health damage to be considered as well. Not to mention all the other pain and destruction yet to be revealed, or to come, should there be a second wave, which seemed likely.

I slid behind the wheel in Jen's driveway and sped off back to Fairfield, trying to forget those morbid thoughts, tuning in a sweet jazzy jam on the radio called "It Girl" by Pharrell Williams. It was being laid out on the airwaves by Steve DiConstanzo through his Radio Base Camp program on local station WPKN. It was a mood upper... until I turned onto the Post Road and reality returned. A line of Masked Cart People six feet apart waiting outside Trader Joe's. A passing car with the driver's pink face mask hanging from its rear view mirror. A sign at a florist: Pansies Have Arrived, Ready for Curbside Pickup. All the empty windows of small retail businesses that couldn't hang on through this crisis, with "Space Available" signs slapped on them. More Masked Cart People at Stop & Shop loading their cars with supplies to help their families get through another week or two or six of quarantine. More Masked People pumping gas at Shell. A lineup at Dunkin' Donuts for drive-up grab-and-go java. A masked Lyft driver shuttling a passenger. Desperate "We're Open" signs everywhere. The Rawley's Drive-In where Martha Stewart had stopped the other day hoping to get a hot dog but found it shuttered. A Masked Man making a delivery in Downtown Fairfield, pushing a loaded hand cart across the road. The Barber Serville shop, where my boys got their first hair cuts, empty and its entrance barred with a large sheet of plywood — it closed after 70 years to make way for an expanded Community Theater renovation. A "Calmness Is Contagious" sign in the window of the Old Post Tavern. Gas stations pushing rock bottom $1.98/gallon prices.

I thought about masks, and masked men, and the phrase "Who was that masked man?" which was often asked at the end of an episode of "The Lone Ranger", a television series featuring a vigilante cowboy and his Indian sidekick, the reruns of which I had enjoyed as a kid. The other popular phrase he uttered was "Hi Ho Silver" whenever he mounted his horse, Silver, and rode off. Some funny trivia: The Lone Ranger called his sidekick Tonto, which is Spanish for "stupid" or "fool"; Tonto called The Lone Ranger "qui no sabe", which translates to "he who knows nothing".

While I worked at home through the morning, I listened to Soulection Radio Sessions on YouTube, to resuscitate the earlier groovy vibe and try to mute reality. Of course, that was difficult these days, as related inputs flow in from all directions, including my email inbox this morning. In an e-newsletter from UNC Chapel Hill, there was an item about a recent book called "Contagion and the Shakespearean Stage", co-edited by Mary Floyd-Wilson, an English professor at the university. She shared that, in the mid-1600s in the absence of modern-day medicine, "People believed that rotting organic matter produced bad odors or smells that could infect people with disease. At the heart of this notion, however, was an idea of sympathetic contagion, which suggested that the afflicted were already 'apt' or primed to receive the infection. Whether the internal corruption derived from imbalanced humors or moral depravity, already corrupted bodies were understood to attract external corruption." As interesting as this perspective seemed was how similar people's thoughts were to modern pandemic attitudes. Crowds were viewed as dangerously infectious. They criticized the wealthy as immoral when they fled the cities in time of plague. They watched for signs of the plague in various forms — signs on sufferers' bodies, quarantined houses marked with crosses, rising mortality numbers. In a greater view, Floyd-Wilson cautioned, "As our circumstances worsen, this pandemic may radically alter people's primary fears, beliefs and political perspectives, and much of this thinking will be influenced by competing narratives about how to read signs and interpret evidence."

Jen had reached out by email to her contact at the APDA to let her know about her "Hope From Home" initiative and shared with me the woman's reply, which informed that the group would be posting a link to her effort on their website and Facebook page, to help spur donations.

Another email inbox curiosity, if you can call it that, rolled in, The Lead-Lag Report, published by Michael A. Gayed, CFA. He assessed the financial situation, from March 23 to present, noting, "The bear market didn't stand a chance. From March 23 to April 17, stock markets staged an impressive rally, gaining 28.5% and retracing half of the losses already. This was in the face of some of the worst economic numbers we have seen since the Financial Crisis, and possibly since the Great Depression itself. As I mentioned in The Lead-Lag Report, weekly unemployment claims have topped 22 million in the last four weeks, and are set to continue into next week. To get some perspective on that number, the peak four-week total jobless claims in the Great Recession was 2.64 million. The Dotcom Bust produced a four-week total of 1.96 million. The early 1990s recession caused 2 million jobs lost over the worst four-week period. In 1982 Double-Dip had 2.7 million, the 1980 Fed-tightening (Volker) 2.52 million, and the 1975 Stagflation had 2.24 million. **Combining all of those hasn't equaled the last four weeks. It's approximately the population of Taiwan, unemployed.** Unemployment jumped to 4.4% in March, but April is set to be much worse."

Stay home. Save lives. Help stop coronavirus. Stay home. Save lives. Help stop coronavirus. Stay home. Save lives. Help stop coronavirus. Stay home. Save lives. Help stop coronavirus. Stay home. Save lives. Help stop coronavirus. Stay home. Save lives. Help stop coronavirus. Stay home. Save lives. Help stop coronavirus. Stay home. Save lives. Help stop coronavirus. Stay home. Save lives. Help stop coronavirus. Stay home. Save lives. Help stop coronavirus. It seemed these phrases and this mantra was everywhere. The drumming was incessant.

Late morning, NY Gov. Cuomo gave his daily briefing, speaking from Roswell Park Cancer Institute in Buffalo. He started with the stats: total hospitalizations flat, net change in hospitalizations down, intubations down. New people diagnosed yesterday, 1,300 — "that is down and that's good news, relative to really bad news happening up until then." Sadly, another 481 people died across the state — 452 in hospitals, 29 in nursing homes. On the upside, he said NY will once again start allowing elective outpatient treatment in counties and hospitals with no significant risk of Covid-19, and they were going to make reopening decisions on a regional basis. The governor's strategy was essentially establishing a blueprint for surrounding states like our own.

Early afternoon, as the rain kicked in, Jen shared by text a polished, video-recorded version of her playing Elton John's "Circle of Life" medley, which won out and would become her offering today in support of the APDA.

Holy ice balls, Batman! At about 3pm, the skies grew super dark, pushing us to turn on lights indoors, and the skies opened up, not only delivering hard rain but ice pellets that ricocheted off our windows, steps and cars. The rain and ice was accompanied by thunder boomers that rattled the house. So voluminous was the hail that I was able to scoop up a handful from the windshield of Phil's car and mold it into an ice ball. Mother Nature was really whacking us in the back of our bare leg with a wooden spoon.

Fed Ex braved the storm to deliver a package I had been expecting — snappy face masks from AnyTown USA. I pulled one on to check the look and fit. It was perfect. I never thought I'd be so excited about receiving a face mask.

As evening rolled around — and following the Weather Apocalypse — I tuned into Pres. Trump's daily briefing, in which he shared, "Twenty states, representing 40% of the United States' population, have announced that they are making plans and preparations to safely restart their economies." He also shared that the Senate had passed the Paycheck Protection Program initiative calling for $482 billion in additional funding for small businesses ($382B), hospitals ($75B) and testing ($25B) — the House would now need to approve. On the topic of immigration, which he had been kicking around, Pres. Trump said, "The noble fight against the invisible enemy has inflicted a steep toll on the American work force as we all know. Millions of Americans sacrificed their jobs in order to battle the virus and save the lives of our fellow citizens. We have a solemn duty to ensure these unemployed Americans regain their jobs and their livelihoods. Therefore, in order to protect American workers, I will be issuing a temporary suspension of immigration into the United States… By pausing immigration, we'll help put unemployed Americans first in line for jobs as America reopens… It would be wrong and unjust for Americans to be replaced by new immigrant labor flown in from abroad. We must first take care of the American worker… This pause will also help to conserve vital medical resources for American citizens." He noted that the pause would be in effect for 60 days then be re-evaluated.

Dad FaceTime called me, a first coming from his end. He said he had begun to think about how he would be different after this was over, concluding that he might actually consider himself retired and that he was okay with not being required to do anything. We spoke about his new-found joy for cooking, one of the things he looked forward to most in his day. We also spoke about some of his girlfriend prospects, one of whom he had seen a bit before the pandemic broke and another, who lived relatively near, that he had only connected with online so far. We discussed how that was an element that had been missing for him lately in this time of isolation and that having someone for whom you have feelings and can share some thoughts is key.

Mid-evening, I FT'ed with Jen as we were both winding down the day. We revisited a conversation about where we might travel when the green light was given, and we thought of the sandy white beaches of Florida's panhandle, the Panama City area. I pulled a few beach photos and texted them to her, which piqued her interest. We also discussed song possibilities for her for tomorrow, thinking that Billy Joel's "River of Dreams" was a good candidate. However, she pulled a video clip of herself playing Joel's "New

York State of Mind" with the great Charlie Karp, who had lived locally and passed in March 2019. It seemed the perfect way to give a shoutout to NYC, remember him and support her APDA cause.

The Nightly News: Global Covid-19 cases passed the 2.5 million mark, with nearly 172K deaths; the U.S. accounted for over 794K cases, with nearly 43K deaths. Worldwide, almost 660K people had recovered, or nearly a quarter of total cases. Southport, CT announced that its Blessing of the Fleet and Street Parade had been canceled. Statewide in CT, cases had passed 20K; deaths topped 1,400. The Westport, CT Police Dept. said it was exploring using a drone that can sense fevers and coughing — if, when, how and where it would be employed was TBA. Our Town of Fairfield, CT gave updated numbers: 306 cases, 37 deaths - still on a climb but noticeably slowing.

April 22. The sun had returned but it was brisk, just 36 degrees outside as I got a pot of coffee going. The air was unusually clear, and a light breeze rustled blossoming trees and flowers that dotted the surrounding landscape. Mother Nature had recovered from yesterday's tantrum and was resting peacefully for now.

It was Earth Day, its 50th anniversary, actually. Back when the celebration was founded, there were few laws protecting our air and water and the Environmental Protection Agency hadn't been established yet. Factories and cars and machines were all pumping out pollution unchecked. But a young senator — and later two-time governor of Wisconsin — named Gaylord Nelson was watching. In Sept. 1969, he called for Americans to come together in the spring for a day dedicated to environmental education. He received such a positive response to the idea that he formed an organization to support it, called Environmental Teach-In, Inc. to help people prepare for the event. Sen. Nelson hired a former intern, Denis Hayes, to be the national coordinator and assemble a promotion staff, while Nelson built a steering committee of intellectuals and students. Because there were unique ecological issues affecting different parts of the country, Nelson suggested each community celebrate Earth Day in its own way. On April 22, 1970, an estimated 20 million Americans gathered across the nation to promote a healthy, sustainable environment. It bridged political parties and led to the establishment of the US EPA and numerous environmental laws. In 1990, Earth Day went global, mobilizing over 200 million people across 141 countries. It has continued to expand since then, however, this year was the first time it would be celebrated virtually.

I got to thinking of the returning popularity of drive-in movie theaters, given that regular brick-and-mortar theaters were closed due to the virus and, on a whim, reached out by FB Messenger to Ginna Paules, who coordinates an annual series of movie showings on our local beach, using a projector and an inflatable screen. I suggested, "Hi Ginna. I hope you are keeping well and safe. I've been reading that, with all the movie theaters closed, drive-in theaters are coming back. I began thinking about the beach films you coordinate and wondered out loud if you could set the screen up in the parking lot at Jennings Beach and create a drive-in experience, wherein everyone could safely stay in their cars and yet come together and escape our confinement for a little bit, to show some community togetherness. You would need to create a way for people to tune in the audio on their car radios, which I'm confident could be figured out. Maybe an attendant at the toll booth can give out a bag of popcorn to each arriving family compliments of one of your sponsor companies? Let me know your thoughts. Best, Mike."

I got an event notice through FB, to attend a virtual tour early this evening of the Stewards of the Land Brewery in Northford, CT, being led by a rep from BeerFests. It was PJs optional, and it took the place of an event that I had planned to attend back when the world was still normal: Food Rescue U.S.'s "Food For All" gathering at The Loading Dock in Stamford, CT. This was usually a very festive occasion with much drinking, eating and fundraising for food challenged populations across Connecticut. Coincidentally, a friend posted to FB an unrelated photo of hundreds of cars lined up to obtain a few pounds of food each from Foodshare in East Hartford this morning.

FT'ed with Jen, re-thinking her song offering for today given that it was Earth Day. We were thinking her choice should be more Earth focused. For a moment, we toyed with John Denver's "Earth Day Every Day (Celebrate)" from his album "Earth Songs", but it was a bit hokey. Then we shifted to the soothing "What A Wonderful World" by Louis Armstrong. It was the absolute perfect choice. Off she went to practice it on her piano.

I received an email from Tripadvisor with the subject line "7 simple ways to bring luxury getaway comfort to your home", offering bedding suggestions, "the perfect slippers", creating a French spa experience in your bathroom, international cocktail recipes, "ultra-cozy" furnishings, and accessories for your bathroom that would give it the look and feel of a five-star luxury hotel. I guess if we're going to be homebound, we might as well live large? I mean, our pandemic doesn't need to be all boo-hoo and shabby, right?

I wished a happy birthday to a friend, Vivien, through FB. She is a very joyous type who loves to dance and my most recent memory of her was grooving in a packed crowd enjoying the Latin beats of the Cosmic Jibaros band at a local club called The Acoustic in neighboring Black Rock.

There were two virtual efforts planned to support Earth Day of which I was aware: a "Drive Electric Earth Day Tribute: EVs Making a Difference" promoting electric car technologies through a Facebook Live program; and "A Virtual Earth Day Concert" presented through Zoom featuring performances by Fairfield County Artists. A third, titled "Transformation", was being presented by Westport-based Beechwood Arts & Innovation, focused on how world perspectives were shifting and becoming aware of what needs to change, with live music, art and special guests.

I received one of now dozens of daily solicitations of its kind by email, from a promotional company alerting "Hurry! Order Now and Save Huge on Hand Sanitizers, Face Masks, Gowns, Glasses and More". It was the new norm. Another came from Office Depot, offering equipment that could help "Enhance your work from home setup".

Mid-morning, I read a stunning revelation from the San Francisco Chronicle that a person who died at home in Santa Clara County, CA on Feb. 6 was infected with the coronavirus at the time of death, which made that individual the first recorded Covid-19 fatality in the U.S., according to just-released autopsy results. That death was three weeks before the first previously known fatality was reported, on Feb. 28, in Washington state. The local medical examiner also confirmed another virus-related death, on Feb. 17, which predated the first known reported case, too. That Feb. 6 case was likely infected in early January, which meant the virus was circulating in the community — and our country — much earlier than documented.

A Reuters item shared a photo of Chinese performance artist Kong Ning, in Beijing, in a dress she made of eight giant plastic inflatable roses over a wire structure and headpiece crowned by a globe, using fashion to draw attention to environmental protection on Earth Day.

Midday, NY Gov. Cuomo did his daily, noting that it had been "fifty-three days since we closed down New York, which feels very long and it's very stressful." Showing his humanity, he added, "I feel it in my own household. My daughters are getting tired of my jokes, believe it or not. How can that happen? I have no idea... We even have trouble now picking a movie at night, because the rule is, if you pick a bad movie, then you're on movie probation. You don't get to pick the next movie... Even the dog, Captain, is out of sorts and relating to stress... but we have to deal with it... And when you look at the reality of the situation, we're actually in a much better place. We're not home yet, but we're in a much better place." He offered the usual stats: hospitalizations and intubations down, but number of new people admitted "still troublingly high" and number of lives lost "still breathtakingly painful", with 474 deaths yesterday — a number, though, that "seems to be on the decline". How tight was the situation? "What we do today, you will see the results in three, four, five days... We get reckless today, you'll see that hospitalization rate go up three, four, five days from today." Going forward, he said, "Truth and facts" have to guide actions.

I didn't realize how much I missed baseball until I saw a friend's FB post noting that, on this day in 1970, New York Mets Pitcher Tom Seaver struck out 19 San Diego Padres (including 10 in a row) to end the game, a major league record at the time. I was only five then but a budding Mets fan, and Seaver, nicknamed "Tom Terrific", was my hero. I lived in upstate New York and our milk cartons promoted free Mets tickets when you mailed in proofs-of-purchase from the cartons — four proofs equaled one general admission ticket. You can bet that my brother and I tried to drink as much milk as we could so my Dad could redeem the stubs and we could travel down to Queens, NY and see a game at the old Shea stadium. Sadly, Seaver was diagnosed with Lyme disease in 1991 while he lived in CT. It reoccurred in 2012 and led to Bell's palsy and memory loss. A year ago, his family announced that he was suffering from Alzheimer's dementia and was retiring from public life. His Topps trading cards would hold a special place in my baseball card collection.

Puppeteer friends known as Mortal Beasts & Deities posted an old photo online of their Volvo wagon piled up with their gear — stilts, giant puppets and show props — and mourned that, for the first time in many years, they had "zero gigs on their calendar". I suggested that they do a performance online and seek Venmo donations, that people were dying for this kind of fuzzy entertainment.

Early afternoon, the "Drive Electric Earth Day Tribute: EVs Making a Difference" popped up, beginning with a catchy ballad shunning gasoline usage. An excerpt: "You're making me cough, you're turning me off, I'm breaking this relationship. Gasoline, gasoline, you're driving me insane. Gasoline, gasoline, the world's in flames. Gasoline, gasoline, I've got some big news. There's someone better, better than you... We had a good run, but now we're done, you're poisoning our atmosphere. You don't even care, pumping dirt in our air, leading on that the end is near."

Mid-afternoon, I listened in to a "Nasa Science Live: Earth Day at Home" FB broadcast, featuring an interview with NASA Administrator Jim Bridenstine, who commented about the space agency's monitoring of the ozone layer, studying crop yields to guide farmers on crop production, and observing what countries are heeding anti-pollution guidelines.

Late afternoon, as the sun burst out, I got inspired to order a bouquet of flowers for Jen, from our local Hansen's flower shop. Shop staff was apparently busy and it rang through to an operator based in Arkansas. I asked how she was faring there and learned that things were more relaxed than they were here. Indeed, they had a little over 2K cases and just 43 deaths to date.

With the mail, a Summer activities booklet came from our Fairfield Parks & Recreation. It was full of planned experiences that I wondered would even happen: live comedy shows at Penfield Pavilion beginning May 21; a concert series at Sherman Green Gazebo starting May 31; Movie Nights at Jennings Beach rolling out June 12; a Dog Days event June 13; swimming lessons kicking off June 22; a Peanut Butter Jam concert series for kids starting June 24; S'mores Sundays at Lake Mohegan sparking on June 28; and a "Dive-in at Lake Mohegan" immersive in-water viewing experience of the movie "Twister", July 31. So much fun planned.

Our CT Gov. Lamont gave his daily briefing for the state, noting over 22.4K cases, up over 2K from yesterday; and 1,544 deaths, up by 121 since yesterday. Our numbers put us in the top 12 among states for total cases, just behind GA and TX. Lamont said that we were "by no means out of the ditch on this."

Pick-up of the flower bouquet was 1-2-3. Hansen's gave me a ring, I shot over, the curbside exchange was made like a Bronx drug deal and I was back home again in an instant.

Spontaneous Chicken Cacciatore ensued — a big skillet full — made from a recipe grabbed online. Pandemic Pasta. Chicken Coronatore. Corona Cacciatore. Whatever you wanted to call it.

At 6pm, I hopped into Beechwood Arts' live FB WE feed, led by Jeanine Esposito and Frederic Chiu. Their "Transformation"-themed broadcast came straight from their home's piano room. The focus steered toward how we will evolve into a new normal — taking stock of what we've learned from this time and incorporating it into how we will go forward working and living. Frederic kicked things off with a piano piece, then it moved into Shakespearean theater, a bit of Romeo and Juliet but with roles reversed, in a split screen Zoom format, with a piano intro from Frederic. The artwork/ artist segment followed, with works of art shown being transformed and then artists appearing in a split screen Zoom format being interviewed for their thoughts about transformation. It was a fascinating presentation overall and I was impressed by the varying technologies being employed.

I patched into Pres. Trump's daily briefing then, in which he took a positive, forward-looking stance, saying new cases were declining nationwide, recent hot spots appeared to be stabilizing, and places like Boston, Chicago and Detroit were getting things under control, with the goal of more states soon to be in a position to reopen. The President turned the mic over to Dr. Robert Redfield, the Director of the Centers for Disease Control, who had been painted earlier in the press as suggesting that the flu and Covid-19 were going to be a double whammy this fall and winter. He said his comments were misconstrued and clarified to say that that time period is going to be "more difficult" but that we will continue to be in a "containment mode so we don't need to resort to the mitigation we had to this spring." Dr. Redfield said that he had confidence in early case recognition, contact tracing and surveillance of the most vulnerable populations along with the American public's continued cooperation.

At 7:45pm, as the sun was doing its dip for the day, I zipped to Jen's, taking the Post Road to Westport the whole way, eyeing Xmas lights circling Tequila Revolucion Mexican restaurant, more Xmas lights wrapped around a tree at a Westport Exxon station, and local TV/magazine personality Mar Jennings zipping by in his low-riding Porsche with MAR-TV plates.

Jen was glad to receive my bouquet but wondered what I was up to given no associated occasion! She poured me tea, we propped her laptop computer on her ironing board in her TV room and we tuned in to the aforementioned Sustainable Fairfield "A Virtual Earth Day Concert" presented through Zoom. Nearly a dozen local performers took turns playing a song each, including Brian Dolzani, Elizabeth Dolan McNicholl, Dan Tressler, John Burlinson, Michael Dunham, Greg Packham, James "Fuzz" Sangiovanni of Deep Banana Blackout, The Bar Car Band and the Vanderwal Family. The sound was a bit clunky at times but the spirit was strong, pulling community together.

We caught the last half hour of "Roman Holiday" from the other night and laughed when Audrey Hepburn as the Princess dismissed an attendant: "You have my permission to withdraw. That will be all, thank you." Jen thought she would adopt that phrase into her own daily routine. On the heels of that film, we enjoyed "Eat Drink Man Woman", a Chinese film from 1994. It featured noted actor Sihung Lung as semi-retired Master Chef Chu living at home with his three unmarried daughters. Their home life is anchored by an elaborate dinner every Sunday, the stability of which gives them a common point as they each deal with romantic relationships and disappointments. It was just pure entertainment for us, centered on life versus pandemia.

News: Virus-infected Broadway Actor Nick Cordero had his right leg amputated the other day as he developed complications. Someone stole an entire truckload of Jack Daniels whiskey from a trailer yard in Atlanta, GA. A sheriff in northeast Ohio busted up an Amish barn gathering in a community being impacted by Covid-19. After canceling its annual tulip festival, an Oregon farm began delivering its flowers to isolated seniors. Air conditioning in a restaurant in China was believed to have spread the virus from an infected person there to 10 other patrons in the space, suggesting that small businesses will be challenged by ventilation systems as they reopen and operate in warmer months. New York state's health department issued, then rescinded, a guideline urging EMS workers not to try to revive people found in cardiac arrest, in order to protect the health and safety of the providers, conserve resources and ensure optimal use of equipment to save the greatest number of lives. A Business Insider story offered a history lesson about how San Francisco emerged from a lockdown too soon during the 1918 Spanish flu pandemic, leading to an even bigger outbreak. Over

2,200 workers across 48 meat plants had tested positive for the virus to date, potentially threatening meat production and distribution. Twenty-two percent of Americans still working reported they were sleep deprived due to virus related anxiety, which was affecting productivity. Worldwide, virus cases surged past 2.6 million, with over 182K deaths (over 714K recoveries); the U.S. accounted for over 830K cases and over 46K deaths (over 83K recoveries). Milford, CT-based Hawley Lane Shoes donated 200 pairs of therapeutic footwear to essential workers. CT Gov. Lamont reported over 22K cases (up by over 2K cases) and 1,544 deaths (up by 121) to date. Ansonia, CT's Midsummer Fantasy Renaissance Faire announced it would not be held this year. A local radio station promoted another big virtual music fest, called "PlayOn Fest", with 65 artists, to stream for 72 hours starting April 24. The South China Morning Post reported that mainland China might have had four times as many infections as official totals stated if broader criteria had been used in identifying them, putting the estimate at 232K cases.

April 23. Wiping away the sleepies, Jen and I discussed her song plan for the day, deciding on Nat King Cole's "Smile". She sent me off with a package of dark sweet cherries. Though it was a Thursday and supposedly morning rush hour, there was barely a car on the road. The absence of traffic made the grayness of the day more bleak and pronounced. I wondered when we would step back out into the sun as I passed a tree with a yarn wrapping incorporating a heart in front of the Westport Fire Headquarters. There was another wrapping further along. Flags were at half-mast in front of Mitchell's Department Store — mannequins in the windows were arranged around the phrase "Get Your Spring On". Numerous businesses displayed Curbside Pickup signs: Sakura Japanese Restaurant, Fortuna's Deli, Gruel Brittania, Avellino's, LobsterCraft and Tequila Revolucion. A bedsheet hung in front of Furniture Consignment II: "P. Trump Save Me".

With a big mug of java in hand, I stepped online, noticing it was an old high school friend's birthday. She was working the pandemic right, boating and dining on fresh fish in Florida.

I read an oil market assessment from CFA Michael Gayed, suggesting it would eventually flow back strongly: "Oil equities are some of the most oversold, underappreciated companies out there right now. And while there's short-term pain in hand for oil companies, the infrastructure globally for oil isn't about to change tomorrow. China's economy already is slowly reopening for business. China is the world's biggest energy importer and already is stocking up on the cheap black stuff. Evidence suggests that for months, China has been amassing inventory. Smart for a country that's expected to rebound strongly once the Coronavirus is contained, for now, and cured later. So while there's no demand right now for oil, it will not be that way forever. And it may take some time. With rock bottom prices, how could you not be in the equities that are levered for a potentially massive bounce? The conditions are there."

I read about Las Vegas Mayor Carolyn Goodman and the flap she created in deciding to reopen the city despite the virus threat and that hotels and casinos are hot spots for the spread. Goodman said the fears were "alarmist" and that businesses should reopen and allow the free market to dictate whether they are "destroyed" by the virus. So many different viewpoints across America about reopening.

Our friend Bob, the owner of Penfield Auto Service, shared online that his tow truck guy, Corey Iodice, was killed while loading a vehicle on the Merritt Parkway in the Fairfield/Trumbull area. It was a crazy happening during this chaotic time.

At high noon, NY Gov. Cuomo gave his usual briefing, noting again that hospitalizations and intubations were down, new hospitalizations were flat around 1,300 but that "lives lost is still breathtakingly tragic" at 438 yesterday (403 in hospitals, 35 in nursing homes). "That number's not coming down as fast as we would like to see that number come down," he added. Cuomo also addressed the challenges the Fall might present when the flu and Covid-19 would be present at the same time. To this regard, I happened to read that a person can contract both at the same time — double trouble to be sure. Gov. Cuomo also shared that a screening of 3,000 people found nearly 14% tested positive for antibodies for the coronavirus, suggesting up to 2.7 million residents across the state may have been infected with the disease.

Our Fairfield First Selectwoman gave her daily report, noting our town cases were up to 334, with 38 deaths. More than half who had tested positive, 117, had recovered. She said our case rate was 538 per 100K, lower than 18 other towns in Fairfield County, which indicated we'd been doing a good job of social distancing. Average new cases per day for the last 10 days was 11.2. A glimmer of good news: "I am working on a plan with our emergency management team to lift some restrictions placed on our outdoor and open spaces. The details will be announced early next week. The approach we are taking is data driven and will not be governed by emotions," she said. "What I *do* want residents to know is that we will be limiting access to certain town spaces to Fairfield residents only," she added, with an encouragement to get our 2020 beach stickers.

My Dad and brother Dave had, a long while ago, planned a trip to Britain for late May this year. As the infections increased across the world, though, the trip's reality seemed more and more in jeopardy. Today, my Dad got the "nail in the coffin" word that it wasn't going to pan out, after having a FT call with his brother-in-law, Bob, who lives in South Wales. Dad had toyed with staying with Bob for a couple of days before he and Dave headed to North Wales. "Forget it," was the short answer, and not just about visiting them, but the whole trip. North Wales was shut tight, Bob said. Bob's son, Matt, called the North Wales Tourist Board and they told him that there were gates across the entrances to villages with signs saying "Turn Around and Go Home." There were also police everywhere, targeting rental cars in particular, and again just turning them around and sending them back where they came from — local residents only. Britishers from places like Manchester had been trying to flee to North Wales for relative safety and were not welcomed. Virtually all public accommodations were closed — pubs, restaurants, inns, b&b's. Bob said that even when *he* goes out in his own car, he's likely to be stopped and asked where he's going and whether or not the trip was essential. Bob said they expect to be shut tight into June at the very least, and maybe into the fall months. They don't expect tourism to open up until December, if then. Bob said my Dad would be wise to reschedule the trip for NEXT May.

Mid-afternoon, global virus cases pushed over 2.7 million (740K recoveries), with over 189K deaths. Of these numbers, the U.S. accounted for over 868K cases (nearly 85K recoveries) and over 49K deaths. Among U.S. states, the ten with the most cases included, from top to bottom: NY, NJ, MA, CA, PA, MI, IL, FL, LA and CT. Sadly, this was CT's debut in this "top ten" category.

Given that it was a raw day, I made a mega pot of chili and kicked back to scroll through my FB newsfeed, happening to stumble on the amazing Norah Jones playing her acoustic guitar and piano and singing live, from home. I had always thought she was so humble and approachable and this live interaction confirmed it. "Thanks for the requests, keep 'em coming! Love, Norah," she posted, encouraging feedback and input.

I had to laugh at a friend's FB status post: "My dream is we wake up like Dorothy in the Wizard of Oz and everyone is healthy and happy and life is good. Oh and don't forget the Munchkins are doing my hair and nails and giving me a massage." Another posted: "I need a tropical beach and unlimited cocktails, stat." I wondered how many of us were hoping we could just flip a switch and Covid-19 would go away.

An update from Gov. Lamont's office indicated that his plan to reopen parts of the state by May 20 may be pushed back. May 20 would instead be the date when a reopening plan was ready for the governor's review. A gradual reopening was more likely in June and would continue through the rest of the year. His office said that the state would also be implementing a contact tracing program so that when someone is infected with COVID-19, public health workers and volunteers would make phone calls and track down all the people that person has been in contact with so they, too, could be tested and potentially isolated. The state planned to bring modern Cloud or app-based technology to the initiative. On a related note, the Westport, CT Police Dept. abandoned its exploration of a drone program to sense fevers and coughing after receiving a lot of pushback from local residents concerned about invasion of privacy and extreme policing, which all of these measures seemed like to many.

At 6pm, Pres. Trump gave his Coronavirus Task Force Update for the day, reporting, "States are starting to open up now and it's very exciting to see. I think it's awe inspiring. We're coming out of it and we're coming out of it well. Really, I'm very happy. The governors have been doing a really good job working with us. It's really pretty impressive to see... The safe and phased reopening of our economy is very exciting but does not mean that we are letting down on our guard at all in any way. On the contrary, continued diligence is an essential part of our strategy to get our country back to work, to take our country back. We're winning this and we're going to win it and we're going to keep watching... for the invisible enemy."

The President detailed a new initiative: "As we continue to develop potential therapies, the FDA has recently begun a national effort to expand access to convalescent plasma donated from the blood of those who have recovered from the virus. The blood of these donors contains antibodies that can potentially reduce the severity of the illness in those that are sick. Nearly 3,000 patients are enrolled in the expanded access program and receiving transfusions nationwide. Convalescent plasma will also be used to manufacture a concentrated antibody treatment that does not have to be matched with a particular blood type."

Putting on his Ronnie Reagan hat then, the President championed, "We have every hope that with the full might and resources of American science and technology and with the courage and devotion of the American people... we will end this plague and together we will restore the full measure of American strength and power and prosperity."

I stumbled onto some hot licks being laid down through a "Watch Party" of a trio of musicians — Rohn Lawrence, Jay Rowe and Trever Somerville — live jamming at a place called the Tipping Chair Tavern in Southington, CT. It was really quite amazing during this time to get all these various inputs, especially from the music world, literally from all over the globe at all levels — homegrown, mid-range and professional. The stage had been leveled.

Another local event, Black Rock Day, planned for June 14, bit the dust when the Black Rock Community Council of Black Rock, CT announced its cancellation. The annual occasion typically offered a truly local opportunity for bonding and all-out revelry, all across the tightly knit neighborhood.

Instead of "going to the movies" this evening, I flipped through Instagram and happened to stumble on a "Quarantine Meditation" session of stress-relieving exercises offered by @thetravelinglight AKA Natalie Torres, a spiritual coach and healing artist. She was literally sitting on her bedroom floor, in a tee and shorts with a green colored facial mask on, performing breathing and stretching exercises for viewers to follow. Occasionally, her dog would make an on-camera appearance, running past and barking.

I spoke with Jen late evening, who had abandoned the Nat King Cole song we had discussed for her daily APDA token and gone back to her classical roots with Chopin's "Nocturne". We collaborated on an accompanying text message, then she posted it to her FB page.

NEWS: Another 4.4 million Americans filed for unemployment benefits last week, bringing the unemployed total to over 26 million. A series of tornadoes that touched down from Oklahoma to Mississippi yesterday had killed at least six people, compounding challenges in the region. NYC Mayor de Blasio announced a "Test and Trace" plan and said that July 4th is still on. A study shared by Nat Geo said a sneeze can travel up to 27 feet, as droplets linger in the air. Germany's iconic Oktoberfest celebration was canceled, the first time since World War II. And YouTube celebrated its 15th birthday.

April 24. Today must have been Mother Nature's day to shower. The rain came down in buckets all night, leaving pools of water on the street, continued this morning, and was expected to last through late afternoon. It would be a stay-at-home day. Wait, it was *already* going to be a stay-at-home day... like pretty much every other day since early March!

I eyed an email that my Dad sent me that had come from his cleaning service, detailing their virus-oriented safety protocols. This included: using EPA-approved disinfectant to sanitize all frequently touched surfaces according to CDC guidance; fresh shoe covers, masks and gloves worn in each house; wiping down of equipment between houses; staff to notify employers if they feel sick and, if so, to stay at home; clients to notify cleaners if they are sick or in quarantine; techs to social distance when they are in the home; use of hospital grade microfiber cloths with built-in bacteriostat which can remove up to 99.99% of pathogens with just water; color coded cloths to distinguish between bath and kitchen usage to prevent cross contamination; dirty cloths from another house never enter your home; all cloths washed using a sanitizing cycle; use of scrubbing microfibers instead of sponges, which are color-coded and washed along with the other microfibers; and use of vacuums with high efficiency filtration that carry the American Lung Association seal. The business operators seemed to have thought of everything and, yet, a slip-up here or there and the virus could be introduced into a presumably sterile, safe environment. I shared that concern with Dad but also offered, "That said, sometimes you have to take a leap of faith and assume they are following all protocols."

This virus and our extended "Coronacation" was really beginning to wear on people I had begun to notice. One friend, whose kids put her over the edge last night, just had to escape for a bit to clear her head. She posted, "I left to go on a drive not knowing where because normally my go-to would be a beach. So I drove by Saint Mary's very slowly and stopped at the end. The lighthouse was lit. It smelled like the beach and it was absolutely beautiful. On my drive, I just happened to hear, all in a row, some of my favorite music. Van Morrison's 'Moondance'. Doobie Brothers' 'Listen to the Music'. James Taylor's 'Fire and Rain', and the Eagles' 'Peaceful Easy Feeling'. Wrapped it up on the way home with Gladys Night and The Pips' 'Midnight Train to Georgia'. After singing and dancing in my car, I pulled in my driveway feeling like me again after a much needed 30-minute break alone. I highly recommend it."

Among the Bible scripture quotations and inspirational messages folks had been posting during this challenging time was a passage that popped up this morning, credited to Indian Author Haroon Rashid: "We fell asleep in one world, and woke up in another. Suddenly Disney is out of magic, Paris is no longer romantic, New York doesn't stand up anymore, the Chinese wall is no longer a fortress, and Mecca is empty. Hugs & kisses suddenly become weapons, and not visiting parents & friends becomes an act of love. Suddenly you realize that power, beauty & money are worthless, and can't get you the oxygen you're fighting for. The world continues its life and it is beautiful. It only puts humans in cages. I think it's sending us a message: 'You are not necessary. The air, earth, water and sky without you are fine. When you come back, remember that you are my guests. Not my masters.'" His thoughts had apparently circled the world, touching millions.

I had to smile about an email I received from an American-made products company showing a photo of a family of four laying on the floor in a den setting, with their bored faces resting on their hands, captioned "Looking for something to do?" and offering below that some fun for all ages: an activities book with wordsearch puzzles, crosswords and Sudoku challenges, and a "Coloring for Everyone" book. Boy, we had really become anchored.

Late morning, I learned that another local favorite restaurant, Westport's Rothbard Ale & Larder House, a German-style restaurant and sister of the recently closed Walrus + Carpenter, was ceasing to be. However, Owner Joe Farrell said a new creation, Walrus Alley, would soon be taking its place, offering American Southern-inspired flavors. He also promised Rothbard would be back as a pop-up from time to time, "especially in October". So all was not lost, in this case, just some consolidation and fine tuning.

From a friend's FB post, I was "glad" to learn that I wasn't the only one who experienced anxiety when making the groceries run. She posted,

"Why do I feel like every day I am heading out to grocery shop like I am on some kind of Mission Impossible? Deep breath... here I go again!" Her message accompanied several photos of empty store shelves that she had encountered recently.

I needed a mission, an outing, and a message through Instagram provided one. It was Stratford Antiques Center in Stratford, CT, just up the pike, letting me know that a 40-year-old "The Legend of the Lone Ranger" lunch box, in which I had expressed interest, was available for purchase and pick-up this morning. So into the car I hopped and motored east on I-95, with my windshield wipers slapping at the oncoming rain and tractor-trailers flying by, to the venue. Not wanting to risk going in, I pulled up close to the entrance and called, reaching a clerk who was aware of the conversation. In a moment, she appeared — masked and gloved — through the door, toting the package, and brought it to my passenger side window. We nimbly exchanged cash — I collected my change in my bandana — and she reached through the window to set the package on my seat. Done and done. With a "Hi Ho, Silver!", I galloped away, a representation of the masked man and his trusty sidekick now in my clutches.

Realizing that Fairfield Craft Ales brewery was in this same neck of the woods, I pulled up curbside hoping to score a four-pack of their Darkness on the Edge of Town Dunkel beer. But the brewery had no Friday pick-up hours, so the detour was for naught.

Back on the highway I went, passing the usual "Stay Home, Stay Safe" digital warnings calling me out for my non-essential travel, and back down through Fairfield I came to take on my #2 anxiety-producing task: getting gas. At Shell, a gallon of regular was $1.99. With a 40-cent discount via a partnership with Stop & Shop, I was down to $1.59. Unheard of in modern times! I filled the car for $26 (normally $45 or more) and had to check my gauge to see if I'd actually received a full tank. Pleased with myself, I finally returned home, immediately engaging in a round of disinfecting — of my wallet, car keys, hands, the lunchbox, etc. Gloves and bandana went in the wash; anything paper went in the trash.

It was NY Gov. Cuomo time again. Total hospitalizations down, net change in hospitalizations down, intubations down. Number of people coming into the hospital "not great news" — slightly down and basically flat, but still 1,200 to 1,300 new infections per day. And the most "heartbreaking" stat: 422 more deaths yesterday (398 in hospitals, 24 in nursing homes). "Dropping somewhat but it's still devastating news," he commented. Further, he warned against relaxing our vigilance, saying, "This is a remarkably effective virus at spreading and growing… The game is just at halftime." He also spoke about missing signs that the virus was around earlier than realized and said the lesson learned is "An outbreak anywhere is an outbreak everywhere", given our ability to travel so easily across the globe; that we can't assume that it will take a couple of months for it to get from one side of the world to the other. In short, our actions here were "too little too late". With that water under the bridge, he was now starting to turn his attention to cleaning protocols, particularly of mass transit systems, given the lifespan of the virus on plastic, steel, cardboard, etc.

There was a flap on the Internet relating that the President, in an aside to a doctor at his daily briefing yesterday, had wondered if UV light and/or disinfectant, given their newly revealed strength at killing the virus, could somehow be translated to a human injection or application —something fast acting, in the spirit of keeping open to any and all possibilities. Of course, the press ran with it, stating that he wanted people to go and inject themselves with bleach. Responding to those headlines, disinfectant makers issued cautionary alerts that people not try that at home.

At the same time, a YouTube video emerged suggesting that the White House staff had all been vaccinated already, through a behind-the-scenes collaboration with a Texas-based company called Greffex. The video said "the Trump gang" planned the pandemic to destroy China and all the USA's imaginary enemies, as well as the unwanted populations of the world. The video explained that there was a microphone leak just before the President's Covid-19 press briefing on April 20, wherein Fox News host John Roberts says, as they are setting up, "You can take the mask off, the case fatality rate is 0.1 to 0.3 according to USC." To which a Fox tech replies: "Really? That's reassuring. Everybody here's been vaccinated anyway." The video went on to state: No wonder Trump tests remain negative for coronavirus even after multiple interactions with infected people. More: The vaccine was purported to be the product of an $18.9 million contract Greffex received in Sept. 2019 from the National Institute of Health's National Institute for Allergy and Infectious Diseases. The video was headlined, "Trump's gang self-exposed: We are ALL vaccinated! Covid-19 is a CIA plot against all mankind!" Conspiracy theories were rife.

My ex, Marlene, sent a text saying she had spoken with our son Evan and that he was considering renting a car and driving here from D.C. to be with Phil and me, as a spirit booster. I replied to her, "He's certainly welcome to, though I don't advise traveling and particularly to our NY metro area where, just in NY, people are dying at the rate of 500 people per day. He is also allergic to Stormy (our cat), which would make him more vulnerable to getting the virus, given a runny nose etc. that he would get. I think it's best to continue to stay home and stay safe until this thing flattens out. They're looking at June here."

Acting on the text exchange with Marlene, I rang Evan and we chatted at length. He actually wasn't very motivated to come up from D.C., as it turned out, or even sure if he could get a rental car these days. Marlene's heart was in the right place though. He had the day off today, which was the first bit of time off he had had since the beginning of the year. He had received his stimulus check, which barely covered a month's rent but was still welcome. He had been staying inside unless he really had to go out, to run, for instance, which he did wearing a mask. He was well stocked up with food — pasta, beans, rice, etc. He was making meals like Spaghetti Bolognese, and freezing portions for other days. About his job, working for SmartBrief, he said that they had their highest amount of website traffic ever last month. He reiterated that his office was going to open back up, at 30% capacity, on May 18. There would be protocols in place: can't sit next to someone, automatic opening doors, have to wear a mask, alternating days in the office. All that was amenable though the only way for him to get to work was via the Metro, which he didn't feel safe riding. Further down the road, his company was planning to transfer him to their NYC office mid-August, though he would be working remotely at first. He didn't mind that as so many of his friends had moved away from the D.C. area. His girlfriend, who works for Microsoft, was also planning to move to NYC, so that aligned well. On a side note, she had just given him a haircut, so he wouldn't look shabby in Zoom meetings.

The mail arrived early afternoon, producing the usual anxiety in handling it. It included the May/June issue of a monthly town magazine that was normally robust with information and advertising but that was now reduced to just half its size. Its editor lamented some of the new vocabulary words we had learned, like "quarantine" and "social distancing", and our new state of normalcy. "We know one day this will be behind us and whether we are in a crisis mode or not, the beauty that spring brings, the joys of gardening, the celebration of our small businesses, and talent of our residents will always be important," she suggested. Articles centered on gardening and family.

Another local coastal publication's editor quoted the words of poet Pablo Neruda, "You can cut all the flowers, but you cannot keep spring from coming." It spoke to the uncertainty we were feeling emotionally, countered by the resiliency of our natural landscape and how that can be a guide for our community. Articles mirrored the monthly fare and also touched on meditation, preserving food without canning, recipes and beekeeping.

Late afternoon, CT Gov. Lamont got on the squawk box with his report. Hospitalizations were going down significantly while testing was going up "in a serious way". Positive cases were at 23,921 in total; deaths were still "a lagging indicator" at 1,764 (up 125 since yesterday). Hospital admissions were down or flat for all counties, which Lamont called "extraordinary good news". Looking out at the nation, he was concerned about flare-ups at food processing places, like South Dakota, and MD and VA with poultry, and vowed to support challenged state residents with expanded access to farmers' markets and food share resources, and to help restaurants with prep and delivery of meals to seniors and those under quarantine.

Phil got word from UConn with regard to summer and fall and planning for resuming instruction — scenarios ranging from most or all courses remaining online to returning to all in-person instruction and residential life with significant safety modifications and accommodations. As to summer, the school decided instruction for all summer terms would be delivered online or remotely through distance education. A decision about Fall face-to-face classes was to be made by June 30, determined by the progress on slowing Covid-19, guidance from public health experts and federal and state government, and the availability of testing. Faculty was told to plan as though courses would be delivered online in the fall.

I dined on leftovers as Pres. Trump gave his daily briefing, reporting "very very significant progress", with new cases down in many hard hit areas. He asked Americans "to maintain vigilance" and noted that he signed the

Paycheck Protection Program and Healthcare Enhancement Act "to keep American workers on the payroll". He also said the FDA approved the first at-home Covid-19 test, developed by LabCorp, which allows, under certain circumstances and with a doctor's supervision, for a test to be mailed to a patient and for the patient to perform a self-swab and mail the test back to get results.

Now a regular end-of-week feature for me, The Digital Friday Night Cafe, shared by email from Music for Youth, provided a wealth of young local musical talents performing classical numbers. There was Camden Archambeau on cello playing Debussy, Cameron Chase and David Bernat on violin performing Prokofiev, and Alexandra Mascoff and Ava Turner on piano, each playing a Chopin selection.

Mother Nature offered a fine end-of-day sky show, with a palette of pastel streaks of pink, amber and blue. It was the kind of sunset that I would normally race over to nearby Sasco Beach to admire along with dozens of other people. But, of course, those times had been suspended and the beach was chained off. Instead, I had to settle for the glow of a neighbor's firebowl two yards over, which lit up the backyard and the underside of adjacent trees.

I poured myself a Godiva liqueur to sip on and savored the Dark Sweet Cherries that Jen had given me the other day, and settled into my lounge seat for the Friday night movie viewing. The selection: "The Eternal", a 1998 horror film featuring Alison Elliott (Nora), Jared Harris (Jim) and Christopher Walken (Nora's Uncle Bill). After a night of drinking, Nora experiences a flashback and bangs her head falling down the stairs of her NYC apartment building. Her doctor advises her to give up alcohol and the couple and their son head to Ireland to visit her grandmother and recuperate. In the basement of the matriarch's palatial home is the body of a 2,000-year-old druid witch, that Uncle Bill has retrieved from a nearby bog. The druid was infamously known as a powerful individual "in touch with the power of nature" who never aged but then fell in love, neglected her spells and lost her power. After the witch and her lover have a child, he abandons her. She tracks him down, kills him and then kills herself. Through the process of transmigration, the druid's soul begins to move into Nora's body, which sends everything into a tailspin of mayhem.

There were two notable passages for me. One was the words of a young girl, Alice, that Uncle Bill had adopted, who was the story's narrator. Studying a puddle on a rainy day much like the one we had experienced today, she says, "In the beginning of the world, the Earth and the sky were one creature and it was the hardest thing to tear them apart. They loved each other so much. And that's why it rains — the Earth and the sky are always trying to get back together."

Uncle Bill offered the other notable passage: "Everything that is, is in the process of turning into something else. We can't know where our pain is from, nevertheless we suffer from it." It just seemed appropriate to our times as so many people are in agony every day and so many souls are beginning a new journey.

Before heading to sleep, Jen and I spoke by phone... and had The Talk... about our personal virus protection regimen when we're out in public and how we disinfect at home. Can you think of a more romantic Friday night conversation? But, honestly, people these days really needed to be speaking about these things, to ensure they were protecting themselves and each other. We discovered our regimens differed somewhat but were no less effective respectively. #inthistogether

NEWS: Female rowers in Venice had been delivering groceries to the elderly by gondola. NBC reported that this pandemic may forever change the touchy-feely nature of hotels, which were eliminating things like mini bars, room service, buffets, riding with other people in the elevator and person-to-person check-in. Global Coronavirus cases surged over 2.8 million (778K + recoveries) with over 196K deaths. The U.S. accounted for 912K+ cases (92K+ recoveries) and over 51K deaths. Among U.S. states, NY had over 276K cases and 21K+ deaths. It was announced that the USNS Mercy would be leaving NYC and the Javits Center would conclude its hospital operations in May. An Iowa woman sewing colorful face masks had been hanging them like Xmas ornaments on an evergreen tree outside her home for neighbors to take as needed.

April 25. The day — Saturday, I think (!) — was off to a fine start. Bright. Crisp. Light blue skies. I hoped it would hold.

I leafed through email, learning that airplane cabin designers have been working on ideas for reconfigured seats with safety in mind. In rows with three seats, the middle seat would be turned around to face the rear of the aircraft and have a transparent shield around it. And "Glassafe" transparent cocoons were being imagined, to attach to the top of existing airplane seats to form an umbrella of sorts around a person's head.

I read about dating approaches that respected physical distance during this pandemic period. Some ideas to kindle the flames included virtual movie night through a Netflix Party extension, a personality quiz date wherein you take online quizzes together to see if you're compatible, going on a QuaranDate (a video pair-up hosted by a neutral third party), staging a video cooking competition and home tour, creating a date in a box (shipping your significant other a box full of everything they need to have the perfect virtual date together) and planning a socially distant date outdoors (bike ride, hike, etc.).

With some alarm, I read that two pet cats in NYC confirmed positive for the coronavirus. At this time, there was still no evidence that pets or animals played a role in the spread of Covid-19, but health officials were keeping close watch for more incidences like this across the country.

Humorously, Miller High Life was offering $10K and a wedding at your doorstep if your ceremony was impacted by Covid-19. Three couples would have a chance to win the package.

I received an email from Dad who shared that his planned trip in July to Macedonia to help build a home with a Habitat for Humanity group had been cancelled due to the virus. As of today, Macedonia had 1,326 cases and 57 deaths, which was a pretty high ratio of deaths to cases. His HFH contact added that it was her understanding that ALL "global village" builds for the balance of 2020 had been canceled.

I realized today was Day 45 of Quarantine — 45 days since our CT schools locked down and panicked people rushed the grocery stores to stock up for the apocalypse. It had been feeling like someone pressed a big pause button and just suspended our lives. We had all been drifting around, kind of aimlessly, not really sure what to do, making up every day as it came, trying to keep ourselves entertained while staying safe. #staysafe #stayhome #staysafe #stayhome

I noticed it was FB friend Constance's birthday today and posted wishes, as well as a song I found that had her name in its title. Its intro line: "Battered, bruised and not yet broken, we stood behind the wall, beholden our unbeaten foe, beholden to no man. We huddled with our arms in hand, our feet out firmly to the floor." It seemed to sum up just what I was feeling, that we had been pummeled by this virus in so many ways, and were huddling but standing firm against its attack.

My phone pinged with a text message from Verizon, my phone service provider. They were letting me know that they were adding 15GB of mobile hotspot data to my plan at NO CHARGE for the whole month of May — a "remember we did this for you when this is over" gesture, I perceived.

As I sipped at a fishbowl of coffee, I glanced out the window and saw neighbors visiting with another family that had strolled up the street. They were all standing six feet or more apart. *So* not human if these were usual times, but smart with regard to staying safe.

The mild weather had brought people out all over, in fact, as I noticed on a drive-out for my two usual anxiety-producing errands: post office and groceries. Pulling up across from the post office and while getting my Personal Protection Equipment (PPE) in place, I watched others flow in, all with masks, including a contractor with boots who pulled a red bandana up over his mouth and nose as he entered, looking like an extra from a spaghetti Western ambling into a saloon.

Once inside, and as I waited in the lobby for another customer to be processed, I eyeballed signage. One was headlined: Please protect yourself and others. Graphics and more messaging was listed: Masks or face coverings required inside our lobby. Keep a minimum of 6 feet between yourself and others. Limit the Post Office lobby to no more than 3 people at a time.

Another sign, from the Department of Transportation, was much more comprehensive, listing a litany of Domestic Hazardous Materials that are prohibited from being sent through the mail. These included: explosives, flammable gas, non-flammable gas, inhalation hazards, poison gas, toxic gas, oxygen, flammable liquids, flammable solids, spontaneously combustible material, dangerous-when-wet materials, oxidizers, organic peroxide, cargo-aircraft-only items, radioactive materials and corrosives.

I was mailing two face masks to Evan, which appeared to be ok to send based on all the regulations. The process was the new usual and quick, and I was out and on my way to Stop & Shop in no time, though $4 lighter for a package that was feather-weight and should have run $1. The USPS had really inflated its costs in a desperate effort to save itself.

Stop & Shop was the usual scene again, which unfortunately included even more shortages than my last visit, of French fries/tater tots, frozen waffles, frozen vegetables, orange juice, napkins, toilet paper, butter, dishwashing products, disinfectant wipes, feminine hygiene products, shredded cheese, bird seed and pasta. All but one shopper was wearing a mask, and she was not at all ashamed of her infraction — no gloves either, touching stuff, gabbing with store staff, ridiculous. Checkout was a process. As usual, I preferred to do the bagging myself to limit touchpoints, which took longer but was more mentally reassuring. Having to show I.D. for beer complicated things, requiring taking off gloves, putting them back on. Same for getting my credit card out and interacting with the touchpad. With sweat beading on my forehead, I completed my business there and made my escape finally, edging by about 20 cars lined up at the Doughnut Inn as I turned out of the parking lot.

The unloading process at home was the new usual labor and, again, gloves, face mask and pullover all went into the laundry for washing and all kitchen surfaces got disinfectant wiped.

I finished just in time to catch, oh joy, NY Gov. Cuomo's daily briefing. Total hospitalizations, down again, "back where we were 21 days ago", net change in hospitalizations down and new cases ticked down to about 1,100 yesterday. In general, NY was "on the downside of the mountain" but "just when you think you're going to have a good day, this reality slaps you right in the face: 437 deaths yesterday (418 in hospitals, 19 in nursing homes), which is actually a tick up." Going forward, "Testing is what we are compulsively obsessively focused on now," he said.

The grass needed mowing, which I did in rapid fashion, hauling the grass bag to our town's yard waste facility. When I got there, though, there was a car arranged across the road turning people back. Apparently, access to that area and dump hours had been abbreviated and I was too late. Back home I came, full grass bag and all.

I spoke, then, with a high school teacher friend who operates a clambake business during the summer. He had about 50 parties booked this time last year but only 15 so far for this year, with no calls in six weeks. "People don't know what's going on or coming next," he said. I reassured him, saying food service support seemed to be pretty strong locally and that it looked like restrictions were going to start to ease and stay more relaxed — if we all didn't go crazy once the green lights were given and drop back to square one, a fear he shared.

My sister-in-law shared an article written by Don Surber, from her W. VA area. It was his opinion that the auto industry, print newspapers, NYC and restaurants were all going to be seriously affected by this crisis, not that they weren't already suffering. His arguments... Cars were sturdier, people were going to worry less about maintaining them and they were barely driving them now, particularly as they were spending more time at home. Print newspapers have traditionally been driven by advertising and, with businesses closed or going out of business, they were losing their sustenance. NYC may revert to the 1970s, given lots of apartment vacancies due to people fleeing the city, floundering businesses as potential visitors are nervous about visiting the pandemic epicenter, tax revenues dwindling and increasing crime. Finally, people had been learning to cook and finding it more cost efficient and social than dining out.

An US Weekly email detailed that Actor Nick Cordero, who had recently had his leg amputated due to a virus complication, had now been fitted for a temporary *pacemaker* after some irregular heart activity. This... guy... is... 41.

I watched from the house another pair of families saying hello to each other, from opposite sides of the street. On the far side, a dad with a face mask seated on a bike towing a covered, wheeled carrier with a kid inside. On my side, a husband and his very pregnant wife. I could only imagine her concerns during this time.

The street activity drew me and my lounge chair out to the front yard where I set up to people watch. Folks passed with strollers and bikes and on foot, sharing wishes of "stay safe". Many of the faces were new to me as locals had expanded their exercise routes. Down the road, there was a virtual block party going on with kids playing basketball and riding bikes, and parents chatting with each other. I wasn't sure how safe all that socializing was.

I spoke — at a distance — with three respective neighbors and we were all concerned that the nice day and subsequent nice days were going to be a problem, especially in our very social neighborhood, and may undo all that we had done to patiently wait things out.

As further evidence of that, DEEP had to step in again to temporarily close some CT state parks due to overcapacity.

Meanwhile, reports were rolling in suggesting that North Korean dictator Kim Jong Un was, at the very least, in a vegetative state and, at best, dead, following apparent heart surgery to put in a stent after a recent collapse.

The air started to chill driving me inside to chow leftovers. Phil went for a ride on his motorcycle, reporting a curious sighting when he got back: in the middle of the now-longtime barren parking lot at Fairfield Train Station, a group of people had gathered to tailgate, complete with grills going and sports chairs and music. He had stopped to visit some friends, too, who were docked at home from college.

I relaxed with a shot of tequila with a slice of lemon and tuned into a FB "Watch Party" hosted by Norwalk, CT's Wall Street Theater, featuring keyboardist Scott Chasolen of The Machine Pink Floyd tribute band playing songs like "Pigs" for a virtual audience.

Mid-evening, I made the dash to Jen's, getting passed en route on I-95 by a Range Rover literally doing 100mph and criss-crossing lanes. Our southwestern CT corridor had become a mad speedway.

Jen and I sat together at her dining room table, having Sapporo beer, Tate's ginger cookies and spoonfuls of Graeter's ice cream, her favorite. Then we relocated to her TV room, hoping to catch PlayOn, the virtual music fest that had been planned for this weekend. It seemed to just be a string of past concerts, though, versus a live experience, so we switched to watching some pre-recorded video bits: Comedian Will Ferrell and Red Hot Chili Peppers Drummer Chad Smith having a drum-off; Ferrell and Actor Mark Wahlberg telling Dad Jokes; late night show host Conan O'Brien, Comedian Kevin Hart and Performer Ice Cube taking a Lyft ride together through Hollywood; and O'Brien serving as a Chinese food delivery person in NYC. It was a real mish-mash of entertainment, a lead-up to Saturday Night Live's second remote-from-home broadcast, introduced by Brad Pitt.

Snuggling up to me, Jen commented that she liked that I am "solid", which inspired me to ask Alexa to play Ashford & Simpson's cheesy 1984 disco hit "Solid", to our great amusement.

News: Global virus cases passed 2.9 million (with 830K+ recoveries) and over 202K deaths. These numbers included the U.S. with nearly a third of worldwide cases, at 946K+, and a quarter of the deaths, at 53K+. Nearly 116K recoveries. Among states, NY remained hardest hit, with over 287K cases and nearly 22K deaths.

April 26. The morning, in Jen's neighborhood, was so quiet that you could hear every nearby bird's distinct call. Suddenly, the peace was shattered by a loud nearby explosion. I hurried out the door, scanned the sky for a potential plume of telltale smoke, and then hopped in my car to go take a look-see, encountering a couple of Jen's neighbors just down the road who had also heard the bang. They had lost power and suspected it might have been a squirrel making contact with a transformer. I did a little loop around to look, but didn't see anything out of place, then just kept going toward Fairfield along the deserted Post Road, past the usual masked shoppers at Trader's Joe's, and all the empty store lots.

A motivator for my get-up-and-go was The Tasty Yolk food truck, which had returned to downtown Fairfield for a few hours the first half of this Sunday. I ordered a couple of "Pigs" breakfast sandwiches and chatted with another truck patron, Jim Keenan, the founder and chairman of the annual Chowdafest scheduled to happen in October in Westport, CT's Sherwood Island State Park, and the Great Mac 'n Chili Challenge, that had been held late January at the new SoNo Collection Mall in Norwalk. Masked in a bandana, Jim told me that Chowda might be in jeopardy, at least with regard to its location, and we both wondered if the mall was even going to survive the pandemic for him to hold another Challenge there. He was grabbing a bite on his way up to Providence, RI, to retrieve his daughter from college after they shut down her campus due to the virus.

I had to laugh at a sales email that landed in my inbox, with the come-on: Show your *personality* with Custom Cloth Face Masks and the opportunity to upload your own photo or choose from one of their pre-existing design templates for the look of your mask. Face masks had become fashion statements and extensions of our selves.

On FB, I noticed it was my friend Dalma's 30th birthday. What a time for such a milestone. I had last seen her, with Jen, at Wall Street Theater, at a totally packed show featuring Comedian Rob Schneider. He was a howl and the virus was not even a twitch in anyone's eye on our local scene.

Jen shared a video clip of CGTN Anchor Liu Xin reporting that she had recently visited the Wuhan University of Science Technology and that, of the hundreds of international students housed there, none of them had contracted Covid-19. The students and teachers apparently had a collective understanding that strict quarantining was necessary in order to protect everybody. Over the several weeks when the virus situation was very bad there, the students were not allowed to leave their dormitory. Xin thought this was important to share with regard to helping people understand why the cases and mortality rate had been relatively low in China. For 76 days, people were ordered to stay in their homes, no exceptions — no popping out for air or for a jog, or over to the grocery store or going out with a mask-optional mentality. Xin said wearing a mask there is a universal instinct. In fact, she said, if you *don't* wear a mask, you feel strange — just the opposite here in America. "It was that kind of awareness to help yourself to help others that really helped cut the path of the contagiousness of the virus," Xin said. In addition, she offered that over 40,000 medics came from all over China to Wuhan to lend a hand. She further reported that, in the epicenter, over 3,600 people over age 80 who contracted the virus survived; among them, seven people over age 100 survived. And apparently the Chinese government assumed all the treatment costs. Traditional Chinese medicine also played a role with regard to treating patients with mild symptoms. Finally, Xin said the average Chinese citizen trusted the measures they were told to follow. Yet another side of this pandemic story to consider.

Today marked First Lady Melania Trump's 50th birthday. The President sent an email to supporters offering them the opportunity to sign an official card and share a short personal note. Birthday celebrations overall these days had been reduced to remote affairs. A Nat Geo editor related attending one recently, sharing, "As I approached the house, I saw the front yard decked out in streamers and balloons. Mom, Dad, and the birthday boy were safely behind a cast-iron fence with a shiny Happy Birthday sign hanging along it. The rest of the mask-wearing party people? Social distancing on the sidewalk or in the middle of the street, one girl sitting atop her father's shoulders holding up a giant handmade card." We had seen the same kind of thing locally, sometimes with a line of cars, with each car blowing a horn as it went past a celebrant's house and/or pausing for a moment to drop off a gift. It was all so disconnected and sad.

That same Nat Geo editor shared the idea of conducting inside-the-home insect safaris given that there are a number of species that nest in our homes. Further, she said parents should be *encouraging* rather than *discouraging* their kids to have more computer screentime, provided it was constructive: education-oriented or to stay connected socially with friends.

A Westport-based author/artist/motivational speaker friend, Amy Ostreicher, shared a thoughtful email, suggesting an approach to occupying our time during this stay-at-home period that was *opposite* to all the virtual tours, game apps, online workshops and livestreamed concerts being promoted — and that was to simply enjoy the stillness, silence and empty space that had resulted from the crisis. She suggested that sometimes "we need boredom to grow, discover ourselves, and learn to trust our instincts." She continued, "There will come a time when we look back on this period with fondness – even a romanticized longing. We will remember when life slowed down, when we could not leave our homes, and we were forced to scale down, focus on what really mattered to us, and pay attention to the little moments — we realize in the small moments, how much there is to be grateful for." She stressed being *in* this moment: "When we stop fighting against the past, stop worrying about the future, and we surrender to being in the world as it exists now, all anxiety disappears because we realize that we *always* have the power to be in the present, we can be happy, fascinated, and in awe of the world we live in at this very moment – it's in *our* hands."

Travel & Leisure queried chefs and restaurateurs about what the restaurant industry may look like post-pandemic and all agreed it would have to adapt and change to the new reality to survive. Ideas included: single-use menus, silverware sealed in a pouch, signs confirming tables have been sanitized, servers wearing gloves and masks, tables further apart, individually packaged meals, reduced occupancy, contactless payments, sanitizer everywhere, strict personal hygiene habits for staff, stronger food safety measures, no-tipping policies instituted to stabilize wages, better worker protection, greater efficiency with regard to food prep and execution, a continued rise of take-out and online ordering, the rise of "ghost" kitchens, a shift in restaurant locations as more people work from home, more zero-waste kitchens, more local sourcing, more tech solutions, more carbs and more foods you can't make at home.

Noontime, NY Gov. Cuomo gave his mostly positive update for the state. The "numbers" were down again, "the descent continues"... now back to where numbers were March 31. Even new Covid cases were down, to 1,000 yesterday, though that was still significant. Still terrible news was that 367 more people died yesterday — 349 in hospitals, 18 in nursing homes — down but still "horrific". Going forward, once rates have been in decline for 14 days, per the CDC, the state could begin to reopen, which Cuomo planned to do in phases, by region, with monitoring.

The day was turning out to be a very raw one, with almost continual rain all morning and winds gusting up to 25mph. More rain was forecast for the balance of the day, through the overnight and into mid-morning tomorrow, with injections of thunder and lightning even.

I was thinking about that 1984 "Solid" song and pulled out the old photo album again from that period, to find a pic of me from that year, wearing a skinny tie, which Jen had said her Dad was also fond of wearing. In the process, I found some other dated photos of friends, took snaps of them and sent them to those respective friends for amusement. I also dove into my Halloween gear again, this time to retrieve a face mask that was an accessory to a medic outfit I had worn one year. Who would ever have thought that I would be using it one day in real life to actually protect myself?

This afternoon was all about reheated chili, a refreshing Black Hog Brewing Co. Granola Brown Ale, enjoying more music from Glenn Roth, Tim Palmieri and Chris Cavaliere, and even catching a tango performance called "Flor De Mayo Project" shared by Chris Dami.

Our Fairfield First Selectwoman checked in with town tallies to date: 365 positive cases, 42 death, 146 recoveries amongst the positives.

I read a piece in VICE that suggested these months will eventually become a blur for many folks isolating at home, according to memory researchers. As we experience a global pandemic, it's odd to realize that we're currently living through a new Big historical event. We'll be telling our children about it, documenting it in history textbooks, and swapping our shared experiences for years to come. "Moments of each day feel unforgettable, because of how strange or tragic they are: the death count updates, the 7pm applause for healthcare workers, watching press conferences with governors and infectious disease experts, grocery store lines around the block, and working from home day after day (for some of us) as the streets of the busiest cities in the world stand still and empty," the article shared, pretty much summing up my experience. "But what exactly will we remember years from now? The unnerving truth is that we may not remember much, because we never do—that's not the way memory works.

We don't remember each minute, or each day or week. We forget people, places, moods, and events," was the opinion.

Not so for those on the frontlines though. "They'll witness the toll on human life firsthand and emotions like grief, fear, and anxiety will heighten their memories. They may end up haunted, the way people with post-traumatic stress disorder (PTSD) are," it suggested. Others would be adversely affected, too. "For people facing other extreme stresses— whose loved ones get sick and die alone, who are jobless and frightened by the economic downturn— traumatic memories might continue to surge to the surface."

Mid-evening, I attempted to watch "Cabin Fever: Patient Zero", a 2014 horror film about a flesh-eating virus that a group of young people contract from the water just off the shores of an unpopulated island in the Dominican Republic while celebrating a low-key bachelor party. It turned out to be a bit too gory for me, with projectile vomiting of blood and melting skin and what not. I flicked it off and rang Jen instead. She was trying to master on the piano and record for posting Chopin's Fantaisie-Impromptu, written in 1834 but not published until after the composer's death. It would be her last installment for her APDA effort but wasn't coming together.

News: The same strip club in Oregon that initiated Boober Eats, sending their dancers on food delivery missions, created a tented drive-through strip club environment. A design group in Austria created some ideas for parks that effectively enable people to social distance from each other. A Long Island man became the first person in the U.S. to be charged with hoarding PPE under the Defense Production Act. Italian winemakers filed a formal complaint against a company promoting APM's (Automated Prosecco Machines) that dispense Prosecco in an ATM-format style. Due to people being locked down in Mumbai, India, over 100,000 flamingos have flocked together and are occupying open spaces there.

April 27. I was awake at first light but the dreariness of the morning didn't inspire me to get up, so I flipped through social media and news on my phone.

One FB post, by Rachel Rhody, was offered as a virtual hug to folks at home who were "seriously beating themselves up because they aren't 'maximizing' their time in quarantine by organizing their closets, repainting, developing a side hustle, becoming a piano virtuoso, exercising themselves into a lucrative career as a swimsuit model, etc." — all the things many people and sites have been suggesting. Rachel said to just hold up and breathe, offering, "If you're feeling adrift, there's a reason. I'm about to drop some first semester nursing school on y'all. It's Maslow's Hierarchy of Needs. Humans have basic requirements (the bottom of the pyramid) like food, water, air, shelter, sleep, etc. The biological basics. If those are met, then the next rung of the ladder is Safety and Security. If we feel safe and secure, then we can climb up and start on our Love and Belonging needs and on up the ladder we go until finally at the very tippy-top is SELF-ACTUALIZATION which would entail all of the cool aforementioned activities. The catch is, you cannot level up until the needs at the current level are fulfilled. If the needs remain unfulfilled, we remain stuck on our current level until the situation changes."

She assured, "Friends, in the midst of a pandemic, we are dwelling in the basement of Maslow's pyramid. How in the heck do you think you're going to kick ass at the highest levels when we can't even find toilet paper for Pete's sake! You physiologically and psychologically aren't built to live your 'best life' right now. Your only job is to live 'a life' right now. A luxury that is being denied many which increases the pressure to really make every day count."

Essentially, cut yourself some slack was her message, and focus on the bottom level: "Are you eating, drinking water, and sleeping at all these days? If so, that is a triumph right now. Are you showering? Eating a vegetable once in a while? Getting some sunshine and fresh air? Keeping some semblance of a sleep schedule? Start there. And be extra gentle and abundantly gracious with yourself. We'll get through this. And right now, getting through is absolutely enough."

Sadly, I came across a post from my friend, Jeanine, at Beechwood Arts. She had sent out an email yesterday canceling their upcoming WE Zoom session, citing a death in the family. Her post this morning shared who that was: "My Uncle Angelo, 95, my Mother's closest brother, died this week of complications due to COVID -19. Both he and his wife, together for 78 years, contracted COVID while staying temporarily in an assisted living facility. Because he was a veteran, he went to a different hospital than she and each were isolated. Before he went in, he slept holding her hand each night. But days later, he died alone."

Jeanine called him an "indestructible survivor – surviving 3 exploded ships in his years of active duty in the Navy and the premature death of his daughter of cancer at age 35." She added, "He never forgot having to bury Marines at sea and often talked, tearfully, about how they died and were buried without their Mothers, sisters, brothers, spouses or others with them or being able to be there." The family found a way to have a wake/viewing and burial during this time and used Zoom to allow his wife, still in the hospital, and his remaining siblings and others to "be there" with him and have some closure until they could all meet in person to share their stories and celebrate him in the way they felt he deserved to be celebrated.

My clever friend Sonal was up to her usual creativity, this time with regard to meals. She said her girls made a Dinner Request Box into which they and her husband each dropped two meal request choices for the upcoming week. Among the pulls was "Thanksgiving in April": roast turkey breast, gravy, Brussels sprouts, mashed potatoes, sweet potatoes, pear-ginger cranberry sauce and jalapeño cornbread.

There was some more good news about the environment, related to marine life in Hawaii. Since the state's residents started staying home and tourism came to a halt, the absence of scuba divers, snorkelers and beach bums was bringing new life to the coral reefs around Oahu.

The Daily Beast shared that Baby Boomers (born between 1946 and 1964) were not happy being isolated. Said one healthy 78-year-old CA woman, "I've been doing Zoom, Zoom, Zoom, Zoom, Zoom. It's not the same. It's boring. I'm tired of doing that. I feel like I'm surviving and not thriving." Before the pandemic, she was involved with a book club and Bible study, and went to the gym three times a week. Suddenly, against her will, she had become a couch potato, lacking mental stimulation, staying up later, watching more TV and sleeping in. Deemed "medically fragile", she may be told to continue to stay isolated after her community starts reopening, which may actually *threaten* her health. Older people "need social interaction beyond what they get via media—such as touch—to feel they are in touch," noted a professor of psychiatry at Duke University. "So functional decline could be dramatic."

The mention of the Boomers group made me think about the various "named" generations of the last century, which began with The Lost Generation (born 1890-1915); The Interbellum Generation (born 1901-1913); The Greatest Generation (born 1910-1924); The Silent Generation (born 1925-1945); Baby Boomers; Generation X (born 1965-1979; Xennials (born 1975-1985); Millennials (born 1980-1994); iGen/Gen Z (born 1995-2012); and Gen Alpha (born 2013 to present). I was smack dab on the fence between the Boomers and the X'ers, which made me a BoomXer? A BoXer? A BXer?

I saw that the French Grand Prix, which was scheduled for June 28, had been canceled due to the virus, further pushing back the start of the Formula One season. The French government had banned public gatherings until mid-July and race organizers decided not to try to postpone the race or hold it without fans. The iconic Monaco Grand Prix, which had been scheduled for May 24, had already been canceled due to the virus. It was the first time the race wouldn't be held in 66 years. Another blow to the racing world.

I noticed that a musician friend, Samantha Preis, had decided to use her downtime to record an album from home. "It will be self-engineered and a stripped-down, honest presentation of myself and my work, as well as a project I can devote my time and energy to over the next month," she shared. It was yet another notable survival approach at this time.

Mid-morning, as I had shifted to my home-based working/dining room/kitchen space, Phil woke up and came downstairs to make a cup of tea for himself. He was in the throes of finishing up homework assignments and preparing for final exams, due to start next week. He had just finished a history paper, something he enjoyed, versus math, which presented a steeper learning curve for him. We decided he was mostly right-brained, being creative and artistic, very adept at writing and hatching ideas. At the same time, though, he also had analytical and methodical left-brain qualities, but more so applied to mechanical things — computers, bikes, scooters, cars. He liked to see the result of his labor and to be hands-on, and math didn't give him either of those benefits.

It popped up that it was my half-sister Nancy's birthday. Often, people conduct fundraisers through FB on their birthdays and she had decided to link with Feeding America, the largest network of food banks, pantries and meal programs in the country, which were particularly challenged at this time.

I had to make a run-out to the post office, a task that had become *less* anxiety producing the more I went. In fact, I was *more* anxious now being on the road than being in the post office. Cars were just zooming past with distracted drivers. It was really a life-risking proposition to be driving these days. Less traffic + anxiety + distraction = more speed + less care + more opportunity for accidents.

I donned my Halloween surgical mask today, feeling like it really *was* Halloween, in combination with the gray day and chilly temps. My post office visit was again routine, and once again outrageously expensive just to send a couple of paperback books snail mail. I wasn't shy about announcing my unhappiness. My flame was tempered only by the outfit of another patron: knee-high rainbow socks with Pikachu faces, camo jacket and cowboy-style red bandana facemask. Rocking pandemic look.

Glad to be out of the house for a bit, I went on a little local tour, passing drivers who were often masked. This had been a frequent complaint online — about lone drivers wearing masks — but I got it. It can be a pain to put on the mask securely in the first place and there was less risk of contamination by leaving it on, versus taking it off and putting it back on repeatedly. Best to be safe and look silly. Folks that did remove them tended to hang them from their rear view mirrors, both for convenience and so as not to contaminate their car seats.

My tour took me all about, by Lesko & Polke funeral home, a center of grief at this time; Shearwater Coffee; Penfield Service Station; and other area businesses and eateries. Doughnut Inn had a line of cars wrapped around it again, as before.

As I made the loop home, I spotted a firefighter friend and his wife walking their dog near the firehouse and pulled over to converse with them — with me on one side of the road and them on the other — speaking to each other as mostly contractor traffic went by. He was anxious to get back to work, thought it was about time to reopen, and believed most town cases were among the elderly, who we could continue to isolate to keep them safe. His emergency calls had been few to none, related to things like cats getting stuck under decks and the like. We agreed about a fear that folks were all going to rush out and clog things up the minute a green light to get back to normal was given, and we knew the town would just slam that door shut again if that was to happen. He also shared that the marina had opened, but just for boat drop-off. Boats weren't allowed to go out yet, the thought being that they would turn into floating parties.

As we chatted, I noticed a group of police officers, all masked, gathering for a photo at the police station just ahead, and drove up to jump out and grab the same pic. We were grateful for their service and putting themselves at risk to keep us safe.

It was late morning when I walked back in the house, in time for NY Gov. Cuomo's daily update. The numbers were down or flat — 1,000 new cases again yesterday — including deaths, though still "tragically high" at 337. Testing-wise, over 7,500 people had been "inspected" statewide, resulting in 14.9% of them testing positive. Among those, the majority were men, which had been the largest group affected across the board with ALL virus cases worldwide.

Early afternoon, I checked in with Jen, who had conquered and was about to post the Chopin piece. In these matters, she was such a perfectionist and it all had to meet her quality standards.

Flipping around online, I read that the board chairman of Tyson Foods, John Tyson, had warned, "The food supply chain is breaking" and that "millions of pounds of meat will disappear" from grocery stores because of virus-forced plant closures. He said that millions of animals — chickens, pigs and cattle — would also be "depopulated", ie. exterminated. The thought added another worry to an already fragile grocery store situation.

In a related story, a Minnesota contract egg farmer said 61,000 of his chickens were euthanized amid falling demand for eggs. The farmer said a crew of about 15 workers arrived in the early hours of April 9 with carbon dioxide to euthanize the birds. Describing the process, he said, "They come in with carts, put them all in, wheel them up to the end, put a hose in that cart and gas them, then dump them over the edge into a conveyor and convey them up into semis and the semis haul them out." The farmer added that four other egg farms, larger than his, saw chickens euthanized in his state in recent weeks.

The Navy's Blue Angels team announced that it would fly its distinctive blue-and-yellow F/A-18 Hornets over the Metro New York area tomorrow, between Noon and 12:40pm, as a salute to frontline Covid-19 responders. The closest they would come to us appeared to be Stamford from a flight path route that was shared online.

As I grew weary late afternoon, contemplating the gray skies and thinking about dinner, a ray of sun burst through, not from outside but on FB, in the form of a thoughtful post by my Dad: "It's possible that any given moment is the most rapturous of our lives… I'm sitting on my deck in the afternoon of a weather-perfect day – Carolina Blue skies, tree-filtered sun, the burble of a small waterfall on Morgan Creek below the house – having just had a perfect lunch – a spectacularly good Caesar salad I made with a crusty French roll and a lemony New Zealand Sauvignon Blanc. I've just fast-walked five miles (after doing ten yesterday) and nothing hurts. Myriad birds are tweeting in the trees and (ironically due to the Coronavirus) there are no motors or other mechanical sounds to disturb the peace. What is Heaven, and how could it be better?… But it isn't just this house or this place or this time or my late parents or my gorgeous late wife – it's my life. Even more, it's the life of my family. My whole family. My grandparents were immigrants who had the courage to accept an uncertain future to escape an unacceptable future. My mother's family fled a starving Ireland. My father's family fled turmoil and economic depression, even religious persecution, in a newly formed and unpredictable Germany. Courage. To leave the only life generations of one's family have ever known. Perhaps that's the strength of the America that's nurtured us – people who dared… And so here I am, indescribably, unarguably happy on a sunny afternoon in North Carolina. Is this the most rapturous moment of my life? Perhaps… Look around you. Feel. Listen. Remember. Revere. Maybe *this* is the most rapturous moment of YOUR life."

CT Gov. Lamont gave his briefing late afternoon, noting that his office's 211 info line had received a lot of calls about our supply chains and food. Lamont had his Commissioner of Agriculture Bryan Hulbert speak to that. Hulbert said the state was increasing SNAP (Supplemental Nutrition Assistance Program) benefits and duration, providing new outlets to restaurants and farmers for their food, working on getting supplies to people in quarantine and looking into availability at grocery stores. The latter was becoming a sore spot for me, seeing the same empty shelves every time I went to Stop & Shop, so I was keenly interested in what was going to be done there. Separately, the governor reported that hospitalizations were down across the board but that 74 new deaths were logged yesterday.

A friend on the creative team at Ogilvy Health and the team #IAMNOTAVIRUS created a six-poster campaign raising awareness about Asian-American hate crimes. Just in the last 30 days, 1,497 bias-based assaults were reported to the Asian Pacific Policy and Planning

Council's hotline. The campaign was headlined "Let's attack the virus, not our neighbors", and depicts the scarred faces of victims.

At the traditional dinner hour, Pres. Trump, who had retreated from the spotlight over the weekend after getting frustrated with various press depictions, led a daily Task Force briefing. He declared, "We continue to see encouraging signs of progress", citing declining or stabilizing case counts in many urban centers, and that "things are moving along" with regard to getting the economy restarted. He also noted that over 5.4 million tests had been conducted across the country, and invited top representatives of big companies like Abbott Labs, Walgreens, Quest and CVS Health to individually report on their progress in broadening that scope.

A Nat Geo article shared that "experts looking for new ways to fight the coronavirus have suggested using hyperbaric chambers, instead of just ventilators, to treat patients. And since hyperbaric chambers are difficult to mass produce, one creative idea involves turning grounded airliners into a kind of hyperbaric chamber by outfitting them as medical wards and allowing the cabins to be pressurized as if they were in flight. The method hasn't been fully tested and there are all kinds of barriers to making such a plan a reality, but the idea sure is fascinating."

In a March article for Stat News, Dr. John Ioannidis, a much-cited professor at Stanford's School of Medicine, suggested that Covid-19 is far less deadly than models were assuming. He referenced the experience of the Diamond Princess cruise ship, which was quarantined Feb. 4 in Japan. Nine of 700 infected passengers and crew died. Based on the demographics of the ship's population, Dr. Ioannidis estimated that the U.S. fatality rate could be as low as 0.025% to 0.625% and put the upper boundary at 0.05% to 1%—comparable to seasonal flu. "If that is the true rate," he wrote, "locking down the world with potentially tremendous social and financial consequences may be totally irrational. It's like an elephant being attacked by a house cat. Frustrated and trying to avoid the cat, the elephant accidentally jumps off a cliff and dies."

I was heartbroken to learn about an E.R. doctor at NY-Presbyterian Allen Hospital who went home to family in Virginia to take a break from the horrors she had witnessed working with patients battling the virus, and committed suicide. Her father shared, "She tried to do her job, and it killed her. She was truly in the trenches of the front line."

CT Sen. Tony Hwang called me out of the blue. He had become a thoughtful family friend over the years and was checking in to see how I (and my Dad) was faring. He had been busy listening to people across the community, relaying concerns up in Hartford and even distributing masks to people. He was set to host a unique "Listening Town Hall" through Zoom tomorrow, that would give business owners and self-employed individuals the opportunity to talk about and share their challenges and frustrations, in light of being denied approval or even access to federal stimulus funds or due to drastic changes caused by public health declarations enacted during this crisis.

Norwalk, CT Mayor Harry Rilling was another local politician trying to lead by example. He and his wife, Lucia, planned a mid-morning "moment of silence" tomorrow to honor United/Food and Commercial Workers they called the "true heroes and *she*-roes continuing to work every day ensuring we are able to procure essentials during this crisis."

In reviewing people's online posts and general dialogue, I was starting to detect building angst, irritation, sadness, anger and depression — a whole litany of emotions that were not common during normal times. People were either falling apart and withdrawing or warring on each other to the point of damaging friendships, blocking and deleting each other. It had gotten so you had to be very careful about the words you chose, how you couched things, what hashtags you used, who you sided with, where your political orientation lay and the types of things you posted about.

A Forbes article was picking up on those negative vibes, too, noting that the "drastic, massive and immediate" measures that were taken to curtail the virus spread had made us far more worried and apprehensive than usual, resulting in "racing thoughts, pounding pulses and ever-present fear" as our new norm.

By mid-evening, I needed a hug and headed for Jen's hoping she could raise my spirits. En route as I was leaving town, a fat kamikaze rabbit darted out in front of my car, causing me to swerve to avoid hitting it. I thought, wow, the universe is really throwing some body blocks today, as I rolled onto 95, which was not only the route marker but seemingly the average speed these days, too. Welcome to the Wild Wild East.

Jen was FaceTime chatting with a girlfriend as I arrived. Her friend was airing some issues she had with her boyfriend and generally throwing all men into the fire. Her comments raised some questions about our own relationship, which we ended up discussing heart to heart, coming to some agreements and resolutions thankfully. We were pretty reasonable people after all and weathering the pandemic as well as could be expected.

Later in the evening, we worked side by side on respective diversions — hers was to draft a letter to parents of students in her piano studio group suggesting how their children could also help raise funds for the APDA by posting performances of themselves online together with a donation link. For my part, I poked around through my newsfeed and on social media.

One item that popped up was an initiative titled "Call to Unite", a 24-hour livestream event set for May 1 offering performances and conversations about overcoming the challenges of the pandemic. It would feature folks like former Pres. George W. Bush, Oprah Winfrey and Julia Roberts.

The Sydney Morning Herald reported that Britain had issued an alert about a possible new virus syndrome emerging in children. Apparently, kids of all ages were presenting with a multi-system inflammatory state that was so urgent it was requiring intensive care across London and in other regions of the U.K. Cases had been building over the past few weeks.

I shared with Jen a Well + Good blog piece about cuddling and its benefits. "Being cuddled is nearly synonymous with being cared for, comforted and loved," according to a clinical psychologist. And in these uncertain times, it was certainly welcome. We had to laugh about some of the cuddle *positions* cited, including the side-by-side Taco Wrap, and the Dish Towel, wherein a partner comes up from behind the other and hugs them as they're doing something else, like washing the dishes at the sink.

News: Global virus cases passed the three million case mark, while deaths topped 207K. The U.S. accounted for over 987K cases and over 55K deaths. Among U.S. states, NY was the hardest hit at almost 294K cases and over 22K deaths. NYC's Mayor de Blasio said the city will close 40 miles of streets to cars in May to provide an opportunity for recreation and expand space for pedestrians to keep social distance. Meteorologists said that 2020 is on course to be the hottest year since records began. Super.

April 28. There was no alarming explosion to make us jump this morning — only the long fingers of the sun poking through the slats of Jen's wooden blinds. She wanted us to make a Home Depot run, so energized us with tea and toast with peanut butter and jelly, and off we went, taking both our cars. Our main mission was to get more than a dozen bags of mulch for Jen's garden, along with some bleach, deer repellant, ant traps, flowers and light bulbs — an all-in-one run. We headed to the Norwalk location, which I was admittedly nervous about as cases in the city were five times what they were in Fairfield. But the big box store seemed to have put in place a barrage of precautionary measures: police outside to keep order, one entry point where a head count is done to monitor store capacity (like the Fairfield location), signage warning people not to enter if they are sick, plexiglass barriers around the cashiers and the self-checkout areas, masks and gloves on all employees, and X's on the floor marking proper physical distances at the checkout lines. We were in and done in a respectable timeframe. In fact, we spent more time in traffic — yes, actual, real-live traffic — on 95 trying to get back. It was the kind of blockage that I definitely did *not* miss along this corridor but it was due to road work which I thought was wise to do as roads were less crowded these days.

After the unload at Jen's, I scooted back up the Post Road, which also seemed strangely busier on this Tuesday, almost as if the reopening bell had been rung.

Midday, the awe-inspiring Blue Angels and Thunderbirds flyover took place over our NY Metro area and, really, it was something to see. Two sets of planes, six in each formation, closely grouped, doing wide circles over the region.

NY Gov. Cuomo weighed in early afternoon with his briefing. In general, overall numbers continued to come down, though another 335 New Yorkers died yesterday. He addressed thoughts on reopening, saying the decision should not be philosophical, political or based on protests, but founded on a factual discussion and done without infecting more people or overwhelming the hospital system. To that regard, he said we should design a system to address that, measuring what is happening in society and calibrating reopening to those measurements. If hospitals hit 70% of capacity or the rate of transmission reached a rate of 1.1, those would be danger signs signaling a pullback would be necessary. He suggested that in Phase One reopening, construction and manufacturing industries would be among the first to be greenlighted.

Broadway Actor Nick Cordero continued to struggle through his virus battle. After surgery to implant a pacemaker, he got a fever that caused his blood pressure to drop slightly. That development meant he had to stay on a ventilator with a trach tube down his throat.

By late afternoon, the day's temps had warmed to the low 60s and the sun made it feel even warmer, drawing me outside to sit in my canvas-backed folding chair. With a beer in hand and some roasted peanuts in a jar lid in my lap, I did some more news scrolling.

Some of what popped up was disturbing. Like the fact that many farmers across America said they had no choice but to cull livestock as they run short on space to house their animals or money to feed them, or both. To make room for 7,500 piglets he expected from his breeding operation, an Iowa farmer ordered his employees to give injections to his pregnant sows that would cause them to abort their baby pigs. Another group of Iowa producers was euthanizing the smallest five percent of their newly born pigs, or about 125 piglets a week, composting their bodies to become fertilizer. Same story in Canada - in Quebec alone, a backlog of 92,000 pigs was scheduled to be euthanized. On a related note, Pres. Trump was to sign an executive order meant to keep meat processing plants open and stave off a shortage of chicken, pork and other meat on American supermarket shelves.

Our Fairfield First Selectwoman invited town residents to tune into a Facebook live update tomorrow at noon, regarding access to our open spaces. I hoped that she would be opening the "gate" a smidge to allow us to get out and about. I sure missed the beach. At the same time, I continued to fear that people were going to go nuts, like the running of the bulls in Pamplona.

There was no doubt the c-virus was going to change the way we traveled in the future. Experts in the fields of aviation, hospitality, cruising, finance and epidemiology gave some predictions and projections. To start, consumers will factor health concerns into their travel choices even more than before, but also think how their visit might inadvertently impact the place they visit. There may be mandates to self isolate upon arrival at a certain destination. Flights will resume between places least affected by the virus and where demand is strongest. There will be fewer choices for travelers as airlines shrink and offer fewer flights. Airlines will stress social distancing, block middle seats, limit people on board and may require proof of good health. People might consider flying private jets for the first time. There will be all sorts of great deals. Hotel choices and room options will be reduced. Airbnb accommodations will be less attractive as travelers consider private residences riskier than hotels. Surprisingly, the cruise industry might sail through fairly intact as passengers have simply moved bookings to next year. Travel agents will make a comeback, being the most knowledgeable about all the new particulars.

Phil's interest in cooking had piqued along with a desire to move away from carbs. After sundown and quite spontaneously, he whipped up a Mexican bean salad, referencing a recipe he pulled from online. It was delicious!

Middle of the evening, it was wonderful to catch a live performance by Mike DelGuidice, presented by Wall Street Theater. Mike was best known as the rhythm guitarist and a vocalist for rock/pop legend Billy Joel's band and as the lead vocalist and pianist for the Long Island, NY-based band Big Shot, which is a Billy Joel tribute band. In this live stint, he was jamming at home on his piano.

News: Top Chinese scientists warned that the virus may be retained in humans and return year after year, like the seasonal flu. An article compared modern day Dr. Fauci to Dr. Tuttle, a leading epidemiologist during the time of the Spanish flu, who also recommended face masks and social distancing. A study indicated that adding a nylon stocking layer behind a face mask would boost protection from the virus. Global virus cases topped 3.1 million, with over 215K deaths. The U.S. accounted for over 1,022,000 cases and nearly 58K deaths. Worldwide recoveries were over 944K. Among states, NY remained hardest hit at over 300K cases and nearly 23K deaths. Some school districts across the country said they were giving up on remote learning and ending the academic year early, after concluding that it was too cumbersome for teachers, students and parents. Airlines, manufacturers and scientists were all working at developing ways to prevent virus spread in aircraft cabins, including the use of UV light. JetBlue became the first U.S. airline to announce that all passengers will have to wear a face covering on flights. Various virus monitoring models showed differing ultimate numbers for U.S. fatalities, depending on the amount of contact reduction — one model predicted 74K American deaths by August. A virus outbreak at a long-term care facility in Holyoke, MA had resulted in 68 dead military veterans and dozens more sickened. It appeared that NASCAR's North Carolina-based Coca-Cola 600 race would get a green flag to run Memorial Day Weekend, though participants would have to social distance and there would be no fans onsite. Also in North Carolina, a pug tested positive for the virus, the first dog in the U.S. to be confirmed.

April 29. It was gray again and forecast to slide into another round of rain in the overnight through the next couple of days. Not at all mood enhancing but appropriate for coffee consumption.

I saw a FB friend's post that made me sad: "My father's wife just called me. Pop's got the virus. So say a little prayer please. He's 92 in a nursing home." Sadly, given the nursing home fatality rate of late, he was probably not going to be around long. Still, I said a prayer.

I also read that the intense inflammatory syndrome virus side effect detected in children in the U.K. had now been observed in three children in New York.

And Irrfan Khan died. He was a veteran character actor in Bollywood movies and one of India's best-known exports to Hollywood. He played the police inspector in "Slumdog Millionaire" and also appeared in the adventure fantasy "Life of Pi". Khan succumbed to cancer. He was only 54.

It was just daybreak and I needed a laugh already, finding one in a BuzzFeed story titled "17 People Who Learned Things About Their Partners During Quarantine That They Were NOT Ready For". An excerpt: "I discovered that my boyfriend doesn't clip or file his nails — he just rips them off with his fingers. He RIPS. THEM. OFF." Another: "My husband silently narrates his emails while he types them in a lively, conversational way, complete with hand gestures and facial expressions." A third: "I found out my partner is a MASSIVE germaphobe! He's obsessed with getting dirt off of everything. He'll even wash unused cutlery if it was on the coffee table. Unused!"

I checked in by email with a friend who operates a local digital arts educational center to see how he was faring. Unfortunately, he was thinking "about shutting everything down and giving up" his space. He was bummed but I knew he was a smart, resourceful guy and would no doubt bounce into a new passion. I suggested he connect with my son, Phil, who had similar talents and with whom he might collaborate. He said he would hold onto his space until end of July and try to monetize it however he could.

Another contact, who handles advertising for a local museum, had his budget turned off to make up for the facility's revenue shortfalls. He hoped the venue would reopen by summer.

Likewise, a friend that runs a skincare business which had to close its doors after being deemed "non-essential" said she was basically just holding on and had no idea when the state might let her re-open.

A travel agent friend also weighed in to say about her business, "Everything is really up in the air right now. Most of my clients have cancelled their travel through the Summer and things are so unknown. Europe is not looking good until next year. I personally don't book a lot of cruises except for Alaska, but all of my cruise clients have cancelled their cruises through October. Once things pick up, I predict travel will first pick up in the U.S. as people will likely want to stay close to home."

A local Chamber of Commerce president gave a status report. As "a small non-profit in the midst of a pandemic", she had shut down spending, commenting, "It is so very tough for all of us. Who could have predicted this! It's really tough for anyone asking for funds because there are so little to go around these days. But I am truly confident that better days are ahead, although probably later than sooner."

A friend that does marketing support for restaurants primarily in Fairfield County was now just doing simple day-to-day business support, with a few videos online and a list of restaurant offerings, though she admitted there were a lot of the latter these days, through free FB portals that well-meaning people had set up.

On the upside, from a local brewery owner, I got some positivity. Though he declared he was "operating on fumes", he had expanded his hours and, in fact, had run out of several styles in cans and was brewing so he had *more* cans to offer. Growler fills were also doing well and he had to order more growler glassware to keep up with demand. "Certainly nowhere near our normal sales levels, but thanks to Connecticut's craft beer drinkers' support for our beers, we are able to keep the lights on!"

I got an email from a local psychotherapist, Mel Schwartz, who shared thoughts on relationships at this time. He said that they often make us "feel like we're under a microscope, as we examine, react and judge each other's actions and intentions" and, "that under the distress of the current COVID-19 pandemic, these interpersonal tensions may feel even more acute, particularly when we're in confinement with each other. This tension can boil over causing us to lose balance and a healthy energy in our relationships."

Jen and I jumped through some hoops to this regard over the past 24 hours, but were thankful that we were able to communicate with each other and express any differences. Soon after we chatted, the pajamas I ordered for her arrived at her doorstep, which she happily FaceTime'd me about and modeled.

A Nat Geo item shared that mask culture is changing. "Humans become frustrated when they can't read facial clues," the piece said. "In many countries, people are also unaccustomed to wearing masks to protect themselves from the pandemic, or they feel self-conscious if others aren't wearing masks. More and more, however, mask-wearing is being seen as caring toward others, as well as protective of oneself."

Another Nat Geo item had to do with asteroids, which we had been reading more and more about and their close passes near Earth — fear-inducing news when you're also dealing with a global pandemic! The piece said that NASA's new mission is to crash a spacecraft into an asteroid to see if this technique can be used to safely divert "potentially hazardous" space rocks from a collision course with our planet.

A triple play for Nat Geo today, as it also reported on "Zoom Fatigue". Wired to look for social cues on video conference calls, people had been emoting more due to the confines of a little box on a screen. The practice could be both mentally and physically exhausting reported participants.

Late morning, NY Gov. Cuomo chimed in, to again report that most of the key numbers were down, with the exception of new hospitalizations for yesterday, which were "up a tick", still at around 1,000 a day, and deaths, at 330, which he called "terrible news". The decline of the latter was "slow at best". And he again expressed caution about opening up too quickly, citing "Singapore talking about a second wave with 900 new cases" and Germany "now seeing an increase" after reopening, with an infection rate that went from .7 to 1.0 in 10 days. "That's trouble," Cuomo assessed.

Meanwhile, up here in our Town of Fairfield, CT, our First Selectwoman Kupchick announced that our open spaces would *reopen* (PRAISE BE!) this Friday, May 1. These spaces included our Jennings, Sasco and Southport Beaches; Lake Mohegan; Carl Dickman and H. Smith Richardson Golf Courses; and the South Benson Marina. Parking would be restricted to residents with permit stickers, which would help keep some out-of-towners away, but did not prevent them from busing themselves in or being dropped off, which could be a problem. Balancing that perhaps was that the beaches and Lake M would only be open to walking — no chairs and no loitering. Penfield Beach was left out of the mix because it has tables where people would be apt to sit and a playground and swings to which kids would certainly dart. But that said, there are no gates from the beach side closing off Penfield and no doubt people would try to access it. I hoped FS Kupchick had planned to put police or "specials" in place to monitor things or we would quickly be headed back to square one. In this reopening process, we would be stepping out of the capsule onto the lunar surface — "one small step for man, one giant leap for mankind."

Mid-afternoon, after responding to a surprising slew of emails, I fork fed myself some leftover pasta. As I did, a kid of about 12, with a surgical mask on, rolled by the house on a scooter, with his mother walking by his side, going up the street. Our new normal.

Late afternoon, CT Gov. Lamont, the other constant with regard to my daily briefing tune-in, gave his report, noting that numbers were generally trending down, though overall cases were approaching 27K and deaths were nearing 2,200. Lamont was joined by several guests, including Ridgefield First Selectman Rudy Marconi, who had personally battled the virus and had been in recovery mode. He stressed, "We cannot open too soon, please believe me. This is a highly contagious, serious virus that we need to be careful with each step we take… Just in my little town of Ridgefield, we've lost 30 people, we're approaching 160 cases and it continues to be a problem. And there are contagious people, and until we can get testing going and we're working at that from every corner imaginable, to be able to control statistics and have a better understanding — have our people feel more comfortable in society — until we get to that point, let's work together, continue to social distance, continue to wear the face coverings… Let's do it once and do it right."

After hand rolling dough to make a pizza and popping it in the oven to brown before laying on toppings, I looked through an email from SmartBrief, which aggregates and teases stories that tend to identify trends across industries. One teaser linked to a Reuters story about how, during this seemingly dark economy, some businesses were actually thriving. One was Ohio-based Lubrizol, which makes the gelling agent used to make hand sanitizer. Procter & Gamble and Kimberly-Clark both had gains on demand for cleaning and personal hygiene products. Citrix Systems, makers of software that allows people to work from home, posted record highs. Amazon and Walmart had added tens of thousands of employees to ship goods to homebound Americans. Other businesses, the article continued, had reinvented themselves. An events business in Utah that revolved around plants was now selling plants and outdoor displays and conducting landscaping consultations via video.

Variety online spotlighted a kids' film called "Trolls World Tour", which Universal released directly to consumers because movie theaters were closed due to the virus. It raked in $100 million, which had encouraged Universal to release more pictures through video-on-demand. On that news, struggling AMC Theaters and Regal Entertainment vowed to never show any more Universal movies. The truth was, those theaters might not even survive this pandemic.

A WCBS radio wire shared that, as ridership had plummeted on NYC subways, the homeless had taken up residence in them. A conductor's video showed car after car on one line with the homeless in every car, sprawled out across the seats surrounded by their belongings. The conductor said it was making riders scared and putting train staff lives in jeopardy.

As I munched on my pizza, I hopped on FB, which led off with a Memory from this day eight years ago. I had noted, "Beautiful day with a great finish! Sparked up the grill to make hamburgers and hot dogs, served up with homemade mashed potatoes and ravioli with sauce. A brewski on the side, a sunny spot in the backyard, and a quick ride to Dairy Queen for dessert and all was good with the world." It seemed like another lifetime ago.

I saw a posting from a local car dealership that drilled home that the car buying experience had certainly changed. To ensure customer safety, it promised smaller staffing rotations, appointment-only visits, everyone must wear a mask, all surfaces are cleaned multiple times throughout the day and all vehicles sanitized and cleaned continuously. Other lures included no payments for 90 days, 0% APR for 60 months, complimentary maintenance for two years and an IRONCLAD lifetime warranty. It was obvious they were hurting for business and ready to make a deal.

My brain was swelling by sundown. An acoustic music feed from Glenn Roth helped with the pain. That led to a Living Room Livestream from

Drew Angus, playing pop covers. Finally, I downshifted into mellow with Chris Cavaliere, who was performing some new material.

News: Global virus cases topped 3.2 million, with nearly 228K deaths (nearly 1 million recoveries). Of this total, the U.S. accounted for 1,060,000 cases, with over 61K deaths. Of U.S. states, NY was still hardest hit, with over 305K cases and over 23K deaths. Gilead Sciences Inc's experimental antiviral drug Remdesivir was positioned to become the standard of care for COVID-19 after early results from a key clinical trial showed it helped patients recover more quickly from the illness caused by the coronavirus. To reach customers, Chicago's Goose Island Brewing had a black van driving around the city with the brewery's phone number and message "Want beer right now?" on the side, encouraging people to call and order drinks, which the van then delivers to them. The van even plays ice cream truck music to attract attention! The Newport Folk Festival and Newport Jazz Festival both announced they were canceling their events for 2020, due to Covid concerns; they aimed to return in Summer 2021.

April 30. It rained all night, hard at times, the drops hammering my bedroom windows and sills with ferocity. Birds insistently chirping in the front tree stirred me to rise. I watched another early riser walk past the house, umbrella in her hand, raincoat flapping, dog leading the way down the street.

I mainlined some java and got on e-mail, reviewing a note from my Dad. A local running store had issued a COVID-19 challenge: run or walk 19 miles total during the week of April 27. The "19", of course, was a play off Covid "19". Dad accepted — though didn't officially participate in — the challenge, walking five miles one day, ten another and four yesterday. He had already walked another ten on the 26th, so all told he had walked 29 miles in four days! On a related note, my brother Dave strolled six or seven miles of the Appalachian Trail atop the mountain upon which he and his wife live in West Virginia. He imagined that "the waking woods were full of furtive bears" and was "chased back out by a developing storm." I shared with them both that I was glad to have my chance to do a bit of walking tomorrow, too, when several of our recreation spaces were set to re-open.

A Travel & Leisure drop offered a look at the "10 Best Places to Retire in Florida". Flipping through each representative area photo and seeing the beaches and palm trees sure looked good compared with the view through my kitchen window at the blanched sky, tree limbs getting whipped around and rain blowing sideways.

On April 24, 1990, NASA launched the Hubble Space Telescope into orbit, where it has recorded some of the most stunning images of the planets and stars around us. To celebrate the Telescope's 30th anniversary in space, NASA and the European Space Agency (ESA) created a tool wherein you can see a capture from space that was taken sometime during the past three decades on your birthday date. It simply required visiting a designated website and entering your birthday to get a pop-up pic of a capture on your birthday sometime over the last 30 years. The pop-up included a description of what the telescope was focused on. I had to try it, of course, and got a capture from 1998 of the five galaxies that make up Stephan's Quintet — a fantastic sight showing bright blue clusters of stars "born from the violent interactions between some of the member galaxies." The look made me feel very humble, like a speck really, and that any of my concerns — no paper towels again at Stop & Shop this week, for instance — were so trivial and inconsequential. We were ants scrambling around on an orb of grassy, rocky earth hurtling through a black void in an orbit around a blazing ball of fire.

Another bit showed how artists in San Francisco's Bay Area were painting gorgeous murals on the plywood boards covering businesses that had been forced to shut down, to try and bring a little life to post-apocalyptic, barren cityscapes.

Colorado-based Dano's Tequila invited me to join in a pay-to-participate virtual Cinco de Mayo happy hour, themed "Cocktails & Culture", to benefit the Bartender's Guild Relief Fund, assisting out-of-work bartenders.

Regarding other virtual goings-on, I thought it was interesting to see how the popular sip-and-paint/sketch format had moved from a brick-and-mortar setting to a virtual space, after I received a FB invite to participate in one. You pay a fee to sign up, pull together some sketching materials then log into a Zoom setting in which an instructor guides your efforts. In this case, spring flowers was the sketch focus.

A New York Post article said that many Gothamites who fled the city during this virus period may not return. NYC's largest moving company, Dumbo Moving + Storage, reported that moves were up 11% this March compared with last March, which was two months before the peak moving season even begins. Dumbo's CEO said those folks have fled to less dense outposts both near (Staten Island, Long Island, NJ and CT) and far (Massachusetts and Washington, D.C.). Many of those emigrants said it was nearly impossible to avoid contact with people in the city during the pandemic, which spurred their flight. Now they were finding new freedom, more space and lower expenses in their new digs. I mentioned this to Jen as she had been considering selling her house and this might be the best time to go ahead with that.

The rain continued to tip down, eliciting a friend to comment on FB, "It's weird, but all these rainy days, when I'd normally be trapped inside anyway, are the ones that really make me FEEL like I'm trapped inside." It was raining in North Carolina, too, my Dad noted in a text message, which he followed up with a photo of food items he had set out on his kitchen counter ready to make a big pot of chili for the day. It was an inspiring thought and I followed suit.

A photographer in our Fairfield area had adopted the great idea of capturing portraits of families sitting on their porches in this time when we are all homebound, as a way to keep afloat and stay engaged in the community.

You know these are extraordinary times when a post on FB exclaims, "Hey bread bakers! BJs has yeast! No flour or sugar (unless you want a 50-pound bag!) but they did have lots of other supplies including paper towels, tp and hand sanitizer if you're looking! Please let me know if you find confectioner's sugar!"

NY Gov. Cuomo gave his daily update, saying numbers were better across the board, though another 306 deaths were reported. Of note, he said the MTA would begin shutting the subways down May 6, every day from 1-5am, to thoroughly disinfect the system. Alternate transportation would be arranged for essential workers.

Early afternoon, after polishing off a bowl of magnificent homemade chili, I checked in by phone with a circulation person at Pequot Library, over in neighboring Southport. She said that the staff had just had a meeting to discuss what protocols to put in place for when they reopen. Those changes might include the installation of plexiglass shields at the circulation desk, masks and gloves for both staff and visitors, social distancing within the library, concerts and other activities held outdoors weather permitting as much as possible, and a move to online and virtual programming. We agreed that it was a sad but necessary direction to take.

In speaking with my library friend, I realized that, this weekend, the Kentucky Derby would have been run, the first of the three big annual horse races. The library was known for hosting a very popular "Derby Day" attended by area residents decked out in fancy outfits and enjoying elaborate tailgate parties next to their vehicles parked on the venue's Great Lawn. One year, the Derby and Cinco de Mayo fell on the same day, which changed the theme to Cinco de Derby and influenced a mix of cultures in the displays and garb. Another fun time crushed by the virus.

Good old Nat Geo said that one of the bright spots of the pandemic had been the increase in pet rescues. Because shelters were closed, adopters have had to see prospective pets via video meet-and-greets, online profiles and curbside introductions. Gaining a companion animal had been a blessing for many, helping to combat loneliness and depression, lower stress and provide a sense of purpose.

I had been thinking about H.G. Wells' timeless novel "The War of the Worlds" and its closing passage, about how microbes killed the visiting aliens that came to Earth to extinguish us. But now the microbes had turned on us and, yet, we were staying strong and defending ourselves. The closing passage of Wells' great book is particularly significant: "These germs of disease have taken toll of humanity since the beginning of things--taken toll of our prehuman ancestors since life began here. But by virtue of this natural selection of our kind we have developed resisting power; to no germs do we succumb without a struggle, and to many--those that cause putrefaction in dead matter, for instance--our living frames are altogether immune."

The aliens were vulnerable because "there are no bacteria in Mars, and directly these invaders arrived, directly they drank and fed, our microscopic allies began to work their overthrow. Already when I watched them they were irrevocably doomed, dying and rotting even as they went to and fro. It was inevitable. By the toll of a billion deaths man has bought his birthright of the earth, and it is his against all comers; it would still be his were the Martians ten times as mighty as they are. For neither do men live nor die in vain." Microscopic allies? No longer. The invisible enemy more aptly, but we will again earn our birthright here on Earth.

I tuned in, late afternoon, to a live video feed from our local Fairfield Museum and one of the staff there talking about and showing old spoons, teapots and pipe bowls and what you can learn from them and their markings and fabrication. So fun to learn like this. And being a spoon and antique collector, this presentation was particularly interesting. Mid-point, I switched over to another Zoom presentation from Fairfield University's Quick Center, an installment in a series called Quick Sessions. This particular session was focused on the decades-old progressive dance group Pilobolus, which I had seen perform in person on a few occasions, once at then SUNY Purchase (now Purchase College). The Zoom interface allowed you to pose questions to the featured team — including Robert Pranzatelli, who was writing a new book about the group — that they could address, so it, in effect, brought you into the conversation. Most delightful was the showing of performance clips from the 1970s. Just brilliant!

It was back to reality around the dinner hour, for CT Gov. Lamont's live daily briefing, which was gradually becoming the leading day-to-day focus for me and many in our state. He opened with a stats update, indicating a general downward trend over the past eight days, though positive cases had reached 27,700, with 933 new cases yesterday, and 89 additional deaths, to total 2,257 in CT. Then he shifted focus and spotlighted his "Reopen Connecticut Initiative" with the aim of kickstarting a general reopening on May 20, assuming certain criteria had been met by then. That included a 14-day decline of hospitalizations, wider testing available, sufficient contact tracing capacity, ample protections for high-risk populations, adequate healthcare capacity and PPE supply, and appropriate physical distancing measures in place. That said, the businesses he was looking to give a go-ahead to reopen included restaurants (outdoor only - no bar areas), remaining retail (apparel, jewelry, etc.), offices (though he encouraged continued working from home if possible), personal services (hair & nail only), museums/zoos (outdoor only), additional outdoor recreation (e.g. camping, mountain biking) and university research programs. All good and measured it seemed. Slowly opening the spigot.

I spooned out another bowl of chili and tuned into Tracy Jo Recalde playing an acoustic guitar and singing in a live format she dubbed "Adventures in Music" Happy Hour. As she played, I opened another FB tab and scrolled away. One item that popped up: Little League International canceled its

World Series in Williamsport. Our local Fairfield team had won the region last year and had WS dreams this year, another opp smashed by the virus.

Mid-evening, I set sail for Jen's, riding a musical vibe and general feeling of renewed hope, confirmed as I left my Beach Area neighborhood passing by the Tree of Hope adorned with red, white and blue lights on our Downtown's Sherman Green. In an unhurried and far less anxious way, I floated west on the Post Road, past strings of white lights strung from poles in front of Henry C. Reid Jewelers, a "One Heart, One Community" sign at the Fairfield Chamber of Commerce's office, the very Christmassy-feeling decor and outdoor music at Tequila Revolucion, lights lining the eave of Westport's Little Barn Restaurant, the cozy Earth Animal business, a glow from The Mumbai Times Indian Restaurant, red neon draw of the Five Guys burgers and fries joint, and inviting facade of The Little Kitchen Chinese restaurant. All these familiar landmarks paddling like mad to stay above water, I was sure.

Jen and I relaxed a while and spoke about her house, her fond memories of it and plans to try and market it, based on what we had been reading about the eager, motivated New Yorkers fleeing the city for the burbs.

We capped our quiet evening listening to a mish-mash of songs through her Alexa unit — tunes by Robert Cray, Otis Clay, James Brown, Marvin Gaye, Ray Charles, Warren Zevon, Lynyrd Skynyrd and Otis Redding.

News: Due to reduced demand, farmers had surplus of many crops, which they have had to destroy or use to feed livestock. An effort called the LEE Initiative's Restaurant Workers Relief Program had turned local restaurants in cities nationwide into relief centers offering to-go meals and other supplies for those in the restaurant industry who were currently out of work. American Airlines partnered with them to donate 25,000 meals that would have been served in-flight. Up to 60 bodies were found stacked in U-Haul trucks outside a NYC funeral home after neighbors alerted police to a bad smell — the funeral home told police crematorium staff were supposed to pick them up after the home's freezer stopped working correctly. More than 3.8 million laid-off workers applied for unemployment benefits last week as the U.S. economy slid further into a crisis fast becoming the most devastating since the 1930s. Roughly 30.3 million people had now filed for jobless aid in the six weeks since the coronavirus outbreak began forcing millions of employers to close their doors and slash their workforces. That was more people than live in the New York and Chicago metropolitan areas combined, and by far the worst string of layoffs on record, adding up to more than one in six American workers. In tribute to first responders, Mattel created a line of toy figures in their likeness. Global virus cases topped 3.3 million, with nearly 234K deaths (1,037,936 recoveries). The U.S. accounted for 1,093,198 of those cases and 63,790 deaths (151,784 recoveries). New York remained the hardest hit state, with 310,839 cases and 23,780 deaths.

CHAPTER 5

THE DOOR OPENS A CRACK

May 1. It had rained through the night, cleansing our surroundings and feeding our trees and plants — Mother Nature's watering can at work. The birds chirped happily. Their chorus was the only sound audible. No cars. No trains in the distance. No planes overhead. It was bliss actually. But I knew this silence — beautiful to me, maddening to others who were too long sequestered in their bunkers — would soon be broken. Today, at least locally, we would be creeping to the water's edge. Dipping a toe. Testing the waters. Stretching. Walking. Seeing each other from afar, reflections in others of our own hobo-like unkempt selves. Blinking as we looked at the unfamiliar site. Hopefully, we would keep ourselves in check. Restrain ourselves from being human. Not hug. Not shake hands. Keep apart. Stay masked, at least for now. Savor our freedom but not abuse it. And if we were good, we could have more privileges, get a cookie, some extra playtime. It was up to us.

It seemed appropriate that the initial step of our local reopening should fall on May Day, a celebration of spring in many cultures around the world — a day of unity, togetherness and rebirth marked with dancing, singing and cake. I hopped on my phone and, at first glance, found the mood online mirrored that spirit. One post, for example, showed a sign: "New month. New beginning. New mindset. New focus. New start. New intentions. New results." I just hoped that we would not have to be using "May Day" in its negative sense, as in "Mayday! Mayday! Mayday!" signaling distress.

Even more fitting was that today marked my late Mom's 81st birthday. To my FB page, I posted a photo of the two of us from 10 years back with a tribute message: "Today, May Day, my late Mom would have marked her 81st Birthday. Born in Great Britain just months before World War II began, she was a trooper who hitched up her boots when times got hard. As a girl, she and her family made ends meet by growing their own food in a backyard victory garden and repairing clothes to make them last longer. As a young woman, she became adept at helping people as a hospital nurse in London and stewardess for Pan Am airlines. In late August 2005, when Hurricane Katrina thrashed Louisiana, destroying whole neighborhoods and killing over 1,800 people, Mom didn't hesitate to go straight to the front lines to help distribute FEMA relief checks to desperate families. She slept on a cot in a crowded school gym with displaced people, emergency workers and other volunteers for a week while onsite. She always rose to the challenge when the occasion called for it.... During these new strange modern times, while the world is again entangled in crisis, she would have been right there to pitch in again, sewing face masks, working food drives, distributing meals, assisting in a hospital or nursing home perhaps, checking on elderly neighbors, reusing, recycling, repurposing and being a community champion.... Her spirit lives through us as we remember her lessons and can-do attitude. I miss you Mom. Virtual hugs and kisses. xx"

Of course, reminders of our current apocalyptic dilemma and its associated fallout crept back in. The first notice was a post from a long-while friend who had worked for years as a nanny for a family down the road, but had just been laid off, presumably due to the economy's downturn. She posted, "All good things must come to an end. I know there are hundreds of people going through the same thing, but I am heartbroken to leave my boys (her charges). Gonna miss them so much. We've been a team since they were born."

Another reminder came with writer Marcel Theroux's discussion of "plague literature". Having reviewed several tomes on the subject, he concluded, "The primary lesson of plague literature is how predictably humans respond to such crises. Over millennia, there has been a consistent pattern to behavior during epidemics: the hoarding, the panicking, the fear, the blaming, the superstition, the selfishness, the surprising heroism, the fixation with the numbers of the reported dead, the boredom during quarantine."

Theroux referenced a passage from Daniel Defoe's "A Journal of the

Plague Year", first published in March 1722 offering an account of one man's experiences in 1665 when a bubonic plague struck London: "Many families foreseeing the approach of the distemper laid up stores of provisions sufficient for their whole families, and shut themselves up, and that so entirely, that they were neither seen or heard of till the infection was quite ceased."

Another passage from Defoe's book addresses the danger of asymptomatic carriers: "The plague is not to be avoided by those that converse promiscuously in a town infected, and people have it when they know it not, and that they likewise give it to others when they know not that they have it themselves."

Theroux also refers to Giovanni Boccaccio's "The Decameron". Completed in 1453, it is a collection of novellas framed around tales told by a group of men and women sheltering in a secluded villa just outside Florence, Italy to escape the Black Death. Boccaccio described the spread of the virus thusly: "It would leap from the sick to the healthy whenever they were together, much as fire catches hold of dry or oily material that's brought close to it. And that was not all. Not only did speaking with the sick and spending time with them infect the healthy or kill them off, but touching the clothes of the sick or handling anything they had touched seemed to pass on the infection."

I needed fuel to make my landing at Normandy or, in this case, my curious visit to, first, Southport Beach, then Sasco and finally Jennings. Jen prepared a couple of fried eggs, some toasted bread, and a fat sausage split down the middle with a ketchup-coated gherkin pickle passenger riding within. Washed down with coffee, it was the perfect ration to spur me to march to my battle cruiser and navigate back roads to the first site of disembarkation.

As I motored along, I passed many joggers and walkers, then a pair of parking control cars who were evidently expecting a crush of visitors. When I pulled up at Southport Beach, a town public works crew was picking up barricades that had blocked the parking lot and loading them in the back of a truck. Already a few local residents had arrived, even before the magical appointed 10am opening hour. It seemed as if the beach and sea were calling, "Give me your tired, your poor, your huddled masses yearning to breathe free", that famous line from Emma Lazarus' 1883 "The New

Colossus" poem associated with the Statue of Liberty. Folks indeed looked weary, war-worn, quarantined out.

I made a single first footprint in the sand, emulating Neil Armstrong's history-making step on the lunar surface. It had been 30 days since I'd stepped on any beach, and that was only to check to see if rules barring people had been followed (they had). Before that, it was March 15, just before the lockdown was complete. I ventured further toward the water, looking up and down the beach, not really knowing what to do with myself. There was a family to the right, and another family down the way to the left, otherwise the beach was empty. Fog hovered on Long Island Sound and the low bellow of a foghorn sounded.

I got back in the cruiser and moved along east toward Sasco Beach, squeezing by police guiding motorists and a work team repairing a gas main that a construction crew had ruptured a day earlier, to the beach entrance.

A young attendant wearing a face mask was at the little toll house verifying beach stickers on windshields. I was the second car in, which put me in an empty long lot.

Again I did a Neil Armstrong, while watching a maintenance worker to my left clean off with a shovel some sand that encroached onto a sidewalk and, to my right, a tractor doing laps around the sand towing a rake that smoothed out the surface. Again I walked around a bit in a somewhat disoriented fashion then fled.

My last stop was Jennings Beach. On the approach, there were No Parking signs on the side of the road discouraging anyone from leaving their car in the adjacent neighborhood. Like Sasco, a masked attendant checked my sticker and waved me through. I hopped out and walked up and over a rise to the beach, finding it even more foggy than the other two that now lay to the west. A lone man walked along the water to my left, a woman and her small children played straight ahead and three teens rolled bikes down a rise to my right. I headed right, with the aim of walking the shore length to Penfield Beach, where I thought we weren't allowed to traverse. It was great to just breathe in the sea air. Then I thought better of that as I neared people and pulled my bandana up over my nose and mouth. Perhaps it was prudent not to go all gung-ho at first, I figured. Baby steps, baby steps. I scored a few pieces of sea glass for my efforts, as people faded into or emerged from the fog like specters.

Heading back toward home brought me by the entrance to Penfield Beach. The parking lot was closed off though police at the entrance said I could park on the street with my sticker. I did so and walked up past the pavilion, its entry points barred with steel gates, to the beach. The little playground and adjacent swings were both barred off similarly, but the beach was ok to stroll. I had a look about then finally returned home. It had been a welcome first excursion.

Grabbing a bowl of leftover Carbonara on top of which I sliced up rotisserie chicken, I settled in front of my computer to trawl through email and social media. A shocker to learn, at least for us local folks, was that Westport's Levitt Pavilion outdoor stage canceled its entire 2020 season of 50 free concerts and related special events. That was always a frequent go-to during the summer and would be sorely missed.

Pop legend Madonna revealed that she had tested positive for coronavirus antibodies. To her Instagram followers, she said, "I took a test the other day, and I found out that I have the antibodies. So tomorrow, I'm just going to go for a long drive in the car, and I'm going to roll down the window, and I'm going to breathe in the COVID-19 air. Yup. I hope the sun is shining."

Coincidentally, a FB friend posted that she had also tested positive for the virus antibodies. She had contact in February with a nail tech who had spent January in China. She got sick and lost taste sensation.

I eyed what I would call a temperature reading of the beer industry during this time, in the Wisconsin State Journal online. The writer, Chris Drosner, confirmed what we knew: "Distributors have stopped ordering kegs, with no on-premise customers to take them." Bottle shops were open and doing brisk business as people continued to "replace drinking out with drinking in". Buying patterns had also changed in terms of quantities purchased: "People who might stop in once or twice a week are now buying for two- to three-week increments, so what had been a six-pack purchase is becoming 12-packs or cases." Customers were also falling back on comfort brands, more of what they knew. Drosner said the breweries he worried about the most were "those whose business model is built on taproom sales. They've already lost that — for how long is anybody's guess. And these breweries are usually the smallest, too, and so perhaps have the smallest cushion for misfortune. They are the ones that need your dollars the most in these difficult times."

Early afternoon, I tuned into another Fairfield University Quick Center "Quick Session" featuring Megan Lewis speaking about "Movers & Shakers in South African Theatre". One artist about whom she spoke was Brett Bailey, who exposed issues of racism and social strife through his productions, noting, "I work in difficult and contested territory that is fraught with deep pain, anger and hatred. There are no clear paths through this territory, and it is littered with landmines."

Late afternoon, Phil, who concluded his UConn spring semester "classes" today and was scheduled to take his sophomore year final exams next week, let me know that his school had canceled its Spring commencement, the first time it had done so since 1914. It also let him know that his summer class would be both online and in person, to accommodate students' varying comfort levels. The school's UConn Foundation also announced that it would be part of a May 5 global movement called Giving Tuesday Now, meant to be a day of giving and unity as an emergency response to CV-19. For its part, UConn was addressing the needs of students facing hardships during this crisis, through a Students First Fund.

Oscar Mayer was running a social media campaign themed "Front Yard Cookout" encouraging people to have front yard barbecues that still respect social distancing guidelines during the pandemic. The company envisioned people safely grilling in their own driveway and waving to neighbors across the street. Tomorrow, it planned to donate one million meals to the non-profit Feeding America and would share up to one million additional meals if fans posted photos of their outdoor setups on Twitter with the hashtag #FrontYardCookout, through May.

Reminding me that the Kentucky Derby would have been run this weekend, Maxim magazine shared a recipe for the perfect mint julep so we could celebrate the derby's heritage at home. On the upside, Kentucky Sports Radio announced a replacement: the Kentucky Turtle Derby, to be aired through YouTube tomorrow evening. Churchill Downs bugler Steve Buttleman was set to sound the traditional call to the post while Broadcaster Larry Columbus would be providing play-by-play "for what will surely be exciting racing action." The idea actually inspired some serious thought about having a Zoom party with friends around the YouTube event, with food, drinks and all.

In his daily briefing, NY Gov. Cuomo announced that schools and colleges across his state would remain closed for the rest of the academic year as virus cases spilled over 300K.

The Miami Times rebuffed conjecture that the pandemic would see a rise in the American birthrate nine months from now. A Univ. of Wisconsin professor said, "Couples are in bed at night on their phones, scrolling through their newsfeeds checking various infection and death totals. That's not conducive to 'sexytime.'" In fact, experts said this pandemic would lead to a *decline* in births, possibly for years to come.

At the dinner hour, with a beer in hand, I tuned into a CTBeer "Beer Together, CT! A Toast to All Keeping Our Community Strong" virtual happy hour. It was a fun way to see some of my industry friends and "socialize" at the same time. Aside from the sipping, hosts Kevin and Jen Mardorf Zoom interviewed brewers. After a bit, I flipped over to local reggae star Mystic Bowie's FB page, to see him singing and grooving from home to recordings he was popping on a record player. Cuts like the Grateful Dead's "Shakedown Street". Next up in my virtual Friday evening round-up were the great young players of Music for Youth in their now usual Digital Friday Night Cafe performances: 18-year-old Sequoia Kessler on bassoon, 14-year-old Joy Xu on piano, Josuéa and Samuel Bustamente doing a violin duet and Julian Shively on cello. A friend invited me to a FB Watch Party featuring a band that was new to me, Dirty Heads. From Huntington Beach, CA, the band had been around about a dozen years, serving up ska, reggae fusion, reggae rock, acoustic music and alternative rock. Their beats and lyrics were really catchy. I don't think I'd been more in tune with music across all genres than at this time. FB friend Dina Montefuscoli put together a mash-up live Zoom talent show with various folks entertaining from home, including comedian Robert Punchur telling jokes ("In this time of quarantine, I considered having phone sex but was afraid of getting hearing AIDS.") and Amae Love singing gospel and playing a ukulele. This was an extraordinary time to be alive.

I was impressed with the spirit and message of a FB post from Amanda, a Chinese-American friend, who shared how difficult it had been to be Asian during this crisis. In its entirety, her un-edited post: "May is Asian-Pacific Heritage month. It's only fitting that this is occurring during a global pandemic in which Asians are being blamed, harassed, & assaulted for. What does being an Asian American mean to me? It means being fetishized in my dating life, the center of coronavirus jokes, only compared to Lucy Liu or Jackie Chan, being told that my people eat dogs & cats so I must too, it means more people than I could keep track of slanting their eyes at me, regularly being asked 'but where are you from?' & being referred to as the Asian friend/family member instead of just simply being Amanda. I know I don't fit into the Asian or American beauty standards. I aim to be my own individually unique self without influence. I am thick & untraditional for an Asian girl. I am not white enough to pass as American. I exist in this muddled grey area as myself. Challenging societal expectations & assumptions. I'm not palatable for everyone, nor do I want to be. But what really matters to me is respect. Be respectful of not only me but of all countries & cultures. The ignorance that exists in the USA towards Asians has been mind blowing to experience. I remember being in a history class in high school & a student said, 'you're Asian so you're Chinese.' At least 1/3 of the class agreed with him. My teacher had to pull out a map to show that China is just one of the countries in the continent of Asia. Another thing that's disregarded is that there's more to Asia than just East Asia. You're forgetting India, Pakistan, Turkey, Sri Lanka, Indonesia, Saudi Arabia, & so many other countries. My goal in all of this is just to say, be mindful. Of micro-aggressions, racism, stereotypes, & prejudice. If there was ever a time that Asian Americans needed allies & for those allies to speak up, it is now."

Moments later, another friend shared a photo of a classroom in China wherein all the students not only had surgical masks on but also plexiglass face shields. She captioned the picture, "School 2020… China does not mess around."

I stepped out in the dewy back yard to put some bread in my bird feeder and happened to look up at the Moon, which had the strangest glowing corona around it. I don't know that I had ever seen the Moon looking like that.

It seemed that quarantine had helped show many people how stressful, alienating and angst producing isolation can be and they had considered that feeling with regard to caged and maltreated animals in zoo and circus environments. Denmark had actually done something about it, announcing that it bought the last remaining circus elephants in the country for $1.6 million to let them retire.

If the pandemic wasn't enough to deal with, 17-year cicadas were set to emerge from the ground in a massive amount being called Swarmageddon, in North Carolina, West Virginia and Virginia. Terrific.

Following an experiment being tried in Lithuania, NYC was considering expanding restaurants' outdoor dining spaces onto the sidewalk and even into the street, particularly since the city was now reserving 40 miles of streets for pedestrians and cyclists only, and may have as many as 100 miles of car-free streets in the near future.

News: A viral disease that causes honey bees to suffer severe trembling, flightlessness and death within a week was spreading exponentially in Britain. Like farmers, beer distributors have had to discard inventory due to reduced demand — one Arizona beer distributor dumped thousands of kegs. A Manhattan nursing home was reported to have over 95 virus deaths. Global virus cases surged past 3.4 million with over 240K deaths (1,093,115 recoveries).

The U.S. accounted for over 1.1 million cases and nearly 66K deaths (nearly 162K recoveries). Among states, NY remained hardest hit, at over 315K cases and over 24K deaths.

May 2. Strong winds thrashing the trees and making things clunk against the house was my alarm signal this Saturday morning, a seemingly gorgeous one as I peered out the window at a light blue sky and bright green budding tree leaves. Stormy was mewing down the hall and scratching at the carpet in the spare bedroom next to mine. It was time to get up.

The day looked so inviting that, while a pot of coffee brewed, I took a stroll around my property, admiring a single purplish tulip standing defiantly tall above an audience of Allium stalks and waving grasses, pink Hyacinths hugging the side of the house and a cluster of purple lilac blooms swinging back and forth like hula dancers above my head. As yet, the buds on my Rhododendron (ro-ro) bush were still tucked up tight, as were the Hydrangeas, for now rehearsing in private for their colorful annual show, one of the only events that would *not* be canceled by this virus. Perhaps the most impressive characters in the crowd though were my agave plants, which produce single towering stalks and white flower blooms. The stalks grow so tall that I have to place a rod alongside each of them to moor and help support them. When their time is done for the year and the stalks dry up like bamboo, I crop them at the base and wait once again until spring for new clusters to emerge, as they were starting to do now.

Immersed in this botanical reverie, it was hard to process that we were still in the midst of a worldwide pandemic. Reminders were easy to find, though, like an update about Broadway Actor Nick Cordero. To add to his misery in his battle with the virus, now doctors were preparing him for a tracheostomy procedure that would allow him to breathe without the use of a ventilator. His wife, Radio City Rockette dancer Amanda Kloots, went to the hospital to pick up his personal items, like his wedding ring and a gold neck chain, so she had a few things to hold onto if she couldn't hold him. Seen wearing the neck chain, she said, "Anything to feel closer to him at this time makes me feel better." Heartbreaking.

I liked that Ellis Island was offering a constructive distraction: personally helping you research your ancestors from home. The landmark's foundation had more than 65 million pieces of data to cull through to help families find ancestors that may have come through the famous immigration hub. For just $30, they were offering to do the research for you.

I thought about our family's own extraordinary capture of ancestral history from Ellis Island: a scan of an immigration log page listing my great great grandfather Anton and his family, registering their arrival here from Germany in 1871, aboard the Hamburg-America line's steamship Westphalia! The crossing from Hamburg was two weeks in duration — from Oct. 4 to Oct. 18. We even had a photo (from a book) of the steamship.

Established in 1847, the Hamburg America Line was the first German transatlantic steamship line. The founders were ship broker August Bolten, ship owner Ferdinand Lalesz and banker Adolph Halle. With support from other Hamburg business leaders, they founded the company under the name Hamburg Amerikanische Packetfahrt Actien Gesellschaft (HAPAG). By 1896, the line owned a fleet of 102 vessels.

At the time my ancestors came over, the ship had a crew of about 120 men, including two-dozen deckhands, a group of officers and petty officers, firemen, coalheavers, machinists, stewards, cooks, helpers, trimmers, etc. It was built in Greenock, Scotland (west of Glasgow) in 1868 by Caird & Co. with dimensions 340ftL x 40ftW x 33ftH. Made of iron, the ship had three decks and a hurricane platform, the latter affording a great lookout for passengers. She was a single screw steamer with a service speed of about 12 knots and was originally built with passenger accommodation for about 90 first class, 120 second class, and 520 third class passengers, but reportedly carried larger numbers on some occasions. She only had one smokestack initially and two masts. Her captain was H.F. Schwensen. The ship was expanded in 1877 to accommodate new engines and more passenger cabin space. She was ultimately scrapped in Genoa, Italy in 1901. I loved these aspects of history and to think about the incredible uprooting and journey my ancestors undertook to make a better life for themselves here in America.

The day became spectacular with each passing hour — brightening and warming with just the right dash of breeze. I did a quick mow and shuttled my grass bags to our town's transfer station, seeing loads of people out on the road — both motorists and pedestrians — particularly at the dump. Car after car hauling junk or yard debris. A new process had been implemented at the yard waste site, with staff masked and directing motorists to drop-off spots as slots opened up, in the safest manner they could manage. I wasn't actually sure how safe things were as the breeze would have carried anyone's cough or sneeze all around the site, but I could see they were making an effort at least.

From the dump site, I motored to our Penfield Beach, parking across the road from the pavilion as I had before. I had to know, on such a sunny day, if people were following town guidelines to social distance. Right off the bat, walking across the parking lot, there was a trio of teens keeping apace of each other and two of them were wearing face masks. Good sign. Actually looking out along the length of the beach, I was further encouraged. Yes, there were more people than yesterday, but they seemed to be keeping apart and only one or two were "loitering", which our First Selectwoman had cautioned against. There was even a guy with a very cool looking fat tire Felt bike who had been taking a spin across the sand.

I clambered back in the car and continued on west through our Beach Area neighborhood, noticing various supportive signs: "A Nurse Lives Here, She Is Our Hero", "Thank You", "Hate Has No Home Here" and "Congratulations Fairfield Prep Graduate". There was even one with a simple red heart with a shell in the middle of it. I was glad to see an overall hopeful, positive, encouraging mood.

I rolled into the Sasco Beach parking lot, which was mostly devoid of cars, and strolled the beach a bit. Again, not mobbed and everyone staying apart and safe. There were even three masked bicyclists there practicing good social distancing. Great!

It was the same story at South Pine Creek Beach. Hardly a soul though so tempting was the site and views. As I was already in his area, I paid a call on my friend Eric, who was celebrating his birthday today. I had him gather his family on the porch and snapped a pic of them as a keepsake. A real estate agent, he was right on top of the trend I had noticed about New Yorkers moving up out of the city to areas like ours. We vowed to have a beer in person at the earliest, safest opportunity. As we spoke, Fairfield University art professor Philip Eliasoph came ambling by with his wife, Gael. They were pacing about the neighborhood, just glad to be safe and well. On my final turn toward home, I passed the Carl Dickman Par 3 golf course and noted several groups at play, all appearing to be safely interacting. It seemed like we had passed our test.

Before heading out for a motorcycle ride, Phil shared a video his brother had posted of the Blue Angels and Thunderbirds flying over Washington, D.C. He had captured the clip from the rooftop of his apartment house. It was fantastic and I was glad he had had the opportunity to see the sight.

The pleasant day further inspired me, this time to fetch dinner and a palatable beverage. I put Nordic Fish, in Downtown Fairfield, in my crosshairs, strolling in with my red bandana pulled up over my nose and mouth and saying, "This is a holdup!" It elicited a smile from owners Frank and Jardar, who were working hard behind the counter. They said the day had been crazy, with the phone ringing off the hook. I had tried to ring them earlier, in fact, and couldn't even get through. Sun + Seafood = Happiness, especially in a beach community. I came away with three salmon fillets, a pound of scallops, string beans and potato salad, the perfect mix for a fine evening banquet.

Then I made a straight shot east to Aspetuck Brew Lab, and my friends there, owners Pete and Tara Cowles. The taproom, which was so jubilant and full of people two months ago, had essentially been turned into a packing/distribution area, with a big, shrink-wrapped pallet of goods and a table topped with to-go bags on it. Their refrigerator cooler was my godsend, offering four-packs of their fine beer to go. I pulled two and chatted with the duo, who looked haggard. "We're working twice as hard for half the money, but managing to keep the lights on," said Pete. He wasn't sure *when* they would be able to open the taproom again, but was glad to have product to push.

Across the parking lot, The Blind Rhino restaurant remained shuttered. Co-Owner Jamie Pantanella, his wife, a couple of staff members and some friends were hanging out in the back. We discussed his situation, which was essentially to maintain a holding pattern. "We were among the first to shut down (on March 15) and we'll be among the last to re-open," Jamie said. His interest was in ensuring that his employees and customers all stayed safe and healthy. And he wouldn't reopen until he felt it was again safe to do so, and his customers could feel comfortable around each other. For now, they were following the reports and daily briefings and riding things out.

As I looped back home, I spied a roadside sign in front of the Lice Treatment Center: "Your custom logo on 2-ply 100% premium cotton FACE MASKS as low as $4.95 each".

We continued to mourn the loss and feel the absence of our sporting events, now into what would have been professional baseball season. While players had been sidelined, many of the teams' *stadiums* were in the game — the *pandemic* game, that is, with fields converted to overflow hospital set-ups, coronavirus test sites, shelters for the homeless, food service centers for the hungry, and morgues.

I noted a shocking milestone had been passed. That of the coronavirus death toll in the U.S., now at over 67K, which had exceeded the number of American fatalities incurred in the Vietnam War (58,220). The war toll had been amassed over the course of 20 years, from 1955 to 1975. In roughly 50 days, we had literally buried that total and had continued to surge well beyond it.

I had to be somewhat amused about Corona Beer's recent advertising slogans, particularly "Miles Away From Ordinary". As applied to the "corona" virus, that sure rang true. We had certainly moved miles away from anything resembling ordinary. More amusing still was what that slogan was meant to represent: "Corona is more than just a beer, it represents a philosophy of living, it is about connections between people and self-expression." These days, it was more like hanging on, staying Zoom connected and self-isolating.

Doubt continued to be cast towards China and its assertions about the origin and presence of the coronavirus. The latest pop came from The New York Post, which said that a 15-page dossier leaked from the "Five Eyes" intelligence alliance — comprised of the U.S., UK, Australia, New Zealand and Canada — claimed that China lied to the world about human-to-human transmission of the virus and disappearing whistleblowers. The alliance also believed the virus may have been leaked from the Wuhan Institute of Virology in contrast to China's story that it came from a local wet market. Overall, the alliance called China's handling of the virus 'an assault on international transparency' and further suggested that its government not only downplayed the outbreak but scrambled "to bury all traces of the disease at home, including bleaching wet market stalls, censoring the growing evidence of asymptomatic carriers of the virus and stonewalling sample requests from other countries." The alliance also believed China had evidence of human-to-human transmission in early December.

NY Gov. Cuomo gave his daily briefing, significant to me in that it still provided another general indicator of how our region was faring. Again, the numbers were all generally down, including deaths, though "that number has remained obnoxiously and terrifyingly high," he said, at 299 for yesterday, bringing the state's death toll to 18,909. Overall, the state had over 308K cases.

A new key focus of Cuomo's presentation was antibody testing. He said 15,103 people had been surveyed — of those, 12.3% across the state and 19.9% in NYC had antibodies for the virus. Among the boroughs, The Bronx had the highest percentage. To support folks in NYC, Cuomo said seven million masks were being given out in the hardest hit areas, at nursing homes, public housing and low-income neighborhoods.

Early evening, I cooked up the salmon fillets and plated them with green beans soaked in roasted garlic, poached scallops and potato salad, with a pour of Aspetuck's Full Send Ale. In short, it was "un dîner extraordinaire". A pandemic culinary highlight, if you will.

Of course, I just had to tune into the Kentucky Turtle Derby, presented by Old Forester bourbon, on YouTube at the appointed seven o'clock hour. Dubbed "one of the most impressive fields in half shell history", it featured eight competitors: Seattle Slow, Green Mamba, Sir Hides-A-Bunch, Galapa-GO, What the Turtleneck?, Rocket to Nowhere, Steve, and American Tortuga. The terrapins were placed in the center of a ring and, at the sound of a bell, they were off... or not off... then eventually off, crawling toward the outer edges of the circle. In the end, it was What the Turtleneck for the win, Galapa-GO in second and Rocket to Nowhere in third. Thrilling! The Run for the Lettuce.

Middle of the evening, as I was in the onset stage of full-on Saturday Night Cabin Fever, I stumbled on friend Holly Danger's appropriately titled "Live from our Living Room, It's Saturday Night Again" show of groovy lounge music with psychedelic kaleidoscopic imagery. I got so worked up by Holly's show that I retrieved a disco ball from my attic bedroom and set it up in the street-facing window in my living room, to accompany the show. It was pretty amazing I had to say, sending a swirl of rainbow-colored dots out around the room. A passing motorist was equally impressed, stopping to step out on my front lawn and take a photo or video clip!

Holly got chatty so I flipped to Desiree Bassett playing a three-song instrumental set of original rock songs from home on her electric guitar.

She was wailing on it and flipping her long, half-blonde mane from side to side. More amazingness.

Hard to imagine, but the night got even better as I stumbled across a feed from the band Twiddle, performing a "Live From Out There" Earth Mama free show. The beats, the disco ball going, some tequila shots flowing… it was all good. Fade to black.

News: The federal government was considering tracking the spread of the virus through sewage systems to predict where the next hotspot may be. The virus could be detected in feces within three days of infection, days before most individuals begin showing symptoms. Deadly "murder hornets" from Asia that measure up to two inches had been found for the first time in the U.S. and may be forming colonies. They could wipe out bee colonies within hours and had stingers long and powerful enough to puncture beekeepers' suits.

May 3: The rain peppered the house in the wee hours of the morning, pushing me out of bed. Some java to get my brain plugged in and I was rolling through news updates.

One story reported that guards at the heavily fortified border between North and South Korea fired shots at each other and that a South Korean guard was wounded. The last time a skirmish like that occurred was in 2017. The timing was notable as it had been just 24 hours since the apparent reappearance of North Korean leader Kim Jong-un, after a 21-day absence. Outsiders were still not 100% sure if he was, in fact, alive and that his "re-animation" had been somehow staged or misrepresented in the government's press.

A man was arrested for camping at Walt Disney World's Discovery Island in Florida. The man said he didn't know he was trespassing, though he would have had to have passed No Trespassing signs and breached two closed gates. The entire complex had been empty since the beginning of the outbreak in the U.S. and its 43,000 employees temporarily furloughed.

As part of the aforementioned 24-hour "Unity" benefit that took place online yesterday, Former President George W. Bush shared a video message meant to spur Americans to come together during this pandemic. He noted, "This is a challenging and solemn time in our nation and world. A remorseless and invisible enemy threatens the elderly and vulnerable among us, a disease that can quickly take breath and life. Medical professionals are risking their own health for the health of others, and we're deeply grateful.

Officials at every level are setting out the requirements of public health that protect us all and we all need to do our part. The disease also threatens broader damage: harm to our sense of safety, security and community. The larger challenge we share is to confront an outbreak of fear and loneliness. And it is frustrating that many of the normal tools of compassion — a hug, a touch — can bring the opposite of the good we intend. In this case, we serve our neighbor by separating from them. We cannot allow physical separation to become emotional isolation. This requires us to be not only compassionate but creative in our outreach, and people across the nation are using the tools of technology in the cause of solidarity. In this time of testing, we need to remember a few things. First, let us remember, we have faced times of testing before. Following 9/11, I saw a great nation rise as one, to honor the brave, to grieve with the grieving and to embrace unavoidable new duties. And I have no doubt, none at all, that this spirit of service and sacrifice is alive and well in America. Second, let us remember that empathy and simple kindness are essential, powerful tools of national recovery. Even at an appropriate social distance, we can find ways to be present in the lives of others, to ease their anxiety and share their burdens. Third, let's remember that the suffering we experience as a nation does not fall evenly. In the days to come, it will be especially important to care in practical ways for the elderly, the ill and the unemployed. Finally, let us remember how small our differences are in the face of this shared threat. In the final analysis, we are not partisan combatants. We are human beings, equally vulnerable and equally wonderful in the sight of God. We rise or fall together, and we are determined to rise. God bless you all." These were sobering, thoughtful words that rose above the clatter of a well-meaning, but slickly orchestrated, spotlighted, commercialized virtual event.

Equally sobering was the experience of a FDNY paramedic who recently woke up from a coronavirus coma with a new lease on life. The last thing 34-year-old Christell Cadet remembered before being induced was telling doctors she could no longer breathe on her own. She was initially hospitalized March 21, after collapsing outside her Queens home upon finishing a shift. Now she was teaching herself to speak and walk again, with the aid of her mom, a nurse, who was also feeding her and monitoring the oxygen tank she needed to breathe. The matriarch was also taking care of Christell's father. Anxious and afraid he might never see his daughter again, he suffered a stroke in early April and lost some of his ability to speak.

While wholly trivial in comparison to Christell's tale, a story I could more relate to was that of San Diegoans who, up until a week ago, had been frustrated they couldn't go to the beach because of stay-at-home orders. A woman there who took her first dip in the water in more than six weeks asserted, "The beach is a part of our lives." Much in the way that the beach is central to what it means to be a Californian, the beach is central to what it means to be a Fairfield Beach Area resident. The coastline closure set off protests there. One CA protester was seen holding up a surfboard marked "Surfing is not a crime." Here, we anxiously but patiently waited things out. At the core, people were just frustrated.

Mid-morning, I went out on another mission to support local businesses, but also wanted to take the pulse of our Fairfield community. Love was the overwhelming vibe as evidenced by signage: a simple heart at the front of a house, a Christmas wreath on a door, a cutout of a cheerleader with the message "Honk for Emme's 10th birthday" and balloons decorating the porch of the adjacent house, a heart labeled THANK YOU in a window, a lawn sign "We will get through this together - a salute to the frontliners", another lawn sign "THANK YOU" in a heart, yet *another* lawn sign "We support our healthcare workers", thank you messages in the window of the Glitter & Grime dance boutique, and hand cutouts and the message "How do you help make Fairfield an inclusive community?" in a window at The Loft. The one sign that went against the pack was handwritten and taped to a glass front door: "Fraud pandemic. .01% deaths. 99% survival rate. Less than seasonal flu. Every business is essential." The beauty of America is that we could have differences of opinion and the freedom to express them, though there were many that will and *do* argue with you on that point, to the extent of dogged unapologetic ferocity.

My mission ultimately took me, first, to Bud's Deli, for their classic bacon, egg & cheese sandwiches. The counterwoman, who was masked, said the business was faring well, like usual, but thought that our area was getting too social too soon and that might be a problem. My other stop was Candlewood Market, a family-run business offering coffee, tea, kombucha and more. Counter girl Jasmine and her sister Mariah made the visit a pleasant one and set me up with a mocha latte to go.

I heard from Jen by FaceTime. She had some quiet time last night, thinking up a business idea to make music-themed face masks. She thought she could expand to other products down the line.

Midday, NY Gov. Cuomo came online to do his daily briefing. Once again, numbers were moving downward, including deaths, 280 yesterday. Apart from the stats, he discussed a recent CDC report, which indicated that West coast virus cases came from China while East coast cases came from a different strain, from Europe. So, while we were watching China, "the horse was already out of the barn" and had arrived here and was spreading in the metro area.

The afternoon became absolutely glorious, drawing me back outside but no farther than the front lawn, where I plopped down a chair in the sun. I'm a people watcher so this spot also afforded me a view of the street and passersby. And there were many. Walkers. Joggers. Kids and adults on bikes. Dogwalkers. And then there were the neighbors performing yard chores — powerwashing a fence, raking leaves out from beneath shrubs, etc.

A Fed Ex truck pulled up and a guy got out to place a package on our porch for Phil. I called out to to the driver, "Stay safe. You guys are on the front lines."

Late afternoon, like a snail, I pulled my head back in my shell, to get out of the increasing intensity of the sun. Temps had climbed over 70, though it felt even hotter than that.

I read a post from a chef who works with a local oyster company who noted this interesting historical tidbit: "During the 1918 influenza epidemic, oysters were the hoarder equivalent of today's toilet paper—stockpiling was ubiquitous, prices skyrocketed, black markets developed. Poachers raided oyster beds—you can often still see the remnants of single-room guard houses built in the middle of the bay where guards with shotguns stood lookout. Why the hysteria? Legend had it that oysters could fend off the flu, especially the rich, briny broth locked inside. As legends go, it was fairly sound science. Zinc has been proven to be an immunity booster, and oysters are zinc powerhouses—pound for pound, these bivalves might be the best possible source of zinc. Back then, oysters weren't raised as cocktail-sized delicacies. Before steaks and chicken breasts, oysters were harvested at full size, providing a major source of protein for communities close to the shore. (Think: oyster stew for dinner.) Full-sized oysters—4 or 5 years old—are a relic, as out of fashion as shoulder pads; but now that restaurants are on intermission (and restaurants account for 90% of oyster sales), maybe more of these beloved bivalves will be given the space to grow into maturity. Savor the benefits of the adult oyster? I think so. If not now, when?"

Dad rang me up through FT to report that he'd had a love interest over for wine and cheese — at a distance — on his deck. The woman came to the house in a mask. They had been communicating online for a while and this was their first time meeting in person. He decided ultimately that they weren't a love match after all, though he respected her smarts and thought she was interesting. He said he was going to shift his attention to another "lead". He also shared that a friend had dropped off 10 hospital grade masks to him, to help keep him safe when he needed to go out on errands — or maybe dates?

After a good chow of leftovers that included the salmon and scallops from yesterday, I popped online to vote for my favorite cars featured in the Connecticut Seaport Car Club's Facebook Virtual Car Show. This was the alternative, of course, to voting on cars in a live environment. The car with the most likes would be featured with a write-up on the Car Club's site; second place would receive a virtual trophy.

In a couple of different online portals, I'd seen a piece circulating meant to put the "hardship" of the current day health crisis in perspective. It ventured, "Imagine you were born in 1900. Many would think that that was a pretty simple time of life. Then, on your 14th birthday, World War I starts, and ends on your 18th birthday. Twenty-two million people perish in that war, including many of your friends who volunteered to defend freedom in Europe. Later in the year, a Spanish Flu epidemic hits the planet and runs until your 20th birthday. Fifty million people die from it in those two years. Yes, 50 million. On your 29th birthday, the Great Depression begins. Unemployment hits 25%, the World GDP drops 27%. That runs until you are 33. The country nearly collapses along with the world economy. If you were lucky, you had a job that paid $300 a year, a dollar a day. When you turn 39, World War II starts. You aren't even over the hill yet. And don't try to catch your breath. If you lived in London, England or somewhere in continental Europe, bombing of your neighborhood or invasion of your country by foreign soldiers along with their tanks and artillery, was a daily event. Thousands of Canadian young men joined the army to defend liberty with their lives. Between your 39th and 45th birthday, 75 million people perish in the war. At 50, the Korean War starts. Five million perish. At 55, the Vietnam War begins and doesn't end for 20 years. Four million people perish in that conflict. On your 62nd birthday, there's the Cuban Missile Crisis, a tipping point in the Cold War. Life on our planet, as we know it, could have ended. Sensible leaders prevented that from happening. Perspective is an amazing art. Refined as time goes on, and very very enlightening."

Mid-evening, with my disco ball whirling in the front window for some cheer, I turned on the boob tube hoping to find something engaging. I turned to classic Westerns, landing on "The Bravados", released in 1958 and starring Gregory Peck and Joan Collins. The plot involved Peck chasing four outlaws who killed his wife. I just couldn't focus on it though and the day's moments spent in the sun had drained me, so I turned in.

News: A naked man apparently under the influence of drugs attacked a bus in New Haven, CT. Global virus cases passed the 3.5 million mark, with over 245K deaths, nearly 1.3 million recoveries. The U.S. continued to be hardest hit, with over 1.1 million cases and over 67K deaths (nearly 174K recoveries). Of U.S. states, New York had the most cases, at over 319K and over 24K deaths. Kentucky Derby organizers said they were committed to trying to make the race happen, in September now. Pink Floyd said it would stream free concerts every Friday to help fans get through quarantine. More than 80 employees of a single Walmart west of Boston tested positive for the virus.

May 4. My cat had gotten into the attic room and was scrambling around after something overhead, stirring me to wake before the sun was even up. I made my usual fishbowl of coffee and sat at the computer, to get an early start on the day.

In a daily email I receive from The Beer Connoisseur, I noticed an article about Newport, RI's Rogue Ales & Spirits and that it had been making a hand sanitizer called Helping Hand, the only one I had heard of from the beer category, though I assumed there were others. Demand for their product had been so great that they had to partner up with a distributor who had access to additional excess beer. Rogue distills the donated beer and adds 80% ethanol, glycerin, hydrogen peroxide and distilled water to it. They package it in 375ml bottles they sell at the brewery and online.

Typically when I returned home from one of my missions — a grocery store run, post office drop, beer or food fetch — I would not only wash my hands but wipe my phone down with a disinfectant wipe. Now a company called Casteify had started making a UV Sanitizer, using the shortest UV wavelength, UV-C, to kill any bacteria or common virus. You simply put your phone in a case like you would a pair of glasses, and plug it in to a USB port for three minutes. Six mercury-free UV lamps inside go to work on disinfecting the entire contents, without the use of any additional cleaning solution.

Given our very pleasant recent weekend, which drew people out all across the region, NYC Mayor de Blasio begged New Yorkers to continue following measures to suppress the virus spread, saying if it bounces back the city's reopening could be significantly delayed. "We cannot afford a boomerang," he said. He had deployed 1,000 officers across the city who were focused on ensuring people were maintaining appropriate social distancing. One officer got into a scrap with a pedestrian who ignored his order to disperse and took a fighting stance against him. The officer pointed a stun gun at him, slapped him across the face, punched him in the shoulder and forced him to the ground. Both ended up being disciplined: The man was arrested on charges of assault on a police officer and resisting arrest; the officer was stripped of his gun and badge and put on desk duty pending an internal investigation.

We had no such reported scraps here in Fairfield. In fact, our First Selectwoman posted a message on her Twitter account to say, "Checked in throughout the weekend to see how our restricted opening of our spaces was going. Happy our residents were following social distancing, with police reminders from @FPDCT. Proud of our emergency management teams' work for the safe use for our residents. #WeAreFairfield."

It didn't seem to be the same story in Westport where State Park managers had to close Sherwood Island for overcapacity.

My brother Dave and his wife, Jill, were out and about as well over the weekend, despite their governor's posted warning "PLEASE STAY HOME!" In their Town of Harper's Ferry, public restrooms were closed, public parking was banned, public trash cans were off limits, the parks were shut and citizens were reminded to practice social distancing. It was funny to see the complete turnaround in attitude, from almost cavalier at the start as the last state in the union to experience the virus, to almost full lockdown now. Still, D&J managed a four-mile stroll from Bolivar Heights to HF and back. Jill sported a t-shirt with the slogan "Don't Cough On Me" with a curled up serpent design, a play on "Don't Tread On Me". They reported seeing some Canadian goslings near the picturesque join between the Shenandoah and Potomac Rivers.

Meanwhile, Pres. Trump said on Sunday, in a virtual town hall discussion broadcast by FOX News, that he believed as many as 100,000 Americans could die in this pandemic after the death toll passed his earlier estimate. He also said he was confident a vaccine would be developed by the end of the year. Despite that toll, he encouraged states to reopen as they felt it was safe to do so, remarking, "We can't stay closed as a country or we're not gonna have a country left." He also said he wanted students to return to their schools and colleges in the fall, even while acknowledging the possibility of a second wave. "We'll put out the embers, we'll put out whatever it may be. We may have to put out a fire," he promised. Finally, he suggested there might be more federal aid going out: "There is more help coming. There has to be," he said.

Mirroring Pres. Trump's assumption about fatalities, former FDA commissioner Dr. Scott Gottlieb, a Westport resident, predicted that 100K will die from the virus by the *end of June*. It was his opinion that mitigation hadn't worked as well as people hoped and he warned that the true number of infections could be 10 times higher. And while numbers were trending down in some of the hardest hit areas, like NY, the numbers were rising in states like Illinois, Texas, Maryland, Indiana, Virginia, North Carolina and Tennessee. Most chilling, he opined, "We may be facing the prospect that 20,000, 30,000 new cases a day diagnosed becomes the new normal and a thousand or more deaths becomes the new normal as well." Like Pres. Trump, he hinted there might be a Fall relapse, and even used similar words to describe the urgency of halting it now: "If we don't snuff this out more and you have this slow burn of infection, it can ignite at any time." Dr. Gottlieb's hope was that, by fall, there would be multiple manufacturers of vaccines that had cleared early stage safety trials and had millions of doses that could be deployed in large-scale studies in cities. In that way, you're continuing to study it, but also using it to contain an outbreak.

I read about concern from environmentalists regarding the mass production of PPE gear, like masks, gowns, face shields and gloves, and where it would all go once it's not needed and disposed of. Their other concern, like mine had been, was that some of those same items carelessly discarded on the ground were finding their way to sewers when it rains and often ending up in the ocean. "The structure of PPE will make it particularly hazardous for marine life," said a Greenpeace USA rep. "Gloves, like plastic bags, can appear to be jellyfish or other types of foods for sea turtles, for example. The straps on masks can present entangling hazards." Over time, these products break down into micro plastics that add to our overall pollution, which was ironic as we were producing plastic to help fight one crisis but contributing to another.

A woman in South Carolina was arrested and charged with aggravated breach of peace and food tampering after being captured on security cameras licking her hands and touching food items and handles and, according to an eyewitness, licking coins she put into a tip jar and saying "It's in God's hands now." It wasn't the first instance of this affront and wouldn't be the last.

The beautiful morning, with temps climbing up into the high 60s, beckoned me to head outside. I thought I would be productive and prune bushes in my front yard. At the same time, that would afford me the opportunity to eye and interact with passersby, of which there were several. A woman with a young child by her side that went past pushing a stroller. A guy walking up the street with a satchel in his left hand. I thought he was heading to the train station, but it was just to his office in town, he said. About the train, he believed it was running on a very limited schedule. Another guy went up the street, with a backpack strapped over his shoulders. I also asked if he was headed to the train. He replied, emphatically, "Noooo," adding that he, too, had a home office around the corner. "It's the perfect commute," he said happily. A mom jogged by with her two young boys running along beside her. Contractors pulled up at a neighbor's house. She was masked, they were masked, it was all so weird these days.

Midday, after chowing a salad with some leftovers mixed into it, I went for a drive around my Beach Area, spotting more signs of support: "Thank You Healthcare Heroes", "LOVE your neighbor (your black, brown, immigrant, disabled, religiously different, LGBTQ, fully human neighbor)" and a biggie leaning against a tree that exclaimed "Celebrate! Support! Thank! All Essential Workers. At 7:00PM daily, step outside, open a window and make some noise, clap, ring a bell, shout! So THEY can hear us! BONUS: You get to see your neighbors! SPREAD THE WORD". Going against the grain again was the resident putting up the handwritten posters. Today the shout was "MEDICAL TYRANNY" and a slew of other exclamations — about 10 signs in all — taped all over his *car*. He was mad and wasn't going to take it any more, it appeared. The neighbors be damned.

The signs along Fairfield Beach Road were of a different nature, advertising RENTAL properties and rooms, aimed at students and New Yorkers fleeing the city. This included a rental sign for the space my ex-wife first rented at the beach when she moved out. I texted her the pic for grins. We were civil like that.

While I was out, I thought I would eyeball the beach again and see what was up. In all, there might have been only a dozen people all told along a two-mile stretch. And keeping anyone and everyone physically distant was a Fairfield policeman manning a four-wheeler going up and down the shore with lights flashing and headlights on. It was the first time in nearly 24 years that I had seen this done. Our First Selectwoman, and the PD, wasn't messing around.

Back in front of my home computer again, I scrolled through this and that. One notification that really bummed me out was from Greenwich Polo Club in tony Greenwich, CT, announcing it had cancelled all of its summer matches through August 30, the date of the first of three final matches originally scheduled for the season. This virus was really wreaking havoc on my usual summer diversions.

I loved the subject line of an email from Dunhill Travel: "Staying home is better with wine." The message promoted a wine deal from Firstleaf with the intro, "Stuck at home, bad. Without wine, very bad", detailing a six-wine deal for $29.95. It was the one thing missing from my homebound hutch. They had set the hook. I needed wine and this was the easiest way to reel it in. Done and done.

Today marked 50 years since the Ohio National Guard killed four anti-war demonstrators at Kent State University in Ohio. These days, stay-at-home orders in various states were drawing out the protestors in large numbers. Thus far no one had been shot but there had been many arrests.

Another historical footnote was the tidbit that home run great Babe Ruth caught the flu in Spring 1918, likely from fraternizing with soldiers at Camp Devens, west of Boston. He was even hospitalized for it but went on to lead the Boston Red Sox to a World Series Championship. A second, stronger wave of the flu prevented a parade celebrating the win. It was the team's only crown of that magnitude for another 86 years.

I had to raise my eyebrows when I saw an item about sportswriter/ historian William C. Rhoden who got stuck in Arizona as the pandemic took hold in March. For his own safety, he decided not to fly and instead rented a car to drive back to the East Coast. "For seven days, my car became a movable quarantine on a trip that stretched over 2,300 miles and through nine states," he said. His journey was noteworthy to me not only because of its timing and my own past travels, but because it was almost exactly what happened to my folks on 9/11. They were, in fact, in Arizona where my Dad was giving a lecture, and all the flights were halted, for days. To return home to North Carolina, they rented a car to make the 2,700-mile slog.

An email dropped in from the Trump-Pence "Trump Make America Great Again Committee" noting that, in just 183 days, Americans will head to the polls to vote in the 2020 presidential election. The team reminded receivers of the email of the duo's accomplishments, citing: Brought two radical ISIS leaders to justice; appointed two conservative Supreme Court justices; implemented the nation's most historic tax cuts; rebuilt our nation's military; and strengthened our borders like never before - the WALL is being finished.

Given a nationwide shortage of paper towels, I noticed companies pushing alternatives, like Swedish dishcloths made from a biodegradable fabric blend of cotton and cellulose. Similarly, alternatives to plastic wrap, also in short supply, were being peddled, like reusable beeswax wrap, which you can just rinse with cold water and dish soap, then air dry flat on a dish rack. The latter apparently keep for up to a year and can be composted.

CT Gov. Lamont checked in late afternoon to give the numbers — everything still trending down, though new positive cases for yesterday were 886; new deaths 61. Our Fairfield First Selectwoman also stepped up to say we had 423 total cases and 72 deaths for the town, with 168 recoveries.

In a worrying development, Mount Sinai Hospital said it was seeing new and unusual COVID-19 related illness in several pediatric patients, like what was being seen in the U.K., and warned parents to be on the lookout for certain symptoms, including abdominal pain, vomiting, diarrhea, low-grade fever, rash, conjunctivitis and/or cracked lips.

As I spooned back some reheated chili, I heard from my Dad by email that a meet-up he had planned for June to Geneva, New York to rendezvous with three lifelong childhood chums had gotten scrubbed, at least for now. The group was kicking around trying to make it happen in September instead, depending on the situation then. Dad's trek up had included stops in West Virginia to see my brother, several other upstate NY towns to which he had a connection — including Syracuse, Schenectady and Albany — and a stay here in Fairfield.

I had planned to go to Jen's mid-evening but she texted and said she was going to come to my place instead, and wanted to go for a drive. That was uncharacteristic of her and suggested trouble in relationship land. We set out on I-95 toward Stratford, where she said a girlfriend had a house she wanted to see. As we rolled along east though, we came across a dead-halt traffic jam caused by an accident between a tractor-trailer and two cars in the other direction that would make our return difficult. So we hopped off the highway before we had even gotten out of Fairfield and looped instead to Southport, to park by the harbor. I was right in my assumption — it *was* a relationship-related meeting, never my favorite topic. I let her say her piece. The grievances came rapid fire as she unleashed them, peppering my brain full of holes. At a certain point, her mouth was just moving with blurred noise coming out. Occasionally, a word like "miserable" would crash through like a hot cannonball and blow a big chunk of my gray matter away, taking billions of neurons with it. I retracted like a clam and basically went into shutdown mode, stopping her in her tracks at a certain point, putting the car in drive and just silently driving us back to my house. There, I hopped out and went inside without looking back and immediately shut off the porch light. It wasn't the adult thing to do but I was having a hard time absorbing the blow and thought it best to just go radio silent. There was only so much I could digest on my plate, particularly in the midst of a planet-punishing pandemic. As far as I was concerned, this was an inedible bit of gristle right now. I turned in, around 10pm, mentally raked at that point.

News. Retailer J. Crew filed for bankruptcy, the first U.S. retailer to do so since this pandemic began. On the upside, it said it would continue with all day-to-day operations and expected to stay in business and emerge from bankruptcy as a profitable company. Global virus cases surged over 3.6 million, with over 251K deaths (1.1 million recoveries). The U.S. remained the hardest hit country, with over 1.2 million cases and over 69K deaths (nearly 182K recoveries). Among states, NY was still suffering most, with nearly 327K cases and nearly 25K deaths. Our own Fairfield had 423 positive cases (168 recoveries) and 72 deaths. With campus life in question, some graduating seniors had decided to take a gap year, attend schools closer to home, transfer to community colleges or even forgo college altogether. Alpacas were being employed in certain areas as therapy animals, particularly to support isolated seniors. Heathrow Airport was setting a standard to prevent virus spread with measures like enforced social distancing measures, blocking off certain waiting area seats, installing hundreds of hand sanitizer dispensers and mandatory health checks of passengers.

May 5. The low thump of music stirred me awake. In my groggy state, I assumed Phil had gotten up early to study and had his music on as he usually does. Then I noticed it was still dark out. What time was it anyhow? 1am. What in the heck? Here I was thinking I had had a full night's sleep and I'd really only gotten a few steps down the path. Fortunately, I was able to drop back off and wasn't up again until first light. Strange things at work in the universe.

Temps had dropped considerably, to the mid-40s, and would only tickle 60 today. And looking at the week's forecast, this was going to be the warmest day. The jeans would stay on.

Over coffee, I read that Victoria's Secret had become another threatened retailer. Like other apparel brands, it had temporarily shut its stores and was struggling. It was just about to make a deal with a group that would take a controlling share in the company, but VS pulled out of it and decided to focus its efforts entirely on "navigating this environment to address those challenges", according to the company's current director and future chair.

I took a little stroll around outside, admiring the pruning and weeding work I had done yesterday. The air was full of the sound of birds. Such a chorus! It was no surprise that there had been a noticeable increase in the number of people birdwatching during this outbreak. Bird sightings and their songs had been a spirits lifter, especially for folks literally confined to their homes and apartments. An online site called Breakfast Birdwatch illustrated just how passionate people had become, being a repository for new enthusiasts' birds photos, videos and stories.

Remember last month when NATO jets intercepted Russian military aircraft over the Barents Sea? Well, Russia had apparently been strengthening its presence in the Arctic region of late, creating new local units, refurbishing old airfields and infrastructure, and founding new military bases along its adjacent coastline. Intelligence sources also noticed a concentrated effort to build air defense and coastal missile systems, early warning radars, rescue centers and various sensors. Concerned about the build-up, our navy just sent three destroyers to the area, the first time Navy ships had operated there since the mid-1980s at the height of the Cold War. Their purpose was "to assert freedom of navigation and demonstrate seamless integration among allies" according to an official statement. Translation: Keep an eye on the Russians to make sure they don't get cute.

For its part, the Navy notified Russia in advance of the ship movement to avoid any misperception.

Meanwhile, in Venezuela, President Nicolás Maduro said his government had captured two American "mercenaries" (ex-Green Berets) and one other soldier whom he said were trying to infiltrate his country to incite rebellion, apprehend its leaders and kill him. The mercenaries were apparently part of a larger group of several dozen men, most of whom were "defectors from the Venezuelan military who had been living hand-to-mouth in camps in Colombia", according to reports. Maduro was tipped off in advance about the impending breach and sent 25,000 reservists to the country's coast. There was a confrontation in which eight people were killed. The mercenaries may have been looking to collect a $15 million bounty the U.S. officials had placed on Maduro, who they had indicted on narcoterrorism charges.

The saga of Broadway Actor Nick Cordero continued. It was reported that, while he was starting to open his eyes after tracheostomy surgery and being taken off sedation, he wasn't responding to commands.

Mid-morning, CT Gov. Lamont tweeted some breaking news: "Due to the ongoing pandemic, in-person classes at K-12 schools in Connecticut will remain canceled for the rest of the academic year. Given the circumstances, this is the best course of action for the safety of students, educators, and staff." I think we all expected this, though the news elicited a collective online "ugh" from parents.

On the aircraft/airline business front, a report shared that General Electric would be cutting as many as 13,000 jobs from its jet engine business, *for good*, in response to what it called an unprecedented and deep contraction of commercial aviation. Orders for jet engines had plummeted as companies like Boeing and Airbus cut back production of new planes. United Airlines was also looking at "right sizing" its workforce, likely in October. Another indicator of the gravity of the crisis in the industry: Ryanair, Europe's top budget airline, said its passenger traffic dropped a whopping 99.6% in April — just 40,000 people flew last month compared with 13.5 million last year.

As the sky grew sunnier and temps warmed a tad, I went on "look-about" in the car — another community pulse check. There was Veres Park with its idle playground equipment and posted sign warning kids to stay away. A lawn sign in front of a house celebrating a high schooler: 2020 SENIOR. Southport's Driftwood Sandwich Shop and Spic & Span Market, offering limited access and takeout, and hanging in there. Across the street, the empty Southport Galleries space, which made me sad every time I passed it. Pequot Library had a large green banner stretched between two wooden posts with a message in stacked white block letters: STAY HOME. STAY SAFE. SAVE LIVES. Two people were on Southport Beach, walking the length of the jetty, adhering to the posted advisory sign with its nine bullets of information. Circling back toward home, I spotted a large American flag hanging down from a wire strung between two trees in a front yard. S&S Dugout on the Post Road in Southport had a neon OPEN sign above the door and the message "TAKE OUT ONLY" scrawled across one window. On the approach to Sasco Beach, a digital sign had been erected, alternating between "SASCO BEACH 2020" and "BEACH STICKER REQUIRED". The beach itself looked beautiful. There were several cars parked there, but only two people on the beach, like Southport. Someone had spelled out (HEART) U MOM with small white shells. A foursome of men was playing a round on the adjacent Country Club of Fairfield golf course. Penfield Beach was also mostly deserted, perhaps a dozen people in all, spread across the stretch from the far end of Jennings in one direction to Lantern Point and beyond in the other. Again, the patrolman with the quad was there keeping watch and scrambling along the coastline to issue warnings as needed.

Early afternoon, there was a flurry of activity at the house next door. Several ladies coming and going, some carrying pots of flowers. It turned out it they were real estate agents staging the house for sale. My neighbor had said nothing about it and I wondered what was motivating their move? Job change? Economic hardship? New opportunity elsewhere? The house would hit the market in two days. "Don't worry, we'll find you a nice family," one of them said when I inquired.

As "el Sol" started to slide down out of the "cielo", I decided to dash out for Mexican food for Phil and me — after all, it was Cinco de Mayo, commemorating the day when Mexico defeated Napolean's French forces at the Battle of Puebla in 1862. My first stop was Señor Salsa, a go-to for us, where the staff was all masked and gloved and doing a brisk business packaging up burritos, taco platters and flan, which I threw a lasso around and dragged back to the car. Then I zipped in the opposite direction to Tequila Revolucion to secure a margarita, colorful fresh-made chips and dipping salsa to go. At home, I re-plated and re-poured everything and put on some "Happy Mexican Traditional Music", with mariachi, guitar and trumpet accents, that I found on YouTube. It managed to be quite the fiesta!

Normally, I would be out and about on this night to one or another CDM party in the area, but I was happy to be able to tune into the Cosmic Jibaros band live streaming from The Acoustic, a nearby showplace. That and a Corona with a sliver of orange was making things all good.

As the concert wrapped, I heard a mewing at the back door. It was Stormy and she trotted in with a just-deceased bird in her mouth, looking quite proud of herself. I wrapped the poor feathered soul in a paper towel, the most precious of commodities these days, grabbed a trowel and gave the creature, still warm, a proper burial in a flower bed out back. Who needed Murder Hornets when you already had Murder Cats?

News: Global virus cases topped 3.7 million with over 256K deaths and over 1.2 million recoveries. The U.S. remained hardest hit with 1,225,675 cases, over 71K deaths and over 192K recoveries. Among states, New York was still suffering most, with nearly 330K cases and over 25K deaths. In CT, hospitalizations had dropped for the 12th straight day, as cases pushed over 30K and deaths over 2,500. A Pennsylvania dairy farmer decided to start bottling and selling direct to the consumer his own milk rather than dump it like so many other farmers had been doing — it sold out in hours. A five-year-old Utah boy was pulled over while on his way to California to try and buy a Lamborghini.

May 6. The singular call of a Canadian goose passing overhead, insistent coo of a mourning dove and frenetic chirping of an unseen bird of the native domestic variety — the sounds of which would normally be drowned out by the rush of commuter traffic as cars would surge through my neighborhood's main arteries and pump along the highway — was my call to rise. The day was a gray one, with temps that would not top 50F, and rain would be rudely barreling in early afternoon for a long stay.

Shower. Shave. Open curtains. Feed cat. Stow dried dishes. Get coffee going. Check and answer email. Surf online newsfeed. The drum of routine. Monotonous sometimes but reassuring in an unsure time.

One item: The White House went back and forth about winding down its coronavirus task force, with Pres. Trump ultimately deciding it would carry on indefinitely, though shift its focus to reopening efforts. Some doctors continued to recommend that the economy stay closed for a longer period of time, but the President asserted, "We can't keep our country closed for the next five years. I'm not saying anything is perfect. Will some people be affected? Yes. Will some people be badly affected? Yes." He added that the states themselves knew enough at this point to manage any new flare-ups.

Pres. Trump got out of D.C. yesterday for the first time in several weeks, flying to Arizona to tour Honeywell's manufacturing plant where the company was making millions of N95 masks for the government. He complimented the plant's employees on their hard work and the quality of the products. "You're part of this incredible industrial mobilization, the biggest since World War II, hard to believe, for an invisible enemy. But it's a vicious enemy, a smart enemy. Like generations of patriots before you, the workers of this factory are pouring their heart and their soul and their blood into defending our nation and keeping our people healthy and safe. You make America proud and I want to thank you very much," he told the group. "In normal times, it would take nine months to stand up one facility like this, but Honeywell has built this in less than five weeks, creating 500 new jobs in Arizona and another 500 jobs in Rhode Island. Together, these new factories will soon produce more than 20 million N95 masks every single month, a truly miraculous achievement."

Our Fairfield police had begun using a drone to get a bird's eye view of the town's recreation areas and determine where officers were needed. The department assured us residents that they were not employing the drones as health monitors (like Westport had proposed with its drone plan), for data collection or any other perceived infringement of people's constitutional rights. In fact, they had already been using drones for a while now, to assist with rescues, as a cheaper, safer and more environmentally friendly alternative to a helicopter.

A friend posted on her FB page an excerpt from a song in the "Annie" musical, "When I'm stuck in a day that's gray and lonely, I just pick up my chin and grin and say, the sun'll come out tomorrow..." And no sooner had she posted it, then the sun peeked out from behind the clouds and shone down a bit — right on cue.

I read a disturbing piece in The Atlantic about delirium that many

Covid-19 patients had experienced in extreme conditions of intensive care. The writer spotlighted the case of Barry Jones, a Florida man who spent nearly a month in the ICU, including 15 days on a ventilator. For part of that time, he thought he was somewhere else entirely. "One day I was in D.C., the next I was in Chicago, riding motorcycles with friends of mine I hadn't seen in years. I was putting my shoes on, walking out of the hospital to have barbecue and a beer. I was all over the place. I was on a boat. I was going back to work. I was vividly, in my mind, doing things." Over FaceTime, according to the writer, he told his longtime partner that a puppy was keeping him company, and that Pres. Trump had given him a tour of Mar-a-Lago. A Kia commercial played when he closed his eyes. He tried to escape and join his family for Easter Sunday. When he was put on a ventilator, Jones hallucinated that doctors glued plastic tubes directly into his lungs.

Spending time in the ICU, the writer noted, especially for anyone with COVID-19, was a dangerous, physically taxing experience. I had repeatedly heard NY Gov. Cuomo say that 80% of people who went on a ventilator didn't make it. But for survivors, the mental toll can be even more severe than the physical one, said the writer, noting that about one in three patients who spend more than five days in the ICU would experience some kind of psychotic reaction, like delirium, becoming intensely and pervasively confused. "Delirious patients may believe their organs are being harvested, or that nurses are torturing them. A spike in fever might feel like being set on fire. An MRI exam might feel like being fed into an oven. Strange figures might appear on the floors, walls, and ceilings of their hospital room," ICU doctors and nurses told this writer.

Late morning, NY Gov. Cuomo conducted his daily briefing, this time from Long Island. As ever, he started by citing numbers: total hospitalizations, intubations, new cases, all down, but in a "painfully slow decline". For instance, there were 232 new deaths (207 in hospitals, 25 in nursing homes) yesterday, which he termed "stubborn" and "distressing", and 600 new cases. With government doing all it could do to prevent spread, he wondered where these cases were coming from and how they were originating. It was characteristically methodical for him to ask this, with his focus on facts. On these 600, they were primarily downstate NY, mainly Long Island, male, African-American/Hispanic, over 51 and working from home, retired or currently unemployed. The fact that they were predominantly at home suggested to the governor that they weren't taking enough precautions to personally protect themselves, with face masks, hand sanitizers and social distancing — the usual prescription for self-care these days. And while stressing that, he also remarked on a new hot spot, in upstate NY's Oneida County, around a vegetable processing plant. No, not a meat plant or a shipping center or a home goods retailer, but vegetable processing plant, where there was a large number of people working in close proximity to each other — further evidence for him to support his discouragement of large gatherings for the foreseeable future.

Gov. Cuomo also circled back to his frequent point that this was a pivotal moment. "People are ready for change at certain moments," he said, and this was one of those moments, alongside events like 9/11 and Superstorm Sandy. So, now, how can we change things for the better?

Finally, with an acknowledgement that today was Nurses Day and of their hard work in the state and across the globe, Cuomo announced that JetBlue was donating a pair of round-trip flights to 100,000 medical personnel and nurses to honor their efforts, beginning with 10,000 NY medical professionals.

In step with Cuomo's shoutout was a FB post by the Fairfield County Children's Choir of a virtual choir performance with contributions from all the member students from across 16 towns singing Simon & Garfunkel's "Bridge Over Troubled Water", from home in a Zoom format. "The song holds a great message for these unsettled times and this video celebrates the power of children singing separately, but together," the page administrator noted. "We dedicate this video to all the frontline health care workers and first responders who have indeed been our 'Bridge Over Troubled Water', and to all the families that are suffering and have lost loved ones." It encouraged a donation to a Covid-19 Support Fund for Bridgeport Hospital in memory of Mary Avila, the grandmother of the FCCC conductor. It was a truly touching and inspiring post.

On a related note, CT Gov. Lamont was at a gathering celebrating National Nurses Day at Hartford Hospital, attended by nurses and staff. Among speakers was the President of Hartford Healthcare Jeff Flaks, who recollected, "It's hard for me to imagine that, eight weeks ago, it was a Friday evening about 10 o'clock, I got a phone call at home and was told we had our first patient who tested positive for Covid-19 who would be admitted to the hospital. And we came into the hospital and several of us, we went up and wanted to be with our team, who had had already admitted our patient — she was there — and we wanted to talk with our team. And I didn't know what I would encounter. I really didn't have an appreciation, but I knew this was a moment in history and I could imagine the fear, the trepidation. I could imagine this was getting real now... What I saw, particularly in our nursing leadership and all of our nurses, was confidence, professionalism, empathy, commitment. It was incredible. I was so inspired, because I left and said, 'We've got this.'"

Our Fairfield town announced that it had formed a Business Reopening Task force led by our First Selectwoman to develop recommendations and guidelines for businesses in response to the Governor's May 20 order. The task force would be discussing the impact on restaurants, retail, salons and other businesses covered under the Executive Order. On a related note, the State had partnered with CBIA-CONNSTEP to assist in the distribution of donated surgical masks to eligible, essential small businesses with 50 employees or less.

In The Strange Case of Kim Jong Un, South Korean intel officials said they believed that the North Korean dictator did *not* undergo heart surgery as reported and had just been laying low during the Covid-19 crisis. Though North Korea insisted there had been no recorded cases of the virus in their country, it was not ruling out the possibility of an outbreak there.

The day sank back into grayness and became more raw temp-wise, with some brief showers mixed in to make a slurry of blah. But that didn't stop me from dashing out and making the rounds to some area businesses to snap and share some pics through social media — in effect, slapping the "support local" tambourine.

I darted first to PACI, a 25-year-old Italian restaurant situated by the Southport train station, where owners Bob and Donna Patchen received me. They had been closed since the state shut down and were just reopening, initially for takeout, though they planned to have their patio dining space going on May 20.

I u-turned, through Southport Village, where the Horseshoe Cafe had also begun offering takeout, and Switzer's Pharmacy still had the lights on. The Southport Volunteer Fire Dept. was quiet as I rolled past and down by Southport Harbor and the yacht club there, eventually working my way north up into the Greenfield Hill part of Fairfield. Testo's Deli & Pizza had a sign in its window: "Everything will be OK", with a rainbow design.

Up on Black Rock Turnpike, Sunny Dae's ice cream store was alight and customers were lined up outside Kindred Spirits & Wine. Alina's Cakes & Cookies winked "OPEN" as did Whoopi Thai Cuisine. Blue Cactus Grill was plastered with signs: OPEN Blue Cactus TAKE OUT ONLY, NOW OPEN, OPEN 7 DAYS, FREE DELIVERY, WE'RE OPEN, Pick-up Curbside.

An elder woman stepped out of a sleek, high-end black Mercedes to step inside FRED's Chef Crafted Prepared Foods. Little Pub was barring any entry and instead accommodating pick-up around the back. A half-dozen people stood six feet apart in a pyramid design waiting to go inside A&S Italian Fine Foods while Puerto Vallarta Mexican restaurant spotlighted a banner offering Takeout & Free Delivery. Billy's Bakery promoted its croissants, pastries, artisan breads, tarts, bagels, cakes and coffee. Chip's Family Restaurant was pushing its usual "Breakfast All Day" proposition while CKC Salon & Keratin Bar expressed "We miss you, stay safe". My parting area shot was that of a mural of a waving American flag installed across three garage bays at Star Fuels gas station. I was glad to see all were doing well and hanging in there.

My Dad emailed me a photo of his homemade dinner: General Tso's chicken with broccoli, which inspired me to make a similar creation — chicken with rice, vegetables and soy sauce, with an accent of ginger. I dished up a bowlful and relaxed computer-side for a working dinner.

There were some amusing virtual entertainments early this evening on Instagram, including Charter Oak Brewing's pair-up with Danbury Library for a Trivia Night, with Star Wars-themed questions in Round One and participation from home. Nati Trujillo-Bound, a yoga teacher with @ bohemeandbody who goes by the handle @fityogamermaid, was doing a yoga stretching session —"Raise your arms up on the inhale, look up, then go all the way down, open the chest, step back the left foot then the right, plank, chest up, head up, downward dog, left leg back, right leg back, long exhale." So pleasant, relaxing and easy to watch.

Over on FB, crazy-haired Tash Neal was delivering the funk with his electric guitar, jamming for Venmo tips. And John Lamb was going space cosmic with a live show banging away at an electric organ, while seated in a high-backed rolling desk chair.

"Come on, it's a pandemic. You can be weird," said my FB friend Carolyn in a video post of herself madly dancing in her kitchen to the disco classic Kool & The Gang's "Celebrate". "Oh, and ignore the hole in the ceiling. I've got a leak from my bathroom!" Equally funny was my bud Mike Bud demonstrating how you could pry a cap off a beer bottle with a staple puller.

The two of them could be in danger of being censored as Facebook announced it had named 20 people to its "Supreme Court" for content moderation. The board included nine law professors, a Nobel Peace Prize laureate and journalists from around the world. "The panel will issue rulings on what kinds of posts will be allowed and what should be taken down," according to NBC News. The move was meant to relieve the company's executives of having to decide. FB's community standards had grown to prohibit not only illegal images such as child pornography but also hate speech, harassment and, most recently, false information about the pandemic.

I read about a new strain of the virus in the U.S. that had mutated into a more contagious version of the Wuhan strain, which came to the East Coast through Europe. The mutation was on the "spike" protein, which the virus used to enter its host. "To date, we have identified fourteen mutations in Spike that are accumulating," researchers said. "The mutation Spike D614G is of urgent concern; it began spreading in Europe in early February, and when introduced to new regions it rapidly becomes the dominant form." The research team warned that future vaccines could prove ineffective against the virus if the "pandemic fails to wane" in future months. That scenario could "ultimately limit the effectiveness of the first vaccines."

A piece from The Beer Connoisseur discussed "The Global Impact of COVID-19 on the Beer Industry". I already knew, from a local litmus reading, that small breweries were hurting. Sadly, "hard work and government assistance, including loans, grants and extensions of sales tax payments, are unlikely to be enough to help small breweries stay in business," the article said, adding, "In early April, a Brewbound survey of 455 respondents across 49 states and Washington, D.C. found 46 percent of independent and craft brewers indicated they would likely close within three months."

In contrast, grocery stores, bottle shops and online alcohol sales had seen an uptick in demand for beer. "In the third week of March, market research firm Nielsen saw U.S. alcoholic beverage sales rise 55 percent," the article stated. "The U.S. is already the world's second-largest beer market, and once widespread quarantining became the norm, online alcohol sales rose by 243 percent and beer sales jumped 34 percent." Enthusiasts also showed more interest in buying beer through alternative channels, like direct-from-brewery shipping, curbside pick-up from restaurants and alcohol delivery apps.

Fairfield Museum posted that, this week, May 6-9, shorelines along the Long Island Sound would be experiencing King Tides, the highest regional tides of the year due to the alignment of both the Sun and Moon's gravitational pull. The group Save the Sound asked for shore residents to take pictures of the coastline during this time as records for regional planners to assess the extent of local flooding and potential effects of sea level rise.

Folks like me that enjoy the ocean were able to take that love to the next level now, tapping into beach cams on either coast of the U.S. One cam in Clearwater, Florida allowed you to see four different views. Another in Santa Monica was trained on the famous Pier. Yet another, up the coast from there, gave live coastal views in Malibu.

Besides throwing exceptionally high tides at us that would push our oceans up, Mother Nature had some more fun planned for us: the Polar Vortex was to unleash winter-like cold across the eastern half of the nation in the next few days, bringing snow to the Northeast and Mid-Atlantic and chilly temps from the Upper Midwest to New England. Frost was even expected in northern Georgia and the western Carolinas later this weekend as this giant air mass settled in and challenged records, making it feel more like early March than early May. "A dollop of wintry mischief" one forecaster called it.

I wondered how the court system was functioning, or even if it was, and Google searched for an answer. According to one site, "In response to public health guidance related to Covid-19, U.S. courts (state and federal) are making modifications including closing courthouses, restricting courthouse access, continuing trials, cancelling non-case related activities, and rescheduling or permitting videoconferencing of oral arguments." The dilemma posed, of course, was that anyone in jail awaiting trial was going to be denied their "speedy trial rights". Some folks proposed releasing these people on no-cash bail or with electronic monitoring anklets.

A friend, Nikki, put up a FB post that seemed to perfectly capture this current moment in time. Not the pandemic overall, but the point at which we had now arrived. The passage began:

Flattening the curve didn't mean stop the infection, but spread it out so that the system could handle it. I am seeing so much anxiety about resuming business, and so much anger about continued regulations. People are feeling the need to catapult to one side or the other, then fight the opposition.

The passage continued: Here's my perspective, from a mainstream medical model. I think a lot of folks have fallen into the idea that social distancing was meant to stop the viral spread. It wasn't. It was meant to SLOW it while we put medical infrastructure in place. It's not perfect, but it's much better than it was seven weeks ago.

A vaccine is a long way off. At some point, people have to be systematically exposed to begin the building of (hopeful) herd immunity. We will likely begin to experience a real increase in cases after reopening. Ideally, that exposure is controlled and calculated, in phases, to allow our medical community to respond adequately, and reduce the number of severe or fatal cases. That's where we are.

Whether you feel like things will be opening too soon, or not soon enough, we were never going to social distance this thing into nonexistence. You now need to proceed as your health, wallet, and conscience allow.

If you are medically vulnerable, you do not need to be a part of what is about to happen. Stay home if you can. If you're not, or if your financial vulnerability trumps your health concerns, you need to proceed in ways that continue to protect yourself, and the elderly and medically vulnerable around you.

All of us need to calm down. Quit telling people who are financially struggling that they don't care about human lives. Quit telling people who are truly at risk of dying from this virus that they are cowering in fear. Remember that until you've walked in someone else's shoes, you should probably be careful in your judgements and subsequent harsh words.

We don't HAVE to choose an either/or proposition and fight. We could choose other ways to be. Examples include but are not limited to:

"I think this may be too soon, so I will continue to shelter myself, and pray/make masks/check on those who can't."

"I really need to go back to work, so I will do so, but I will be careful and try to protect myself, my family, and those around me with healthy strategies."

See how those positions allow each of us to do what we need to, and also respect those who are choosing differently?

One thing that allows us to do this is humility. I can acknowledge that I am not an epidemiologist/economist/whatever, that I am making decisions based on my understanding of complex subjects and my own personal health and financial situation, that I am not all knowing, always right, and an expert in all fields, and that each person around me is doing their best too. We can make different choices and still be a supportive community. We can learn and evolve in our understanding of these issues.

End of passage. And well put.

As the night sky grew moister and inkier, I followed the Yellow Brick Road past the sleep-inducing poppies to the intensely flexible dancer/therapist/pilates instructor @venuschun's live video feed on IG. In her tomato-red crop top and shredded jeans shorts, she coached, "Inhale to arch, undulate your spine, articulation, all fours, toes tucked or untucked." Together with some machine-generated background music that she was pumping, the session was mesmerizing.

I stumbled into a Watch Party of the Dave Matthews band, a free feed courtesy of a provider called Nugs. The show was previously recorded in front of a live audience, a setting I really missed — the cheers, the yells, smoke wafting above the crowd, the urgency of the jam, the connection between audience and performers, a psychedelic light show on multiple screens, flashing strobes, people swaying, an aroma of sweat, perfume and beer. Oh to be in the room!

As sweet was a "Live in Isolation" clip recorded the other day by the members of The Doobie Brothers band playing their 1974 classic "Black Water". Each of the four members were playing from their respective homes, which were interesting to see in their own right. They really looked like they were having a great time — together yet apart, making glorious harmonies, strumming the pandemic out of our collective consciousness. The clip wrapped with a video patch-in of loads of other people and families joining them to sing the song from their own homes. The "show" supported Feeding America.

As the night grew whiskers, and I found myself watching a GIF clip of a praying mantis devouring a hornet, I knew it was time to turn in. Hasta Mañana, space cowboys.

News: Pres. Trump appointed ally and fundraiser Louis DeJoy to serve as the new postmaster general for the U.S. Postal Service, effective June 15, to try and lead the government agency out of its current mess. The President's newly created Space Force released a recruitment video, addressing potential cadets, "Maybe your purpose on this planet isn't on this planet." The group had become the sixth branch of the U.S. military this past December and welcomed its first class of cadets from the U.S. Air Force Academy graduation in late April. The last time a branch was added was in 1947 when the Air Force split off from the Army. Gold's Gym filed for bankruptcy, citing financial stress due to the virus crisis. On the upside, the chain said it wasn't going out of business, just realigning itself to meet challenges. This year, high school graduates from Flagler County, Florida would get to drive across the finish line at the Daytona International Speedway to get their diplomas handed to them. The ceremony was set to happen May 31 for the county's two high schools. Alabama police were searching for a rooster that had aggressively attacked people at ATMs — the "suspect" remained on the loose. Global Coronavirus cases passed 3.8 million with over 264K deaths, 1.29 million recoveries. The U.S. remained hardest hit with 1.26 million cases and 74,200 deaths, over 206K recoveries. Among states, NY had over 330K cases and over 25,436 deaths. Very scary was a new report of virus-afflicted, oxygen-deprived "happy hypoxics" showing up at hospitals, thinking they were healthy but really very badly off with deep lung distress.

May 7. I woke up at daybreak as I tend to do, feeling groggy as I had stayed up way longer than I had planned. When I climbed into bed last night, I was tired but not yet ready for sleep, so surfed on my phone. Scrolling through my Instagram feed, I got a notification that @charlie_britz was going live and, out of curiosity, clicked on it. And there was Charlie, a lanky, long-haired bottle blonde with six-inch stiletto heels, jeans shorts and an abbreviated tee, in a room that was lit up in a blush pink glow, with sheets covering windows behind her and a stripper pole in the middle of her space. To the accompaniment of some chunky rock music by Tool, she began writhing across the floor, and gyrating, and curling like a serpent around the pole. Occasionally she smacked her chunky heels together with an attention commanding WHACK. And at the end of each song, an article of clothing was peeled off. The shorts went first, courtesy of a zipper that went all the way from front to back and fell off of her in two halves. Led Zeppelin's "Whole Lotta Love" was playing when the tee came off… "A-way, way down inside, a-honey you need-ah, I'm gonna give you my love, ah, I'm gonna give you my love, ah oh…" A lacy lingerie set got shimmied off next, revealing just a black bra and black panties and a massive serpentine tattoo on her left torso. It was a steamy, IG-busting show, to be sure. I had no idea my feed contained such entertainments.

I continued to scroll and stumbled on a friend who I knew of late to be a homemaker and mother of two elementary school-aged girls. What I *didn't* know was that she had found a new passion for dancing on TikTok, in a style not so unlike Britzy. There were two recorded clips she had put up, both set to music, and both of her sexily gyrating and looking way too hot for a Los Angeles-based homemaker mom.

Wednesday night had become the new Friday night.

Coffee was a good fixer for the cobwebs that cloaked my brain, and the day was starting out to be a pleasant one, sunny and headed to 62F for a high, so that helped to perk me up as well.

While doing my morning FB rounds, I received an invite from a family acquaintance to like a page called "Marine Fit". Our family friend was a former Royal Marine Commando turned fitness instructor and he was offering "Free Daily Workouts During Lockdown" to help "people keep active, stay healthy and keep motivated during these hard and difficult times." I assumed I would be notified when he was holding a session and thought I might give it a look. Lord knows I needed to shed some pandemic pounds.

I imagined that, with so many events cancelled and other activities prohibited, that camping would be a popular pursuit this summer. I think others thought the same as I began seeing stories pop up highlighting gear like a double tent cot that sleeps two and is elevated to keep you off the cold hard ground, and a circular suspended, netted hammock. Another rising push was behind giant lawn games aimed to "bring supersize fun to your backyard". These included giant bowling and criss-cross connect sets.

I read about the emergence of BYOC (Bring Your Own Covid) parties,

201

like in Walla Walla, Washington, wherein infected and non-infected people come together to hang out and ensure *everyone* gets the infection, the thinking being that the infection is inevitable and why not speed up the process? Maybe it wasn't as crazy as it sounded. You might say it was a "novel" idea.

The virus may have jumped from animals to humans as early as October 6 last year, according to researchers who looked at 7,000 genome sequence assemblies gathered from around the world to determine their most recent common ancestor. And data showed that the first confirmed infection was actually November 17. The research further confirmed this virus' ability to quickly mutate and adapt to its human hosts. No doubt that this was a tricky, nasty beast.

In Santa Rosa County, Florida, what was meant to be a prescribed, controlled burn on a private property, had gotten out of control fueled by high winds, low humidity and drought conditions. By early evening last night, it had grown to more than 2,000 acres, shut down portions of Interstate 10 and forced the evacuation of area residents as it threatened about 1,100 residential structures — 336 of which were in the fire's direct path. It was dubbed the Five Mile Swamp Fire. I immediately thought of the devastating brushfires in Australia earlier this year.

At the appointed hour of 10am, I got on a FaceTime call with my Westport-based Hawaiian artist friend Jana. We hadn't seen each other in ages and wanted to catch up. She said life had been a little "chaotic" since the pandemic's start, but not wholly different. "I like being home. I'm quite happy being home, and having the kids around," she said. The differences were that she suddenly had more time and couldn't go running with her kids anymore. Instead, "feeling a little selfish", she would go for a run on her own, usually late at night when no one was around.

Of late, her time had been occupied having Zoom calls with family, which was not as intense as being on Zoom calls of a professional nature. She had also been working on new artwork. At the beginning of the year, she was working on a koala drawing using charcoal recovered from the Australian bushfires, and hoping to expand that approach into murals. But then Covid-19 crushed any opportunity for her to introduce that work in a public gallery setting. Now she was working with a saber-tooth tiger image, with large fangs, which represented to her "a silent scream" speaking to the horror behind the coronavirus, but also badassery.

The devastating aspect of this public health situation aside, she thought that this was an "amazing moment in time", as did I. For her, the quarantine started March 12, which was Day 1 for me, too, when the local schools closed very suddenly. The local closures, we knew, were spurred from the infections that started at the Westport private party; she was acquainted with the hosts and some of the guests. But even before that event, she thought the virus was in the community. She believed her younger son may have contracted it in early March, as he was experiencing some uncharacteristic nausea. And there were also a "few people with weird sicknesses" in the area.

She was partially prepared for the event though unintentionally so. Because she works with many toxic paint substances for long periods of time, she was fortunate to have a small stockpile of face masks — seven to start, three with filters, of the N95 variety. One thing she wasn't prepared for with this whole crisis was the "divisiveness of people" — the partisan split, geographic division and polar opposite attitudes being displayed. She was also disturbed by anti-Asian sentiments, though hadn't personally experienced it. "I'm usually brown and get the brown racism. People think I'm Latina," she said.

Jana admitted that the start of all this was a bit bewildering, but she found some purpose through volunteering — to handle food shopping for an elderly, immune-comprised Redding woman. The overall community volunteer initiative was started by a Staples High School student. Jana's charge would email her a detailed list of items, often including photos of products and containers, and pay her through PayPal. Jana had been doing the shopping at Caraluzzi's, a small grocery store and market in Newtown, CT, which seemed to be consistently well supplied.

As we were speaking, her phone alarm went off, reminding her of an errand — to pick up food for herself at Gilbertie's in Westport, where a Farmers Market there was struggling to exist. Jana had pre-ordered online and went to collect, "bringing" me with her. Arriving there, she donned her mask and went to a pick-up point. It was an almost military scene, with staging areas, tables with goods, and masked staff. It was Jana's first time trying this. She wished she had ordered more based on the intricacy of doing it. I wondered if she had considered starting a home vegetable garden. "I don't like worms," she answered, to my great amusement. (But saber-tooth tigers are just fine.)

We continued talking as she returned home, marveling at the fact that we could even do that. I noticed how long and bushy her hair had gotten. She said she'd recently dyed it as it had been "75% white".

As we wrapped our near hour-long call, I asked what she wanted to do when she felt that it was safe enough to really get back out and about. "I want to swim and get the boys back into sports. Get on an airplane and not be worried. And travel, to Hawaii," she said. Coincidentally, she had had plans to go to Milan and Barcelona in March, which turned out to be two of the hardest hit areas in the world by this virus.

Late morning, I received an email from a cosmetic surgeon friend, who announced that his office would be reopening May 20. It was interesting to know how they planned to accommodate people in their tight quarters. Their safety measures included: all patients will be temperature screened at the building entrance, you MUST wear a mask to enter the building, waiting room organized to provide six feet of distance between chairs, appointments limited to patients only (limit of one companion), staff wearing gloves and masks at all times, designated areas to allow social distancing at check in and check out, credit card payment encouraged to limit touch points, payments made over the phone prior to appointment to limit time in the office, and telemedicine appointments encouraged for consultations and follow-ups to limit in-office traffic.

My Dad shared a link with regard to the Wales visit plans he had had, which pretty much banged the final nail into the coffin for the trip. The link was to the Shropshire Star, a Welsh newspaper, that reported the First Minister had "warned that rushing to ease lock-down restrictions will only risk a second wave of coronavirus, and more problems down the line." The Minister said he "believed the virus had now peaked in Wales, largely as a result of the social distancing measures which had succeeded in stopping the spread." Still, he warned people to continue to be vigilant. "Personally, I don't think anybody needs to travel more than two miles. If you want to get some exercise, do it near to where you live. You don't need to drive out to a beauty spot," he said.

With Mother's Day just a couple of days away, CVS offered a shareable message about mothers, summing them up as: The stay-up-all-nighters.

Boo-boo kissers. Movers and shakers. And taxi drivers. The bonus moms. Grandmoms. Foster moms. The aunt moms. Sister moms. Mentor moms. And fur moms. To all the moms. We heart you.

Early afternoon, I happened to stumble into a Fairfield Theatre Company livestream performance shared by none other than my friends Lez Zeppelin, the Led Zeppelin tribute band with whom I welcomed in 2020 on New Year's Eve, a moment that seemed *so* long ago in time now. The four members were performing together from their respective homes in a Zoom collaboration, and it was nothing short of fantastic and heart-warming.

Periodically, I will take work as a photographer and realized that tonight I was supposed to have covered Operation Hope's "Motown Magic Gala". Now, that community help group was scrambling to organize food drives to help support neighbors in need.

I read in Us Weekly about pop star/actress Miley Cyrus and her view on the public health crisis. "I know I'm in a unique position, and my experience with this pandemic is not like most everyone else's in my country and around the world," the 27-year-old said. "My life has been pushed on pause, but really I have no idea what this pandemic is like. I am comfortable in my space and able to put food on my table and I am financially stable, and that's just not the story for a lot of people." One way she *did* do some public interface was by donating 120 taco meals to hospital staff in her area in April. She also adopted a rescue dog.

I received an email from the University of North Carolina, from where my eldest son graduated and my Dad had taught, congratulating this year's graduates. "We did not want this weekend to pass by without taking a moment to celebrate you," the Chancellor stated. "While we are not together in person, we are hosting a 20-minute Watch Party on Facebook and YouTube at 10am on Sunday, May 10, to view the videos and greetings from all over the Tar Heel community to recognize your day." The school said it would announce at the end of the month its plans for a postponed in-person commencement ceremony.

I had to accomplish two missions this afternoon: yard waste drop-off and a grocery run. Happily, I wasn't feeling the anxiety as before and simply and mechanically grabbed my PPE (bandana and gloves), tossed the bulging leaf bags in the trunk and headed out, steering around people who had come to tour my neighbor's house on its first day on the market.

The yard waste drop-off station didn't have the militant reception as before. No reception actually. I drove in, did my drop and back out I went. And I took a leisurely loop through our beach area in the direction of the store, passing a cop blocking the already barricaded entrance to Veterans Park, numerous kids on bikes — very few of them masked — past the sealed-off Penfield Beach parking lot and up Beach Road, where I spotted real estate friend Suzy. She didn't have a mask and we spoke through the passenger side window of my car. She told me of her grown daughter Camryn and a job she had had lined up with a high-end dressmaker in Miami that fell through when Covid exploded on the scene. Suzy asserted that it was time for us to get back to life.

Stop & Shop's lot was full but not oppressively so, and people were all masked — both shoppers and workers. I spontaneously adopted a one-glove-on-to-steer and one-glove-off-for-grabbing stuff method that served me well. Navigating the aisles like a skier zooming around moguls, in no time — and happily finding 95% of the store stocked for a change — I was at and through the register, back to the car and back home, to Phil's helpful hands in receiving the booty — the groceries, that is. My booty didn't need helping. Perhaps it was beyond help. Who knew anymore?

Scouring my email, I read a NEW 102.7 NY radio blast about pop star Kesha and her "rear rejuvenation". In short, in quarantine, she was having her boyfriend apply a nightly age-defying "butt mask". She had also taken to applying men's beard dye to color her eyebrows. The same email detailed the bizarre name SpaceX Founder Elon Musk and his "Electo-Fairie" girlfriend Grimes' newborn baby boy: X AE A-12. Its derivation was a mashed potato pie of meanings that involved an unknown variable, elven spelling of AI, a favorite aircraft and a favorite song. Whatevs.

The girls were at it on Instagram live again — @laurensimpson teaming with @valentinalequeux doing a tag-team exercise session, focused on abs, which they seemed to have already perfected judging by their chiseled midriffs. "We don't want to be using our hip muscles here, we want to be isolating our quads," suggested Ms. Simpson. God Bless her.

Nat Geo took an interesting, though not new, focus today, expanding on the thought, "When nature is sick, we're sick." Essentially, "rampant deforestation, uncontrolled expansion of agriculture, intensive farming, mining and infrastructure development, as well as the exploitation of wild species, have created a perfect storm for the spillover of diseases from wildlife to people," she stated. Further, "Future pandemics will happen more frequently, will kill more people, and will cause greater economic damage unless we start recognizing the inextricable links between human health and the health of the planet, its ecosystems, and its nonhuman living creatures."

On a related note, a former wildlife inspector for the U.S. Fish and Wildlife Service said that, while public conversation had been focused on the illegal animal trade, "the diseases that simultaneously hitchhike into the country on *legally* imported wildlife continue to go largely unnoticed."

Our Fairfield First Selectwoman provided an update for today: 448 total positive cases, 181 of which have fully recovered, and 79 deaths to date. Eighty-five percent of the latter had occurred in nursing homes. These "congregated settings" were becoming a last stop for many across the board, across the world. She also announced additional reopening: tennis courts at Gould Manor Park and at the high schools, a middle school and an elementary school. The H. Smith Richardson Golf Course would also open, May 15. Finally, the parking lots at Jennings and Sasco Beaches would open earlier, at 8am, along with Lake Mohegan, for residents.

Early evening, I just had to have me sum Sasco sunset. A favorite viewing spot, the beach front was just three minutes from my home. It was a popular idea it turned out, with more than a dozen cars lined up and several people paired off and out and about. I sailed in, dropped anchor and went on walkabout myself, spying a peace sign made with shells right off the bat, likely created by the same person that made the Love U Mom design the other day. I walked the length of the beach and beyond, to Southport Beach Club where idled bleached white Adirondack chairs waited for squatters. The sun was dropping quickly over the posh colonials and historic homes on the other side of Southport harbor, so I did a spin-around and flip-flopped my way back, watching the sky glow with tones of pink. It was a much-missed view and swallow of Sound life.

News: Global coronavirus cases exceeded 3.9 million with over 270K deaths, over 1.3 million recoveries. The U.S. remained hardest hit, now with 1,289,028 cases and nearly 77K deaths, over 215K recoveries. New York continued to suffer: 337,170 cases, 26,365 deaths. Meteorologists gave early warning that an unseasonably out-of-whack, potentially record-breaking snowstorm was headed for the Northeast and New England. Get in line behind the Murder Hornets, oh, and the non-native Gypsy Moths which were threatening to infest a county in Washington state, to the degree that the governor issued an emergency proclamation saying the agricultural and horticultural industries of the state and economic well-being and quality of life of its residents were in jeopardy. Denmark may have defined what live concert events will look like going forward, debuting a "drive-in" concert last week, wherein audience members watch and listen from their cars, like at a drive-in movie.

May 8. TGIF, right? Gloomy morning. Very still. No cars to be heard. Bird chirps very very pronounced. Trees absolutely still. Not the slightest breeze. Refrigerator humming. Coffee pot gurgling. Clock ticking. It would have been easy to spiral into madness at this moment without distractions.

A friend's FB post perfectly summed up life as we currently knew it: Well..... we were supposed to be at Logan airport boarding a flight to Cali right now, for an awesome long anticipated two week vacation that my family and I have been looking forward to for months. But nahhhh...Instead I'll get my fat ass out of bed, get in my car and go get my coffee, drive around in circles for about 30 minutes, then try to find a supermarket that doesn't have a line of 50 people to get in the door so I can get some fucking Lysol, paper towels, and tp that they won't have. Then maybe I'll hit the post office because that's always a fucking joy. Hell if I'm really daring maybe I'll drive by my buddy's house, beep and wave from 200 feet away with two masks on my face. I guess after that I'll head back home to stare out my window at my fucking crazy bat shit neighbor raking his woods all day and dumping what he rakes in his woods. Heck, if all goes well and the airlines don't fold, I can rebook our trip spring of 2030."

I happened on a breathtaking YouTube clip called "Swans for Relief" which featured 32 premier ballerinas from 22 dance companies in 14 countries performing a Le Cygne (The Swan) variation sequentially with music by Camille Saint-Saëns, rendered by cellist Wade Davis, in support of a Swans for Relief charity. Each dancer performed from her own home or studio space and all the segments were edited together into one run, then all shown in one concluding parting shot. The sad sound of the cello and beautiful, graceful moves of the dancers seemed to capture my morning mood.

There are experts across the globe whose job it is to think about potential catastrophes to help governments plan for them. Every year, they collaborate to compile a Worldwide Threat Assessment document, referred to as "a distillation of worrisome global trends, risks, problem spots and emerging perils." Beyond future pandemics caused by increased human encroachment on wild habitats, there were apparently eight other major f-bombs that scientists and national security officials were concerned about "that are real, identifiable and stand a chance that is more likely than not of occurring — at some scale, ranging from mild to catastrophic — in the next five to 50 years." To start, there are increasing attempts by adversaries to manipulate or delete data or otherwise raise public doubts about whether reported reality is real reality, e.g. changing broker information, manipulating bank records, doctoring audio to change words people are saying and/or hacking a media account to disseminate a false story to injurious effect. More than ever, biosecurity is under the microscope: concern about lab accidents, bioterrorism and biological warfare. Massive technological disruption is another hot topic as everyday society becomes more reliant on interlocked tech systems that were not originally designed with security in mind. The fear there are cyberattacks on power grids, banking systems, healthcare networks, satellites and stock trading systems. And how about an unexpected electromagnetic pulse being thrown out by the sun or from space that fries the guts of the globe's circuitry? Don't forget nukes, which are omnipresent but fall to the back of our minds these days — specifically where countries stumble their way into an accidental "WarGames"-like nuclear armageddon. Of course, there's climate change, which is and will continue to occur despite all of our efforts to slow it down, resulting in more severe weather, food and water shortages, sea level rise and geopolitical instability. Let's throw into the mix global reordering of power, which we're already seeing as America, China and Europe play chess with each other. While we're at it, let's put catastrophic earthquakes out there — in the U.S. alone, threats include a fault off the coast of Oregon and Washington, one running from Missouri to Oregon, and one stretching across Utah and Idaho, along with the much-anticipated San Andreas fault promising a "Great California Shakeout".

On the climate change note, a just-published study noted that "extremely humid heat that is more intense than most Americans have experienced has more than doubled in frequency in some coastal subtropical regions of the world since 1979." Apparently, "temperatures of 95F — which render ineffective the human heat response of sweating to shed heat through evaporation, leading to hypothermia — are already occurring for short periods of time at a few weather stations." Geographical examples include the Persian Gulf shoreline, coastal southwest North America and northern South Asia. The study warns that "highly populated regions of the world will be rendered uninhabitable sooner than previously thought for parts of each year." Researchers urged people to take wide-ranging prep steps now to adapt to the heat.

I read in a Vox article about the unique dilemma of RVers, specifically, the approximately one million Americans who live full time in recreational vehicles. Their owners include traveling nurses, retirees and digital nomads living on the road by choice or for financial savings. Their challenge now, though, since Covid-19 stormed our nation, was finding a safe place to shelter, finding a doctor and staying employed. "We do not live in post-apocalyptic rigs worthy of a feature in a Mad Max film," said the RVer writer. "Water tanks and propane tanks need to be filled, food runs out faster since we stock a mini-fridge and cabinet, and trash needs to be dumped. Most of this setup is far from pandemic proof."

Quite out of the blue, Jen FaceTime'd me. We had been incommunicado all week. She was dressed in a robe and sipping coffee, and looked like she hadn't slept very well — her eyes were slits. She wanted me to know that a worker from Andersen Windows had appeared at her home to replace the sliding, multi-paned glass door adjacent to her dining room that a student of hers had shattered unintentionally with a rock. I had been involved in the process of getting the contractor to schedule an installation appointment and come out, which is why Jen called, I assumed? But, to be honest, I didn't know *what* was going on in her head.

Mid-morning, Phil came downstairs to make tea for himself as he prepped for his final final exam of his sophomore year, scheduled for early this afternoon. I told him about Jen's call, which sparked a dad-son conversation in general about women, our personal preferences with regard to them, where we each want to be in two years' time when he graduates from college, and his mom and what she was thinking about future-wise. It seemed to us like some big shifts would be coming in the not-too-far-off future, for us all. I hoped they would be positive, life-enhancing ones.

With rain expected to arrive at midday, I gave the lawn a fast mow and hauled the grass clippings to the dump. In, out, no fuss, no muss. Then I went drive-about, as usual, to see what I could see. In the Fairfield Beach Area, a giant American flag hung from the front of a second floor patio deck. A "Congratulations to Emma Rauth", Class of 2020 Fairfield University sign was attached to another second story deck. A child's drawing with the message "You Are Our Heroes" was taped to a living room front window. Zipping up to Fairfield University, I did a u-turn past the guard shed. The security people there were all masked and overseeing students retrieving belongings they had left behind when school was closed two months ago. Around the bend, there was a congrats lawn sign to Julia, a 2020 grad of Laurelton Hall. Further on, there was a giant cutout of a heart attached to two upright posts at the back of it, on a lawn. A pink banner with various stitched hearts hung from a tree branch. A rainbow of multi-colored heart cutouts was taped inside a front window. A wreath of tulip tops was attached to a front door. Wreaths of forsythia hung from the large wooden front doors of St. Pius X Catholic church.

In the lot at the latter, I spied a group of nine people, all but one of them masked, with poster board signs, "You Got This Chris, Feel Better" and "Get Well, Wishing You a Speedy Recovery", preparing to do a "get well drive-by" past the house where their skateboarder friend was rehabbing from a broken leg after a skating accident.

Looping back down toward downtown, there were more signs: "Thank you first responders, essential workers & healthcare heroes!"; a "THANK YOU!! From Your PTA Family" sign at Riverfield Elementary School; a simple THANK YOU, BE SAFE sign on another lawn; "AN AMAZING EDUCATOR LIVES HERE" sign; and BEEP, an amazing CREC educator lives here.

On a banner hanging on the perimeter fence at Fairfield Ludlowe High School was the message "FLHS Families Appreciate Teachers and Staff!" It was clear Fairfield's pulse was beating hard and strong for one another.

To reward myself for my outing — and because I was hungry and missed this particular venue being open — I zipped to Nauti Dolphin

Pizza for a sausage calzone to go. The masked co-owner brought it out to my car as I pulled up.

I arrived back in time to tune into another Quick Center Quick Session, this one with the topic of how live performance theaters were holding up during this time and what was planned for the future. The moderator mentioned that a lot of theater was currently happening through Zoom, for an audience of "Zoombies", a play off Zombies, she joked. I think she had just invented a new vocabulary word.

A sobering milestone was reached late afternoon: Global coronavirus cases exceeded a staggering 4 million cases, with over 275K deaths, and 1.375 million recoveries. The U.S. remained hardest hit with 1,317,852 cases and 78,463 deaths, and 221,723 recoveries. New York was still the state suffering most, with 340,472 cases and 26,581 deaths.

I remembered Pink Floyd was offering free Friday concerts, through May 15, so this was my second-to-last opportunity to catch one. They were actually pre-recorded video captures of past shows. The featured show was from Oct. 20, 1994 at Earls Court, London, UK. The footage was restored and re-edited in 2019 and re-released in early Jan. of this year. It was quite amazing to witness, having been a long long time fan.

A Mental Health article that popped up through Bloomberg news suggested that the next Covid crisis could be a wave of suicides, with a study predicting 75,000 American "deaths of despair" over the next decade, fueled by isolation, anxiety, economic hardship and substance abuse. The suicide rate in the U.S. had already been rising for the past two decades and, in 2018, hit its highest level since 1941.

Within an email, I saw a picture of a RAD POWER electric bike and clicked through. I had been interested in the technology since getting a chance to ride a couple of different versions locally. Now I was thinking that this was finally the time to buy one, certainly since there was hardly anywhere to go now that "summer had been canceled". Phil thought he would just do some quick comparison shopping for me, which he did, confirming this was a good choice and value. Minutes later, I had paid for and ordered a RadRover Electric Fat Bike Version 5 in black!

I received an email from UCONN noting that tomorrow, Sat. May 9, marked UConn's first-ever virtual commencement ceremony. "While we may be apart, we can still show the Class of 2020 that UConn Nation is here to celebrate all that they have accomplished," it stated, offering ways parents could support the occasion: view UConn Nation's videotaped words of encouragement, update your FB profile picture with an image of the Huskies mascot and phrase Celebrating #UConn20, wear your best blue and white, and tune in to the virtual commencement.

Another email rolled in, from Chilton & Chadwick "Global Real Estate Concierge", with a word about the real estate market. "With all of the tragedy Covid-19 has wrought, there is a silver lining, at least for Connecticut real estate," it began. "From the high end to the low end, we're seeing multiple offers, cash deals and, quite simply, one of the busiest markets we've ever seen before. Buyers are streaming out of New York City in a way I can only liken to refugees, and they're giving the Connecticut real estate market a steroid injection that we have needed for some time." For stats evidence: In April 2019, there were 605 single-family home sales across Fairfield County with a median sales price of $440,000. In April 2020, there were 608 single-family home sales across Fairfield County at a median sales price of $480,000 - an incredible 9.1% increase. The numbers are similar for Litchfield and New Haven counties, which have increased in the same time period 27% and 10% respectively." The mindset? "Buyers are largely thinking that if Covid-19 re-emerges or if we respond to the next pandemic as we did to this one, that they would much prefer to be in a suburb with space and land for their families than locked down in a New York apartment." The bonus? "On top of this surge in demand is a serious inventory shortage. Deals at all levels are seeing multiple offers and bidding wars because there is so little for buyers to choose from."

My FB friend Amanda, who is Vietnamese-American, was bumming out again online. She was upset over a case in Georgia — a young black guy being shot to death while out jogging. Phil was headed out for ramen and I messaged her to see if she wanted him to pick up a bowl for her, being a Fairfield local. She had already made chili though. We continued "chatting". I asked how she had been spending her time during this pandemic. "Painting, hosting Zoom events (BINGO, trivia, drunk history), kayaking, hiking, helping my friend/roommate at her brother's restaurant, spending time with my parents and siblings. I help them school my little brother while they're working," she replied. On the kayak note, I suggested we take my kayaks out together — I had been itching to go — on the next warm, clear day.

I hadn't connected the fact that 1969's celebrated Woodstock Festival was held during a time when another pandemic, H3N2, was circling the globe. According to an article by the AIER (American Institute for Economic Research), "The flu spread from Hong Kong to the United States, arriving December 1968 and peaking a year later. It ultimately killed 100,000 people in the U.S., mostly over the age of 65, and one million worldwide." In terms of lethality, "it was as deadly and scary as COVID-19, if not more so, though we shall have to wait to see."

The article writer was five years old at the time, which was just a bit older than me. He had no memory of it. "My mother vaguely remembers being careful and washing surfaces, and encouraging her mom and dad to be careful. Otherwise, it's mostly forgotten today." He wondered why that was: "Nothing was closed by force. Schools stayed open. Businesses did, too. You could go to the movies. You could go to bars and restaurants." And Woodstock took place in August 1969, during the worst period of death. Further, the stock market didn't crash, Congress didn't pass any related legislation. The Fed Reserve sat still. There were no social distancing enforcements, curve flattening or banning of crowds, etc. etc. More important at the time was the Vietnam War, the moon landing, the civil rights movement, student protests and the sexual revolution.

"The only actions governments took were to collect data, watch and wait, encourage testing and vaccines, and so on," he added. "The medical community took the primary responsibility for disease mitigation." Hopefully we would be looking back on this period at some distant point and trying to answer the "Why was this different?" question.

I read that even the White House was not "immune" to the virus, which was concerning as a threat to our highest leadership. Two days ago, one of the President's personal valets tested positive; today, VP Mike Pence's press secretary was also confirmed for the virus. The White House said Pence and Trump are both tested daily and that tests are given to anyone with whom they meet. Other staff were being checked now as the two aides came in contact with up to a dozen other people.

Instagram was full of entertainments again, in the form of live feeds. There was the lovely @sanadanielle giving makeup tips, @cameron_ dettman playing "Hey Jude" on acoustic guitar and singing, @melaniesop and her roommates making mochi rice balls and @baddcheeta doing her dj thing playing amazing beats.

I finally turned in but didn't step through the door into sleep until a couple of hours later. Keeping me up was very strong winds battering the house and rain drumming down on flat surfaces outside — car tops, windowsills, the roof. So I started "surfing" again.

One thing I was really getting frustrated about was the testing process for the virus. I was really anxious to know, in particular, if Phil and I had had Covid-19. To this regard, I read that Americans "now have two FDA-authorized options to choose from. On May 7, the FDA granted an emergency use authorization for at-home saliva collection developed by a lab at Rutgers University. The lab, RUCDR Infinite Biologics, joins LabCorp's Pixel at-home nasal swab test, which was authorized by the FDA on April 21." So, now, Americans could spit in a tube from the comfort of home, mail it in and find out if they had the virus.

New books were apparently emerging that were aimed at easing children's anxieties about the coronavirus and explaining the pandemic in simple terms. One called "The Big Thing" told the story of a school kid who becomes afraid of the goings-on and finds that all colors have turned to gray, flowers are no longer attractive and cupcakes have lost their sweetness — until her teacher asks her to look for silver linings — the lesson being that there's always a bright side in something dark. Another story was titled "My Hero Is You, How Kids Can Fight Covid-19", a collaboration between U.N. agencies and international NGOs translated into nearly 40 languages. It took children ages six to 11 on an adventure around the world to explain how to stay safe from the virus and manage difficult emotions in unfamiliar situations.

In Australia, around 4,000 wild brumbies (free-roaming feral horses) were going to be killed or re-homed while pigs, goats and deer were going to be shot by gunmen from helicopters, to remove them from Kosciuszko National Park in a move to help native wildlife recover from a hellish summer of bushfires.

I admired the artwork of NYC-based artist Sabeena Jindal, who used a lot of iconic imagery to make collage-style artworks. I was so impressed that I reached out to her to see how I might go about purchasing a piece.

The provocative headline "You might need a reservation for the beach this summer" begged a review of the related article, which was exactly what some beachgoers in Spain would be required to do this summer, thanks to Covid-19. "Canet d'en Berenguer, a Mediterranean town located just north of Valencia, will only allow 5,000 daily sunbathers on its local beach, around half the usual number, in order to maintain social distancing. These spaces will need to be reserved in advance via a mobile phone app," the article stated. I wondered if such a process might be adopted at our own beaches — but hoped not.

A Reuters article suggested that psychology would be very much in play as countries slowly reopened and we would all have to make individual choices about how — or if — we were going to get back out there. Each of us would have to ask himself, "Are we comfortable going to the office, or taking public transport to get there? Will we visit friends and, if so, should we wear masks? Can our kids go on playdates?" One psychologist opined that humans are naturally risk- and loss-averse, so where the potential penalties outweigh the possible payoffs, most people will play it safe. At the same time, our habits often guide our decisions — this lockdown hadn't been long enough to change habits that were long ingrained, and so we would be likely to fall back into those. And, yet, people were also notoriously bad at predicting their own behavior in unfamiliar situations — we might think that we would stay inside even after lockdowns lift, but that doesn't mean we would.

The nightcap was @yomaly.santiago dancing around in a crop top and pajama pants while drinking a very generous pour of white wine. The bleach blonde with black eyebrows came teasingly close to exposing her bare upper assets each time she raised her arms above her head, much to the delight of three dozen mostly men that had tapped in to watch and encouraged her with text messages.

News: NYC's Comptroller predicted that 1 in 5 workers would be jobless by the end of June and the unemployment rate for this quarter would be 22%, an unprecedented number in the post-WWII era. In another example of food producers getting smart, Florida farmers had begun selling their produce directly and quite successfully to consumers, to avoid dumping it due to distribution system breakdowns and mass restaurant closures. Six people were arrested in the Bronx for taking part in a large-scale heroin and fentanyl distribution network and the DEA seized 120,000 glassine envelopes, some of which were marked "*coronavirus*", "*Black Mamba*" *(Kobe Bryant's nickname)*, "*ISIS*", "*Hiroshima*" *and* "*Antrax*". *The U.S. unemployment rate hit 14.7% in April, the highest rate since the Great Depression, as 20.5 million jobs vanished in the worst monthly loss on record. In addition, 5.1 million other Americans had their hours reduced in April, which meant less income and, so, less spending. Roy Horn, of the Las Vegas duo Siegfried & Roy, died at age 75 of coronavirus complications.*

May 9. My eyelids were practically stuck shut when I arose this morning, bathed in sun streaming through the openings in my bedroom curtains. The sky was a perfect cloudless blue but the treetops I could see were whipping back and forth. A big wind pattern had settled on us, bringing with it temps for the day that would not top 46F, with a wind chill factor making it feel 10 to 15 degrees colder. Winter in May, lovely. Come on 2020, give… us… a… break.

Like the Beatles song, "I found my way downstairs and drank a cup" and put on a favorite radio station in the area, 95.9 The Fox, which was cranking some Guns 'n Roses. The caffeine combined with the ax grinding and sun pouring in even more intensely served to perk me up.

As ever, pandemic reminders happened quickly. This morning, it was three women walking down the street, spread six feet apart across the road, each wearing a face mask and, because of the wintry weather, winter coats, knit hats and wool gloves.

I was excited by the prospect of my morning mission: driving up to Reed Intermediate School in Newtown, CT to drop off all my accumulated cans, plastic water bottles and glass beer bottles. The organizing group wanted these items sorted out from one another to make redemption on the back end easy. The money they would then receive for the redemptions was to be donated to the local FAITH Food Pantry. It was a wonderful idea and I was glad to make the drive up. Not to mention that it was an excursion and chance for me to see what was happening during this pandemic outside of my immediate area.

I did the sorting, loaded up my trunk with five 13-gallon trash bags full of bottles/cans and set out at 9:15am. In my own neighborhood, I passed several solo joggers and walkers, each with bandanas around their necks should they have a close encounter and need to use them. Once on 95, I motored under an overpass that had a sign hanging from it "Nurses, Doctors, Hospital Staff, You Rock!", next to a large American flag.

I-95 was still a speedway, which law enforcement seemed to finally recognize, putting up digital messages like PLEASE DON'T SPEED, HELP OUR HEROES and setting up several speed traps along my route. Despite those warnings, a pickup truck passed me doing a solid 90mph.

A Mohegan Sun billboard cooed, "We love you Connecticut #inthistogether". A digital billboard, sponsored by Bridgeport's Street Factory Comedy Club, offered "Thank You Nurses".

As I turned onto the Rt. 25 connector heading north, the wind really kicked up, pushing my car around.

DrewbaQ barbecue joint in Monroe promoted curbside/takeout service. Seven Maples Gift & Garden was open for outside sales. Other places were "By appointment only", drive-through and takeout/delivery.

Blue Line Firearms & Tactical had a yellow "do not cross" caution tape ribbon strung across the whole front of the shop, appearing to bar access. I wondered what that was all about?

A roadside Farm Market housed under a tent appeared to offer locally grown produce. The staff and visitors all wore face masks.

A big sign screamed HAND SANITIZER, with "1-ounce spray bottle $4" in smaller letters.

Other shoutouts along the route: "All Healthcare Workers, 50% Off", "You Are Our Heroes!" and "Thank You, Be Safe" (in a big red heart design).

I located the Reed school, joining a line of cars funneling up to the drop-off site, where there was already a mountain of trash bags full of bottles and cans, and a group of masked-and-gloved volunteers doing the collecting from people's cars. They were all good spirited and seemed appreciative of the donations.

I took a more rural route returning home, passing a couple of horses grazing on a small farm and adverts for Pansies, Sheep Manure and Veggies. Even on this fairly untrafficked passage, there were signs like "Thank you for all the essential workers", "Heroes Work Here" and "Thank You to All the Helpers".

While up in this neck of the woods, I had hoped to call on Newtown's Reverie Brewing or Monroe's Veracious Brewing, to pick up some beer-to-go. But both didn't open until noon and it was only 10am. So I zigged to Monroe's Warehouse Wine & Spirits instead, strolling to the walk-in cooler at the back of the store to fetch some long-missed Two Roads Espressway Cold Brew Coffee Stout beer. The cashier was stationed behind a big plexiglass barrier and payment was by card via a processing machine, like the post office. As easy as 1-2-3.

Passing by some more signs, for TOILET PAPER and CASE WATER, I decided to make a "scenic" detour to the East Main Street area of Bridgeport, to take a pulse reading there. It was literally looking like the DMZ, with lots full of destroyed building debris, many vacated businesses and a long line of masked people waiting to cash checks at a MoneyServ place. I spotted a favorite place called Harlan Haus, a German beer hall, and thought I might score some takeaway. But it was shut up tighter than a beer barrel and there was no indication that they were even offering any curbside or takeout food.

When I finally got back to home base, Phil let me know that a boating safety class he was going to take in person had been moved to a virtual format, and he needed to send a check to sign up. I took care of the fee in exchange for his promise to wash my car and clean the dashboard on the next nice day.

Phil had no sooner finished his school semester, then he was busy again doing computer fixing and software upgrading work with local clients. One friend with whom I connected him came by with a laptop that needed attention. She was masked and we chatted for a moment in front of my house. She said that life hadn't really changed so drastically for her as she works from home anyway, like I do. The grocery store had been her place to run into neighbors and socialize but now everyone had been doing their best to avoid each other there, so that aspect had been taken away. She didn't mind wearing a mask either, she said, as it covered scars on her nose where she had had some sun-damaged skin removed.

As we were talking, my next door neighbors pulled in. They were already speaking to someone that had interest in buying their house. We agreed it was an excellent market. They hoped to get full fare.

My friend Amanda checked in. We had settled into a regular FB messenger chat pattern now. She was busy preparing food for Mother's Day tomorrow, a menu that included breakfast pizza, fruit salad with Cocowhip, broccoli salad, green Middle Eastern Shakshuka poached eggs, Russian meringue pavlova dessert with berries and a mimosa bar. It sounded amazing.

NY Gov. Cuomo got on the blower for the expected stats update. All the numbers gradually going down, including new cases, to 572 yesterday, which was equivalent to the number on March 20, at the very beginning of New York state's outbreak onset. Still "heartbreaking every day" and "infuriatingly constant" was the death toll for yesterday: 226 (173 in hospitals, 53 in nursing homes), despite all the state's best efforts to protect people. A new topic in his briefing was a "truly disturbing" priority concern — how the virus may be affecting very young people. "We were laboring under the impression that young people were not affected," he said. "And yet hospitals have reported 73 cases of children with symptoms similar to Kawasaki Disease or Toxic Shock Syndrome, an inflammation of the blood vessels that can cause problems with their hearts. It has already taken the lives of three young New Yorkers." These children were positive for Covid but didn't show the classic virus symptoms. In response to this new development, the CDC was creating criteria to distribute to hospital networks nationwide.

There were a couple of good things to come from this crisis. One was notification of a partial refund of the fee for Phil's dormitory space, since he only occupied the space for less than half the time he should have been there — 42 days there, 55 days out. And he wasn't even there for all of the 42 days — his Covid-like sickness kept him away from the dorm for six days.

The other upside was a $41.94 kickback from my auto insurance company. They called it a "Stay-at-Home Auto Credit", which they would be spreading out in equal installments over the remainder of the policy period for the current term.

Fairfield Ludlowe High School parents were busy cooking up ideas to celebrate this year's graduates. One mom posted in a school forum: "Ok, I just figured it out with help of hubby...went to Google Earth and counted parking spots at Jennings Beach...OVER 700!!!!!!!!!!!!!!!!!!!!!! BTW, there are 380 graduates at FLHS...not sure how many at Warde...but seems like the very perfect spot for a drive-in movie style graduation...make it short and sweet...one carload per family, streamed for the rest of the town. Streamline it (for bathroom considerations) with a quick slide show, music, speeches, drive up service, broadcast over the radios or streaming. FunFlicks does a graduation ceremony, very short fireworks at end...everyone decorates their cars and people on the streets go outside to wave to any graduates coming home." It sounded like a great solution.

In an incredible stroke of what-in-the-hellness, it began snowing here just after 5pm. Really coming down hard with huge flakes. But it only lasted about five minutes before changing to a weird heavy rain-like sleet. Just incredibly bizarre and unexpected, especially for ... May 9. #wtf

Through a personal contact at AFC Urgent Care here in Fairfield, I was able to find out about getting personally tested for the coronavirus, to see if I had the antibodies and had had the virus when I suspected I did, back in mid-January. He connected me to his office which steered me to the group's website, wherein I was guided to set up a tele-call later this afternoon with one of their providers, to be interviewed about my symptoms. In the meantime, I filled out online some required information related to my health history, personal details and insurance info.

The provider and I had a poor video connection at the appointed time, so we simply spoke by phone. I described my symptoms — body aches, chills, fever, headache, pink eye, styes, swollen and cracked lower lip — and she assessed that it was "reasonable to test me". Her admin made an appointment for me for first thing tomorrow morning at their office, where they would do a simple blood draw to send to a lab. She anticipated results in about five days, though she added it might take as many as 14, but the lower number had been their experience. We discussed Covid-19 in general. She called it a "perfect storm of a virus" and said that it was "checking all the boxes as the perfect virus to infect everyone". She had been in medicine for seven years, she shared, but had spoken with other MDs who had been in practice for 30 years or more and they said "never have they seen anything like this before."

I had to laugh about the squawk that was going on with regard to the hair salons reopening in CT as of May 20. Local ladies were all for it and couldn't wait to get fixed up, but they were balking at the safety measures that had been put in place, which were extensive and limiting, really only allowing for *partial* hair service. The regulations included: maximum 50% capacity, appointments only, waiting rooms closed, workstations six feet apart, physical barriers where possible, contactless payments preferred, tools soaked in disinfectant between clients, hand sanitizer and cleaning wipes at entrance points, high-contact areas and bathrooms cleaned frequently, limit conversation where possible, employees to wear facemarks and face shields or eye protection, employees to provide clean smock for each customer, customers to wear facemarks or cloth face coverings, increase ventilation and airflow where possible and, finally — and this one was the kiss of death apparently — blow drying hair will be prohibited.

Dad sent me an email letting me know he and my brother Dave had decided to go to the Moab Desert in Utah, in place of their now-postponed-until-next-year trip to the U.K. They planned to go May 23 and would be exploring there for a week. Then Dad was going to come see Phil and me here in Fairfield. Dave had rented an off-road Toyota Tacoma for the drive-about. I was concerned that they were going to be flying and, actually, that they were going to be anywhere near an airport or airplane. At the same time, I was curious to ultimately hear about their experience.

Dinner was a thrown-together, multi-ingredient salad along with a pour of the Espressway beer I had snagged today. The combo was a satisfying match. I chowed while sitting at the computer, keeping one eye trained on the outdoors, which had grown ominously dark and increasingly tumultuous, actually looking like a hurricane or tornado — maybe even a Sharknado — was about to strike us. The weather soup ultimately brewed into snow or sleet or freezing rain come to pelt us again, combined with very strong wind gusts that bent the trees over. Dozens upon dozens of people posted all over Facebook their captures of the crazy conditions. It was just another jaw-dropping event in the 2020 lineup that had *so far* brought us bushfires, earthquakes, the pandemic, destructive killer tornadoes, massive Murder Hornets and a Gypsy moth infestation.

Feeling like it was a night in December rather than an almost mid-May evening, I stumbled onto a pre-recorded concert featuring Dead & Company, that originally took place Feb. 24, 2018 at the Smoothie King Arena in Louisiana. I spotted Fairfield, CT-born John Mayer up there on stage, and George Porter Jr. It was a smooth jamming show.

I was so pleased to hear that Newtown's FAITH Food Pantry Drive was a HUGE success, as described by Maple Craft Foods, the organizer: "Dear Newtown. This morning's Can/Bottle & Food Drive to benefit the FAITH Food Pantry was AWESOME! We planned for two small dumpsters worth of donated refundables (about four cubic yards), and a truckload of donated food/personal items. We should have known better because THIS IS NEWTOWN!! We ended up needing three HUGE dumpsters, and three small ones because YOU dropped off 110 CUBIC YARDS of plastic bottles and cans!!! And...YOU donated FOUR truckloads of food and other high demand items!! And....YOU donated hundreds of dollars in cash, checks and gift cards!! And, so far, YOU have ordered 20 Hot Family Meals from our website that we will bring to the Food Pantry for you!! So thank YOU Newtown for being YOU!"

It was interesting to note why the Apollo 11 astronauts were quarantined when they returned from their historic moon landing mission in July 1969. According to Travel + Leisure, NASA feared they might have brought back a "moon plague". There was lots of debate and fear about it and that the moon might host extraterrestrial microorganisms that were dangerous to humans. Immediately after the capsule splashed down southwest of Honolulu, rescue divers clad in biohazard suits from U.S. Navy recovery helicopters scrubbed the hatch with iodine and threw Biological Isolation Garment suits into the capsule for the crew to put on. They and the module were then sprayed with bleach and immediately flown to an aircraft carrier where they were marched straight into a mobile isolation unit. Astronauts Armstrong, Aldrin and Collins then spent 88 hours in a modified 35-foot aluminum Airstream trailer on the USS Hornet, which NASA called the Mobile Quarantine Facility. It was basic, with six airplane seats, a small table and some bunk beds. After the carrier docked in Hawaii, the entire MQF, with the astronauts in it, was flown to Ellington Air Force Base in Houston, Texas and put into what NASA called the Lunar Receiving Laboratory. The crew spent 15 more days in the LRL behind an airlock, with ultraviolet light to kill any exotic bacteria and microbes. Everyone working in the LRL had to shower and be disinfected at the end of their working day, and they agreed to be indefinitely quarantined themselves if Moon pathogens escaped. Eventually, they were cleared by NASA's surgeon and driven home to their families.

I dropped into bed about 10 or so, and again had difficulty falling asleep right away. Once again, I found myself enjoying, in a one-sided fashion, the company of what I will call Instagram Circus Performers, like @mysterygirlradio, a dj type who was redefining "Saturday Night Live" with rap and hip-hop jams she was playing and lip-syncing to.

The Los Angeles-based homemaker mom was back on TikTok, this time dancing to Megan Thee Stallion's jam "I'm A Savage", the chorus of which goes, "I'm a savage (yeah), Classy, bougie, ratchet (yeah), Sassy, moody, nasty (hey, hey, yeah), Acting stupid, what's happening? Bitch (whoa, whoa)."

@anjlmusic, a singer, songwriter and producer, was looking lovely and brown, with an infectious smile and playful goofy attitude, crooning some original songs. I checked her recent profile posts to get some insight into her mindset. One from April 6 noted, "Life always continues to go on, no matter what. I'm sure a lot of us have been feeling lonely, isolated, bored, maybe even depressed, I know I have. I say, communicate and keep close with those who bring the sunshine to your life. Do little things that make you better than the person you were yesterday — and by that I don't mean you have to come out of this pandemic with a brand new bod, or with the next great hit song... but just do something, even something little, that keeps propelling you forward... just as life moves." Another post from April 18 noted, "This quarantine has given me a newfound confidence in myself. I've been working on my craft, working on my body, learning and doing things to love myself more. I'm eating good, and I'm surrounding myself with people that make me happy but also push me to be my best. That's all you need really."

@mariathattil, a 2020 Miss Universe Australia Finalist and spectacular looking, shapely girl in her own right, was modeling outfits, with periodic wardrobe malfunctions along the lines of Janet Jackson's infamous half-second breast exposure during the live halftime show of Super Bowl XXXVIII on Feb. 1, 2004, in a team-up with Justin Timberlake. But Maria's thoughts, judging by her posts, were deeper than she made herself seem. "If this time in our lives has taught me anything, it's that you need to romanticize the seemingly insignificant details in your life because that's when you start 'living' and you find magic in every day. Today, I'm in love with the feeling of fresh air in my lungs after a run and letting my hair down to savor that first sip of an almond latte on a Sunday." Drilling deeper, she shared, "Create the highest, grandest vision possible for your life, because you become what you believe. I'm often asked about confidence, positivity and motivation — and I think one of the most useful things I can share is that all of those things are built in the trenches. My sense of self-efficacy and faith is strengthened in moments of darkness, hardship and loneliness.

It's when I'm confused, hurting or uncertain of horizons ahead — but I still make a choice to have faith in myself, to be mindful of my intentions and energy and even if I slip up, be patient with myself. I think it's dangerous to misrepresent life as being purely an upward trajectory of growth and consistent positivity without acknowledging that a trajectory like that isn't possible without having hardship to fuel it. Even the most successful, happy people have dark moments. If you're human — it's peaks and troughs. I just think that when you're in the troughs, having a vision for your life that motivates you to persevere toward more positive horizons will build confidence."

Maria offered another perspective, on Coping With Change and COVID Anxiety. "Understanding my neurochemistry and the mind-body connection is how I cope with anxiety and uncomfortable change. How do we wake up every day and function in a global situation that is unfamiliar, unprecedented and uncertain? By changing perspective. It sounds simple. You will see quotes on the power of perspective, and I know that in drastic times, it can seem fluffy and cliché, and for me I need more. It's my mission and passion to understand the science behind perspective, and how conscious intent influences our energy, and therefore how we experience life. Choosing to use language that focuses on what you 'have' as opposed to living in a place of 'lack' can mean the difference between anxiety and resilience. It's: 'I am so lucky to have X, Y, Z in my life and I can't wait to get back to it' as opposed to 'I miss this, I'm stuck at home and can't do this.' Choosing to activate elevated emotions like 'gratitude' and 'inspiration' as opposed to suffering creates higher vibrational energy, which means we tap into something bigger in the quantum field: that which we can't see, where possibility and creation lies. Elevated emotions like that signal our genes to express themselves in a way that improves immunity, too. Choose to navigate this territory by searching for a silver lining and opportunity, I promise it'll change the way you experience reality."

In a trifecta of deep thought, she also shared, "I have a new appreciation for the ability to do something as simple as run outside, feel the sun on my skin and breathe fresh air. Now that the influx of places to go, people to see and things to do are reduced, I'm savoring and noticing the simple things in a more 'awake' sense. I'm working, exercising, e-socializing and creating from home; I've been making day plans (even for days off) to make sure that being at home for a prolonged period doesn't bleed into a blur. Choosing to appreciate what I (a) have and (b) can do at home is one way to be present comfortably in this period as opposed to wishing it away. We need to stay home to save lives and #flattenthecurve. Every day is a gift and can be meaningful if I choose, as we #LockdownForLove."

News: Music legend Little Richard passed at the age of 87 and was mourned online by musicians everywhere. Mexico had put a stop to its domestic beer production in early April, deciding that brewing was a non-essential activity. The ban has led to the smuggling of beer from the U.S., essentially fostering a "beer black market". A Ohio restaurant owner installed clear shower curtains around tables to comply with state orders to keep diners safely separated. Celebrity Chef Guy Fieri raised over $20 million for out-of-work restaurant employees. The snow squall that we experienced yesterday tied a 1977 record in NYC's Central Park for the latest snowfall of the year. Returning beachgoers left 13,000 pounds of trash on Florida's Cocoa Beach, prompting a crackdown and proving that humans are a lost cause — that we just don't learn from our experience and that any promises folks made to be more protective of the environment just went right out of the window. Global coronavirus cases topped 4.1 million, with over 280K deaths, 1.444 million recoveries. The U.S. remained hardest hit with 1,347,309 cases and over 80K deaths, with over 238K recoveries. Among states, NY had the most cases, at over 343K, and nearly 27K deaths. China reported 14 new virus cases as a high-risk area resurfaced. Similarly, South Korea reported 34 new virus cases, the highest one day number in a month.

May 10. Mother's Day. A bittersweet occasion for me having no mother in person to celebrate and now with a relationship with another mother put on pause, likely a permanent one. The day deserved a song, a tribute, to my Mom first, but also to all the mothers out there handling unprecedented challenges and fears and rambunctious children stuck at home, along with spouses who may also be home due to losing their job. It seemed appropriate to acknowledge this weekend's bizarre wintry weather, too. And, so, on my personal Facebook page, I made the following tribute: "We Need a Little Christmas" is a popular Christmas song originating from Jerry Herman's Broadway musical "Mame", and was first performed by Angela Lansbury in the title role in that 1966 production. Angela was a Londoner. My Mom loved her as a fellow Brit and enjoyed the show as well. Mom was always very cheery and singing songs around the house while she worked and at the holidays. This song was one of them, and she would likely have been singing it this weekend given this blast of wintry weather we've been hit with here in the Northeast. Perhaps she even had something to do with sending this harmless burst to us, to spur us to burrow in our homes, light a fire, make some cocoa and snuggle with our families. Seeking a little cheer, many of us during this Covid-19 crisis have put wreaths back on our front doors and strung up lights in our trees, which would certainly not have been out of place with the powdery dusting we received. With a big smile and bouncing around to the music, Mom would be singing this now… (Song lyrics inserted)… Happy Mother's Day, Mom. Thanks for the cheer. Virtual hugs. I love you and miss you. We're fighting the good fight down here. We remember what you taught us. Don't worry, we got this. Your loving son, Mike. XX" I posted this passage with a photo of Mom taken at Christmas in 2011 at my Mom & Dad's home in Chapel Hill, North Carolina, sixteen months before she passed from pancreatic cancer.

It was a fitting start to the day, I thought, and aligned well with what was turning out to be a bright, sunny morning that would evolve into an even brighter warmer day, with temps aiming to hit 60F. It would be pleasant enough for folks to get out and celebrate their Moms in the best way possible given the myriad of restrictions that remained in place for our safety and as precautions to prevent the further spread of Covid-19.

On my agenda, of course, which I looked forward to with both excitement and apprehension, was my appointment to get tested for the virus antibodies. Had I had a bout with the disease in January? I was so curious to know. I re-checked the address for the AFC office where my blood was to be drawn: 1918 Black Rock Turnpike, Fairfield. 1918. As in the year the Spanish Flu killed off 50-100 million people worldwide. *That* 1918. Coincidence? There's no such thing, according to my Dad.

I got on my way around 9am, passing more lawn signs on the way — the great new dominant communication devices these days. "HATE WON'T MAKE US GREAT", speaking to hate crimes and biases that have been emerging. A congrats to a Providence College graduate. Another congrats to a Fairfield Warde High School graduate, tagged #mustangpride, referring to the mascot. "Health Care Heroes Today and Every Day!" posted in front of My Salon Suites, a corral of independent hair care salons.

I pulled up at AFC and the receptionist, Julie, ushered me in and to a patient room. Soon, a tech, Amber, appeared, to draw my blood. She assessed that I had "deep veins", and tried a draw twice at the elbow of my left arm and then twice from a vein on the top side of my left hand. Nothing. Concerned about continuing to stick me, she summoned a practitioner, Janet, who then tried a vein at the top of my right hand. Success, but a slow draw, during which I tried a couple of things of my own initiative to spur the blood to come out — deep breathing, making a fist, etc. Finally, Amber was able to collect in a small tube the 3ML (about 1/10 of an ounce) the lab required. They put bandages on the "prick" sites, let me know I would likely have results within 48 hours and sent me on my way. All in all, a pretty efficient process, I thought.

I went wide, as I tend to do, on the ride back, going to the northeastern part of Fairfield to see what I could see. Again, more signs, but different. Like a lawn sign "NO TOLLS" which was unrelated to the crisis and revisited a sore issue in the state. In a window: INSPIRED. AMERICA. BE STRONG. In front of the Sunrise of Fairfield assisted living facility in big, cap, free-standing orange letters, "THANK YOU HEROES". Then I passed some fellas playing a round of golf at Brooklawn Country Club, the shuttered-for-the-academic-year Fairfield Warde High School, the dark McKinley Elementary School, a couple of spirits shops, Andros Diner, and a bustle of activity curbside at Hansen's Flower Shop and Isabelle et Vincent French bakery. Near the latter, I was fortunate to stumble on the good old Tasty Yolk food truck from which I scored a couple of "Pigs" to shuttle home. My last look was at a half dozen lawn flamingoes and a sign in the midst of them that read: "We know you might be feelin' blue, Stuck inside nothin' to do, So here's our flock six feet apart, We hope it brings joy to your heart." The family had been "flocked". What a great community gesture.

When I got back home, I made a much-needed pot of coffee… *and called Jen.* I knew she would likely be home alone and felt I should *at least* wish her a Happy Mother's Day. She was still in bed, in the pajamas that I had given her (she pointed out) and seemed happy to hear from me. She mentioned the weird weather yesterday — I agreed it was certainly out of season. We closed by wishing each other a good day.

I took a loop around my property and had a quick word with a neighbor who was strolling by with his two young girls, giving "mom" a little peace to herself. He remarked about the odd weather yesterday, too, and we were both happy that the temp would be rising.

A while later, NY Gov. Cuomo gave his briefing. Hospitalizations down, intubations down, new cases 521 which was "down but still very high" and "right back to where we started this hellish journey (Mar. 20)". Deaths were also down, at 207 yesterday, equivalent to the number late March, about a week into the lockdown. Despite that number being better, Cuomo remarked that it was "still terribly high". Most disturbing was that, of those fatalities, 164 had been in hospitals while 43 *were in nursing homes*, a stat that segued into the next part of his briefing, the "top priority" topic of nursing homes and how to better protect their residents and seniors.

To that regard, Cuomo said that NY state had the highest population of nursing home residents, 101,518, of any state in the country. And yet, NY ranked 34th in terms of the percentage of deaths in nursing homes compared with all deaths in the state (West Virginia had the highest share, at 81%). Still, how could the state be doing a better job? It was already restricting visitations except for end-of-life and requiring PPE for staff. But now he was implementing the following: if the home couldn't give the highest care, the residents were to be transferred out and facilities could potentially lose their licenses. Staff would be tested twice a week. Hospitals couldn't discharge a patient to a nursing home unless the patient was negative for the virus.

Cuomo's other focus of concern was on the children: the NYS DOH was actively investigating now 85 *cases* of the COVID-related illness in children. Finally, he was looking at May 15, the date later this week when NY's PAUSE order was set to expire. The state would be assessing all parts of the state to see which areas were safest to begin re-opening.

The day became very pleasant as it wore on and I plopped down in my back porch folding chair for a bit, watching Phil work on his motorcycle, which he set up near the back patio. Then I cooked up a pasta, sausage and veg dish with marinara and plopped down at the computer, with some classical music as a peaceful background.

"FOMO" (Fear of Missing Out) popped up as a term for a legitimate human reaction to crisis. With much of our summer plans canceled by Covid-19, a psychologist suggested some ways to temper it: thinking outside the box, not letting life reflect the current situation and doing what you can to take control of your own reality, while also taking the safety of others into consideration.

On another "mental" note, it was suggested that talking to yourself sometimes can actually be a healthy thing. It allows us to sort through our thoughts in a more conscious manner. It also sparks memory and creates a stronger association between language and visual targets. All good to note as many of us were spending so much time by ourselves these days, my Dad as an example.

There was a great sun glow coming from the west that lured me to get in the car and zip over to Sasco Beach for a little walkabout. The sailboarder guy was there, packing up from his afternoon outing. I paced out to the end of the jetty to look out over the Sound, did a loop up and back on the beach, and then motored back through my Beach Area neighborhood, seeing a couple of guys from Sea House Clambakes masked and gloved delivering lobsterbake dinners to an Oldfield Road home, a trio of teens biking, and various joggers going to and fro. Penfield Beach looked clean and the flats were visible as it was low tide. I walked out and around a bit, coming up past the kayak racks and then shuttled back home.

The IG Circus had begun, led by @julie.meka, who was showing us her family's barbecue gathering and introducing viewers to various guests, including her pop. Julie terms herself a "restaurant entrepreneur". She posted her desire to go to Jamaica as her "first trip after lockdown."

It was worthy to note that today was Day 60 of Quarantine — that is, 60 days since our local schools shut down and everyone went panic grocery shopping, on March 12. Sixty days since our lives drastically changed, potentially for good. Certainly we may never do some things the same again. Time would tell.

The Pentagon seemed to be preparing for the worst as it looked forward toward that potential Second Wave that had been threatened. As an illustration of that forward planning, the government reactivated its underground command center — NORAD's Cheyenne Mountain in Colorado — as backup homeland defense headquarters for the duration of the pandemic. Its personnel was living in isolation to prevent them from contracting the virus. Carved out of solid granite and fitted with 25-ton steel doors securing the entrance, the facility was designed to survive a nuclear attack. Buildings inside sit on giant 1,000-pound steel springs to absorb the shock of a nuclear blast. At its peak, it housed 1,800 U.S. and Canadian military staff living in dormitory-style housing with access to cafeterias, food, water and electricity.

Just after nightfall — as I was setting my disco globe going in the front window — a Channel 3 TV news guy popped up on Facebook with an early warning about an "afternoon situation" tomorrow. He was broadcasting from home and had broken his leg, so was hobbling around and trying to avoid his dogs as he switched from one display to another. He reported that potentially severe thunderstorms, small hail and gusty wind was headed for our area, to arrive in the 1-8pm window. Sure, why not? This was the pandemic. All normal weather bets were off!

I turned in at my usual time but wasn't able to drop off straight away. The star performer was @ikadewiyoga aka Ika Dewi, a Balinese yoga teacher with a YouTube channel and all. She was silently performing stretches at first, expecting folks that had tuned in to follow her I supposed. I checked her profile and sparked to one recent post: "When this is over, may we never again take for granted: a handshake with a stranger, full shelves at the store, conversations with neighbors, a crowded theater, Friday night out, a taste of communion, a routine check-up, the school rush each morning, each deep breath, a boring Tuesday, the beach, life itself." Good stuff.

Another Performer was @jennieislate aka Jennie Gall, a self-described entrepreneur, mother of three boys and two Bengal cats, a pilates studio owner and, apparently, an enjoyer of whiskey, as she presented various ornate, high-end bottles and offered some background and tasting notes.

Then, in Circus Ring #3, there was @kaylafitz3 aka Kayla Fitzgerald, who had appeared in the TV series "Amazing Race", Season 30, and was a Sports Illustrated "SISWIMSEARCH top 15 competitor. Indeed, "Fitz" was fit and, tonight, was joined by a friend and the two of them were going through a step-by-step process of making a healthy salad, while sipping from colorful goblets of wine.

News: A 26-year-old surfer was attacked and killed by a shark in the Santa Cruz area in Northern California. Ironically, the adjacent beach was only open for water sports; otherwise, it had been closed to the general public from 11 a.m. to 5 p.m. daily, due to Covid-19. Very dry conditions, record high temperatures and strong winds had led to more fires — over a dozen — in northern Florida.

May 11. My sleep was not great. I woke at 1, then again at 3, and finally, for good, at 5:30am. For a bit, I lay in bed and checked news stories...

One was about Antartica and the fact that it was the only continent in the world that had managed to remain virus-free. And because the region was descending into winter, when it would become completely cut off, it would likely *stay* virus-free, for the near term at least. Around 5,000 people called the icy continent home — scientists, researchers and the like, residing and working in 80 or so bases. Despite the harsh climate, an admin there shared by email, "I really don't think there's a person here right now who isn't grateful to be here, and to be safe." A British colleague of hers, who worked as a field guide, shared that, being so far removed, he didn't realize how serious the situation had become. "I remember the reports coming out of China in early January," he said, "then the first U.K. cases, and thinking that this was something minor and far away, that wouldn't affect me. It dawned on me gradually, as it spread and grew in prominence in the media." At the same time, it was difficult for him to connect to the event. "It's like being on the Moon and looking down. We can see what's going on, but it's a long way away," he said. The region, of course, had tourist appeal — over 78,000 people were expected to visit during the 2019-2020 season, but stations began putting restrictions on visits early in the year as the virus began to spread around the world. The region was later put into lockdown, with all tourist visits canceled. That took place after a close call, in which a group of Australian and New Zealand passengers on a visiting ship evacuated after nearly 60% of those on board tested positive for the virus.

Another story discussed why near-empty planes continued to fly during this time. For American, for example, 99% of their flights were less than 20% full. One recent JetBlue flight was forced to fly from New York to Albuquerque, NM with only *six* passengers on board because of *who* was on the return flight: medical professionals going to NY to help with the virus response, flagged as high priority. While airlines had grounded most flights (three-quarters of their capacity, in fact, reducing traffic by more than 90%), they were locked into instances like these, either because of operational reasons, transporting flight crews, travelers with essential business, key top customer clients or families headed to funerals, births or other life events. American's SVP for network strategy said, "As strange as this sounds, now our obligation to customers has actually never been more important and, also, unfortunately, never less profitable." I wondered how Mom would have dealt with this crisis, if she had been a stewardess today. I guessed with the professionalism, sense of duty and cheer she had always exuded in times of hardship.

I read the awful news that a police officer in an SUV patrolling a beach in Indian Shores, a town in Pinellas County on the west central coast of Florida, accidentally drove over the hips of a 66-year-old man lying on the sand. Neither her speed or any impairment were factors — she likely didn't see him. It made me think about the cop in the quad at our own beach. His vehicle was much smaller but he was whipping it around when I saw him. And yet, no one here was yet allowed to lie on the beach, so at present there was no opportunity for him to run anyone over.

With a cup of coffee in hand, I peered out the window and was really glad to see that a couple had moved into and begun to furnish the adjacent house. No, not my neighbor's house next door, but a large red birdhouse in my backyard. A couple of small domestic birds — house wrens — had apparently signed an imaginary contract with my invisible broker and were busy this morning loading in twigs and making it plush for, no doubt, some new little occupants they were expecting. I would be glad in coming days to see their activities. There were four compartments, with four "windows" per compartment. The couple appeared to have moved into the ground floor west space. Let's call it 1W in an area I began referring to as Uptown West (the actual orientation geographically). A lovely spot, really, with great morning light, a park nearby (the open lot on the other side of my back fence), adjacent to the Botanical Gardens (my garden of sea grasses and wildflowers), a short jaunt from a popular midtown restaurant (my bird feeder), patio access and late afternoon shade, especially welcome in the summer, provided by overhanging maples.

I'm sure my Westport-based artist friend, Nina Bentley, would be pleased about my new feathered tenants, too. She built my birdhouse as a commentary about rising property prices in her town. Small white tiles glued to the front, now faded, had spelled out "Westport Affordable Housing" and, initially, there were a few decorative birds glued here and there to the outside. I won the structure in a silent auction presented by Project Return, a local therapeutic group home residence supporting adolescent girls in crisis. Local artists volunteered to create a wide array of creative bird abodes that guests could bid on — 100% of the funds were dedicated to the charity. Originally, Nina's birdhouse lived inside my house but it occupied a lot of space and wasn't being appreciated like I thought it could be. A light bulb went off in my head and the expression "for the birds", meant to describe something useless, took on a completely opposite meaning. A couple years back, I bought a metal post with a brace meant to connect to and support a mailbox, attached the birdhouse to the top of it and placed it upright and level in a hole in my garden, securing it in place with poured cement. Like the other "cat" birdhouse on the opposite side of the garden that I had recently refurbished and re-installed, I even fitted it with a copper roof to help protect it from the elements. I photographed the modified finished structure and sent the pic to Nina, much to her delight and amusement. Now I had just left her a phone message to share the wrens story, and check on her at the same time.

I had been receiving "your weekly boost" emails from Fitbit, the company that makes the wrist-worn exercise tracking device of the same name. The missives offered supportive messaging about balance, nutrition and workout tips aimed to get users moving. My eldest son Evan had bought one of these devices for me a couple of years back, for Father's Day, and, initially, I got a ton of use out of it, challenging myself all the time to go further and take more steps, set new personal records. But then one day it fell into disuse, and stayed disused, sitting sadly in a clay bowl with other wristbands and knick-knacks. And, now, here was another of those emails in my inbox. A lead-off encouragement: "If the line between weekdays and weekends is getting blurry, try these tips to put the fun and relaxation back in your Friday-to-Sunday stretch." Another nudge: "No gym, no problem — Fitbit data shows how users everywhere are getting creative with exercise these days." Yet another poke: "If you've got someone at home who's down to sweat it out with you, these partner workouts are a perfect way to mix things up." Very smart marketing, with messaging tailored to the pandemic and its resulting effects and restrictions — blurred sense of time, closed gyms, exercise companions limited to family or intimate partners. They even offered an opportunity to join an upcoming high-energy workout session on Instagram Live every Monday through May 25. All of this spurred me to pull the battery from my wristband, pop it in the USB charging accessory and get it prepared for the beach walks I had begun taking again, now that we were allowed back to the shore.

I was suddenly on a high, until the next email, tagged "11 Body Odors You Shouldn't Ignore". Though no doubt replete with helpful health information, I didn't want to topple the Jenga tower of good feeling that I'd just built! Delete.

Beer Connoisseur elevated me again, with its daily email that included a bit about a Belgian Pale Ale beer called Pride & Purpose that a Richmond, CA brewery had just released. Its push: "Pretty much everything about our daily lives has changed, but one thing has stayed the same: our love for the city of Richmond. The city of 'Pride and Purpose' has always been defined by industriousness, perseverance, grit and determination, and we proudly stand with our neighbors as we navigate the road to recovery. As a small business, we have been affected just as much as everyone else by the COVID-19 pandemic, but we're dedicated to doing our part, and what we do best is craft great beer." Further, the brand pledged to donate 20% of the proceeds from the sale of this special release to support the Richmond Rapid Response Fund, to meet the immediate and ongoing needs of its community during the pandemic and beyond... Another example of smart marketing. A nod to America, #stayingstrong message, small business appeal and charity hook. Win, win, win, win for all.

An email from Sacred Heart University dangled the opportunity to join the school's Athletics and Alumni Association for a virtual lunch May 13 to celebrate Bobby Valentine's 70th birthday. Together, with three former New York Mets — Ron Darling, Wally Backman and Lee Mazzilli— Bobby would be sharing stories about the 1986 World Series Championship and talking about baseball's past, present and future. To participate, you just needed to make a minimum donation of $10, which I immediately did, that would go to help support student-athletes. Notably, Valentine managed the Mets and was the current executive director of athletics at SHU. Darling was an All-Star pitcher who played for the Mets from 1983-1991. Backman was a second basemen for the Mets from 1980-1988. And Mazzilli was an All-Star outfielder who had two stints with the Mets and managed the Baltimore Orioles in 2004 and 2005. They were all childhood heroes of mine.

An email from our Bridgeport Sound Tigers hockey team brought the sad news that, this morning, the American Hockey League announced that its 2019-20 regular season and Calder Cup Playoffs had been officially canceled due to Covid-19. "While we know this is not the outcome we were all hoping for, the health and safety of our players, fans and staff remains our top priority. As we now shift our focus to the off-season, we will be devoting our time and energy into creating a memorable experience for you, your friends and your family during the 2020-21 season," the email detailed. IF there is even going to *be* a 2020-21 season, I thought to myself.

Mid-morning, my phone flashed and beeped with two alerts from MyRadar: "Light rain starting in 20 minutes" and "Risk of severe weather in your area within the next 24 hours." Welcome to life in 2020.

Phil called down from upstairs suddenly, "Dad! There's a possum with three babies on its back in the backyard!" Sure enough, there it was, a scruffy-looking Mama possum with three sizable babies clinging to its back! I had never before seen this live (a possum with babies, not just a possum in general) and certainly not up close and personal in my backyard! For a bit, I watched it prowl around, under Phil's car, around the back of the house, under the neighbor's car. I even researched possums to get the 411 on what they eat to see if there was anything I could offer them. Their diet was pretty broad, like a raccoon's: small rodents, insects, worms, slugs, snails, frogs, birds, vegetables, berries, nuts, fruit, garbage, pet food and bird seed. Thinking quickly, I scooped up some trail mix, put it in a shallow dish and placed it near where it had paused. But it got spooked and scurried under our back gate into the adjacent wooded lot. I expected it would be back though and assumed it had a nearby burrow. Apparently, they don't make their own shelters — they take cover in dens and nests abandoned by other animals like skunks or foxes, or they will live in a shed, old building, cavities within rocks, brush piles, hollow trees and fallen logs. There was a brush pile immediately on the other side of my back fence and I'd put money on it that they were in there. I took the tray of trail mix and tossed its contents over the fence in that direction. My Wild Kingdom moment of the morning.

Just past the noon hour and being mindful that rain would eventually be arriving, I decided to dart out to just clear my mind, heading in the direction of the beach. I motored first past Roger Sherman Elementary School, which both my boys had attended. Signs barred each entrance to the fenced-in playing field: "FIELD CLOSED, NO TRESPASSING". It was sad to see these spaces banned and disused, when normally they would be centers of laughter, exercise and friendly competition. But, of course, they had to be closed for those very reasons — many people in close quarters could potentially create a virus flare-up with so many asymptomatic carriers about.

Another big sign red-flagged the school's playground: BE SAFE, STAY OUT DUE TO COVID-19. The sign was positioned near the road, in about the same spot where good old Mr. Wright the ice cream man used to park his truck to serve treats and give out free squares of gum to students after school. Now the spot just looked lifeless and sad.

A redeeming high point was all the signs lining the school's parking lot: "WE HAVE AMAZING EDUCATORS!" each of them read at the top, with the names of individual teachers written in at the bottom. So thoughtful.

I pulled into the lot at Jennings Beach as a Fairfield police SUV was pulling out, and parked in a spot. Stepping wide around a discarded face mask laying on the ground (this was becoming maddeningly commonplace), I walked up and over a rise to the beach and turned east toward the long cement fishing pier. I regarded the inlet and, beyond that, the South Benson Marina, noticing that many local residents had put their boats in the water, ready for the season. As I stood there, I noticed one of several benches facing the water, with a small plaque reading: In memory of Marilyn Lawton Riley: "Sun, seagulls and a good book is all it took. 2013." Nice that.

The tabled seating area at Jennings Pavilion was devoid of people, of course. Posters there advertised summer ice cream and popsicle treats, seeming throwbacks to a whole other period of human history. I wondered if these were something we would ever be able to enjoy at the beach again, or if the snack bar there would even be able to open. Heck, if the operator would even be in a financial position to open it. Maybe he had already scrapped the business and moved on.

Circling back to the Post Road, I spotted a "Vehicle Sanitation Done Here" sign in front of Maritime Chevrolet. It was the first time I'd seen such a thing. This was way beyond the kind of detailing and interior cleaning done at car washes.

I noticed that Circle Diner had put a large, almost mini billboard-sized announcement by the road, practically shouting "Open for Take-out,

Outdoor Seating Available 5-20-20". It seemed like a desperate cry for business.

At the adjacent Circle Hotel, two guys worked from the basket of a cherry picker to whitewash over a mural that said "Hey Good Looking" that had been there for the past several months. I called up to one of them asking if it was going to be replaced by another mural, getting confirmation that, yes, Westport artist (and my friend) Leslie Cober-Gentry was going to be creating a Springtime-themed mural in its place. I was excited for her!

A sign on the door at Craft 260 Kitchen & Beer Bar said "Keep Calm, We Have Food & Booze To Go". I would have ordered a burger but they didn't seem to be open. What was certainly open though was a new Mexican Food, Pizza & Deli takeout place called Takito Feliz. The couple that owned it was inside and eager for business. Both wore face masks — his breathing was causing his glasses to fog up, which had become a common problem for the bespectacled among us. In terms of other safety measures, they had hung clear plastic sheets from the ceiling to screen off the order counter. I asked for what turned out to be a very delicious Torta — a Mexican sandwich consisting of breaded chicken, avocado, lettuce, onion, tomato, mayo, jalapeños and Oaxaca cheese. I promised the couple I would help spread the word about their business.

Moving east, I circled through the back neighborhoods of Black Rock, eventually steering by Showcase Cinemas, a favorite movie theater. It had closed January 20 and was boarded up with plywood. Its marquis, that would normally list what was playing, was bare. Heartbreaking.

OSG MRI, a diagnostic imaging business, had a colorful THANK YOU sign and big heart in its window. The heart appeared to have been signed by staff, though I couldn't be sure.

Up in the Whole Foods Market shopping center, a Five Guys burger joint had an OPEN sign, drawn by a child, in the window.

As I pointed my 15-year-old boat of a car back toward home, I thought that, since I had some time, I would swing by and see my friends at Penfield Service Center, to get the oil and transmission fluid changed and just get another business owner perspective during this pandemic. I chatted with Bob, the owner, about the craziness of the whole situation, how he decided to just press on with the business instead of shutting down and taking a loan, and all the sanitizing they had to do all the time to keep everyone safe. Bob had a loyal base of customers, anyhow, and that certainly helped matters.

We talked about my Merc, too. It had served me well over the years, but was the wrong kind of vehicle for me at this stage in my life, being divorced, a mostly empty nester, not driving a family around any more. I didn't need a big sedan but a light-duty pickup, not too large, something to make dump runs and Home Depot treks in, but that still offered a comfort factor.

There was probably no better time, actually, to consider a new vehicle, and if we needed to flee to the mountains and congregate with rebel forces should the country go south, like in that "Red Dawn" movie, then I would have a new, trusty ride that could tackle hills. So, on that note, I put my resident gear-head, Phil, on the case of finding and recommending to me a new ride. We put the "wheels" in motion, reaching out as a first step to the very Chevy dealer that had the car sanitation sign out in front of it that I had seen earlier, to inquire about their Silverado, one of three pickups that Phil thought would be right for me. The other two were a GMC Canyon and a Ford Ranger. It was suddenly exciting to consider the prospect of having a new vehicle, something I hadn't had in over a decade.

The weather warnings we received really didn't pan out, though a couple local areas reported some thunder and hail. Here in my Fairfield Beach Area, the afternoon went from gray to rain to sun to gray to hard rain back to sun, more rain, then a clearing and wind. It just couldn't make up its mind, behaving like a child having a hissy fit.

A Nat Geo article painted a picture of what a post-pandemic commute might look like: touchless payment, seats spaced farther apart on divider-filled vehicles, drivers isolated in ventilated compartments, occupancy a quarter of what it was, and passenger flow monitors that detect when there might be overcrowding to reroute people and spread them out.

I read about the case of a 54-year-old California man who spent 64 days in the hospital battling the virus — half of that time on a ventilator — which attacked all his vital organs (heart, liver, kidneys). His recovery was so unexpected that doctors and nurses started referring to him as "our miracle patient".

In a look at how the rental car industry was handling virus challenges, an email from Alamo shared their Complete Clean Pledge, to make customers "feel confident and excited about traveling again when the time is right". To that regard, they promised that "all vehicles rented from Alamo are cleaned and sanitized after every rental. In addition to washing, vacuuming and general cleaning, we use a disinfectant to sanitize with a particular focus on more than 20 high-touch points throughout the vehicle." The email shared pictures of both the inside and outside of a vehicle and labeled touch-points which included key/key fob, steering wheel, steering column, seat belts, center console, door interiors, door pockets, interior door handles and more.

News: Ireland sent a six-figure donation to Navajo and Hopi families to help them get through the pandemic, as a thanks for a donation by the Choctaw Nation to the Irish more than 170 years ago, when Ireland was starving during the 1845-1849 Potato Famine. Connecticut was experimenting with creating Covid-only nursing facilities for elderly people affected by the virus, as a way of protecting other healthy seniors in assisted living venues. A guy in Florida staged a protest in Pinellas County to urge the governor to let gyms reopen, mainly to get gym people back to work. When news crews arrived, participants started doing push-ups and squats on the street. Another downside of the pandemic was a sharp reduction in donated organs and transplant procedures. In part, the reduction was because transplant centers were unable to use organs from deceased individuals who showed evidence of virus infection. As if the Covid crisis didn't present enough challenges, an unusual strain of hepatitis that can pass from rats to humans was spreading in Hong Kong, where it was first discovered in 2018. Scientists were baffled as to how it "travels" and what could be done to prevent future infections. China's Wuhan city, the birthplace of the pestilence that we have been confronting, said it was planning to test its entire population of 11 million residents for the virus, after a handful of new cases emerged in recent days. Global coronavirus cases surged past 4.2 million with nearly 286K deaths, 1.5 million recoveries. Among countries, the U.S. remained hardest hit, with 1,378,077 cases and 81,225 deaths, 259,092 recoveries. Among states, New York was still most impacted, with 345,987 cases and 26,874 deaths.

May 12. I was up an hour before sunrise. Why? I had no idea. As usual, I wasn't ready to spring right out of bed, so scrolled through all the things I normally scroll through.

The morning was clear but a little chilly yet — 43F with a real-feel of 36F — so I let the shower water run a while to get the bathroom steamy. And as I did, I peered out the window, catching an eyeful of an enormous red-tailed hawk, the size of a Boeing 707, circling ominously above the trees at the back of my property and, in particular, over the brush pile that I suspected contained my new possum friends. You could see the fear the hawk created, as squirrels and other birds scattered and fast flew away in a multitude of directions.

After I put a pot of coffee on, I strolled out back to put some seeds in the bird feeder and to just check on my friends. I didn't see Mrs. Possum or the kids, and The Wrens were happily chirping and hovering around their new home, so the "community" appeared to have gotten through the brief panic intact.

We'd all been moaning about canceled events but could you imagine the heartache of not attending one that had been held for the past 5,000 years? Since 3,000 years before Christ was born? But that was exactly what had happened at Stonehenge, in Wiltshire, England, perhaps the world's most famous prehistoric monument, which served as an enclosure where prehistoric folks buried their cremated dead. The English Heritage group that maintains the site decided to nix this year's June 21 summer solstice celebrations "for the safety and well-being of attendees, volunteers and staff" in light of the Covid-19 crisis. The charity planned, however, to stream a ceremony on its social media.

A family went all out to make their son's 7th birthday a memorable one during this pandemic, creating a drive-in movie theater setting so the boy could watch a film with his friends. They called their project the "Quarantine Movie Cinema", or QMC for short, transforming the outside of their home with a 12-foot screen and supplied treats and tickets. There was even a red carpet runway made from red tablecloths and a giant popcorn box prop. The boy's guests watched the film with him from their cars, parked curbside, while he and his family watched from the living room couch, which they had hauled out onto the front lawn.

I popped back outside for a stroll around, spotting my neighbor across the street busy in his yard. He asked how I was doing and I replied, "Another day in pandemic paradise." He said, "At least the sun's out," to which I said, "But it still feels like December." He agreed, "Yeah, it *is* a little chilly."

I had forgotten what fun it was to wear my FitBit bracelet, given its interactive nature with my iPhone. Mid-morning, for instance, I got a notice that I had earned a Penguin March Badge, for walking 70 "lifetime" miles. That is, I appeared to have walked 70 cumulative miles since owning my

FitBit, which equated to the distance of the "March of the Penguins" — the annual trip Emperor penguins make to their breeding grounds. I was apparently doing "swimmingly" well.

I read a Kaiser Health News bulletin that indicated that seniors had begun to modify their living wills to specify "no intubation", that is, if they contracted the virus, they did not want to be put on ventilators to try and save them, which is usually fruitless at that stage. Said one Denver senior, "I don't want to put everybody through the anguish."

Another item suggested that Americans were creating a new economic threat by "slashing their spending, hoarding cash and shrinking their credit card debt as they feared their jobs could disappear" during the virus crisis. These were smart strategies, of course, in the face of uncertainty. In fact, in March, U.S. credit card debt fell by the largest percentage in more than 30 years while "savings rates climbed to levels unseen since Ronald Reagan was in the White House." The downside of "hunkering down" though is that it "poses a risk to the recovery in an economy dominated by consumer spending," a so-called V-shaped recovery that can't happen if consumers are sitting on the sidelines.

I was in the mood to bust out of jail again, to parts not recently visited, so hopped in the car and started heading east toward Bridgeport, following the Post Road initially. I revisited the Circle Inn, the side of which was now white, awaiting my Westport artist friend to start her mural work. Then I took a loop over to the waterfront, specifically St. Mary's by the Sea, where there was a popular walking path at a cliff's edge. There was a Bridgeport patrol car parked right at the start of the path and red signs with white letters at intervals along the curb saying "NO PARKING this side of the street, tow away zone, temporary Bridgeport Police Order". The city really did not want you loitering there for any reason, but was permitting walking and running, which many people were doing. It was nice to just be able to pause and look out at Long Island Sound for a moment and see Fayerweather Island Lighthouse, which had stood strong against the elements since 1808. Further along, I looped in and out of the parking lot at Black Rock Yacht Club and would have done the same at Port 5 National Association of Naval Veterans' clubhouse, but its gates were shut tight, and blocked by two cars.

In contrast, I was happy to find the gates open at Captain's Cove Seaport, though there were "Social Distancing Please" signs posted here and there. Yachts, motor boats and sailboats all stood in dry dock, waiting on a GO signal that would hopefully come soon. Other than a couple of guys walking about, the property was deserted. I strolled the sun deck and looked out at the harbor, and had to crack a little smile seeing a 15-foot tall wooden toy soldier statue with a surgical mask slung across its nose and mouth. Another upside was a sign on the door of the cafe there, which read "Opening Day, Friday May 22nd". I knocked on the door to catch the attention of someone cleaning inside to confirm the veracity of the post. I was glad for permittee Jill Williams that she would be able to restart her business.

Around the bend, I visited my friend Michelle's cafe, South on Bostwick Cantina & Grille, which was also not open and there was no word or posting or phone message to indicate when or if it *might* reopen. There was another police car parked on that road and, in general, the city seemed more militant in feel than Fairfield. Almost everyone had masks on, no matter what they were doing — walking, outdoors working, strolling with a pet.

Back towards home, the Hole in the Wall sandwich shop, where it was rumored a staff member had contracted the virus and died, teens waited on the patio for their orders to be ready.

A little before 2pm, I summoned Phil and the two of us drove to Maritime Chevrolet back out on Fairfield's Post Road. I was keeping an appointment I made with sales person Nelda, who was going to show us a Colorado light-duty pickup truck. We approached the front door and reviewed a sign tacked to it which listed extensive rules. "WELCOME! We're glad you're here", it began, but then got down to business, led with a graphic of a STOP sign: "Please stop here until we come to greet you. Proper face covering is required beyond this point. To ensure the safety of our community, we've implemented the following: Only 2 clients in our reception area at once. Everyone is to keep a safe 6 feet apart. If you are sick or experiencing any flu-like symptoms, please do not enter our facility. We will welcome you back when you're feeling better. Your vehicle will be disinfected prior to & after any vehicle servicing. Ask us about PermaSafe complete vehicle sanitation."

I may have jumped the gun by opening the door myself for, as soon as I put one foot inside, I was met quite sternly by a manager who held up his hand and said, "STOP" and "Can I help you?" He was masked as were two other employees behind him. I told him we had a test drive appointment — he had us wait outside for Nelda. I had to say I was put off, as that was our first touchpoint. Nelda emerged moments later, wearing a stylish black face mask, and actually held out her bare hand to shake mine, to which I took a step back and said, "Whoa, we're not supposed to do that." And she said, "Oh my gosh, you're right, I'm so sorry." It was an awkward moment and was likely going to be a repeated scenario as we all gradually came back together again in public spaces.

Nelda led us to our test drive vehicle and I had to share with her that I was miffed about the aggressive reception. She apologized on her manager's behalf and explained that his mother and sister had both recently died from Covid-19. I was sorry to hear it, but thought that maybe he would be better off taking some time off at home. She seemed to agree but didn't say so, and popped inside for keys, a contract and plate. Phil looked over the truck while I peered over a barrier at Mo's Wine & Spirits, which was fulfilling orders from a table in front of their building; and at Wash Tub Laundry, which had a green poster board sign in the window: "We are open. Stay 6' away from others. Start machine. Go to your car in between wash and dry." These were certainly different times and this was how businesses were adapting. Really, it was surreal.

Finally, after Nelda disinfectant-wiped the keys, door handles and steering wheel for us, and I had signed a liability waiver, we climbed aboard for a fast loop around the neighborhood, except it was anything *but* fast. The dictated route was more congested than it had been in recent times and we really couldn't let the truck out any faster than 10 miles an hour — certainly not ideal for getting the feel of the vehicle. But the ride in general seemed like that of a Nissan Pathfinder I had owned in the past, right down to the exterior and interior colors, and I was satisfied. The challenge now was for her to find the model and color I wanted amongst their regional associates, as the model I preferred was not on their own lot. And that was how we left it, for the moment.

I had the opportunity to speak with two other dealer representatives — one at Ford, about the Ranger, and one at GMC, about the Canyon — during the course of the afternoon. The GMC lead seemed pretty much a no-go — in short, we weren't singing the same song. Ford, on the other hand, seemed the most promising, even compared with Chevy, though accessories could be an issue at this time as plants and subcontractors were either closed or at bare bones operation. I could always add the accessories on later, I figured, so I told the rep, whose name was Evan like my eldest son, not to let that hold him up.

The sun had really burst forth by late afternoon, though it was quite windy, gusting up to 25mph. Phil and I had a nice visit from some family friends, Shivani and her mom, Dinal, who came to drop off a face mask that Shivani had sewn herself that had a UConn Huskies design on the front. She had been making these for medical students and healthcare workers as a community support effort. Like Phil, she was a UConn student, though a year ahead of him — about to be a senior vs. a junior. The two of them, who didn't know each other before, hit it off and she offered to be his tour guide at the Storrs campus, IF they were able to go back to school there in person this Fall.

One remarkable comment that Dinal made was about a recent encounter she had with a shopkeeper. The business person made a joke but couldn't tell immediately if Dinal thought it was funny, because the lower half of Dinal's face was covered by her mask. But then the shopkeeper look at the upper half of Dinal's face and said, "Oh, I can see your eyes are smiling." It was a sad realization, as so much of how humans communicate is done by parts of the whole face working in tandem to provide expression and reaction. The cock of an eyebrow, a blink, a wide-eyed look, a tear, a wrinkle of the nose, a frown, a gape, a smile, a grit of the teeth, a smirk, a lear. There were so many facets. Communication is a challenge for many; miscommunication is even more of a difficulty. The masks weren't helping at all in that department.

NY Gov. Cuomo sparked to life from Binghamton State University, starting his briefing with the usual stats — all down, even lives lost, though still high at 195 for yesterday, "back to where we started." He thanked New Yorkers for changing "the trajectory of the virus" and added that the state was "making real progress". That said, though, he cautioned that "it's no time to get cocky, no time to get arrogant. This virus has deceived us every step of the way. We have been behind it from the beginning." And the latest concern was the inflammatory disease caused by the virus that was now affecting *100* children. "Parents around the state and around the country are very concerned about this and they should be. If we have this situation in New York, it's probably in other states," he commented. With regard to the push to reopen the state, he advised, "Inform your actions by what happened in other places that went through the same process."

Our CT Gov. Lamont also piped up, presenting his set of *our* state's stats, which were all continuing to trend downward, too, while testing increased.

Speaking of testing, I was hoping to have heard back today from AFC with regard to the results of my blood draw and antibody analysis. Then I thought that perhaps the 48-hour turnaround timing was measured in business days, which didn't include the Sunday I went to the clinic, so that would put the return at end of day tomorrow (Wed.).

Having tested a higher percentage of its nation than any other, Icelanders were boldly stepping back into the world: gatherings of up to 50 were being permitted; high schools and colleges resumed classes; and all businesses except bars, gyms and swimming pools were reopening. The entire country, though, was ordered to self-isolate from the rest of the world for now, and anyone arriving from abroad had to undergo a 14-day quarantine.

On the topic of international countries and reopening, three Baltic nations — Lithuania, Latvia and Estonia — tried a little experiment, letting their citizens cross each others' borders, in effect creating a travel bubble. A similar alliance was created between New Zealand and Australia.

When bad things happen in the world, good people rise to the occasion and bad people look to work the situation to their advantage. It's an ages-old certainty. On the personal side, today I had to deal with a criminal element hacking into some of my accounts and charging my credit card. The fix process required password changing and bank reach-outs. In the world beyond, shuttered restaurants were increasingly getting targeted and broken into by thieves focused on grabbing liquor and tech equipment. Then there were the innovators, the survivalists who figure out how to get by when the chips are down, like hard-hit movie theaters, for instance. Some of these, like the Pickwick Theatre in Chicago, had been taking online orders for popcorn and other snacks, which were delivered to customers curbside, or they had been streaming their movies online for $10 a ticket.

In the continuing saga of Broadway Actor Nick Cordero, his wife reported that he had awakened from his coma and was following commands, which indicated his mental status was coming back, but even opening and closing his eyes was taking all of his energy and he was so weak that he couldn't close his mouth.

A study conducted by economists at several top universities projected that more than 100,000 small businesses had permanently closed since the virus outbreak was declared in March. That was about 2% of all American small businesses. Restaurants, in particular, had been pummeled.

For the first time ever, Doctors Without Borders had sent a team on a rare mission within the U.S. (versus somewhere overseas), to the Navajo Nation to assist the population there with pandemic response. The people there were struggling as they didn't have ready access to food and water and had high rates of diabetes and hypertension, which made them more vulnerable. The largest tribe in the U.S., it had reported 100 fatalities thus far.

Dropping in bed to scroll, I saw that the Instagram Circus was active again, led by @charlie_britz pole dancing and wriggling again, with a projection behind her of stacked red neon lettering: GIRLS GIRLS GIRLS, like a strip club might advertise. And, like a club dancer, she was doing her thing again, with her big chunky shoes and all, for Venmo contributions.

Long-haired, puffy-lipped, Bang Energy "Elite Model" @misserikagray was chatting with and taking questions from fans. A trilingual star of MTV's Wild 'n Out series, she commented in a post about her life in quarantine, saying that she had "become a full-time dog mom" and been "social distancing on our daily walks to the end of our street and back. I'm staying safe and kicking boredom to the side with Bang (an overt product plug on her part)!"

A news feed pic of a friend, Jamie, also popped up. A R.I. resident, mom of four children ages 10 to 15, and recently divorced, she said she was staying single "and the world is ending so can't mingle."

News: The U.S. Army was seeking to have a wearable device that can detect if the user had been infected by Covid-19, allowing for the quick quarantine of those who test positive, to limit the spread of the virus. A new epidemic had emerged: Folks were getting so used to being home that they were getting anxious about going out — essentially, coronophobia was turning into agoraphobia. With the streets nearly empty in neighboring Bridgeport, the owners of all-terrain vehicles and dirt bikes had been using them as their own race course. Now the city's Mayor Ganim was fining them and confiscating their rides.

May 13. Up with the crows again after a spotty sleep. Bright day, but only in the mid-30s this morning. Was this May or March? On the upside, the forecast called for a warm-up to around 60.

As the sun climbed up in the sky, I got an email from my AFC contact to let me know "We got your result at 8pm last night and it was negative for antibodies." So there you had it. I guess I hadn't contracted the virus despite the weird symptoms. Should I have been happy it didn't get in my system, or concerned as I would be less tolerant than if I had successfully battled it? I posed that question to my AFC friend. He agreed that I would have been more resistant though added, "but the CDC still can't determine how long the antibodies stay in the body. Just use precautions and you should be fine. I know some people say they wish they had the antibodies so they're protected, but with the virus there are so many unknowns." I wondered then, if I didn't have it, then *Phil* probably didn't have it, that his late March case must have been a bad flu. My friend said that I might have gotten lucky and that that was the problem: "It has so many similar symptoms as the flu, back in March it would have been hard to tell the difference."

I heard the phrase "Do The Five" tossed about during a live radio broadcast and had to confirm what that was. Apparently, it referred to a Google home page update back in mid-March that urged doing these five things to fight the coronavirus epidemic: (1) Hands. Wash them often. (2) Elbow. Cough into it. (3) Face. Don't touch it. (4) Feet. Stay more than 3ft apart. (5) Feel sick? Stay home.

At noontime, I tuned into the Virtual Lunch with Bobby Valentine. It was in a Zoom meeting format and required me to download the Zoom application to participate, which I did. This was my first time ever operating in the Zoom space on my own. I felt a bit like a digital pioneer, though really I was at the end of the wagon train at this point in the pandemic. Zoom had become so popular with so many people, despite there being incidences of criminal elements hacking into people's video sessions, and other antics.

It was enjoyable to view the discussion and hear what the players had to say about highlight World Series moments and star players. At the end of the session, Bobby raffled off some of his personal memorabilia to the first 70 people that had donated $100 when they registered for the Zoom session.

Middle of the afternoon, as the air warmed up appreciably, I rolled out to motor around my Beach Area neighborhood, an in-depth street by street prowl, to see what I could see. Signage ruled the day again, with one congratulating a Roger Ludlowe Middle School graduate; another made of wooden fence slats arranged horizontally and painted like an American flag, with the phrase "Thank You Essential Workers" scrawled on it; a large yellow happy face on a front door; another congrats to a Greens Farms Academy grad; a Happy Birthday banner draped across a garage door; a Be Safe Stay Out Due to Covid-19 sign barring entry to the playground adjacent to Jennings Beach; and a Stay Safe, Open May 20 hand-chalked sign in front of the Urban Hair & Co. hair salon on the Fairfield - Bridgeport line.

The other dominant sighting was people, more and more these days. Two young men dressed in Hawaiian shirts carrying fishing gear and walking toward Penfield Beach. A pack of seven teen girls in shorts walking too closely together without any sort of PPE. Three women strolling near the marina, each with a face mask on and evenly spaced apart. That cop whipping around in his quad again, this time in the parking lots near the trio. A couple walking a nature trail running alongside the inlet leading to the marina.

Then there were just the off-beat sightings: a bright yellow vintage Chevelle parked in a driveway; the first literally flowery strokes of my artist friend Leslie's mural on the side of the Circle Inn; and the Face Masks for sale sign that had become a fixture on the Post Road and was now joined by a large stuffed polar bear wearing a face mask that was propped upright in a red sports chair.

The area mood overall? Eager. Happy about today's sun. Ready to get back to life. Preparing for the door to swing open. You could feel the build up. We were just a week out from the first big step out here in Connecticut.

The general vibe even inspired me to break out some steaks and slap 'em on the barbie for a home-enjoyed meal that included garlic mashed potatoes and steamed broccoli. Phil sat with me and we talked about his motorcycle and some frustration he had with it today, working on a valve. "It's never easy," he decided. He was right about that in so many ways.

As I was cleaning the grill, I heard some rustling from the yard of the neighbor diagonal. It was a woman in her mid-40s perhaps, organizing some logs in the corner. I thought she was a new move-in (the house had been for sale) but she was the real estate agent representing the property. She said she was hoping to seal the deal this Friday. An elder couple who had lived in Fairfield, moved to California then moved back to Fairfield, was going to be the new residents. I looked forward to meeting them.

The IG Circus started early this evening, with @cocokomatsu, a pleasant-looking Toronto, Ontario-based Japanese girl available for modeling and photo shoots. She seemed to be doing her laundry when her LIVE alert popped up, but it turned out she was folding a whole bunch of new clothes she received from a fashion company and would soon be modeling. A late March post on her IG page asked, "How's your quarantine going? Mine is meh." She missed going out to eat, particularly Asian food, and had been sifting through old photos on her laptop.

@djzenes was just that, a DJ with Russian-Israeli roots based in L.A. "in love with life and music" according to her profile. When her LIVE feed popped up, she was working a turntable at a rooftop lounge and a girlfriend was standing near accompanying her beats with a violin. She was all about keeping a positive mindset during this time: "When your mindset is strong, nothing can break you. This is an amazing time to discover ourselves and dive deeper into our passions and dreams. It's an amazing gift to receive a break from the universe and think about where you want to put your energy."

Fleur-de-lis tattooed, jument-maned @cassie.curses was up to no good in her live feed, sans vêtements with the exception of a skimpy soutien-gorge and equally abbreviated paire de culottes, each of which avait un coeur-shaped piece of fabric in the zones critiques, si tu vois ce que je veux dire. Teasing and accommodating her nearly 500 viewers, she even provided un volte-face to present and remuer her ample derrière. One of her recent page posts offered the same view and a face looking back that expressed désagréable violation, with the caption, "The face I make when I'm watching the news and I hear that quarantine will be extended for one more month." Another post showed a picture of her sitting up on her knees in a transparente négligé, with duct tape X's masking her tétines, a black masque covering the lower half of her face and an index finger up to her mouth area communicating a "shhhh" gesture. As her profile description noted, she was LIVING HER WORST LIFE, with a play on "worst" referring to her attitude impertinente.

I gradually tired of the Circus and dropped off, only to be bulldozed awake again, at midnight, by the thunderous, nerve shattering and seemingly endless sound of a long freight train snaking through town and shredding the absolute stillness of the night, like a monstrous wave might get up on its hind legs and come tumbling head over heels forward, taking out and mercilessly pounding into mincemeat everything in its path — so utterly dominating that no one would escape its fury. Yeah, it pretty much sounded something like that (!).

My wave analogy had a connection to a USA Today story detailing the tragic drowning of five experienced surfers off the coast of the Netherlands after a storm left a huge layer of foam in the water that, combined with strong winds and high waves, thwarted a rescue attempt. Only one member of an original team of 10 was spared — the other team members' bodies had yet to be discovered.

It seemed Mother Nature had her panties in a twist again, as wrenched as Cassie Curses' undergarments I decided as I stumbled on another weather f-bomb: a monstrous typhoon drawing a bead on the Philippines, expected to make a direct hit. The island country was already in peril from the coronavirus, with nearly 12K cases and 800 deaths to date.

News: Ethiopia and Somalia were seeing the worst "upsurge" of desert locusts in 25 years, and Kenya for 70 years, hitting during the growing season in these regions and complicated by the coronavirus. The U.N. Food and Agriculture Organization (FAO) estimated up to 25 million East Africans would suffer from food shortages later this year. World trade in goods was set to slump at a rate not seen since the global financial crisis in 2009. Merchandise trade was down 3.0% in the first quarter from the final three months of 2019 and by a further 26.9% in the second quarter, said the United Nations Conference on Trade and Development (UNCTAD). Year-on-year, these figures would be falls of 3.3% and 29.0% respectively. A 26-year-old Wuhan, China man suffered chest pain and a collapsed lung after a 2.5-mile run. Doctors found his left lung had compressed by 90 percent and his heart was moved to the right side of his body. They believe the condition resulted from wearing a mask while running combined with already being susceptible to a spontaneous pneumothorax. The face mask appears to have put him more at risk for a problem. The inflammatory disease related to Covid-19 was now being seen in children in the Boston area. A survey showed that moms had been driving around aimlessly and blasting music during quarantine — I even documented one a while back! Shoppers had begun to shift their spending pattern at the grocery store from hoarding and stockpiling to penny pinching as jobs dried up and money got tighter. An Irish pub north of Dublin had been delivering beer and potato chips by drone to its customers stuck at home. Global virus cases continued to surge upward, now at over 4.4 million cases, with nearly 297K deaths, 1.6 million recoveries. The U.S. remained worst off, with 1,426,241 cases and nearly 85K deaths, with nearly 307K recoveries. Among states, NY was still suffering most, with 350,582 cases and 27,282 deaths. A top restaurant in D.C. planned to seat mannequins dressed in vintage clothes at tables adjacent to diners so the room looked more filled and guests felt less awkward, due to limits on capacity inside as they re-opened.

May 14. I woke an hour or more before dawn, which seemed to be par for the course with regard to my sleeping habits of late. I kept myself amused for a while with social media memes, then gradually migrated to the shower, the coffee pot, the cat throw-up on the living room carpet (didn't need that), the cat dish and finally out the door to just feel the morning coming alive. I heard the distant whoosh of traffic speeding along on I-95 (mostly truckers these days, who must be so glad to have readily passable roadways) but, other than that, it was very still. Sure, a car now and then, but nothing like the "old" days (February!). The birds had taken over the airwaves, sharing their chirps and tweets louder and prouder than even our President, who was well known for his off-hour pings. The air temp was only 37F and I could see the puffs of my breath in a generous beam of the Sun's rays, beaming from between two houses across the way and reaching her arms out for me. I was only too glad to accommodate her, positioning myself directly in front of her, in her sweet spot, owning her for that moment, letting her caress and embrace me, warm me. It was our private meeting, our secret tryst, unbeknownst to anyone around us, though no doubt she had other partners. But here, now, she had me, and I had her. The rendezvous literally took my breath away.

The topic of the sun was a "hot" one of late, as increasing evidence showed that Vitamin D might help minimize the Covid-19 contagion. In fact, it was suggested that quarantine and home confinement was keeping the sunlight and this needed vitamin, largely supplied by the Sun, from us. A professor of medicine at Harvard Medical School suggested the deficiency may likely be the underlying cause for the high percentages of virus cases in parts of northern Italy, like Lombardia, Emilia-Romagna, Piemonte and Veneto, a region still making the transition from late winter to early spring when light is abbreviated. Darker or olive skin, which many Italians have, tended to resist sun exposure, too — in general, Vitamin D deficiency was more common in Italians and Mediterraneans. Hence, stay-at-home orders may have exacerbated the contagion, not reduced it.

A friend who works for a local assisted living facility checked in with me. She said she was "fortunate to be working from home and supporting the team... our caregivers are on the front lines, too — and we are working tirelessly to support them and keep them safe, but they are continuously being put at risk every day." An early April post on her IG page showed a photo of her kind-faced grandmother leaning on a railing and the caption, "We were supposed to be there with my Grandma to celebrate her 99 years of life today. She came out of the house, my family gathered in her yard holding signs and we sang to her virtually instead."

That typhoon I read about last night, called Vongfong, had made landfall as a Category 3 storm and was pummeling the central Philippines with a big left hook, about 350 miles southeast of the capital of Manila, unleashing a barrage of flooding rainfall, landslides and damaging 115mph winds. It was the first named storm of 2020 in the northwestern Pacific Ocean.

WHO's chief scientist, Dr. Soumya Swaminathan, had few hopeful thoughts to share in a recent interview. She warned that it could take up to five years before this virus pandemic came under control. She said a vaccine appeared to be the "best way out" but there were lots of "ifs and buts" about its safety, production and equitable distribution. The exec director of the WHO's emergencies program went so far as to opine that the coronavirus "may *never* go away." In recent months, the number of people across the globe living under some sort of confinement reached four billion — over half of the world's population of 7.8 billion.

Checking email, I noticed that Dad had sent me a message just after midnight: "I'm exhausted. I went out through the garage this afternoon to dump some trash and discovered that my big workbench had collapsed. What a mess. Broken glass, screws and nails and paint cans all over the floor, my serious saw slewed against the wall, the little library I'd been repairing down, awful. I didn't build it in the first place; it was there when

253

we moved in thirty-some years ago. The 2x4 that held up one end had pulled out of the wall and down it all went. Apparently it had just been nailed into the cement in the first place. I don't know how it lasted that long. Fortunately once I sorted out the wreckage there wasn't much damage to things that mattered. So I rebuilt the bench far more securely, organized some of the stuff better and even did a little cleanup. It was a lot of work and it took all afternoon, though. Sigh." I was sorry for his calamity, glad that he wasn't standing there when it collapsed and wished I had been there to help him repair it.

Travel & Leisure shared that an airport in Lithuania had turned its parking lot into a massive drive-in theater space screening international films. My mind instantly flipped back to the suggestion I made to our town clerk to stage this kind of thing in the Jennings Beach parking lot here in Fairfield. I wondered where she was with that idea, if she had even pursued it. I decided to send her a FB message with a link to the airport story as a follow-up to my idea, and to also ask her about the American flags sponsored by families thought that I had. She got back to me to say the "field of flags" got nix'ed but other options were being explored.

A whole new boom was happening for businesses that produce signage, particularly lawn signs, as I had been illustrating. But there were further aspects of the signage biz taking flight: "Social distancing cues": Counter top displays and posters that list guidelines for interaction, and floor graphics that show people where to stand. It was a good time to be a sign maker.

Apparently, it was a great time to be a sex toy manufacturer, too, as so many of us were single and couldn't mingle, isolated at home and staying safe, not daring to seek partnership. A company called LELO was "right on top" of the situation, you might say, enticing women in particular with "come-ons" like its SONA sonic clitoral massager, described as "clitorally mindblowing". Its promotion included a comical cartoon-like video, testimonials, reviews and three-step instruction for use. Amusingly priced at $69. It even encouraged users to write in and "share your dirty thoughts", through a Facebook portal. Further, it offered that SONA "plays nice with" its whole family of other products including the gourd-shaped GIGI, hook-shaped HUGO, slim-lined SORAYA and tricky looking TIANI.

For an hour mid-morning, I kept company with reps at my Bank of America, whom I called about the fraudulent recurring Hulu charge made to my account by someone who had hacked into my info. The first person I spoke to, whose name I didn't catch, had me destroy my current card and ordered me a new one. While she was doing some screen updates, she remarked how she hadn't been getting any spam email or telemarketer calls these days. I agreed with that assessment. Checking email first thing in the a.m. was actually a pleasure, getting maybe five emails in all rather than 40! And to not have to dodge solicitation calls was a bonus, too.

When we were through with her department's aspect of the process, she transferred me to another person, Charity, in tech support, to have me update my banking application version and show me how to access my new card virtually in advance of receiving my physical card. I commented how appropriate her name was during this time when charity was needed more than ever before. She mentioned how her Mom had just celebrated her 74th birthday April 24 and how she couldn't be there to fête her in person because of her mom's underlying asthma condition. I shared that my Dad had marked his own birthday recently, with Dave joining him and the gas masks and all. Returning to an account note, Charity said I could always reach out with questions to "Erica", the bank's equivalent of Siri or Alexa, which functions as an online assistant. I asked where the name came from and Charity said it was short for "America". Of course I had to then say Erica with a Texas drawl, as in 'merica. At the end of our call, I thanked her for her help and wished her well with her "charity" work. I know, I was slinging a buttload of Dad jokes her way, but she seemed highly amused and not off-put at all. It was one of the more entertaining customer service calls I had ever had. I didn't expect that at all.

Late morning, I was hoping to get a gander at the National Guard's C-130 transport plane flying over the region, as pre-promoted and specifically scheduled. I stood in the street. I looked up in the air. To the west. To the east. To the north. To the south. I checked a live feed from News Channel 12, from its helicopter. The plane was up but it was impossible to tell where, and there was no audio guidance either. I consulted with one neighbor. I consulted with another neighbor. I did some more looking. And I finally gave up. The best I was going to get was the live feed look.

Disappointed about the flyover, or lack thereof, I hopped in the car and sped over to the commuter parking lot off Imperial Avenue in Westport, to check out the Westport Farmers' Market. Well, the much reduced version of it, anyhow, with ten vendors. And this was not a set-up that you could stroll around, like in past years. Oh, no. You had to go online to the WFM's website, pre-order what you wanted from the vendors and schedule a specific time that you would be at the market, held from 10am-2pm, to pick up your order/s. As a friend of the market, I was at least allowed in and to say hello to and photograph each vendor. I had to say, the set-up was very efficient and well run, but sadly sterile and militant as well. There was no charm, no happiness, no life. All the vendors were masked and, instead of having all their vegetables, bread, seafood, meat, flowers and condiments proudly and beautifully displayed on their tables, there were just clusters of stapled brown bags with pick-up info on them. I couldn't see how we were ever going to get back to normalcy.

As I was near to Downtown Westport, I did a wide circle to encompass it, seeing the site of the former Rothbard Ale + Larder House restaurant now transformed as Walrus Alley. And I did a drive-by of the Westport Library and a big tree in front of it that had a massive yarn wrap with letters stitched into it vertically spelling out A-KNIT-DOTE (antidote). Completely disheartening was my tour of Main Street, the bullseye of the Westport community. It was literally a ghost town. About 10 shops were empty, flagged with space available or for lease signs, etc. Others deemed non-essential were still temporarily closed. A few spaces were being renovated. The only business that seemed to be functioning at all was Rye Ridge Deli. I masked up and strolled in to the latter, ordered a sandwich, paid for it through a confusing touchless remittance system and was off.

I followed the Post Road back to Fairfield, stopping roadside to eye some art installations attached to a chain link fence across from the Fairfield Cigars shop. Made of wood squares with letters painted on them, wired to the fence, one spelled out: Create World Peace. Another: Be-Y-U-tiful. A third: Always Leave A Trail of Color Behind. The creator of this installation had a friend perhaps in my Beach Area, illustrated by a post in their front yard with a message down the side of it: May Peace Prevail on Earth.

Back home for a moment, I scooped up and went and donated to Operation Hope's shelter several pairs of shoes Phil had outgrown. A masked guy that met me at the door seemed thankful — it was hard to tell with his face covering. I also popped to the post office finding a rush of people looking to do business there as well. One was Callie, a senior at Fairfield Ludlowe High School. She was graduating this year of course — the ceremony was long ago scheduled for June. She didn't think it would happen in person and instead would be facilitated with online acknowledgement and private family moments. She had been accepted to Northwestern but wasn't sure if the university was going to have in-person classes this fall. What a bummer I thought, to have such a muted high school finish followed by an uncertain path forward.

CT Gov. Lamont gave his briefing. Numbers down, with the exception of deaths, which were up a tick yesterday, at 94. Still all generally trending down. The state's focus now was on increasing testing, and communicating with and protecting the vulnerable.

NY Gov. Cuomo also weighed in, with a similar story about numbers declining, though many lives were still being lost — 157 yesterday. As to reopening plans, he had blessed two-thirds of the state to go ahead on May 15.

Our Fairfield First Selectwoman also checked in. We had 502 positive cases (199 recovered) and 91 deaths. Numbers overall were trending down. The Town gave out 7,200 face masks to local businesses to support their safety measures. The parking lot at Penfield Beach was going to reopen now, but at 50% capacity and to residents only as of Sat. May 16.

A WCBS piece discussed what college was going to be like in the Fall, when kids arrive on campus. It was theorized that social distancing would be required, both teachers and employees would have to wear masks in the classroom and elsewhere where distancing wasn't possible, and there would likely be frequent health testing. I shared this with Phil — we agreed it didn't sound like much fun at all and wondered how they were even going to pull it off. Phil thought he would probably have a better, more free and safer time staying at home. He had reserved a spot on campus, but could they make him go if he didn't feel comfortable being there? We guessed things depended on how the summer went and if a second wave reared its ugly head.

Financial analyst Michael Gayed weighed in with market predictions, expecting both the bond and stock markets to crash. He cited inflation starting to get lift off, consumers petrified of going to shopping malls, vast unemployment, increasing federal debt due to enormous stimulus payouts, expenditures to fight the pandemic, rising oil prices, cost-push as people get out again, food shortages, and higher prices at grocery stores. Just put all these things in a blender and mix and you've got one helluva toxic cocktail.

The IG Circus got an early start again, led off by the retailer @ freepeople, which featured this tall blonde dj playing some snappy tunes with a catchy disco beat. The segment was meant to encourage people to join their #MovingTogether challenge in support of @mentalhealthamerica.

There was @devilishemi, taking questions from some 125 fans. She was another Bang Energy drink pusher, spending her quarantine time watching movies at home, walking her fur babies, working out and contemplating cutting her hair.

@theviolindiva, Sarina Suno, was working both a turntable and an electronic violin, to produce a live show airing from a nightspot in New York. The jet-setting, NYC-situated Japanese musician, dj and composer posted in early April, "Hope everyone's staying safe and well. I've been taking a social media hiatus for the last couple of weeks and using this 'stay at home' situation as an opportunity to fully focus on creating new music with my team. I've also been editing some of my live performance footage, which I'd never had a chance to work on before. Let's stay upbeat and virus free everyone."

@monica_jambagle popped up on the IG stage next. She was having her own solo party at home, with music cranking and colored lights flashing around her room, and clad in just a strapless black bra and high-waist underwear with garter straps hanging down, entertaining some 60 fans that had tuned in. MJ, for short, was an Asian fusion of Filipino, Spanish, Vietnamese and Chinese. I couldn't determine her occupation, other than party girl. A recent post shared, "I've been taking risks and eating good. PSA, please spread awareness of #covid19 and encourage others of healthy habits. Please don't forget to wash your hands, wear 95 mask and limit contact with others. Together we can fight this virus."

@lualeiteflex was another player. She was broadcasting live *from bed*. She appeared to be a flexibility and strength consultant, from Águas Claras, Brazil. She spoke in Portuguese only but I could pick out a few words here and there — enough to basically understand what she was communicating. Her page posts consisted of a lot of photos of her bending and stretching herself in the most amazing ways.

News: NJ announced it would be opening all its beaches and lakes for

Memorial Day, with limitations, including strictly enforced social distancing.
Global virus cases continued their upward climb, at the pace of over 100K new
cases per day, now at over 4.5 million cases and nearly 303K deaths, 1.7 million
recoveries. The U.S. was still hardest hit, at 1,454,202 cases, nearly 87K deaths,
over 316K recoveries. NY remained the epicenter, with nearly 353K cases, over
27K deaths. The USDA said it would access $470 million of its Section 32 funds
to purchase domestic food directly from producers and provide it to food banks.
The department's kind-of-bizarre shopping list included $5 million worth of
asparagus; $30 million of catfish; $30 million of chicken; $120 million of dairy
products; $20 million of Atlantic fish such as Haddock, Pollock and Redfish;
$25 million of orange juice; $5 million of pears; $20 million of Alaskan Pollock;
$30 million of pork; $50 million of prunes; $15 million of raisins; $35 million of
strawberries; $10 million of sweet potatoes; $10 million of tart cherries; and $50
million of turkey products. The downside to their good will was that deliveries
weren't intended to begin until July.

May 15. They say some of the greatest ideas come to people when they
are in the shower. This morning was one of those lightning bolt occasions.
For the past year and a half, I tried renting out rooms in my house, to
mixed results. Having three unoccupied bedrooms just sitting there had
been a continuing source of irritation for me. How could I make these
spaces useful? Today, I connected the dots between the various houses
being marketed in the area and the rooms in my house and thought why
not market one room in particular, on my second floor across from the
main bathroom, to all these househunters looking for residences in the
area? Many were from out of state, like New York, and likely didn't want
to be hassled going back and forth to the city. If they could stay in a safe
local space that was cheaper than an area hotel, that would be a bonus,
right? I took a photo of the room, the bathroom, the kitchen and the front
of the house and created a one-sheet flyer with all the info and pics. Then
I emailed the flyer to the real estate agent who was representing the house
next door, who had given me her card. She, of course, was vetting her clients,
so that aspect was already taken care of. And I assumed she would be
anxious to let her clients know about my room as it would be helpful added
value and accommodation for her pitch. It was a win-win, I thought. She
immediately emailed me back in agreement. Done and done.

This development — and some java — created a bright glow on a day that had started gray and rainy, though one that was also expected to soar to 75F, which would be the mildest temp we had experienced yet this year. I thought it might even be an unseasonable record-breaker. And why not? Nothing else that Mother Nature and the Universe were dishing out in 2020 was normal.

That bright feeling didn't last as an article rolled into view that imagined what hotels would be like moving forward. How utterly depressing the experience was going to be. Safe, sure, but so devoid of any pleasure that the prospect of a stay was tremendously bleak, the fun completely sucked out of the experience. New measures and implementations would include frequent sanitation of airport transfer vehicles, complete property sanitation, suspended valet service, no bellhops, sanitized bell carts, temperature checks of guests, no communal buffets or snack stations, branded PPE provided, lots of social distancing signage, congregating discouraged, one-way pedestrian flow, no physical check-in, single person/family-only elevator occupancy, plexiglass partitions shielding lobby staff who would also be masked and gloved, seals on guest room doors indicating they haven't been accessed since last cleaned, no decorative accessories or pens/writing materials, no minibars, newspapers online only, electrostatic sprayers and ultraviolet light technology room cleaning, carpets steam cleaned every week, no buffets, limited or no restaurant access, no paper menus (relegated to the wall) and touchless payments.

My bright mood further faded as I looked at "stunning visualizations" of what the novel coronavirus, SARS-CoV-2, looked like at an atomic level. Bearing nicknames like The Death Star, The Flowered Planet and The Devil's Gobstopper, this "riddle wrapped in a mystery inside an enigma" that can't survive long outside a living mammalian host, this nasty little brute is governed by a 30,000-base genome coiled up inside its core that directs it to find a passage into a body and, once it has dug its spikes in and clawed its way ahead it starts replicating itself like mad, sending millions of copies of itself on to other cells in the lungs, heart and gastrointestinal tract. Eventually, this zombie army attracts the attention of its human host's immune system. In some hosts, there would be a swift and effective shutdown. Others would end up fighting through weeks of misery and either emerge depleted or suffer multi-organ failure and die an awful, agonizing death. Its diameter was 1,000 times smaller than that of a human hair and varied in form, though was often spherical and studded with about 90 spike proteins. Frightfully, each time this beast replicates, about 30 mutations can be expected to occur. The only hopeful note with this unwelcome enemy was an envelope protein that creates a favorable environment for the virus' replication that, when altered in a lab, makes the virus unable to copy itself quickly or accurately. Scientists say vaccines might focus on making that disruption happen.

CT Gov. Lamont popped up for his daily briefing to report that hospitalizations were down 40% from the peak a few weeks ago, but that jobless numbers were up to 500K claims in the state — "the stuff we haven't seen since the Great Depression, much worse than what we saw in '08, '09," he commented. In fact $1.3 billion had been paid out in Connecticut — half of that toward traditional unemployment, $25 million to gig workers, and "true-up" benefits from the Fed meant to last through July 31. Lamont also noted that 65% of businesses had received Paycheck Protection loans, to get them through to June/July. In terms of equipment to help support business re-openings, he said the state distributed 50,000 thermal temperature readers.

Regarding Gov. Lamont's statement about jobless numbers, I wondered what the local impact was, specifically in my town of Fairfield, so visited online the Connecticut Dept. of Labor's site, clicked on an "Initial Claims" Excel sheet by town and pulled up Fairfield, which reported figures through May 3. For the first nine weeks of the year, there was an average of 22 claims per week. For the next nine weeks, March 8 through May 3, the weekly average exploded to 437. The weeks of March 22 and March 29 were the peaks, as all went to hell in a hand basket, with a high of 854 that first week and 790 the second. There were cautionary notes: "Because of the pandemic related events, claims are being filed at historically unprecedented levels creating processing backlogs of 3-5 weeks."

I drilled deeper, looking at claims by job category, across the whole state this time. March 22 was the toughest week, with the majority of initial claims being filed then. Of 21 categories observed, the hardest hit for that week were Retail (11,289 claims), Health Care & Social Assistance (10,245), Accommodations & Food Service (9,763) and Self-Employed (5,425). I imagined that, more or less, the results tracked similarly across all U.S. states.

I got some good news, from my contact at Ford, who had not only found a Ranger light-duty pickup that met my specs but he secured it for me with a deposit and said he would be picking it up for me from Queens on Monday of next week! We agreed also to have me bring my Merc over in advance of that, so they could assess its value for trade-in purposes. No problem.

This perk-up was une cause à célébrer that was worthy of a walk at Sasco, so over the hill and through the lot to sand and surf I went. Strolling about, I noticed a pregnant mom and said, "Looks like you've got a newbie on board." She said she was due in September, which launched a chat about the anxiety of being pregnant at this time. She thought, though, that by Fall things would be a little more normal — or at least that our new normal would not be so anxiety producing. It turned out that we knew each other — we met last Fall when she was a bartender at a local pub and I was there to catch the NFL season-opening games. It seemed so long ago that I was in an atmosphere wherein people were elbow to elbow in close quarters with not a care in the world about cooties.

A little further down the beach, a family was sitting on a blanket, which I had thought was a no-no per town guidelines, but it seemed that the police were letting that go, perhaps because this was a family unit and not unknown to each other.

Circling back to my car, I stopped for a moment to speak with a mom and her adult daughter tailgating in the parking lot. The woman was a nursery school teacher at a local church and had injured her foot in a fall, further compounded by excessive walking. It was wrapped in one of those big boots. Her work with kids made me think of the new inflammatory disease that had sparked up — she said she was very concerned about it.

I pulled up stakes there and re-anchored at Penfield, noticing that the parking lot had been divided into two halves by iron fencing. The half to the right would stay unoccupied while the half to the left would be for parking under the recently enacted 50% lot occupancy rule.

The beach itself looked big and beautiful and I didn't see our quad cop friend, thankfully. I had thought his presence was a bit much and really not required. People seemed to be doing a good job of keeping apart without the local gendarmes breathing down on them.

I walked out on the low tide flats to the water's edge and started along it, when someone called my name. It was my foodie friend, Jess. She went to hug me then pulled back, remembering that we're not supposed to do that. It was a crazy realization, life was so upside down. She was in the same position as me with older children at home, taking refuge from school for now.

A single, small fishing boat with a canopy was sitting out in the Sound. It was the first boat I had seen out there this season. Down the way, a kid was laying in the hold of a giant inflatable unicorn. And I can tell you with certainty that *that* was the first *unicorn* of the season I had seen, too.

Looking past some more floats and out along the shore to Lantern Point, I saw a sight that would have been wonderful at any other time: about forty students all clustered together, sunning and mingling. It was this kind of close social contact that I thought might get us all back into trouble but, at this point, people were going to be people and do what they do without little hope of stopping them. And either we were all going to get sick or we weren't. The fates would decide.

Exercising much more responsibility, three girls were sitting evenly and well apart from one another on a nearby jetty. They were Fairfield Ludlowe High Schoolers happily practicing proper social distancing. Likewise, another trio of girls was walking in a spaced-apart triangle shape across the flats — keeping apart yet hanging together. Yet *another* trio of girls — roomies at an adjacent house — were swimsuited and sunning on towels spread apart on the sand. I chatted with them for a minute, remarking on how weird it was that we could be enjoying the beach like this when the world was going to heck.

U-turning, I spotted a family arranged around and sitting atop a lifeguard chair. The matriarch of the family was Japanese, from Yokohama, where the tires are made. She said she was a cook and maintained a blog on Instagram showing her daily creations.

Back home, I gobbled a sandwich and eyed email, sparking to one from the local suds joint, Aspetuck Brew Lab, promoting a new release in tribute to American Craft Beer Week: All Together IPA, a worldwide collaboration hosted by Other Half in Brooklyn. A 6.5% New England-style IPA, the brew promised bursts of flavor "from Citra, Mosaic, Simcoe and Cascade hops". A portion of the proceeds were to be devoted to the CT Hospitality Employee Relief Fund. I had to get my hands on a four-pack of this limited release I thought, and shot over to the Lab.

The day really crested nicely, reaching the anticipated high, before cooling back down and delivering a light breeze and rosy sky. It was a delight to sit on the back porch for a spell, with the sun on my face and a pour of the new All Together in my hand.

Early evening, the IG Circus, my new diversion, fired up, led by Shiamak Davar International, a large academy teaching Bollywood dancing, which was exactly what I stumbled into — a split screen wherein one dancer at the bottom was teaching some steps to the dancer at the top.

I stepped into another split screen, maintained by the Fairfield Comedy Club, with comedians Beecher at the top and Joe Gerics at the bottom, pre-promoting an online show later in the evening.

@suburbansensi was jamming on his guitar, playing some psychedelic reggae jam funk.

@alexisren, an apparent model, was dressed in a white bralette and lounge pants and was alternately applying makeup and dancing to some background music, to the enjoyment of nearly 14,000 fans. One of her recent posts commented on the pandemic: "After all of this, let's not forget what matters. Connecting to one another on a soul level is life itself. Remembering that it's not our accomplishments that make us lovable, it's our ability to be eye to eye with each other — continuing to expand our minds so we can expand our hearts. The world is full of shiny things that will distract us from the wholeness that we are all capable of creating within. We can turn this crisis into evolution if we choose. Let's choose to evolve, choose to be better for ourselves and others. Choose to be love so that it heals us."

@playwithjade, aka Jade Elliott, was one long, brown, lean, dancing machine with purple lips, a bright yellow halter top and black denim jeans. She was promoting a new video titled "Take Me Home", playing the song track.

I had forgotten that I was following @kaiagerber, lovely spawn of Randy Gerber and supermodel Cindy Crawford. She was as delightful as her mom, with the same doe eyes. In a post at the beginning period of the pandemic, she shared, "I know we are all feeling isolated right now, so I was trying to think of easy ways we can stay connected (beyond just scrolling) and decided I'm gonna start a book club. I read a lot on my own, but would love to be able to talk to you guys about it... so every week I'm gonna post a book to my stories and the following week I'll jump on live (sometimes with a friend, writer, guest, etc.) so we can all talk about the book that week! I want to start with a new favorite I'm actually rereading right now: Normal People by Sally Rooney." This particular evening, Kaia's guest was none other than her mom!

The Acoustic in Black Rock had a funk band in-house, The Breakfast, and was broadcasting them live out into IG Land. Great beats.

@breenaylaya, aka Breena Ylaya, a Gaming Video Creator of Filipina, German and Italian stock that produced almond-shaped eyes set into a perfectly sculpted face atop a slender frame, was applying makeup and responding to a dozen or so fans. The live format allowed you to type in comments or questions for the presenter to see. I fired off some phrases in Tagalog — Mahal kita and modelo ka ba among them. One of her recent page posts asked, "If the world was ending, you'd come over right? You'd come over and you'd stay the night. Would you love me for the hell of it? All our fears would be irrelevant." (From my perspective, I would have to answer that in the affirmative). She also commented on the term social distancing, saying she did not like it "for its subliminal psychological effects. I prefer the term 'physical distancing' because 'social distancing' seems to feel so much more isolating. I hereby suggest that we consider saying 'physical distancing' to each other so that we are not constantly reinforcing this notion of aloneness during quarantine. We are not alone. Together, we are temporarily separated. Words have power. Thoughts?" Another post, in late March, found her wrestling with the whole situation: "Why so serious, you ask? I mean we're in a freaking quarantine, so yeah… I had a dream that I was out shopping for my sister. It's the little things you miss when you have to stay at home for weeks. I see all the simple things I miss in my dreams. A part of me feels like I may have trouble seeing my sister for our birthday in June… and that makes me sad. But we all must try our best to stay safe and positive." She had participated in a photo shoot that same day, noting, "It was fun for me to shoot these portraits today. I miss shooting and the outside world. To be honest, it's been very cold and windy in L.A. Going from the tropical weather of the Philippines to the cold in L.A. has been very weird for me. I love being in the sun and now I'm stuck inside. What are you all doing to pass the time?? The days all feel the same right now."

News: Brooklyn had been hit extremely hard by Covid-19, with a staggering loss of life — more than any other county in America, more than all but three states, with 4,312 deaths as of May 12. Confirmed cases totaled over 50K. Gyms reopening in certain places were defining how that environment was safely going to work, with face masks, distance between workout stations, thorough wipe-down of equipment by users, complete daily sanitation, etc. Wealth distribution was shifting from categories like banking and consumer services to technology, due to Covid-19. Germany had entered a recession after two consecutive quarters of negative GDP growth, due to the virus. Airports had installed vending machines offering for purchase personal PPE like face masks and gloves. This virus outbreak had forced many people to postpone health screenings, which may ultimately result in an alarming number of new diagnoses of cancer and other diseases. National parks and other tourist draws were beginning to reopen including the Grand Canyon, Rock & Roll Hall of Fame, NC's Outer Banks, Yellowstone National Park and Las Vegas' Strip. Almost three million more Americans filed for unemployment last week, bringing the total to over 36 million. Criminals across the nation were increasingly using the threat of spreading the coronavirus to commit violence and cause mayhem.

May 16. I was up wayyyy too early this morning, but ultimately glad for that as the quiet time allowed me to get to some things I'd meant to. Like organizing the contents of a desk in my kitchen area. And updating the programming and personal info for my FitBit. More thoughtfully going through accumulated email. And responding finally to an Ancestry DNA kit I had sent for in early December 2019…

I had been hesitant to order the DNA kit in the first place, reasoning that I had lived all of my life believing that I was composed of certain specific ethnic strains — half British, quarter Irish and quarter German — and to find out otherwise would be disruptive. But my Dad had done his, which led to the confirmation that he was 53% Irish (from Leinster and Ulster, Ireland), 41% Northwestern European (likely Germany), 4% French and 2% Eastern European/Russian. We translated all that as mostly German/Irish, no surprise. My late Mom had done the DNA test, too, which turned up surprising — or maybe not so surprising — info. Specifically, long thought to be 100% Welsh (from Wales, in Great Britain) she turned out to be mostly German, which we thought accounted for her height (5'9", quite tall for her generation) and strong can-do demeanor. And the Germanic-ness actually made even more sense given that the Saxons came from Germany to Great Britain. So, the presumption was that I would be, perhaps, a good 75% German and 25% Irish and not at all British, or very little anyhow. I have to admit I had always *felt* more German than anything, given my attention to detail and organization, traits often associated with Germans. Of course, there was my passion for beer and German food, too, but that may be more trickle-down from my Dad.

Interesting note about the Saxons and why they migrated to Britain. One school of thought portrayed them as attackers and said that, in the fourth century AD, they raided the shores of south and east England, then-controlled by the Romans, either displacing, absorbing or destroying Romanized British kingdoms there.

Another school said Saxon warriors were *invited* to England's shores, to help keep out invaders from Scotland and Ireland. One historical account said a king called Vortigern asked the Saxons for help against the Picts and invited two Jutes (Germanic people believed to have come from Jutland in what is now northern Germany) called Hengist and Horsa to Britain in AD 449. Notable was that the words "Wales" and "Welsh", in fact, came from the Saxon (and Anglo) use of the term "wealas" to describe the people of Britain who spoke Brittonic, a Celtic language used throughout Britain which later developed into Welsh, Cornish, Breton and other languages.

Another motivating reason for the Saxons' migration was that their own land often flooded and made it difficult to grow crops, so they were looking for new places to settle down and farm. Britain was a relatively short leap for them to make.

The process with the kit I had received involved first activating myself online with a provided code, offering answers to a series of personal questions (birth year, gender, etc.), giving my consent to apply my results toward greater DNA research being conducted, and to agree with the sharing of information that would show a link between me and other people that may be a DNA match. I would expect the latter to include my mom and dad, of course. Could there be other surprises, like my Dad's discovery of a long lost daughter, now my half-sister? We would see.

The DNA "offering" was a 1-2-3 activity — spit into a collection tube, screw on a top that released a sample stabilizing fluid, put the sample in a pouch, put the pouch in a small pre-paid return box and drop the box in the mail. Six to eight weeks for results, perhaps longer at the moment given this pandemic, which wasn't at all an issue when I first received the kit.

Just attending to the kit inspired me to do some other long overdue things and so I set about reorganizing my home workspace; polishing my wooden dining room table and changing out the runner; repurposing a cellphone holder from the car to work for my home office space and better facilitate FaceTime calls; organizing my wearable accessories which hung from a small rack of hooks near my back laundry room; fixing two high-back stools and moving them to the basement while replacing them with two antique tractor seat stools that I owned, integrating one of them as my new desk seat. They jokingly say organization is the sign of a sick mind; I decided I must be very ill. And very German!

Another measure I took was to actually put on some of the wearable accessories that had so long hung idle. Jen had not been a big fan, which made me think I had also outgrown them, but I guess I hadn't. So, in addition to the FitBit bracelet on my left wrist, I put a braided leather anchor clasp bracelet on my right wrist, a neck chain with a Guinness bottle cap serving as the "charm" and a silver ring on the pinky of my right hand. The latter, actually, was a fond keepsake. It was the end (about 1-1/2 inches) of a fork that had been truncated and bent into a loop, and it had writing on it identifying it as a commemorative piece from the 1939 New York World's Fair. It was particularly cool to me for that reason but also because 1939 was my late Mom's birth year, she had lived and flown out of New York as a stewardess, and she and my Dad had worked the 1964 New York World's Fair together — she as a model and my dad as a young GE executive presenting his company's "Adventures in Science" program.

As the noon hour approached, I grabbed Phil and the two of us drove in the Merc to the Ford dealership in Bridgeport. There, the used car manager, Joe, masked, looked over my car then took it for a spin around the block. When he returned, he connected me with Evan, the rep with whom I had been dealing, who was also masked. As I hadn't test driven the Ranger yet, he passed off keys and Phil and I took her out for a run. It was love at first sight. I liked her feel, special qualities, curves and playful spirit. We were a match made in Heaven, more suited to each other than my real-life partners apparently. I gave Evan the thumbs-up to take things to the next level: retrieve the vehicle, connect me with the owner and start to put a contract together.

The day had really heated up — it was all of 75F, glorious, almost tropical. The lawn needed a mow and the mower needed a lawn — the two were united in grass shearing nirvana. I scrambled around on my hands and knees after, trimming grass the mower wasn't able to reach, pulling out dead plant stalks, installing two tiki torches and watering some fine baby grass that was fighting to grow in some shady areas of the lawn. I was only too glad to help these little blades flourish.

It was the ideal afternoon for a barbecue, some normalcy, a taste of summer living by the shore. I fired up the grill, poured a brew and got a Mac 'n cheese side going inside on the stove. In the process, I heard rustling again from the yard diagonal — it was our new neighbor, Casey, the returnee from California. I passed over a beer as a welcome gesture and we spoke about his inspiration to move back to the area — his wife Wendy missed her family here and needed to tap into her local health care team about an issue. He shared that he had three kids, older than my own, scattered about the country.

Phil and I dined al fresco at the back patio table, which he had cleaned off for me — its first sanitation of the season. We kicked back with some music from his mini squawk box, enjoying grilled Italian sausage, the Mac and a salad, with a local brew for me. It was so wonderful just to relax like that, to forget about face masks, ventilators, intubations, food shortages, nursing home horrors, daily briefings, refrigeration trucks stacked with bodies, families saying their final goodbyes through windows.

Puffy clouds paraded across a pastel blue sky as the sun grew tired of holding itself up in the air and retreated behind the Earth. It was firebowl time, the first of the season. Like Tom Hanks' FedEx employee Chuck Noland stranded on an uninhabited island, I rubbed two sticks together and, thumping on my chest, declared, "I… have… made… fire." It produced a glorious glow and warmth, which was welcome as a chill set in. We parked my Adirondack chairs around it, and a convenience table for the accommodation of my beer, a tippler of tequila and a Monte Cristo cigar that had been encased in a glass tube waiting on release.

As I sat there, I struck up and maintained through Instagram messenger a dialogue with Joan Chew, the keyboardist of Lez Zep, whom I had enjoyed seeing a couple weeks back on a Zoom session with her fellow bandmates. I found her intriguing given the contrast of her on-stage, low-slung guitar badass self and her yoga practicing, cat-loving shy New York City apartment home self. I extended an invitation to her to escape the city for an overnight, to take advantage of my spare room and a little kayaking, cooking out, beach strolling, etc. I think she had interest but, really, didn't know me at all. I surmised that she would definitely have to have a strong feeling of comfort and ease about coming up and reassurance that she was not going to get infected up here either. The former was completely understandable; the latter was a consideration of the new normal. You couldn't just be spontaneous these days, to satisfy a curiosity about them, and just roll the dice and throw caution to the wind. I wasn't sure how long it would take to melt the ice cube, but I was willing to hang in and apply some good old college persistence.

Returning to my "corona cocoon", I hopped into the FB-IG-Email stream to look for standout piscine pop-ups, netting a troubling story about an explosion today at a downtown L.A. commercial building that significantly injured at least 10 firefighters among 230 that were on-scene battling a huge blaze, that later spread to surrounding buildings.

My hook landed in another denizen of the deep, a piece noting that police in Elizabeth, NJ were using drones to look for people not social distancing in areas their patrol cars couldn't access. The image of Terminators combing apocalyptic landscapes to hunt down and extinguish humans came to mind.

There was no maritime humor in the next story to jump out of the murky bog that had become the news of late: an eight-month-old boy in the U.K. contracted the Kawasaki disease related to Covid-19 and died after suffering a ruptured aneurysm. His devastated mom cried, "I can't believe I carried him for longer than he was alive. I will never be whole again." The child's inflammation began with a rash that looked like a sunburn, a temperature and swollen lymph nodes. He later developed severe sickness and his hands and soles of his feet turned red. Then he started vomiting. He was admitted to the hospital the next day. A heart scan found multiple coronary aneurysms, enlarged arteries and fluid. He died the next night.

It was no mood improver to read the NY Post headline, "The sun has entered a 'lockdown' period, which could cause freezing weather, famine." Apparently, the sun was currently in a period of "solar minimum", with activity on its surface having fallen dramatically. Experts — and there were a lot of them these days — believed we were about to enter the deepest period of sunshine "recession" ever recorded, as sunspots had virtually disappeared. The sun's magnetic field had become weak, allowing extra cosmic rays into the solar system, and those posed a health hazard to astronauts and polar air travelers, affecting the electro-chemistry of Earth's upper atmosphere, and could help trigger lightning. It wouldn't be the first time it had happened — the phenomenon was called the Dalton Minimum which occurred between 1790 an 1830, leading to periods of brutal cold, crop loss, famine and powerful volcanic eruptions.

Then there was the awful continuing saga of Broadway Actor Nick Cordero, still in ICU but now battling a lung infection, left over from when he went into septic shock. His ever-attendant wife said doctors were "doing everything they can to clean it out every day but it's just not getting better."

A leaked database from a Chinese military-run university suggested that the country may have at least 640,000 Covid-19 cases, substantially higher than the 80,000+ cases it had reported. That larger figure reflected cases in 230 cities that arose from early February to late April.

News: Global coronavirus cases surged past 4.7 million with over 313K deaths, and over 1.8 million recoveries. The U.S. had over 1.5 million cases and over 90K deaths, with over 339K recoveries. NY had over 358K cases and over 28K deaths. Mother Nature threw another tantrum today, with high winds and heavy rain knocking out power to 35,000 electricity customers in the Northeast, while the southeast coast of Florida was getting smacked by a tropical storm and flooding.

May 17. I was up wayyyy too early yet again, after a sleep period that went from about midnight to 5:30am, but with interruption for about a half hour at about 1:30am. My sleep patterns had been running weirdly, though there was nothing particularly concerning me, well, other than murder hornets, impending hurricanes, new virus mutations, impending stock market collapse, retirement savings wipeout, second wave infections and the like.

I was not alone in having a disrupted sleeping pattern. In fact, I was lucky to be able to sleep at all, a luxury that many were not being afforded. A feeling "like everything was unraveling, all of the time, with no end in sight" as a Wired magazine article put it, had become commonplace. Sleep experts were seeing a spike in insomnia, that is, the inability to sleep, or to fall back asleep if you woke in the middle of the night, with no obvious impediments to explain it. "During times of increased stress, sleep is often the first biological system to malfunction," said a sleep and anxiety center director, and "a pandemic is stressful like magma is hot." Further, sleep deprivation not only makes your brain slower, but it weakens your immune system and increases the likelihood of all kinds of mental and physical woes. The other complicating factor was that our becoming more sedentary as we had stayed at home made falling asleep even harder. Plus, we were all looking at our electronic devices a lot more and that blue-spectrum light emanating from our screens tells our brains to stop producing melatonin, the hormone that regulates our sleep-wake cycle. Throw into the mix a morning without routine — no office to report to or regular daily structure — and you had a perfect potpourri of pandemic puss.

Really, nothing surprised me much anymore, including the reveal that specialist sniffer dogs were being tested to see if they could detect the coronavirus on people. A U.K.-based group called Medical Detection Dogs had already trained certain canines to identify the scent of malaria, cancer and Parkinson's. If effective, the dogs could be used to screen people, including the asymptomatic. It would be a fast and non-invasive process and help ensure that testing resources were only used where they were really needed.

An NBC piece said that entrepreneurs, engineers and architects were hard at work redesigning doors or finding solutions to opening them safely as our aversion grew to touching doorknobs and fear rose about spreading C-19. One think group created a CleanKey, a "key-shaped pocket tool with a hook on the end that could open doors of up to 70 pounds without the user's hands ever touching the door handle. It could also be used to press elevator buttons, keypads or touch screens." A 3-D printing group in Europe created "a device that can be installed on an existing door handle that allows the door to be opened with a forearm instead of a hand." A London-based analytics group had suggested voice-activated doors. Some had even proposed removing doors from places like meeting rooms and offices and putting them in storage until things changed.

Late morning, I needed to crawl out of my pandemic papoose and go native on the plains of Fairfield, or something like that. I nudged Big Betty in the rib and off we trotted toward Black Rock. I wanted to gallop by my artist friend's mural at the Circle Hotel to see how it was coming along, and discovered it was about 85% there. It was quite something to undertake I realized, given its nearly two-story high by an equal distance wide size, accomplished from a cherry picker, while getting cooked by the sun, chilled by the air or whipped by the wind, depending on ol' Ma Nature's mood.

The second half of the trail led me to Penfield Beach, where I was able to park for the first time this season since the new 50% lot capacity ok was given last week. The temp was only in the high 50s, hence there weren't many folks around. The majority of those onsite were walking along the shoreline, some with face masks, most without. And there were a few "rebels": a couple sitting at a picnic table, a mom and her two kids on a beach towel, and a woman in a sports chair sunning.

What struck me this visit were the steel gates around everything, which wasn't new, but impacted me this time. I knew it was for our own good but it all felt very prison-like. Pandemic prison. Pandemic penitentiary. Devil's Island pandemic penal colony. Corona Correction Facility. Fairfield Prison Blues. And I was Papillon, the francophile safecracker convict feigning insanity from my solitary confinement and seeking out quirky Louis Dega to go over the wall and into the leaky boat to escape our hellish island. Of course our escape would be fruitless as somewhere out there a Mother Superior was waiting to turn us in.

And, so, it was back to my prison again, perhaps to string coconuts together to make a raft for my next escape attempt. Or — and this was the plan that I *actually* pursued — have a rotisserie chicken sandwich, fine local hoppy beverage, some slices of sharp cheddar cheese and crescent-shaped slivers of apple in a glorious spotlight of sun in the cradle of my canvas lounge chair on the lush green carpet that was my front yard.

From this perch, I was able to conduct my neighborhood orchestra, cueing the dad, his daughter and their poodle to cross from stage left. And the neighbor with his arm in a sling, his wife and their eldest daughter to enter from stage left. And the neighbor and his daughter from across the street to pull into their driveway and unload groceries.

Like the director I made out to be, I called from the orchestra seats to ask the accomplished high school senior about her graduation celebration and college plans thereafter. A drive-by cheer was the first bullet; the second was to be at Loyola in Chicago by Fall. I shared my appreciation for the Windy City, as I knew it, at least, from my last visit in Fall 2003. Lincoln Park, Oak Beach, the deep-dish pizza, jazz scene, ribs joints.

I tuned into IG Live and a familiar face: Brooklyn-based DJ Rekha, spinning some Bollywood jams at home. I had seen Her Majesty of Music Marvelosity on a number of occasions, all at Westport's Levitt Pavilion where she would lead a summer highlight B-Wood party, attended by hundreds of people, with music, dancing, on-stage dancers, dance instruction and a psychedelic visual projection show. From that grand stage, she was now reduced to playing from her living room, standing in front of a shelf that held a decanter of whiskey and a large container of Clorox wipes. Still, she managed a tune-in of some 150 people, and was glad to be thanked with Venmo contributions.

My Westport artist friend Nina Bentley dialed me up, seeking a book, and asked if I'd heard about her husband. In early February, the two of them were hosting a modest dinner party at their home when he said he didn't feel well and went upstairs. A guest went to check on him and found him incoherent. They rushed him to Norwalk Hospital where he was diagnosed with a brain tumor. Good God. Leveraging medical connections within their family, they were able to get him transferred to Yale Hospital in New Haven, where doctors performed surgery to remove the tumor, sawing away part of his skull to get to it in the process. He survived the operation, they brought him home and he had been recovering and making progress there since. While monitoring him, she would sit on her porch swing and wave to kids passing by the house.

I pulled up NY Gov. Cuomo doing his live daily check-in. I guess the guy didn't even get Sunday off to spend with his family? No, he had a sick state to tend to and that trumped family. The numbers were down yet again, he reported — "a good day across the plate" — with the curve gradually, gradually, gradually flattening out versus the steep trajectory it took at the onset beginning in mid-March through the third week of April. And, yet, 139 more people died across the Empire State yesterday — "still shocking". But overall, numbers were back to where they had been at the start of the nightmare that was to follow, a solid 78 days ago. And people were feeling that long haul, he said, in a number of ways, including mentally. He cited a study that said 38% of Americans were experiencing "serious mental distress." To address this new "men-demic", the Mental Health Coalition had established a website, howareyoureally.org, encouraging people to call in and discuss how they were *really* feeling, as often our way as humans is to not be so overt about our emotional and mental state. We say "fine" and "good" when someone asks, but that's really just a kneejerk, a placater, an auto-response. "You can't be fine, we're going through hell," Cuomo said. And while the MHC was trying to fix people's heads, the Guv'ner was banging a metal spoon against his TEST-TRACE-ISOLATE pot, pushing diagnostic testing like a $5-an-hour sandwich board barker, as a means to monitor the spread of the virus. On an unconnected side note, Cuomo announced that the state's horse-racing facilities and Watkins Glen car racing track could re-open, though without fans onsite for now.

As I started to get Lobster-y red in the sun, I folded up my lookout station, checked in with cellmate Phil and organized a Mac 'n tuna salad that made the jailhouse rock.

It was time for my own version of the six-o'clock report. You could call me Chet Brinkley, my nom du plume for the evening, bringing you all the news that was fit to print, at least in this book...

In Brooklyn, I saw a photo of people sitting around in Domino Park near the Brooklyn Bridge. Large circles had been marked on the grass, each at a measured distance from another, which indicated where people needed to squat in order to observe proper social separation.

Were we headed into a new Cold War? No, but maybe a Cold Shoulder. Namely, America snubbing China-made products according to a Bloomberg news pop. Forty percent of 'mericans said they would not buy products from the "Red Dragon" anymore. Fifty-five percent of the same group (about 1,000 adults surveyed May 12-14) said they didn't think China could be trusted to follow through on its trade-deal commitments signed in January to buy more U.S. products. Seventy-eight percent of these same patriots said they would be willing to pay more for products if the company that made them moved manufacturing out of China. Sixty-six percent said they favored raising import restrictions over the pursuit of free-trade deals as a better way to boost the U.S. economy. Big talk but would they walk the walk when they were walking through WalMart?

Speaking of China, a new study — and there was a limitless supply of these — suggested that the virus that emerged in the Wuhan animal market was taken there by someone already infected and did not originate there. "The publicly available genetic data does not point to cross-species transmission of the virus at the market," said Alina Chan, a molecular biologist, and Shing Zhan, an evolutionary biologist. They said they were surprised to discover that the virus was "already pre-adapted to human transmission" and added "The possibility that a non-genetically engineered precursor could have adapted to humans while being studied in a laboratory should be considered." The statement gave credence to President Trump's claim that the virus began in a Wuhan lab, though was counter to the U.S. intelligence community's conclusion that the virus was "not man made or genetically modified." The questions continued to mount.

"Weird coronavirus baseball", that's what we would be looking at if the MLB started its season without fans, said the New York Post. On Friday night, the League sent a 67-page 2020 Operations Manual to the Players Association, with regard to "cobbling together" a game plan. The "proposal" included a ball bag full of safety/health protocols and enough dizzying adjustments to life at the ballpark and on the field to shake a bat at (e.g. social distancing in the dugout, a ban on spitting, fielders encouraged to retreat several steps away from a baserunner in between pitches, no out-of-town scores on the scoreboard in order to limit people at the stadium). Literally, it was down to this "sanitized version of the national pastime" — or no version at all.

Phil cut his own hair. Yep. He went into the bathroom, took scissors and buzzer in hand and, over what seemed like a half hour, went to work on the bowl of spaghetti that had come to be the main dish of the follicular feast being celebrated on the top of his cranium. When he emerged, I expected to see someone who looked like an extra from the set of "The Last of the Mohicans", with patches of exposed scalp, but, lo and behold, he actually did a fine job, and perhaps shed two pounds in the process. It was tapered, even, well-shaped. Bravo, mio figlio. Molto bene. Moments later he retrieved the drop cloth from the bathroom that he had spread out on the floor to catch the shearings. Over the back fence they went. Hey, it's organic.

My teacher/clambake caterer buddy called to check in. He said business had been going great, particularly his and his partner's strategy to get pre-orders from a whole neighborhood and then show up to distribute the meals. He spoke of an old college roommate who had been supporting the efforts of a church in Norwalk and the Father there, to feed 120 families every Friday from its kitchen. My bud asked about my Dad, who I said was well and safe at last check, emptying his wine cellar and making creative daily meals.

It was disco-ball-in-the-window and social media scrolling time. Sadly, there were a lot of posts from grads having celebrations that weren't quite what they expected and, yet, they were still grateful for the support from friends and family. Said one, "Today I should have been at my graduation ceremony, celebrating the completion of my masters degree from the University of New Haven. Instead, I'm lounging on my patio drinking champagne and eating Mexican takeout." Another family had created a mock appreciative audience of stuffed animals sitting in three short rows of patio chairs "cheering" on their grad, who was in full cap and gown in the backyard.

I read about some social distancing gone mad, like a man in Rome who strolled through a market wearing a six-foot in diameter disk fashioned out of cardboard, looking like planet Saturn. Or a guy in New York wearing a triangular wire structure as wide as the roof of a garden shed. Or a person wearing a full beekeepers' ensemble.

Talking about people flipping out, about one in five people on Facebook was suddenly creating and sharing avatars of themselves. It was apparently spurred by FB itself, which had just introduced its own avatar this week, to compete with the popular Bitmoji avatars. In reaction, a friend posted, "If I had to rely on recognizing people by their avatars only, I wouldn't know who anyone was." It was a poke at the rudimentary nature of the figures. Another friend, dismayed about the trend, posted, "Marked safe from Avatar Creation" with a little pennant graphic. Yet another friend, a woman, posted her avatar and it had no hair, not purposefully. In her comments below it: "I did this wrong. Ugh." A friend advised, "You can edit it. Just go back into your avatar and add some hair, LOL." These people had WAY too much time on their hands.

Phil told me about kids in the neighborhood that were up to no good today. Middle schoolers perhaps, who, with too much free time, were riding around being destructive, keying cars and such. He mentioned that older kids were no better, sharing that he saw a photo on SnapChat of about 200 university kids stuffed in a beach house having a party. If even one of them had the virus, it was going to be everywhere as each infected kid went back to their home states and families. I suggested Phil look out for the younger kids when he went out riding his scooter, that they don't throw something at him. I told him that he did NOT want to have to go to the hospital at this time. He agreed, saying he really should wear a helmet. I said I should probably *order* a helmet at this time, too, so I would be ready to ride when my electric bike arrived. On that note, I did some quick research, googling "cool bike helmets for adults". The search produced quite an array: some simple and geared to skateboarders, one carbon helmet with a mouth on it that made it look like the creature from the sci-fi film "Alien", one with a visor that looked like the face shields healthcare workers wear, traditional-style styro bike helmets, a folding collapsible helmet, one called a "nutcase" (a case for your nut, which is slang for skull), one that looked like a baseball cap but was hard shelled, one that looked like a fighter jet pilot's shell and one that looked like a jockey's cap. The funniest perhaps was the one for over $300 that had airbags built into it, which would immediately expand on hard contact. I told Phil I wanted something old school and, sure enough, right next to the airbag model, there was a half-face vintage Harley helmet, complete with goggles. It was on sale and had my name ALL over it — click, click, checkout, come to papa.

I turned in about 10 but, of course, turning in these days didn't necessarily mean sleeping. I scrolled, instead, reading about an Alaskan man who was making a 14-hour trip to Costco every week so he could supply his small city with groceries amid the pandemic. He owned a wholesale store in Gustavus and had been going by boat (a 96-foot-long converted military landing craft) with his staff to the state capital, Juneau, about 50 miles away, to restock on essential food and supplies. His store was the only place around where his area's residents (450 of them) could buy these items. Normally, the food and supplies would be shipped *to* his store via a ferry, but the ferry wasn't running during the pandemic. Some bad storms had also damaged Gustavus' dock, so it wouldn't have been able to tie up anyhow. "Alaskans are fiercely independent and resourceful; you really have to be, to survive here. So when a problem arises, we don't typically look to someone else for help, we just find a way to do it," he said.

The supply run reminded me of the same kind of run that Leo DiCaprio made with Tilda Swinton, as Richard and Sal respectively, in the 2000 drama "The Beach". Sal is the leader of an off-the-grid commune hidden on a pristine, uninhabited and restricted island in the Gulf of Thailand and the supply run is to Ko Pha Ngan, the closest mainland city. All the islanders put in their individual requests for things, including personal hygiene products, magazines, etc. The scenario, actually, was not unlike the supply run I was going to make today — that one critical outing wherein you try to get everything you need in one shot to bring back to the fortress to get you through another ten days of your isolation.

I saw a post, and received an invitation actually, to a "CT Liberty Rally", set for May 20 at Hartford's Capitol building. The cry: "Calling all concerned citizens! Calling all patriots! Calling all yearning for freedom! It's past time! You need this rally! Calling for opening all businesses now! Calling for ending the mask shaming! Calling for truth! Calling to end the lockdown! Calling to our Liberty now!" The organizers mentioned that an Idea Box would be provided so that rally attendees could submit their own grievance letter, to be shared with the governor. The wearing of a patriotic or Hawaiian shirt was also encouraged. "Governor Lamont is right", the call to action continued, "May 20 is an important day. Let's show His Excellency how important it truly is." A reminder: "Maintain Social Distancing."

L.A. mom was on IG Live again, a late night installment lip syncing about "why momma needs her happy juice" while sipping a goblet of red wine.

Finally, before I laid my head to rest, I thought (out of the blue) of my friend Hang in Hanoi, Vietnam. A travel agent in her home country, she visited Westport in early March 2018 to give a presentation titled "Irresistible Vietnam", at Saugatuck Congregational Church. She spoke of Vietnam, shared photos and displayed cultural items. She was born at the end of the Vietnam War and grew up in Hanoi during the hardship of the country's reconstruction period. Her mom was a textile factory worker and dad was a chemistry teacher at Hanoi University. Hang couldn't afford to pursue medical school as she hoped, but was an excellent student and went ahead with joining the tourism industry. And now, two years after our meeting, she was surviving another war, with Covid-19. For its part, her country was barely affected, with just 324 cases (of which 263 had already recovered), and no deaths. However, her travel business was being adversely affected. On her business FB page, on May 1, she posted, "COVID-19:

We're In This Together. This is a challenging time in all of our lives. We're all experiencing this for the first time together, and are reasoning our way through it. I hope that you and your families are caring for yourselves and each other as best as you can. I hope we all take stock of how we can individually and collectively make our society a better place. Disasters, as unfortunate as they are, can bring out the best in people. We are reminded of the simple things that make life beautiful: helping a neighbor, embracing our community, putting other's needs before our own." She also shared that Vietnam had shipped about a million Dupont protective suits to the U.S. to help our healthcare workers fight the virus. Her country's relative stability had allowed it to send medical aid to other nations as well, like Laos, Spain and five European countries.

News: National Parks were starting to reopen and, with those reopenings, park officials were cautioning visitors to be wary when touring again, as the resident animals had made themselves pretty comfy in our absence, boldly coming out in the open — even tortoises sunning in the middle of the roads. As of May 15, a total of 231 of 3,143 counties across the U.S. had no reported coronavirus cases. The long stretch in some counties likely reflected an undercount from limited testing, but in others, it likely also reflected the benefits of being relatively cut off. A Texas cafe owner had been rolling with the punches to stay afloat, selling as groceries such supplier-delivered items as eggs, milk, bacon, hamburger meat, chicken, cheese and flour; offering his own brand of household sanitizer called Corona Killa; and marketing packages of margarita mix he called Corona-rita. A Canadian air force pilot died after her jet crashed into a British Columbia home during a celebration for frontline workers in the coronavirus pandemic, authorities said. The Krispy Kreme donut chain announced that it would give 2020 grads a free box of 12 donuts if they showed up at a location in their full cap and gown graduation outfit.

May 18. It was gray, but that was ok, today was my day, I was on my way. I was feeling particularly sing-songy this morning, and that was surprising given that I had about five hours of spotty sleep. I was more punch drunk than anything most likely. Still, I looked forward to the day as there was so much on my activity menu (for a change): the dump for trash, yard debris drop-off, Home Depot, Nina Bentley's, Ford, Stop & Shop and laundry (which was already in the washing machine). You would think I would be less excited about these usually mundane tasks but, hey, we were in the middle of a pandemic, sooo… you get what you get and you don't get upset. Any excuse to get out of the foxhole for a bit and roam the battlefield.

I noticed an ironic dilemma developing. Now that C-19 testing services were widely available, relatively few people were showing up to have them conducted, far short of targets set by independent experts. A Utah health department spokesman suggested it might be because people don't want to be tested, they don't feel like they need to be tested, or they're so mildly symptomatic that they're just not concerned that having a positive lab result would actually change their course in any meaningful way. The only meaning that my own test had to *me* was satisfying my curiosity and knowing if my blood would be useful or not to someone currently infected. The other head scratcher for me was that the health folks didn't know how long the antibodies stayed in your system. So I may very well have had C-19 but nearly four months passed before I was tested and, by then, those antibodies may have dissipated.

A related article, actually, said that testing positive for C-19 antibodies doesn't necessarily mean you *have* them. For example, in a population in which the infection rate is five percent, a test that is 90% accurate could deliver a false positive nearly 70% of the time.

Mid-morning, I launched myself into action, loading the Merc's "six-body" capacity trunk for its last transfer station/dump run of our decade together. The lady clerk in the pay booth at the dump greeted me as I pulled up and realized she also needed to pull her face mask up over her nose. We both admitted to being tired of doing it, to which she shared, "At least I'm getting my hair cut Wednesday." I made quick work of the process, hurling trash here, emptying grass clippings there, then b-lined for my artist friend Nina's, in Westport, to drop a book.

I passed Fairfield's Hyundai dealership on the Post Road on the way — it was dark and empty as was its car lot. Another Covid casualty.

The Dunkin' in Southport had a 16-car line snaking around to the drive-up window. Coffee sales were booming around here these days.

The Exxon in Westport had two huge American flags draped on the exterior brick walls of its mini-mart — a bold and proud patriotic display.

I pulled into the drive at Nina's quaint property and placed my book package in her mailbox. At the foot of the post was an oval rock, painted pink and lettered, "We are in this together."

I u-turned, heading back towards Fairfield, passing what was once a large Pier One Imports store, now also completely vacant and wearing a sad "For Lease" sign around its neck.

Aiming for Fairfield's Home Depot, I hopped on the highway, or should I say I-95 Speedway, where even a granny passed me doing a robust 90.

The parking lot at HD was packed and no less perilous. Almost every space was occupied and people were darting out and backing out and steering carts this way and that, like busy worker ants carrying grains of sand to build a hill. Pulling into a slot finally, I noticed the tailgate of a truck two spots over was emblazoned with an American flag design. I praised it to the landscaper who stepped up and started to transfer his purchases to his truck's bed. He gave me a business card should I need that kind of help.

I noticed the entryway to the open-air garden department was now open (it was gated the last time I visited). I started to stroll in when a cashier barked from her toll booth-shaped enclosure, "You have to go around to the main entrance." Like hell I was going to walk 300 yards to that entry, walk the 300-yard length of the store back to the garden department and then the 30 feet I needed to go to grab three measly bags of topsoil. Against her protests, I proceeded in. A line of masked people looked on — the ladies had scorn for me, the men seemed to support me though didn't flinch. I decided I didn't give a rat's ass either way, collected my dirt, bypassed the ridiculous line and self-checked out inside the store. All in all, the visit took me less than five minutes — another minute to load the car.

From my vantage point, I saw a vintage Jeep Cherokee across the aisle. It had camo trim. Brilliant. I had to take a pic and give the driver a thumbs-up. Then an older man pulled in down the way from me, in a Toyota, though he had an American flag face mask. It was an interesting clash of loyalties.

Extricating myself from the lot was as sketchy as my arrival, with a real risk to bodily or automotive harm. I was pointed to Stop & Shop now, and took a short cut through the Bed, Bath & Beyond lot. From a masked employee just outside the entrance, I learned that the store would re-open on May 22 for curbside pickup of pre-ordered merchandise. I'd always liked this cavernous retailer and was glad it had survived the shutdown.

Stop & Shop was a whole different experience this visit, the most positive one of the pandemic I would safely venture to say. And I let my pleasure with that be known, going into Mr. Chatty mode. Right off the bat, I spied a shopper with a paisley face covering like mine and said, "Bandanas are in this year!"

Then, to a curvy girl with a generous bottom retrieving a carton of ice cream from a freezer case, where I also needed to fetch a container, I said, "We're stuck at home and can't go to the beach, so we might as well eat ice cream." She replied, "What's a beach body? That's *sooo* last year." I returned serve, "Curves are in." She won the point, "I'm all in for that."

To the guy counting and checking eggs in a carton because his wife told him to or else, I said I was just glad to *see* cartons of eggs *at all*, given the two-month long run on them. As we spoke, a staffer in a long white lab coat-like smock passed us, stopping at intervals to spray and wipe refrigerator case handles.

In the frozen vegetable/pizza aisle, I nabbed a diminutive bag of Italian meatballs that claimed to have a 52-count inside. To a woman nearby I said, "52 count? Maybe 25." To which she said, "Maybe they're marble sized — or not even meatballs." Ah, yes, a surprise pack, par for the pandemic.

The frozen foods aisle was practically a boulevard compared with some of the narrower aisles and maneuvering around people in them, particularly if you were going the opposite way of the aisle direction markers, was like some warped waltz — Johann Strauss' The Blue Danube Waltz adapted for the detergent and all-purpose cleaner department. The composer, incidentally, wrote the great work on commission for the Vienna Men's Choral Society to uplift the people of that city who were on the skids after losing the Austro-Prussian War in 1867. His inspiration was Karl Isidor Beck's poem about the beautiful Austrian river. And now the thought of it was inspiring me to whirl and step, from cat food to French fries, and broccoli to pine nuts, from smoked ham to tortilla chips.

There actually *was* music emanating from the store's PA system, though it was far from waltz-like, falling more in a pop/r & b category. Still, it put the spring in my step! And it was much better than hearing the usual drone voice of late thanking us shoppers for our patronage and reminding us to social distance and to observe directional cues and oh are you aware of all the cleaning and disinfecting we are committed to do for your safety, blobbity blobbity blah. The particular-ness of this crisis was wearing on me. Complementing the upbeat-ness were the laughs and joking manner of the deli crew, a pre-pandemic throwback. A new vibe was building, I was starting to feel it all around. We were splitting our cocoons, wriggling, starting to sprout wings, beginning to make the metamorphosis — our grand osculation — from Lepidopterous, leaf-eating inchworms to grand, winged Cressida. Call me Vanessa... or maybe not. Unless you're Greek.

Miracle of miracles, I actually found both toilet paper AND paper towels, exclaiming to a passing shopper, "White gold!" Generally, in fact, the store was pretty well re-stocked, with the exception of disinfectant wipes and related cleaning products. I *did* find a spray bottle of all-purpose cleaner that I thought would work well in tandem with paper towels.

As I entered the fruit and vegetable arena, Emile Waldteufel's The Skater's Waltz, Op. 183 was toe looping through my head. I executed a Lutz in the vicinity of the lettuce, an Axel by the asparagus and a Salchow near the string beans. As I was getting ready to perform a crowd crushing, rarely tried quintuple jump near the baby carrots, I spotted across the rink a familiar fan, my pal Daphne, also a Fairfield resident. Her mane of blonde hair was particularly equestrian and full I noticed, and she had kept herself quite fit. And can I say she was rocking her onyx N95 and its porcine nose plug? We Morse-coded each other with our eyes, genuinely glad to do a figure eight together. I suggested a cocktail. She said, "Or two." I closed with, "Or seven," amusing other shoppers around us who sympathized.

As I rounded the avocados to head down the back stretch, I noticed a pair of women with matching masks and asked, "Are you guys sisters?" They laughed for, on closer inspection, I realized they were mother and daughter. The masks had concealed so much of their faces that it was hard to tell that at first, which must have been a delight for the mom, perhaps not so much for the daughter.

Checkout was not the hassle it had been to date and I even let a staffer bag my groceries, unlike past visits where I would freak if someone else touched them, almost barking at one on one occasion. In fact, it was this very bagger and, recognizing that, I told her I was sorry I had been so hypersensitive. It was just such a foreign and awful anxiety before. But now I was joking and relaxed, so much so that, as I was leaving the store, I spotted Daphne again and asked if she wanted to go kayaking later this week. "I would love that!" she said.

Later, she would text me, "Hey Mike! Thanks for saying hi today! Made my day! So great to see you! I am free Friday starting at 4pm. But low tide is 5:18pm that day — so it's the perfect time to walk out to the lighthouse. It's awesome to be out there at low tide. Would you be up for doing that instead — six feet apart?! I usually start at Jennings and could meet you along the way if that works for you." I responded, "Hi Daphne! Yes, great to run into you as well! There's something so warming about seeing someone familiar during this crazy time. You look wonderful btw. And you were rocking your N95. Sure, sounds great about the jetty walk. I love that route. Let's meet in the lot at Penfield Pavilion at 4:30 and follow the tide out, u-turning as it starts to inch back in, yes?" It was on.

Back home again, I unloaded and put away the groceries, and unloaded and placed at the back of the yard the top soil.

Evan from Ford reached out to say he had retrieved my Ranger from Queens and was having it detailed. He was aiming for us to do paperwork tomorrow and seal the deal and, to that regard, gave me their best number. It clicked for me. Now I would just need an insurance card and certified bank check. Little did I know those were going to be challenges to accomplish. I had already tried to ring my insurance broker this past Friday, now it was late Monday and my message to the main voicemail had spurred no word back. Smartly thinking, I pulled up the email of a contact on staff and called his associated number, leaving a message with him as a backup. As I popped into town to visit the bank, one of his associates called and got the ball rolling for me. Unfortunately, my bank, it appeared, had "temporarily closed" according to a sign on the door, which provided no other information. I headed down the road to another branch. Same deal there, only the ATM was available. Seeing a phone number for security, I rang it and got a person that steered me to a third branch in town that he knew was open. I assumed the chain had consolidated itself for now to protect both its employees and customers. I was right as I spotted a teller there from my branch. This was my first time in a bank since the pandemic started and I had to say, I felt weird wearing a bandana and looking all bank robber-like. It was one thing to feel that way in a seafood market; quite another in a financial facility.

Like other businesses had done, they had tacked floor graphics down at intervals leading up to the tellers, each an attention-getting red square with white letters, marked "PLEASE STAND HERE to Maintain Social

Distancing". And staff was now behind plexiglass shields. What they hadn't thought much about was the commonly used pen on a chain. If ever there was a germ spreader, it was this little writing instrument. I asked the teller if it had been wiped. She said, "I wiped it when I came in this morning." Great, that was just 100 customers ago, many of whom grasped the same implement. Squirming in my shoes, I took hold and filled out a withdrawal slip. As I was waiting to receive my bank check, I noticed the face covering of a fellow customer. It was paisley patterned, finely appointed and with straps sewn on to loop around one's ears. I complimented,"Great mask." She replied that a friend had made it for her. I wondered if the fabricator was our family friend Shivani.

When I arrived back home once again, I reported my success to Ford Evan (vs. *my* Evan) and that I was all set on my end to close tomorrow. Then noticing the daylight waning, I jumped right to the task of spreading some grass seed on bare patches and covering it over with the soil I'd purchased earlier. Some hosing down followed, a little trimming of branches that hung over the patio, laundry folding and, with bittersweet attention, cleaning out of the Merc.

I was certainly glad that I would soon be in a new vehicle, after 10 long years, but reflected fondly on the run I had with this one. The road trips to my Dad's in North Carolina. The leisurely car rides all over the state. The innumerable dump and Home Depot runs. Shuttling the boys back and forth from their local schools when they were just tykes. The trunk had strands of hay in it from the bales I hauled to protect some lawn seeding last summer. There was sand, too, which had shaken off my beach chair last summer. Bungee cords I used to hold the trunk closed when its contents were bulging out. Several dozen receipts in the glove compartment from service work and parts and tire expenditures over the years.

Perhaps most interesting was the original Vehicle Description from the dealership (Michael Jordan's) in Durham, NC, from 2005. I never knew my car color was Arizona Beige. Or that it had been assembled in St. Thomas in Ontario, Canada. Or that it had been shipped by rail to NC. Or that the only optional equipment my Dad, its first owner, had ordered for it was a front license plate bracket. I guess it was already pretty loaded for its time. It had been a sweet ride.

Speaking of Dad, he shared an email early evening remarking that it was the 40th anniversary of the eruption of Washington state's Mount St. Helens and a memory about an experience that took place a week afterwards from a vantage point nearby: "I was speaking in a town on the Columbia River to a group of International Paper wood products people and the local town fathers. Longview, Washington. It was an odd room, long and I was on one end. The side of the room to my left was a long window. About halfway through my presentation, I became aware that I was losing the audience. They were staring out the window and looking kind of agitated. I took a peek myself and discovered that the mountain was belching a new bunch of smoke and ash from what was left of it -- the top had been blown off in the original explosion. I think I sort of finished what I was saying, but there was no way I was going to keep them for long. I was pretty good in those days, but NOBODY is good enough to compete with a volcano!"

News: Global C-19 cases soared past 4.8 million with nearly 317K deaths, over 1.8 million recoveries. The U.S. had 1,527,951 cases, with 90,980 deaths, over 346K recoveries. NY had 359,847 cases, with 28,325 deaths.

May 19. Absolutely GAWgeous morning, though brisk, at 55F but feeling a few degrees off that, particularly with the wind at a consistent 15mph. Unfortunately, the forecast was calling for some cloud-up, starting late morning. Basking in the day's start, I was inspired — well, really, mandated — to go outside and take the hose around to spray the newly re-seeded grass patches. I was determined to have a fully green and lush yard this summer, and so far I was succeeding. There was no excuse not to, given our homebound, introspective condition.

I may have gotten a little too close to Wally and Wanda Wren's apartment, for they suddenly appeared atop my adjacent fence and then Wally flew to their front door to check on the state of affairs. They seemed satisfied that there had been no intrusion or foul committed though and took no further action, though they did keep an eye on me as I moved away to another part of the yard.

I noticed, by the way, that they had also claimed the west loft space, perhaps for in-laws, visitors or for themselves, while their kids-to-be were nesting on the ground floor. Better view, lots of morning light.

Thus far, there had been no takers for the more modest Downtown East space, despite its refurbishment and roof upgrade. Sure, it didn't get the morning sun like the Uptown West space, but it got a nice blast in the afternoon. And it sure didn't have the roominess of the other place either, but these were two different districts. The West 70s vs. the Lower East. The tax brackets couldn't be compared. The Downtown space was also surrounded by lovely plant life, that was just exploding below. Sooner or later, I said to myself, it would get a taker.

I heard a repeated honking and thought, "Damn impatient drivers!" but it was just a lone Canadian goose flying past overhead. Maybe a real estate agent taking a market reading?

I got my first full-week FitBit summary of my exercise and sleep activity and, clearly, I had lot of work to do, with just 16,406 steps recorded over seven days and an average of 5.75 hours of restful sleep per night. But to my credit, I had been pretty computer bound writing, researching cars and monitoring news. The stats were going to inspire me to do more, though, and that was the point.

I read on Fairfield Ludlowe High School's community page about parents trying to salvage graduation for their matriculating seniors. "There is still hope for a modified in-person graduation at Ludlowe!" typed one parent. "Gov. Lamont needs to grant a reprieve for our students to be together one last time (with masks, six feet apart). Please consider reaching out to state officials if you believe this can be done safely... there were more people at Home Depot this weekend than we could potentially have on Taft field."

I'd been enjoying 90.7 WFUV radio streaming on-air in the background while I worked at my computer. What I liked about the Fordham University Bronx, NY-based station was that it wasn't trying to do double duty as a music concern with a political agenda. It was just pure, good and diverse music designed to make your day better, or at least that had been my experience thus far. Can you lose with a jam like Wild Cherry's "Play That Funky Music"? Oh, lawd, lay it on me. "I'm funkin' out in ever.. y... way." Just want to "Lay down and boogie and play that funky music 'til you die."

Paci Restaurant was planning to deliver several trays of their amazing meatballs to the Fairfield Police Station, to thank the officers there for their service, particularly during this pandemic. CT State Senator Tony Hwang had planned to be on-hand to assist with the delivery. I met with him and the restaurant owners, Donna and Bob, at Paci and, together, we convoyed over to the station, trotting the trays upstairs to a briefing room.

Pre-pandemic, that room would have been packed with officers every day. But because of the risk of the virus, the briefings had been suspended and the room had sat idle. By setting the trays in there buffet-style, we instantly turned the room into a cafeteria. The officers were thankful for the delivery and appreciated our confidence in them.

Back home early afternoon, I caught a live feed featuring Vice President Pence leading the Seventh Meeting of the newly formed National Space Council, at NASA's headquarters. He was onsite in particular to herald an upcoming May 27 Kennedy Space Center event, detailed as such by Spaceflight Now: "A SpaceX Falcon 9 rocket will launch a Crew Dragon spacecraft on its first test flight with astronauts on board to the International Space Station under the auspices of NASA's commercial crew program. NASA astronauts Doug Hurley and Bob Behnken will fly on the Demo-2 mission. The Crew Dragon will return to a splashdown at sea."

Said VP Pence, "Welcome to the Launch America edition of the National Space Council. We are one week and one day away from when America will return American astronauts on American rockets from American soil to space. And it's an extraordinarily exciting time in the life of this program... This has put into practice President Trump's vision for renewed American leadership in space... This comes at an important time in the life of our nation. We found ourselves over the last many months dealing with an unprecedented pandemic that we've seen the American people respond to, from our healthcare workers to first responders to leadership at every level across the country. We have stepped forward and met this moment as a nation. But now, as of today, when all 50 states are in some measure beginning to reopen, when we see encouraging signs of beginning to put the heartbreaking losses that we've experienced and the case numbers declining that... it's a time of great hope and a great encouragement... even the news yesterday of a promising new vaccine being developed is giving hope to the American people that we'll get through this. And when the history of this time is written, we'll record that we got through this together, working together as Americans, under the leadership of this President and full partnership with all of our governors. With a whole of government, a whole of America approach, we've responded. But it seems to me altogether fitting that as the American people come every day closer to that day that we put the coronavirus epidemic in the past that we're approaching such an exciting time in the life of our nation, whether it be the launch of the Space Force or whether it be the launch of American astronauts back to space next week, this is exactly the kind of leadership that has ever inspired our nation throughout my lifetime and I know it's going to be a great inspiration to the American people when we see those rockets fire next week."

On an added NASA note, a journal called Space shared, "If you've found yourself enjoying certain aspects of being isolated due to the coronavirus pandemic, you might be just the kind of person NASA is looking to recruit for a new study. NASA is collaborating with Russia's Institute for Biomedical Problems to study how the human body might hold up to the physical and mental strain brought on by the long-term isolation space travelers would experience during a potential journey to Mars. To conduct the research, NASA is seeking volunteers willing to be isolated in a lab in Russia for eight months." I sure thought a lot of us might qualify — the usual stay-at-homers, to be sure.

The time came to pick up my Ford Ranger! With Phil on board, we took our last bittersweet ride in the Merc, spotting people jogging and trucks towing boats to the marina, all very positive signs as we neared our state's reopening tomorrow.

Coming off the highway and around to the dealership, there was my shiny and new truck curbside as we pulled into and parked in the Park City Ford lot. Sales guy Evan and I reviewed all the inclusions on the vehicle's sticker and the operation, if applicable, of those items. Included was an application called Ford Pass, which would track my tire pressure and engine oil quality, and enable remote access and ignition. Then we moved inside to take care of the paperwork. With copies of signed documents, Phil and I were on our way, driving back home in this wonderful new, solid ride. I was so pleased, and when I backed into the driveway, I stood there a while admiring it.

Then I remembered "The Lone Ranger" vintage lunchbox I had purchased at the height of the pandemic and decided to give my truck the same nickname. The stars had definitely aligned on this one.

CT Gov. Lamont held an afternoon briefing, citing more "good news" with regard to declining numbers, and then quickly turned the talk over to FDA Commissioner Scott Gottlieb, who happened to be a Westport resident and acquaintance of the governor's. Gottlieb spoke about steps going forward, which were going to be critical to preventing another wave. "As we go away from population-based mitigation, basically trying to suppress the infection by implementing measures on an entire population, which is what we've been doing, now we are trying to target the virus itself and trying to support people who are infected, get them identified and get them tested, and we're going to be dramatically scaling testing resources in this state and try to track down people who may have been in contact with them and offer them testing, and offer them interventions to try to enable them to self-isolate, and make sure that's not punitive, that people are encouraged to get tested." Talk about a run-on explanation! But he was dead on with this strategy and, so, there was the plan.

In doing some workspace organizing, a business card for Japanese artist Natsumi Goldfish turned up. I think I had seen and liked her work at an art fair in NYC. I reached out to say hello and ask how she was faring. We had some dialogue, even to the extent of meeting up at some safe point — an artist and a writer spending an inspired "working" day together.

Phil and I skipped on preparing a real dinner. Instead, he took two soft avocados and whipped them up into a bowl of guacamole, which we enjoyed with tortilla chips and a splash of tequila, for me anyhow, as a celebration of my new ride.

Several news articles I'd read today were worth speaking on. The first was the news that 30-year-old 2008 "Twilight" film star Tyree Boyce and his girlfriend were found dead in Las Vegas. While their cause of death was being investigated, Boyce's heartbroken mother shared that he was a talented chef and was in the process of starting a chicken wing business called West Wings. "He created the flavors to his perfection and named them after West coast rappers. Snoop Dog, Kendrick Lamar, Roddy Ricch, The Game, etc.," she said. "He had flavors like Tequila Lime Agave... those were my favorite. A Hennessy Maple flavor, oh man, just so damn good." The idea was brilliant.

Another article addressed what some colleges and universities planned to do come Fall. A handful announced they would bring students back but shorten semesters by canceling fall break and ending in-person class time after Thanksgiving. Other schools had plans to cancel nearly all in-person classes through the semester. Among those mentioned was Ithaca College, which my Evan attended for his first two years. It planned an in-person semester start on October 5, giving staff time to plan, prepare and align toward a common goal.

At 6:30am on Dec. 31, 2019, Dr. Lo at Taiwan's CDC woke to an alert on his phone. His colleagues in the media monitoring unit had observed social media posts about a pneumonia of unknown cause in Wuhan. The original posts in China were quickly removed, but screenshots had been reposted on PTT, a popular online forum in Taiwan. Some commenters feared a resurgence of SARS. Lo looked at the reports and suspected something else, something new. He told his colleague to reach out to the WHO. Around 1:30pm that afternoon, the Wuhan Municipal Health Commission announced 27 cases of pneumonia related to a seafood market. It said their investigations found "no clear human-to-human transmission." (Three weeks later, the Chinese about-faced and confirmed that person-to-person transmission *was* taking place.) Taiwan didn't wait to step up precautions and the day the news broke, the island began instituting health screenings for all flights arriving from Wuhan. Those early actions made a huge difference in Taiwan. As of today, they had a total of 440 cases, with seven deaths, and all but 39 people had already recovered. This certainly damned China, but how was the world going to hold the Red Dragon accountable?

Speaking of China, the government there had just put the city of Shulan under Wuhan-style lockdown after fresh Covid-19 cases were discovered. The city is close to the border of Russia, where cases were at 300K, now the second hardest hit country in the world behind the United States. All villages and residential compounds in Shulan had been closed off, and only one person from each household was being allowed out for two hours every second day for essentials. Residential compounds had also been restricted to just one entry and exit for emergency vehicles, and non-residents and other vehicles were barred. Public places, schools and public transport were also closed. The fresh cases had no known history of travel or exposure to the virus. Hundreds of people were apparently under medical quarantine.

I read about the saga of an American cruise ship employee who had been stuck on his original ship — and then a second hospital ship — for 62 days in an Italian port after testing positive for Covid-19 in early April. He had been tested seven more times so far, receiving a mixture of positive and negative results. He had had many very bad days, some good, and would often break down sobbing.

Experts shared that, if you were sheltering in place and working from home Monday through Friday, your days and weeks were starting to blend together. And with no weekend plans, weekdays and weekends seemed much the same, with little to distinguish them. People were starting to develop enthusiasm gaps and declining moods.

In another illustration of how some restaurants were rolling with the punches, one L.A. eatery was creating fun, packaged TV dinners in kitsch foil trays that conjured old-school microwave meals. Another restaurant, in Austin, Texas, was creating Date Night Boxes filled with everything you need to have a virtual date (choices of meals, snacks, drink of choice, incense, dessert, activity cards and a link to a music playlist). A Chicago restaurant offered a meal with champagne glasses, LED candles and stemmed roses.

Finally, a report detailed which states were leading "working from home drinking". We see you Hawaii... and Virginia... and Rhode Island... all boozing it up during the 9am-5pm window.

I dropped into bed late evening for a restless "nap", my head full of anticipation for tomorrow.

News: A new crisis had been declared, that of mortgage forbearance, after four million Americans failed to make their monthly mortgage payments.

CHAPTER 6

CATAPULTING INTO THE VOID

May 20. The Big Step-Out. The Reintegration. The Rejoin. The Reunion. Whatever you wanted to call it, it was going forward, come hell or high water, and the consequences were going to be the consequences. The cards were going to fall where they may. There was no holding anyone back anymore here in Connecticut. Like the wave that first swept over all of us, this new tsunami of energy was sweeping forward and taking any naysayers, doubters, critics and arm crossers with it, subjecting them to our collective fate, be it good or bad, or in virus terms, positive or negative, either of which would be an outcome of our reopening for which we were going to have to wait. That is, would our "coming out" and coming back to together spur a wave of new virus cases or were we going to be good? This was the gamble. There was no other game on the table. Phase 1 of the state's Re-Opening was officially under way at first light.

I arose even *before* that first light, unable to contain my excitement, and maybe a little "insomaniacal", a new term I had coined indicating somewhat maniacal behavior derived from insomnia. Actually, my behavior was not crazed at all, just fervent and eager to accomplish so much at once. I was firing on all cylinders with a new-found desire to achieve a myriad of short-term goals.

This a.m., one very desirable goal was to drive my new truck! I just couldn't wait to get behind the wheel again and almost neglected to put on pants as I rushed out the door and hopped in. That feeling, combined with a need to see the sun rise on this particular momentous re-opening day, spurred me to race over to and park at the Beach Road Seaside Garden, in my Beach Area neighborhood, steps from Jennings Beach, about a mile from my house.

The sun was just coming up over the scrubby beach greenery and sea grasses that lined the ridge and separated the beach from the neighborhood, which was parted up the middle by a wooden walkway. Honestly, I felt like over-the-top stunt driver Evel Knievel strapping himself to his rocket-propelled Skycycle X-2 — more like an airplane than a motorcycle and actually registered in Idaho as such — for his momentous attempt at shooting from one cliff to another over the Snake River Canyon on Sept. 8, 1974. With tremendous energy and anticipation built up inside, I propelled myself up the "rails" and off into the thin air, the sun low and blinding at first. Unlike Knievel's landing though, which was at the bottom of the canyon as the rocket was pushed back by prevailing winds, mine was soft and sandy, landing with both feet and with Long Island Sound laying before me. It was a beautiful, hopeful, milestone moment that buoyed me to a level that I hoped would carry me forward and stay with me as we rolled our reopening dice.

Returning back home, I watered the yard as was my routine for the moment, enjoying all the various bird chirps as I had been doing in the absence of the traffic whoosh. It was bright but nippy out, in the low 50s. I pulled up the collar of my pullover, to keep my neck warm and tried to avoid the cold mist from the hose as the wind pitched this way and that.

Over my fishbowl of coffee, I scrolled through IG, connecting with one unusually early live feed, from busty lovely @maria_zabay, a "presentadora de TV y eventos", "actriz", "escritora" and "guionista". She was hosting a chat with @carolinawilkins, another Latina, for which I didn't stick around. It was a conversation and I'd found that format to be boring. If they weren't circling a stripper pole, bending like a pretzel, spinning jams or dancing, I wasn't interested!

So I delved into the news portal and pulled a couple nuggets out. One story, from Axios, offered that the virus was creating new kinds of work. First, contact tracers, for which a force of between 100K and 300K was needed. There were already several thousand people doing the job, getting paid $17-$25 an hour. It could be done from home via phone. Another post-pandemic job was going to be that of temperature checkers, who would station themselves at offices and schools and other public places, to screen people.

New York magazine proposed that the pandemic was the latest preview of the climate-change future. "We have been shown repeatedly, and yet do not learn, that we live within nature, subject to its laws and limits and brutality, and that many of the fortresslike features of modern life that we once assumed were unshakable and unmovable turn out to be very fragile and vulnerable. But it is not just metaphorically true that the pandemic is showing us a preview of the climate-change future, it is also literally true, because the global economic slowdown has meant a reduction of air pollution, which, in general, cools the planet by reflecting sunlight back into space — perhaps, in total, by as much as a half-degree or even full degree Celsius. Less air pollution means, as a result, warmer temperatures. And though the decline in pollution produced by the coronavirus is not total, the reduction may well be enough to make 2020 the warmest year on record and produce a summer defined by extreme heat. In other words, we will be living through climate conditions we wouldn't have otherwise encountered for at least a few more years — living through something like the summer of 2025 in 2020." Joy of joys. Could this year get any more WTF to the nth degree?

Related to my electric bike purchase (about which I received an email saying it would likely come in June), the CT Mirror posted that Covid-19 was creating boom times for CT bike shops. Specifically, the impact of closures and work-from-home orders had spurred adult recreational bike sales in March that had ballooned by 121% compared to the same month a year ago. And the boom was coming at a time when bike shops had remained open, having been deemed essential businesses. Unfortunately, at the same time, pandemic-related factory shutdowns and work restrictions had created major supply chain problems, which I was now party to.

Ford sales guy Evan checked in by text. He was attempting to get my truck registered but said the DMV was "down". Computer systems? Staffing? I wasn't sure, but they told Evan they would call him if and when they were back up. In the meantime, he was headed to the dentist. "I woke up with some type of infection I think," he wrote. "My whole left side is swollen and my wisdom tooth is absolutely killing me." He said he would touch base with me as soon as he heard anything. I was sorry for his grief, and the DMV news didn't cause any immediate disruption, so all was good for now.

If you know the Fairfield, CT Beach Area then you know The SeaGrape is THE classic, must-visit iconic beach bar. It had been there for decades and seen many a college student go in and out. The current owner, in fact, Peter Collins, was a Class of 1984 Fairfield University graduate. It seemed like the perfect starting point to celebrate our state's Phase I opening. So I trucked over, located a seat "equidistantly physically distant" from three surrounding tables and ordered up — what else? — a Corona beer. It was a popular decision I noticed, doing a visual scan around of drink choices. The other heavy favorite was a frozen margarita. The menu was taking some action, too, as trays of nachos and salads indicated. It was a bubbly, carefree student-heavy crowd here, and the majority were wearing masks — stylish ones at that. Informally surveying a few of them, there was a Saratoga Springs girl, another from Belmar, NJ, and a guy and his mom from Lyme, CT. The students were mostly finishing up their year here, as seniors, and those destinations were their home ports. I chased my Corona with, well, another Corona, and enjoyed a spot of sun and idle conversation about drinking games, before circling back home.

There, I caught a briefing from NY Gov. Cuomo, who reported that numbers were down yet again, with the exception of deaths, at 112 for yesterday, which was actually up a tick. Summing up the overall trend, Cuomo said, "It was a fast spike up and long road down, now stabilized with where we were before the dramatic increase." So where were any new cases coming from? Minority and low income areas, where tests were conducted and high positive percentages discovered. On average, 27% of individuals were testing positive in any given NYC borough. Cuomo said the city's results would probably track with situations in minority and low-income communities elsewhere across America.

CT Gov. Lamont's briefing mirrored the same numbers trend-wise. The #1 principal mission now in the state was public health and safety, science-driven decisions, being prepared with PPE, leaving businesses the choice to open or not, and having an adaptive plan that could nimbly scale or roll back based on real-time critical health metrics.

Our own First Selectwoman weighed in, too, saying she was "grateful for how everyone in our community has come together and sacrificed in an effort to protect everyone in our Town." She quoted some numbers: 531 residents positive for the virus to date, 99 had lost their lives, 212 had recovered.

I had had enough of briefings by late afternoon and wanted to get over to Paci Restaurant to see how *their* patio opening was going and to support it however I could. It was quiet at first when I arrived, but it was Wednesday after all and early for folks that usually just went out to dinner. The handful of couples already there were having cocktails or wine and an appetizer. I sampled a cocktail, too, a Donna-riti, a martini named after Donna, the restaurant co-owner. As I tend to do, I struck up conversations here and there, with a couple celebrating their ninth anniversary; a guy who served as a crew chief in the Air Force during the Vietnam War; another guy born in Italy and friend of the restaurant who brought several pods of homemade dough and volunteered to make some pizza; a woman who grew up in New Rochelle and frequented some of the same local discos I had back when; and a girl who had been laid off from her events planning job and was looking for new employment.

Singer, songwriter, guitarist John Torres was amongst the crowd. We knew each other from the local music scene. He had used his quarantine time to craft and record a new song.

As the sun sank, along with the temps, and after I had killed a glass of wine and plate of charcuterie, I offered a good night and thanks and scooted over to Sasco Beach. There was a solid crowd there — a mix of teens, young parents, dads on the way home for dinner and single couples, who were all glad to be out in the fresh air and feeling some degree of normalcy.

News: For many college students, a gap year was looking attractive this year if on-campus time wasn't going to be possible. The Norwalk Seaport Association announced the cancellation of this year's very popular Norwalk Oyster Festival, due to concerns about Covid-19.

May 21. I was up a full hour before sun-up, actually energized and looking forward to the day, deciding to test my new truck and its abilities. Was it pandemic worthy? If civilization fell apart and we had to retreat to Dave's up in the mountains, was this the ride on which I could depend? To a radio tune that pumped out the distinctive lyric "What doesn't kill you makes you stronger", I motored over to our Home Depot and quickly went about loading up a cart with materials: three bags of topsoil, a bag of starter fertilizer, three bags of paver base crushed stone, two bags of black mulch and, this was the tester, 24 16" x 16" red brickface step stones weighing a good 15 pounds each. I was going to do some yard work, the main highlight of which was extending my patio at three corners.

I had brought a large plastic sheet and set that down in the truck bed and, as I had loaded everything onto the cart, I now uploaded everything to the truck, resting all items on the sheet. The Ranger took the burden well, barely registering a suspension dip and, carefully, I drove home, trying to avoid bumps and craters in the road so as not to upset the load. And as I had loaded the cart and uploaded to the truck, I now unloaded from the truck to points in the yard where materials were needed. And immediately, as the sun rose up in the sky, I took on the tasks at hand: putting down the top soil where my resting kayaks had created a big bare area in the lawn, spreading mulch behind shrubs at the front of the house, digging up a bush by my back shed to make room for the kayaks to now rest there and taking an ax to the overgrown bush to whittle it to a small size and put it back in its place. Mostly though, my time was spent addressing the patio, removing the grass in shovelfuls in the spots where I wanted to extend the pavers.

I also made another jaunt out, first to good old Bud's Deli, my go-to for bacon, egg & cheese sandwiches. There, I happened to run into First Church Congregational's Reverend David Spollet and, not having heard a clergyman's insight on this whole pandemic, I tapped him for his thoughts, asking first if God was punishing us. "God has better things to do," he replied. "This is nature." And he expressed that politicians were taking advantage of the situation to satisfy their own agendas. Deli owner Ed agreed on that point, and it didn't matter which side of the aisle they were from.

As I came back up Reef Road, I noticed landscapers seeing to the property that had been 7-Eleven and asked one if they could confirm that a coffee place was going to replace the longstanding quickie mart. He said, yes, probably in July and it would be a similar convenience-type place, catering to local residents and the college crowd I presumed, as the other had.

A second stop was Hemlock Hardware. I considered myself a pick-up pro at this point and, pulling up in front, called the store owner locked inside and asked for his smallest bag of grass seed. He located one, held it up for me to see, I read him my credit card info over the phone and he set the bag outside for me to grab, with a receipt stapled to the side. Welcome to the pandemic shopping experience.

Before setting back into the yard work, I called Ford's Evan to follow up about my registration. His mouth was "still very very swollen", the infection had not gone down and he was going back to the dentist, but he had succeeded in getting my reg ready, leaving the paperwork with an associate at the dealer. I shot over there, collected the papers, and had the plate switched out from the dealer tag to the plate that had come from the Merc. As I left, I let them know, "I love my truck" and offered a namaste.

Back home again, I sprinkled the seed, hoed it in, moved a seagrass plant to the other side of the yard and started laying and leveling the pavers. I worked efficiently and methodically well into the afternoon as air temps warmed, finding a stopping point for the day and heading out for a bit, first to Sasco. There, I pulled into a parking slot and just stayed in the truck, with the engine off but radio on, surveying the beach. I was surprised to see people laying out in beach chairs as, per the First Selectwoman, no one was supposed to do that until the 23rd, but no one seemed to be stopping the "offenders". I had to marvel at the odd sight, too, of two women with face masks on in their respective sports chairs positioned six feet apart. Was this going to be a commonplace view this summer?

I couldn't have been sitting in place for more than 15-20 minutes when the radio shut itself off, explained by a message on the dash that said to the effect that the radio was being turned off to save the battery. Hmm, ok, sort of a short time but a good measure, right? My truck didn't want me to be stranded. I got it. So I just decided to skedaddle at that point and assumed the radio would just come back on as I got going. But my dashboard screen remained dark and the radio inoperative. Maybe the battery just needed to recharge for a while? So I drove around through the neighborhood and then stopped over at Penfield to take a quick walkabout, figuring a rest and reset would fix the situation.

In that walk-around moment, I spotted a girl with a Sacred Heart University sweatshirt on, sitting on a beach towel. We spoke for a few moments, wherein I learned that she had just graduated with a nursing degree, was planning to return to her home in Bristol and was preparing to take her "boards" this summer. There was certainly never a recent time when great nurses were more needed.

Well, the few moments of truck rest didn't fix the radio and so I drove home and called a tech at Ford Pass. I think they were located in the Philippines, as that was the background of the "guide" I reached. We went through various steps but were unsuccessful in correcting the radio issue. So I called the Ford dealership who explained the truck had various protection sensors and that I just needed to drive it around a bit more, to restore the battery power, though I had only had the radio on while at rest for 15 minutes. I did as he said, even driving to the dealership hoping they could do a quick fix, but it had already closed for the day.

I returned home and put Phil on the case, while I poked around in the yard a bit more. He suspected it might be a fuse but didn't want to mess with it. Better to see the dealer tomorrow was the decision.

I hosed myself off ultimately, created a salad and kicked back with Phil in our "cinema" to watch "Inglorious Basterds", the much acclaimed Tarantino film that I had never gotten to see. It was the usual QT off-beat gore-fest, much to my delight and, though entertaining, the day's labors caught up with me. We knocked off at the halfway point.

News: Hotels, gyms, movie theaters and bowling alleys could be allowed to reopen in Connecticut on June 20, said CT Gov. Lamont, and restaurants would be able to offer indoor dining. Global coronavirus cases pushed way past 5.1 million, with over 332K deaths, and 2.055 million recoveries. The U.S. had over 1.6 million cases, with nearly 96K deaths, nearly 372K recoveries. New York had over 364K cases, and nearly 29K deaths. Yankee Stadium was being turned into a drive-in concert movie venue this summer in light of major league baseball games being on hold due to the pandemic. Norwalk, CT decided to put up concrete barriers on the road in places like Washington Street so that restaurants could create pseudo-patios to comply with outdoor dining only rules.

May 22. Again I was up an hour before sun-up but I had had a mostly solid rest. I did some quick watering in the yard and, with a mug of coffee at hand, got online. I tried to call my Dad, too, but he must already have set off by car from North Carolina for my brother Dave's. They were scheduled to fly out of Dulles Airport tomorrow, out to Utah, to tour the Moab area for a week.

I saw on Fairfield Ludlowe High School's Facebook forum a note from the Superintendent of Schools, Michael Cummings, getting an early start on addressing the topic of re-opening in the fall. "While we are still a long way from re-entry dates, we are better understanding the need to plan for different scenarios, and what each of those scenarios entail. Each potential idea of an answer raises at least three other questions of how the logistics will need to be addressed," he said. The scenarios included in-school instruction, distance learning and "some hybrid of the two" — more review would follow the first week of June.

The State, in the meantime, was collecting input and thoughts from middle and elementary school students about the distance learning experience. At the same time, Cummings and his team were working on finalizing the last dates of that type of instruction, which was being complicated by the need for students to return materials and devices in a safe way, a process that might require staggered drop-offs over a number of days.

Along those lines, Vox said the CDC had released new guidelines for reopening schools (as well as places of worship and public transportation), including recommendations for staff and students to get their temperature checked every day and daily disinfecting of classrooms and buses. It also offered criteria that must be met for two weeks before reopening: a decline in the number of confirmed cases, a decline in the number of cases requiring intensive care, a decline in the number of people presenting at Emergency Rooms with flu-like symptoms, a downward trajectory in positive tests as a percentage of total tests, producing faster test results, and showing an ability to care for all cases without crisis care.

More countries and U.S. states were reporting cases of the inflammatory disease related to Covid-19 that was afflicting children. The cases had doubled in just one week, with pediatric patients in 13 countries now and more than 300 cases across 27 U.S. states. New York, alone, had 157 cases and at least three children had died from the disease. The CDC had now given it a name: Multisystem Inflammatory Syndrome in Children (MIS-C), also called Pediatric Multisystem Inflammatory Syndrome (PMIS). Gov. Cuomo said that in some ways it was more frightening than Covid-19 because it could cause inflammation of the heart's blood vessels, leading to what was essentially a heart attack in a child. There was still more unknown than was understood, which seriously affected the decision making about kids physically returning to school in the fall. For now, summer school was definitely going to be provided through distance learning. As for day camp,

Cuomo said, "As a parent, until I know how widespread this is, I wouldn't send my child to day camp." As far as I knew, though, day camps had not yet been prohibited or disallowed, but now they were certainly swinging in the hammock of uncertainty.

Since all 50 of our states had reopened to some degree, we were suddenly in harm's way. That said, how could we reduce harm to ourselves? A Washington Post article offered four harm-reduction strategies. Determining relative risk, that is, assessing proximity, activity and time for a potentially risky activity, with regard to being near others who might be infected. Pooled risk — in other words, choosing what groups you hang out with, depending on whether they are low or high exposure types. Cumulative risk, that is, deciding what activities are most important to you to pursue, assuming that all activities put you at risk. And collective risk — there being a sound public policy in place for a community that helps reduce risk, e.g. mandates about mask wearing in public, a ban on large gatherings, surveillance systems in place to detect if and when infections rise, a willingness to reimpose restrictions. There were particular concerns with the upcoming Memorial Day holiday that would force new decisions and affect risk calibrations.

A New York Post article ventured that people's noses may make them more or less vulnerable to the virus. "The receptors that let the virus inside cells are more common in the noses of adults than children", indicated a recent AMA report. Three hundred people were studied and the expression of the ACE2 gene was much higher in older age groups.

Looking ahead to the Memorial Day weekend, weather forecasters said it would be mostly warm and pleasant across the nation, though parts of Texas and Oklahoma were expected to be hit with repeated storms with possible flooding because, of course, this was 2020, when everything had to be fucked up in one way or another.

Seven popular U.S. restaurant chains were struggling to survive, according to Eat This, Not That. They included Friendly's, which had already been struggling and closing locations; IHOP, which had shuttered multiple locations in the past couple of months; Ruby Tuesday, which had also been struggling for a while; Houlihan's, which had been in Chapter 11 bankruptcy; Joe's Crab Shack, which had started to close long-standing locations; Dave & Buster's, which temporarily closed all 137 of its locations and furloughed 15,000 employees during this time; and Hard Rock Cafe, which may struggle for a year before it gets back to pre-pandemic traffic.

That cyclone that was headed for India the other day did, in fact, make landfall, killing more than 80 people and leaving thousands homeless, compounding the Covid-19 crisis. The storm wiped out bridges, trees, electric lines, homes, health centers, schools and businesses. The wind from the very dangerous weather event reached over 100 mph.

During this pandemic, I had been considering a road trip, and more so now that I had an interesting and reliable vehicle. Travel industry experts confirmed "this will be the year of the road trip", according to a Washington Post piece. One-third of Americans, in fact, said they planned to hit the road this summer, and there had already been a spike in RV rentals and purchases. But the plan was not without risk during this time. The good old "experts" were saying the eager-to-travel should consider a few things: Pack with the pandemic in mind, carrying face masks, hand sanitizer, disinfectant and hand soap, particularly for those occasions when you have to visit a gas station, rest stop or food/supplies place. Make as few stops as possible to minimize contact or do it strategically, e.g. drive-throughs, curbside food pick-up at restaurants or stores. Steer clear of crowded destinations. Do your homework to know about restrictions that will vary from region to region.

More disheartening news in the saga of Broadway Actor Nick Cordero, whose wife said, "Things are going downhill." While he had awakened from a coma, he was having a bad time of things. She asked for prayers.

In the real estate market, though we had been seeing a boom in interest in this region, apparently U.S. existing home sales posted their largest decline in nearly 10 years. The slump was driven by an upended labor market and economy, which had undercut demand for housing. Specifically, existing home sales, according to Reuters, had plunged 17.8% to a seasonally adjusted annual rate of 4.33 million units last month. The percentage decline was the largest since July 2010. The report followed data showing a record collapse in homebuilding and permits in April, too. The drop aligned with a fallout in retail sales and manufacturing production, leading economists to predict we were headed for the biggest contraction in gross domestic product in the second quarter since the Great Depression. Industry watchers said the worst of the housing market slump was probably behind us but it could remain subdued for a while due to so many people being out of work.

Regarding the retail aspect of this pandemic, the whole environment had changed because of it. Masks mandatory in stores. Shelves rearranged to separate items more definitively. Every other fitting room closed. Cashiers surrounded by plexiglass. Touchless payments. No sampling, e.g. trying on makeup, playing with toys. Now, instead of trying to get shoppers to hang around, stores wanted to get them in and out as quickly and safely as possible.

The government and private labs were all in an intense rush to develop a vaccine, but The Hill said that 1 in 4 people had little or no interest in getting it, noting the speed of development, according to a poll. And apparently the interest level was divided along party lines, with fewer Republicans interested.

Mid-morning, I got a callback from the Ford dealership with regard to my radio issue — bring it on over, they said. I complied. While tech Jose looked at it, I enjoyed the sun and walked around the lot, admiring other Rangers, F-150 pickups, the new Mustangs, an F-350 Super Duty truck, a Ford van shuttle for disabled veterans, Ford's parts delivery vehicle and a badass Ford F-150 XLT 4x4 with a Road Armor winch, tow hook, Rigid fog lights, Mayhem rims and more. Ultimately, my Ranger came out of the examining room with the diagnosis: Loose connector at the back of the radio. Easy fix, good as new and off I went back home.

I returned to my patio work, peeling away a large square of grass at the front right corner, transplanting that removed grass to a bare spot where the kayaks had stood and then prepping the square with crushed stone to receive the paving blocks, which I set in place. I finished the corner off by brushing sand into the cracks, swept the whole area, shuffled the grill, firepit and bar around and, finally, rewarded myself and my sore body by relaxing in one of my Adirondack chairs with a beer... followed by, you guessed it, another beer.

Really, I would have been happy to have continued to relax in that spot, to nap even, but had an appointment to keep with my friend Daphne, who I had planned to meet at Penfield Beach late afternoon. So, over I went, finding "summer" had arrived a day early. Not the actual first day of the Summer Solstice, of course, but the vibe of summer, which really was not to have begun until tomorrow, the day our Town had set for folks to be able to set out chairs and beach towels and swim and play frisbee and spike ball and, in general, congregate with each other in a less restrictive way. In fact, when I got to Penfield and strolled onto the beach, a Public Works guy was just then nailing a sign to the back of a lifeguard chair that read, "SOCIAL DISTANCING RULES IN EFFECT", with three distinct bullets below that: No more than five in a group; Wear face coverings when physical distance cannot be maintained; Keep distance of 15 feet between blankets and chairs.

Well, looking up and down the beach, I can tell you that these guidelines were being violated left, right and center. It seemed like any other day of any other Memorial Day Weekend ever since the beaches became recreational destinations for humankind. But, really, at this point, people were going to go ahead and be people. They knew the consequences. They were big boys and girls. So let the dice roll was the move, and let's see how we were all doing in a couple of weeks. I crossed my fingers hoping for the best.

Among the groups were neighbors from my street and their friends. As I waited for Daphne to appear, I chatted with one of the friends, about the "reopening" and the places I had already visited, including The Grape. For his part, he and his wife had had a meal at Aurora's, a Latin place right in our downtown.

Daphne came along anon, looking like the Sacramento-bred Cali girl that she was, with her long blonde hair flowing, Aviator glasses, leotard top and yoga pants, with a light jacket tied around her waist in case she needed it — which she definitely didn't as the temp was tickling the mid-70s. Still, right at the shore, as the sun goes down, you never know. The breeze can kick up and drive down the temp, particularly where we were headed, which was out along an old cow path that leads to our Penfield Reef Lighthouse. We talked about its history, and the ghost of the light keeper that haunts it, why cows were walked out on this jut of land and, in general, about the beauty of the site. Other couples strolled past and there were quite a few fishermen trying their luck. It was a very pleasant stroll and we gobbled in big mouthfuls of sea air, much to the glee of our lungs that had really only known stale inside-the-house air since mid-March.

Back home again, I used some new all-purpose cleaner, that I had bought on the last Stop & Shop run, to clean off the outside of the grill.

Then, while Phil made a salad inside, I grilled up some fat Italian sausages and steak cubes, and we dined at the patio table. Phil spoke of wanting a new vehicle. It was his habit to fix up a vehicle, drive it a while and then sell it off to find a new "project". Though he was only 20, he had been through four cars and a moped already. Now he was juggling a Nissan Versa, a Suzuki motorcycle and a gas-powered scooter and talking about changing out the bike. I preferred that he just relax and enjoy his current stable of motorized equipment, but supported his intentions if that was what he wanted to do.

He washed up our dishes and went for a drive while I cleaned the grill surface and then relaxed a bit more in one of the Adirondack chairs. I even added two candleholders and lit candles to add to the setting, which illuminated a generous bowl of ice cream I decided to have as an earned day capper. I was in bed by 9.

News: A White House butler, Wilson Jerman, who worked under 11 presidents, from Eisenhower through Obama, died at age 91 from Covid-19. In another illustration of Mother Nature's erratic behavior, powerful storms hammered Charlotte, North Carolina this afternoon, killing two people and leaving behind widespread tree and power line damage; the storm spurred a tornado, too, which touched down in Cherokee County, South Carolina. Brazil jumped to No. 2 in the world with regard to coronavirus cases, at over 350K and deaths numbering over 22K. NASA and SpaceX said they were a "go" to proceed with their historic crewed flight on May 27. Hertz filed for bankruptcy amid a sharp drop in demand. The U.S. successfully tested a laser weapon that could destroy aircraft mid-flight. A passenger jet crashed in Karachi, Pakistan killing 97 on board when it came down in a residential area — a survivor said all he could see was fire. Fairfield First Selectwoman Brenda Kupchick announced that the town's Fourth of July fireworks display would be canceled due to a state order against large group events, aimed at minimizing virus transmission. "We were holding out some hope that we might be able to put them on, but given the gathering order from the governor, we don't see how it will be possible," she said during her daily briefing. Global coronavirus cases pushed past 5.2 million with over 335K deaths, 2.1 mllion recoveries. The U.S. had 1,621,727 cases, 96,377 deaths, 382,244 recoveries. New York had over 366,357 cases, 28,885 deaths.

May 23. Because of my early turn-in, I was up at first light. It was quite foggy out and lightly raining. It was probably fortunate people set up and enjoyed the beach yesterday as today it wouldn't have been possible. I paced around in the backyard looking at the patio, feeling it was missing something: a planter and tropical plant at one corner, yeah, that was the ticket. So off I went to Home Depot, encountering a bicyclist at a midway point, cycling toward me out of the mist, like a Ghost Rider on the Storm, dressed in black with a black motocross helmet and black bandana covering the lower half of his face, a Grim Reaper on his rounds, pumping away madly at the pedals.

At HD, there was mainly contractor traffic, and those jobbers were in and out quickly and methodically, no hanging around and getting in the way or being nuisances. The few regular shoppers that were there were mainly collecting plants. They were masked, and some were gloved. Ahh, yes, pandemic big box, fun for all. Well, make way, people, The White Tornado was here (I announced in my head), on a run taking care of business this weekend.

HD was still doing the one-entrance routine, with a head counter counting heads. I swooped in, went straight to the garden department and made a tactical strike, picking up a bag of potting soil, a teal-colored plastic planter, a succulent plant that had very pointy tips (and that was "tips" for those of you scoring at home) and, for good measure, a "Windy Wings" flamingo plant stake which had moveable wings.

On the way back home, I called in at Chef's Table cafe, which had recently re-opened. The air was tropical — warm and moist — and it was spurring me to want to eat something tropical, like a breakfast burrito. I explained my craving to Owner/Chef Rich and he ordered up a wrap with scrambled eggs, bacon, salsa and avocado slices.

I spoke to a couple of the staff as I was waiting on my sandwich. A girl there was from El Salvador, where she still had some family. The cases there numbered 1,819 as of this morning, with 33 deaths. I knew that both Central America and South America, particularly Brazil, were really starting to get hard hit.

Another staffer there said his sister had contracted the virus, as well as her husband. Both had recovered, though his sister was taking longer to get back to her normal self. She would get winded easily from doing simple tasks.

For Rich's part, he said he had been ok mostly sitting out the last couple of months, and his employees had been collecting unemployment.

He said the payments from the government were generous to the extent that it was hard to get his people back — they were making more money being unemployed (something I had heard a lot) — but it all worked out in the end. About the job market in general, he said he had heard that recent college graduates were having trouble finding jobs so were signing up for more school, to get their Master's degrees. Why not, right?

When I got back home, I went straight to setting up the pot at the corner of the patio and, boink, popped that flamingo right in the middle of the pot. I think I was more psyched about the flamingo than anything, to be honest!

One side note, that I *had* to mention, was the warning on the underside of the pot (the diameter of which was 12 inches it was worth noting): "WARNING, Children can fall into bucket and drown. Keep children away from buckets with even a small amount of water in them". First, the only imaginable child that would fit in this pot would be a brand spanking newborn, and how would a newborn get access to this pot? Frankly, this was a silly alert. There, that was out of my system now!

Standing back from the patio and appreciating all that I had done, I still felt I could do more. That was the problem with being mostly homebound in a pandemic, you start to eyeball everything around you. How could I fix this? I should get to that. Why haven't I updated this? I should clean this out, etc. etc. etc.

So what hit my radar about the patio was that the original pavers needed a good scrubbing to return them to their original color, the seams needed to be weeded and four bricks were needed to finish off a back corner. Soooo, back to HD I went, this time finding the parking lot completely packed and the chaos like the last time I visited during "consumer hour". It was that risk of bodily harm feeling, of getting backed over, or struck, or having something fall on you. People were just so anxious and intense at this time.

With some direction from a masked staffer, I located what I needed and joined a line of shoppers shuffling along like lambs to slaughter into a slotted corral marked with X's on the floor, waiting for our number, our time, our call to the chopping block. With a cashier that might as well have been a butcher for the lack of regard she showed me, I settled up and bolted.

Well, bolted from the *store* anyhow. In the *parking lot*, I took my time, trying to find the safest egress, to avoid a collision or encounter.

On a side note about my face mask choice for the day, I was feeling that I needed something Memorial Day-ish and remembered that I had a woman's stars-and-stripes swimsuit upstairs in a drawer. Ok, that sounds totally weird, I know, but the deal was that, after I got divorced nine years ago, I thought I would pursue a couple of passions — writing and photography. And with regard to photography, I always thought it would be fun to be a model "clicker". I started inquiring of Facebook friends that were models if they were interested in being my subject matter and, to my surprise, they were agreeable. From Facebook friends, I progressed to women that I met out and about, always shooting for fun, just to make great photos. My talent became noticed and then women started to approach me for photos, and headshots, and portfolio pics, and themed scenarios, and so on.

Along the way, at a model showcase in Manhattan actually, I met a Korean girl named Grace. She was quite stunning, but also very approachable and friendly. I invited her up to Fairfield to do some patriotic-themed photos as a lead-up to July Fourth. And for the shoot, I purchased online a stars-and-stripes bikini. Super cute, and Grace looked stupendous in it, as she interacted with a huge American flag along the local shoreline. Well, when our shoot concluded, she left the suit with me. I washed it, put it back in its packaging and then stowed it away. I would have thrown it out but that seemed such a waste, particularly since it had only been worn once. But I couldn't very well give it to someone else either. As it sat at the back of a drawer, it became forgotten — out of sight, out of mind as they say. Like all the bandanas in with the Halloween stuff. Forgotten until a use presented itself, like a patriotic-themed face mask! I had even seen a couple of recent videos online wherein people had taken briefs or underwear and turned them into face masks. I was sure I could do the same in this case.

I examined the bra top first, and while the cups were padded and would be a good filter, the "triangles" were too small to amply cover the lower half of my face. So then I examined the bottoms, finding the back end fit over my nose and mouth and, that if I tucked the front side up into it, I had a workable mask, particularly if I safety pinned the front part to the back part. And both the top half and the bottom half had respective strings so that I

311

could secure them at the back of my head. The bonus was that the fabric was breathable, so it was a win-win.

I took a selfie with my "mask" on and posted it to my social media, much to the delight of friends, several of whom wanted to know where I bought it! To the greater public, I said it was home constructed, and only revealed the actual source to one friend through a private message — her husband had seen it and wanted one!

Late afternoon, after the rain had bucketed down for a bit, a familiar pair of people came walking down the road — Glenn and his daughter Lauren, walking their dog, Duffy. We had kept tabs on each other through social media but were more glad to see each other in person. We spoke of this unusual time and, as we did, I noticed Glenn wincing periodically. It turned out he had developed shingles, and not the kind you put on your roof. Apparently, if you had had chickenpox as a kid, the virus that it springs from stays in your system and can present itself again in your 50s and 60s as shingles. It was not fun, that was clear, except when you combined an anticonvulsant like gabapentin with gummy bears and started tripping, seeing exploding porcelain birds and the like. Talk about sucky timing — rashy, knife-to-the-ribs pain erupting during a time when you also have to worry if you're going to contract another virus that could kill you.

At some point I mowed, reducing the bright green blades to manageable stubble, like I later reduced the hair on my head and around my ears. That was one plus to be folicularly challenged during a pandemic — you didn't need to sit on pins and needles waiting for a salon or barber to open back up. You just took matters into your own hands. Much like you had to do as a single person in a pandemic, or is that TMI?`

My phone lit up with a Red Alert message, an auto dial from our First Selectwoman. She wanted to remind us all that the CDC recommended that we wear face coverings when we couldn't be at least six feet apart from each other and that, at the beach, we needed to keep our blankets and towels respective to our group at least fifteen feet away from another group's same gear. Also, lifeguards would be on duty this weekend, from 10am to 6pm, and police officers would "be available for any questions" (read = arrest your ass if you weren't following the rules). The beach bathrooms would remain closed per state directives, but portables had been brought in to meet "needs". I guess the thinking was that a portable can only accommodate one person, so that prevented multiple people being in the same room together at once. What that *didn't* address though was, if someone was infected and used the portable and someone else went right in afterwards, they put themselves at risk of contracting the virus. Hmm, so there was *that*. The FSW also mentioned that athletic fields and parks would be open, but not for play, just for socially distant relaxing or strolling. Our First Selectwoman concluded that, while we were not able to come together for our traditional celebrations, she hoped Fairfielders would keep veterans and their sacrifices in mind. She added, too, that our local public service TV station would be airing video on Memorial Day Monday of past holiday celebrations here in town. Hurrah for the red, white and blue.

Cuomo chimed in today. More "good news". There had only been 84 deaths in New York State yesterday. Oh boy. Though, actually, this *was* good news. Anything under a hundred deaths per day in New York from this viral beast was to be commended, though "still a tragedy".

Early evening, thoughts of Jen were dancing in my head. It had been almost three weeks since we went all but radio silent with each other. I broke the silence, texting: "How are you, honey?" She immediately texted back, "Are you sure you have the right number?" Nicely played. "Yes, of course," I replied. Then she FaceTimed me. She was at Westport's Compo Beach, walking, and flipped the camera view from herself to the water view. "Come pick me up, and bring water. I'm freaking thirsty!" she said, effecting what I called "boss mode". I had just made a spaghetti and meatballs dinner for Phil and me, which we had enjoyed at the dining room table. So there was a degree of clean-up and put-away to do before I could head out. But head out I did.

As I motored over, she peppered me with texts. "I don't have a mask." "Are you sure it's ok?" "Are you safe?" "I am walking back towards Long Shore Pearl." I was driving and didn't see any of these messages en route, so was startled to find her walking along the road a good half mile from where we said we were going to meet. I screeched to a halt. She looked up, cocked her eyebrows and climbed aboard. "You've gone crazy. *We've* gone crazy," she said.

She looked about the truck and actually complimented me on the purchase. I told her about the electric bike and the patio and rearranging furniture in the house, oh, and the wine club, which I backed out of but still got my first shipment. In fact, I had the Malbec from that group with my spaghetti this evening.

We circled back to her house but didn't go in at first. She wanted to finish her walk, so we walked together. I grabbed and held her hand and we did the loop through her neighborhood, returning to her house... where a great reunion was enjoyed. Later, she said she had tried to FaceTime me earlier, expecting to catch me at something I shouldn't have been up to. But I was at my desktop computer. And we both admitted to being stubborn and not contacting the other, expecting to make the other crack. So I guess I became the one who gave in, as she continued to maintain radio silence. But I don't think she could have held out much longer— she had been wearing my pajamas at night, after all, as a way to keep me close. So maybe she was not so strong after all.

We had some milk and Tate's cookies, of all things, in her living room later in the evening before sacking out. Then, for some reason, we awoke at 3:30am and started chatting. She was still interested in getting a place in Austin, Texas while I was still keen on Florida's Gulf coast, which she called the Redneck Riviera. That just forced me to adopt my redneck accent to make references to moonshine, Nascar, baby Jesus, skeeters, crawfish and banjos, all to our great amusement. Of course, none of those things were a part of the area I had in mind, and I had shown her photos of some of the properties there that we might enjoy. Rightly so, though, she had a concern about how, as an Asian girl, she would be perceived down there. And we spoke about her students, whom she had congratulated for "surviving pandemic piano lessons".

News: Global coronavirus cases shot past 5.3 million, with nearly 341K deaths, 2.178 million recoveries. The U.S. had 1,647,043 cases, with 97,687 deaths, 403,312 recoveries. New York had 367,936 cases, with 29,009 deaths.

May 24. I rolled at first light, making my ride from Westport back to Fairfield, past flag banners lining Downtown Fairfield's Post Road and a large banner that had been attached to the gazebo on our Sherman Town Green, shouting, "THANK YOU to our veterans & all who serve!" It had been posted by Al DiGuido, the founder of the charity group Al's Angels and owner of Saugatuck Sweets, the ice cream shop directly across from the Green.

A wave of tiredness came over me, forcing a two-hour nap followed by a sit for a bit outside in one of my Adirondack chairs. It was partly sunny and on the chilly side, hovering around 60, and wouldn't get much warmer than that.

Phil brought to my attention a jetski that was being sold privately in Westport. It was 26 years old and not currently running, but seemed in good shape and Phil thought he could easily fix it. And it appeared to come with a trailer, all for a modest price. We had discussed owning one and having it as a fun summer diversion. Maybe this was our opp?

My Dad and brother checked in first from Dulles Airport, which was empty, then Denver Airport, empty as well. And they shared in-flight pics of mountain ranges, red rocks and their PPE disguises.

There were some recent news items I had seen and wanted to address…

A New York Post article spoke of a Florida woman who miraculously survived "a terrifying attack by a pack of dogs" only to end up contracting the coronavirus while recovering at a rehab center. The woman's daughter described the attack: "She was pretty much being tossed around like a chew toy by the four dogs. She's a tiny little woman, so the fact that she's alive is amazing." The woman's son-in-law described the aftermath: "Her skull is gone completely from here to the entire back. Her leg, it was pretty much eaten away. They had to shorten her leg two inches to make all of the blood vessel connections." Her injuries were so severe, in fact, that she flatlined twice amid several surgeries, he added. She survived Covid-19 but was still recovering from her horrific dog attack injuries.

I read about a couple of Los Angelenos, Shelby and Wes, who met through the dating app Bumble, who were developing a relationship in this strange no-touchy time. After a number of text messages and phone calls, they met for a date — he stood outside her apartment, they spoke through a window and shared a bottle of wine and some carbonara through the portal. Over the next four weeks, their quarantine love story blossomed and attachment deepened, though they hadn't even dared to hold hands. But more meals got shared through the window as well as gift exchanges — she made him a bracelet with block letters spelling "howdy", a nod to a text message about his Texas roots. They often discussed what they would do when some normalcy returned, like going to a favorite restaurant or to a local park. "In a really weird way, it's kind of given us a chance to not be distracted by just going out on a nice dinner or going to see a movie," Wes said. "For me, it feels a little bit more personal... I don't know any other time that we would have so much availability to get to know each other." He added, "It really sells the whole being-in-grade-school dating thing."

According to BuzzFeed, in the 1940s, women were led to believe they needed to wash their vaginas with Lysol or else their husbands would leave them. The article offered an ad as proof, with the narration: "She was a Jewel of a Wife... with just one flaw. She was guilty of the 'ONE NEGLECT' that mars many marriages. LYSOL helps avoid this." A seemingly obvious fact, Lysol is a toxic chemical when it comes in contact with delicate tissues in the body. Women would regularly complain about the product giving them vaginal burning and blisters.

A NYT article offered that "the role of the automobile has been reinvented in the coronavirus era", turned into "a mini-shelter on wheels, safe from contamination, a cocoon that allows its occupants to be inside and outside at the same time." Drive-in theaters, as I had noted, had been experiencing renewed interest. People were picnicking from sedans and pickup trucks. Birthdays, baby showers and graduations were being celebrated by drive-by waves from the car windows. Drivers were meeting up and parking side by side to chat with each other. There were curbside pick-ups of groceries, hardware and toilet paper. Laundromats were taking in bundles handed off through car windows. Cars had allowed their owners to widen their worlds, to go beyond Zoom video calls. The auto had become the *ultimate* PPE.

A Cable News Network story shared that people were emerging from isolation with stuff to donate. They had turned their attentions inward, to their home environments, thinking over a period of months about the things they didn't need any longer. I had done that very drop-off recently with Phil's shoes. And I was *sure* I could shed a bunch of my *own* things if I could confirm that a local thrift store was available to receive them. Until such confirmation, though, I would sit tight.

College students across the country were bumming out in big numbers. According to Forbes, 20% were more depressed, 11% were more anxious and 16% were more lonely. A peer-to-peer counseling group said, in fact, that "Pandemic anxiety is almost three times more worrying to this age group than any other stress-creating experiences pre Covid-19." It was mainly all about the unpredictability of the world, and the reality that when things are unpredictable, they're very hard to deal with, suggested a psychologist.

As summer approached, NPR discussed the risks associated with various activities. To start with, it all depended on your age and health, the prevalence of the virus in your area and the precautions you were taking during the activities. The article was quick to say "there's no such thing as a zero-risk outing right now." Beyond that, an epidemiologist put it down to four factors: time, space, people, place. Essentially, the more time you spent and the closer in space you were to any infected people, the higher your risk, and indoor places were riskier than outdoors. A colleague suggested, "Always choose outdoors over indoor, always choose masking over not masking and always choose more space for fewer people over a small space." Take going to a party for instance, to lower risk, it was advised to avoid sharing food, drinks or utensils — to make it a BYO-everything party.

And it just so happened that I (and by association, Jen) was invited to such a gathering this afternoon: a birthday party for my Westport artist friend Sholeh. And, in fact, guests were advised to bring everything they needed. I packed up sports chairs and a cooler with drinks and snacks and, at around 3pm, set off to pick up Jen...

We were fashionably late for the mid- to late afternoon fête, held in Evan Harding Park near the Inn at Longshore in Westport. Covid-19-looking decor hung from the trees, and a table was set up with soft drinks, hard seltzer and wraps from Gaetano's, a local deli. Folks were Sunday trendy and most attendees had face masks, though they were hanging around their necks, as were our own. We set up my folding camp chair loveseat and a fold-up aluminum table, opened beverages and milled about, snapping pics, enjoying the water views and catching up — at a safe physical distance and devoid of handshakes or hugs — about what we had all been up to over the past three months.

The host's daughter, Nicolette, had given up her NYC apartment lease to move home with her parents. They were having fun doing Tik Tok shows together. Another artist friend, who goes by the nickname Sooo-z, was showing off her homemade mask. Ann from Manila was the only guest wearing her mask, but that didn't last long. She had three sons with a Scottish man she met in the Philippines. Hema, a divorced mom of three boys (5th grade to age 19), was juggling homeschooling, dishwashing and house care. Christian rock singer Elayne had been doing some live streaming of her original songs. Magazine publisher Tracey was on hand with her beau. It was an interesting mix of folks and a pleasant way to spend a couple of hours.

Jen wanted to swing by Southport Beach, which we did for a bit, where I suggested we just keep going into Southport and grab a bite at Paci Restaurant. Co-owner Donna was there to greet and sit us down, at a sunny table. We snarfed up some water and bread and enjoyed some chicken scarpiello and pasta bolognese. Donna was glad to see us "lovebirds" and we were glad to see her, and to chat with a family at a neighboring table. They were playing Eye Spy, and Jen's pink lipstick was the answer to one set of clues. That kicked off a conversation about the booming real estate market in this area, Jen's waffling about selling her house, homeschooling challenges, and the kids missing their classmates.

I took Jen back to her home via a scenic route and u-turned towards Fairfield, taking the Post Road back. At Southport, I scooped by the harbor inlet and dropped down to Sasco, where I pulled in and went on foot to snap a couple pics of the sunset, always a treat from that vantage point. There were a fair number of people there, paired up, some masked up and all glad for the fresh air and rosy sky.

Catching some news late day, WCBS Radio reported that Pres. Trump had ordered the closure of travel to the U.S. from Brazil as that country recorded the second highest number of virus cases compared with America. He had already banned certain travelers from China, Europe, the U.K., Ireland and Iran. He had not yet moved to ban travel from Russia, which had the world's third-highest caseload.

NY Gov. Cuomo said today that pro sports leagues in New York — the NFL, MLB, NHL, NBA and WNBA — could begin training camps as the state continued "preparing for a new chapter in this saga". He added, "We want you up, we want people to be able to watch sports to the extent people are still staying home. It gives people something to do. It's a return to normalcy. So we are working and encouraging all sports teams to start their training camps as soon as possible." Cuomo also said veterinary offices could begin to open Tuesday. State beaches had already opened; campgrounds were going to open tomorrow. Regionally, the Mid-Hudson area and Long Island were set to reopen as well.

News: Global coronavirus cases climbed over 5.4 million with over 344K deaths, 2.257 million recoveries. The U.S. had 1,666,829 cases and 98,683 deaths, nearly 447K recoveries. New York had nearly 370K cases and over 29K deaths.

May 25. Memorial Day. In a surprise to no one, the area was struck by a White Tornado, creating deep ripples, in particular, in our Fairfield Beach Area, upsetting patio furniture, taking the very finish off paving stones, soaking grass and pummeling populations of area birds and farm animals. Okay, so it was me. Yes, I was the White Tornado, moving my chairs off my patio so I could spray and scrub my paving stones, spraying down new seeded grass, and then preparing grill food including teriyaki chicken, bbq pork chops and bacon-wrapped peeled shrimp, refrigerating it all for a moment. It was a spontaneous attack for me, mostly unplanned, but supported the goal of having a meeting of the "Asian Wives Club" at my home this afternoon.

Explanation needed, of course. Really, the idea popped into my head at yesterday's birthday gathering in Westport. Wouldn't it be nice to have some people over for Memorial Day? So when I returned home, I FB messaged a Norwalk friend and his Korean wife and a Danbury friend and his Taiwanese wife. This morning, I shared a handwritten invitation with my soon-to-be-moving next door neighbor and his Filipina wife. With my Jen and her Malaysian/Chinese background, and my son, Phil, whose heritage is half Indian, on hand, this would truly be an "Asian Collective".

Speaking of Asians, I got an email greeting from my Darien, CT-based Japanese artist friend, Nobu, who shared, "Hope this mail finds you well. This is Memorial day we have never thought of. We miss the parade, American flags, bagpipers and familiar faces. I hope my painting will bring you little smile." She attached a colorful, patchwork rendering.

Nooooo, don't mess with my beer festivals, C-19! My very real anguish was a response to an email announcing that The Great American Beer Festival, the largest of its kind in the U.S., had pivoted to an online-only event taking place in mid-October. The real-ness of our crisis was hitting home (insert tongue in cheek here).

On a related beer note, our local brewery, Two Roads, in Stratford, announced a major initiative to help CT restaurants recover from the effects of Covid-19, with a plan to offer them a substantial "Back On the Road" discount on a selection of its fresh draft products, from June 1 thru July 31. Two Roads was also working with its distributors to split the cost of refunding retailers for draft beer that was no longer fresh enough for sale.

An email rolled in from Road Runner Sports with a spotlighted graphic, "Thank Goodness for Running". The message acknowledged how tough 2020 had been so far and expressed the hope that receivers "take a moment not only to remember what makes America so great and make new memories with family, but also to remember why running is important to you." And on that note, it included some inspirational messages from associated runners. Like Elizabeth: "Running means that in the midst of everything going on, I'm still able to maintain a key part of my daily routine: my morning run!" And Deivid: "Thank goodness for running. Through running I have met the most amazing people and seen the most amazing places." And @ontherunfit, who shared, "Right now, running means freedom. With so many things that we aren't allowed to do right now, running is one constant."

I knew that Fairfielders could not let Memorial Day go by without some sort of recognition or celebration, on a public face, that is. And so I ventured out, toward our town's Honor Roll wall, listing the names of over 4,000 veterans. I found two families at the site, who were mourning the cancellation of the parade, and just wanted to be a part of *something*, *anything*, related to the day. Well, I think I made their day showing up, as it brought us all together in spirit. And, as we stood there, magical things started to happen. Down the road, we started hearing horns tooting, emanating from a mini convoy of cars — perhaps 15 in the lineup — full of families waving flags and calling out. Then up the block came marching a merry band of folks led by local personality Kevin Jennings carrying an enormous American flag suspended from a staff. His followers included fireman Joe Rainis and family, a couple of veterans and the wives or family members of veterans. All carried smaller flags and other patriotic decor. They came together in front of the wall, where Kevin addressed the group and all that cared to wander over and listen. He told tales of his ancestors and their service and invited others up to speak about their own. The "ceremony" was about five minutes long. I hovered for a while afterwards then took a circle through town, seeing Kevin again, just him, carrying his monster flag on the side of the road near the Community Theater. He was determined to be a one-man Memorial Day parade.

As I rounded my way back home, there was the *other* one-man band, Al DiGuido, in front of his Saugatuck Sweets ice cream shop, preparing a barbecue of all-American hot dogs and hamburgers, for the community to feast on, while accepting donations for his Al's Angels charity. Across from his shop, all his patriotic decor, banners and signage flapped in the breeze. It was a glorious sight.

There was a musical note to that scene, too. First off, a bagpiper strolled onto the Green and stood by the Gazebo to play "Amazing Grace" and "God Bless America". Then, redheaded, lanky Sophia Brooks, a trumpeter, took her turn. A 2018 graduate from Fairfield Ludlowe High School and rising junior at Gettysburg College, she stood atop a picnic table on the Green to play Taps. Traditionally the final call of the evening in the U.S. military but also a fixture at military funerals, the tune was created by Oliver Willcox Norton during the American Civil War to honor his men who were resting in Virginia after a seven-day battle. Our own community had earned the song for the now 75-day battle we had been fighting against Covid-19.

Talk about Pandemonium! Early afternoon, a Fairfield Animal Control van pulled up on our street and was going property to property looking for a small white long-haired dog, a chow-chow I think, that had escaped from its owner. I helped locate it in a yard across the street, where the investigating officer was able to corral and collect it.

My guests started arriving at about 3:30 and, really, we weren't quite sure how to act around each other. With the first couple to arrive, from Norwalk, I elbow bumped hello, defaulting to safety. I would have loved to have hugged them, of course, particularly given their party contributions: custom cigars from NYC's Nat Sherman Townhouse near Bryant Park and a bottle of Beringer Bros. Bourbon Barrel Aged Red Wine Blend. Notably, the legendary king of luxury cigars, Sherman opened his first shop in the Big Apple in 1930. It fast gained a reputation among the glitterati — movie stars, famous athletes, gangsters, pretty much anyone that enjoyed a fine smoke.

My Danbury friends entered the back yard wearing matching face masks. They had pre-announced on Facebook that they were coming: "We are going to our first get together since this pandemic started. Memorial

Day cookout with some friends. Time to start living again." They were the more cautious and unsure among us, but no less eager to "thaw" out. They brought a couple of wonderful desserts.

Then Jen showed, in Memorial Day white slacks and a pastel violet button-down sleeveless top and, well, just looked delicious. As tasty were her *own* food offerings: a strawberry shortcake, pita bread squares and chive dip, Cape Cod potato chips and an arugula salad with strawberry slices and croutons. She would later tell me, "I was determined to make you happy."

Any "ice" between us all melted quickly, particularly as we started a game of cornhole, using the wooden platforms that my woodworker friend Joe had custom made for me a couple of summers back. Some local brews and Malbec wine helped create the Puddle Effect.

A fourth couple was going to round out our group, from next door, but he wandered over, with a mask on, to say his wife and baby were sleeping and that he had been working with a lot of Covid patients and didn't want to get anyone sick. So our Asian-American quartet was narrowed to a trio.

Before settling in to eat, we decided to take a rip around in my pickup, with all but one adult riding in the back bed. "I haven't ridden in the back of a pickup since high school," Danbury exclaimed. "This is fun!" Norwalk squealed. "This bed is clean," Norwalk 2 observed. Danbury 2 was my inside passenger and peered out the back window hatch. Anon, we were at Penfield, which looked particularly pandemic paradisiacal, with clusters of folks sunning, circled up to chat, swimming, grilling and boating. We went and eyeballed Sasco, too, which was at capacity but the guard there allowed us a loop-through.

With our moods elevated, I fired up the grill, sounded the bugle and sent my brave, marinated pork, chicken and shrimp minions into the face of battle. It was a fiery skirmish, involving flamethrowers, boiling oil and metal implements, and when the smoke cleared, their hulking charred corpses lay scattered across the field of combat. I plucked them from the fray, placed them en masse in pyrite crypts sealed with aluminum foil, and presented the martyrs to my eager cohorts, who bared teeth like hungry wolves at the sight.

And did we feast? Not a word was spoken, other than the occasional satisfied grunt, a lick of the chops or clash of a utensil against a dish. More beverages followed, glasses raised in victory. We had won the day and patted our bellies in great satisfaction.

Danbury was first to depart. We thanked them for their service. Norwalk hung tight, unveiling their smoking equipment, plump stogies and magic elixirs as I created a pyre that was suitable for gods. We enjoyed its warmth and glow, the midnight blue sky, the rustle of the canopy of leaves above us and idle chatter.

Finally, Norwalk went on leave, as did Sgt. Jen and her squadron of bowls and plates, leaving Phil and I to straighten up the base and retreat inside. The evening entertainment in the Mess Hall at Fort Mike was the second half of "Inglorious Basterds", which completed our conflict-oriented themes for the night.

News: Global coronavirus cases surged past 5.5 million cases, with over 347K deaths, 2.315 million recoveries (not quite half). The U.S. had 1,686,791 cases, with 99,311 deaths, 451,745 recoveries (almost 1/3). New York had 371,193 cases, 29,231 deaths. Cases worldwide continued to grow at over 100K per day.

May 26. Rain had fallen in the overnight, onto ground that had been warmed by yesterday's late afternoon sun, which was now resulting in a heavy fog that had settled in and shrouded everything, like steam on the lenses of glasses. I took a lap around the property, checking to make sure the fire in the firebowl had gone out and that there was no remaining debris laying about from the party. I tore up a slice of bread, too, and placed the bits on the ledges of the bird feeder. And over a cold brew coffee, I scrolled through email.

One amusing story was about a sandwich chain called Potbelly, which was testing "Alone Time Parking Spots" for parents, stressed by quarantining with their families, to find some peace and quiet away. The chain created these in the absence of other traditional pre-pandemic escapes — going for a drink with friends or to the gym — that were now considered health risks. The dedicated spaces were identified with signage that included a graphic of a family of four with a line through it and further explanation, "Children and Conference Calls Prohibited".

At noontime, NY Gov. Cuomo gave his daily, this time from the NY Stock Exchange building, which had just reopened for in-person trading. The facility was operating with fewer people and all those were wearing masks. It was a historic rebirth. The governor said "the numbers" continued to trend downward — "still coming down the mountain" — including deaths, which were at 73 for yesterday, which would be abhorrent at any other time in history, but was the lowest it had been since the beginning of the pandemic.

Cuomo commented that Memorial Day signaled a turning point in the year, when we typically transition into a summer mode. The state's mid-Hudson region was reopening today and Long Island was set to reopen tomorrow, having met all their criteria to do so. Each region was assigned a regional control group whose job it was to monitor the numbers and to jump on any clusters of new cases. "See a little movement and pounce on it," Cuomo advised. NYC was still another story, with cases continuing to rise, particularly in minority communities among people that had been staying home and/or were unemployed. Testing in those areas was being done so intensely that zip codes that were hot spots could be called out. The 10467 zip in The Bronx was most problematic, followed by the 11691 and 11368 zips in Queens, and 11226 zip in Kings County. My ex-wife Marlene had grown up in the 10462 zip in The Bronx, which shared a northwestern border with worst-hit 10467. If her parents were still alive and living there, she would have been worried sick about them.

Phil got inspired to go on a solo kayak excursion, strapping one of our crafts to the roof rack of his mobile and heading out. As the temp slid into the 70s and the air grew muggy, I worked away at email and social media, getting a world pulse reading.

Reflecting on yesterday's party, I was concerned to read a Vox story that said "the greatest Covid-19 risk is being around breathing, laughing, coughing, sneezing, talking, people." Well, that was us lot doomed. Though, for our part, we were pretty good about social distancing, had a huge bottle of hand sanitizer within arm's reach and weren't sharing food. Rather, we were each selecting our own pieces from the serving dishes. Hell, maybe there was some cross-pollination, as it were, but damn how could there not be a little — from shared serving spoons, cornhole bean bags, chairs. We just couldn't be so worried every moment. At some point, you had to assume risk — or stay home in your cave and never venture out.

If schools reopened for in-person learning this Fall, who actually was going to show up? A USA Today piece suggested that there would be a

LOT of empty seats. To start, 1 in 5 teachers said they were unlikely to return to reopened classrooms. Separately, 6 in 10 parents with at least one child in grades K-12 said they would be likely to pursue at-home learning options instead of sending their children back. The disruption in traditional schooling, in fact, might have even *longer term* effects as doubt heightened that a true safe institutional environment could be provided. Sadly, it was students that were going to suffer in the end, likely falling behind and becoming socially disconnected and dysfunctional.

An email from Fathom accurately summed up this very moment in time, nailing our reality, and offered a challenge to make it better than it might be. "This is usually the time of year when NYC forces summer into bloom. Rickety bistro tables cram into impossible outdoor spaces, playground basketball courts draw sideline crowds, sunny park benches become prime real estate, and rosé bottles pop as the sun passes over the yardarm. To say that this is an anti-climactic start to summer is the understatement of the century. Though New Yorkers stay positive, the frightening realities of the pandemic are playing out front and center here. Even as things slowly open up, we're looking at a season filled with discrepancies, uncertainties, and anxieties. Can we also make it one filled with explorations, learnings, new routines, and a redistributing of psychic and physical resources to those in need?"

Nat Geo spotlighted a six-by-six-mile volcanic island called Tristan da Cunha, located in the South Atlantic Ocean roughly halfway between Brazil and South Africa, noting it remained safe from the virus. Its nearest neighbor was 1,500 miles away and it had no airport. The island's leader, James Glass, said, "All we have for our protection is our isolation and our faith."

Higgins Group private brokerage hit me with an email commenting on the market in Westport, confirming, "We have had a surge in rentals the past couple of months with NYC renters particularly wanting furnished houses with pools and paying a premium for them. Now that the renters are settled in, I believe we will start to see even more increased demand in the sales market. Our inventory levels are particularly low — down almost 32% from the same time last year and the numbers of closed sales are up a significant 42% for the same time period. Our sales prices have remained stable year on year, however we are seeing multiple offer situations so as we see more closed inventory over the next month or so, our prices should reflect that demand." Yet another blessing for sellers here.

For a Covid-19 vaccine to be ready to use, world bodies have predicted timing of delivery of anywhere from a year to 18 months, best-case scenarios. That was a LOT quicker than the usual five to 10 *years* it can take. So, how was the development going? Much faster than normal, with first human trials conducted, as we knew, just two months after the virus was identified. As of May 15, WHO said there were 110 candidate vaccines in preclinical evaluation around the world, and eight in human Phase 1 and Phase 2 trials.

AXIOS said the CDC was warning of "aggressive" rats as the virus lockdown put humans and their waste out of reach and made the rodents hungry. In New Orleans alone, hundreds of thousands of the nocturnal beasts were searching much farther for food, and in daylight hours. In March-April, Wash. DC reported almost 500 rodent-related call-outs; Baltimore had 11,000 proactive calls and 311 online requests. In NY, the rats were even turning on each other, eating each other's young and battling for food.

The Independent said a "once-in-a-decade" storm hit western Australia over the Memorial Day weekend, leaving more than 50K households without power and causing much structural damage. This system was the remnant of the storm that clobbered India last week and just kept on going. Mother Nature was just *furious* with us, it seemed, and I feared she had a whole lot more tricks for us as we stepped further into Atlantic hurricane season.

BBC News shared the story of a couple who dropped out of life, bought a van, packed it up and went on the road... and now were halted by the virus. Radka and Ivar met in central Norway in 2016. Both were caretakers for the same disabled man - she was night shift, he was day. They would meet for five minutes every day as the shift changed. She had previously hitchhiked from Russia to southeast Asia and was preparing to do the same from Argentina to Alaska. That plan morphed to traveling the Americas by van, starting in Chile after transporting their vehicle from Germany across the Atlantic and through the Panama Canal. They set off this past January, aiming for southern Argentina. Then they started to hear about Covid lockdowns in Europe. On March 15, the borders closed behind them in Argentina. Camping had been banned country-wide, so they had to hide out and wild-camp. When the weather allowed, they paddled on a nearby lake or went running. They rope-climbed trees. They washed in the local water. Running out of cooking gas forced them to a city, where they learned the crisis was deepening. They were intercepted by police and escorted to an apartment a friend secured for them, where they were mandated to quarantine inside for two weeks. They ultimately learned of repatriation flights out of Buenos Aires and hopped a plane, leaving their van behind.

The front page of this past week's Sunday NYT featured little human figures representing the nearly 100,000 American lives lost to the coronavirus. It was what the Times did best, capturing a historic or historical moment — that had no bearing on politics or party membership — in a dramatic way. Select figures were called out, e.g. Cancer survivor born in the Philippines. Loretta Mendoza Dionisio, 68, Los Angeles.

The WSJ said there were some glimmers of economic recovery happening: American air travelers numbering 300K a day now (in good times, that was over two million), hotel bookings starting to uptick, mortgage applications being filed and new business applications perking up.

A Korean company called Okyung International had developed an antiviral chemical that could be applied to clothing during the textile finishing process to make the apparel anti-microbial as a defense and deactivator of the Covid virus. It was the first of its kind to be proven effective.

A Welsh zoo said it may have to kill hundreds of animals because of the risk of them starving to death due to a lack of funds amid this pandemic. It would first try to re-home them but, failing that, would have to euthanize them. They had funds to last for another week.

Coronavirus shutdowns in Canada were creating a condom shortage which may lead to another health crisis of sexually transmitted diseases. Nine of the country's 10 provinces had declared STI outbreaks before the virus even *arrived*. Shelter-in-place directives impeded access to prevention, testing and treatment as clinics culled back services to make room for Covid testing.

Phil and I were both concerned to learn that a 23-year-old UConn senior was being hunted by federal, state and local authorities for killing two people and stabbing another this past Friday, in Willington and Derby, CT respectively. He was said to have had mental issues for years — we wondered if they were exacerbated by this whole public health crisis.

My eyes were getting tired reading and the day was too pleasant to be inside, so late afternoon, I took a spin in The Lone Ranger, to our Penfield Beach. It was dotted with people but not being monitored by lifeguards or police as on the holiday weekend. Despite that, people seemed to be behaving. And it all looked normal... until two teens in swimsuits approached from their beach towels — wearing face masks — heading to the snack bar for ice cream.

I putzed around a bit back home then went and picked up Jen in my lunar module, rocketing with her to the Inn at Longshore in Westport, executing a perfect landing in the lot at The Pearl restaurant there. I noted social distancing advisories in the lot, which spoke to folks who had decided to come and dine on the Inn's great patio. As Jen and I set off on foot across the great lawn behind the restaurant, we looked back to see staffers in face masks attending to diners under strings of white party lights.

The pathway Jen and I fell into was not an uncharted area; on the contrary, a handful of other explorers had come to admire the view or share a sunset beverage. We bounced along the terrain and watched our blazing sun, too, reflected on the still surface of the adjacent life-sustaining body of water, long ago named Long Island Sound. We clambered along a rocky stretch, did a u-turn and returned to our module, planning one other quick jaunt, to a manned satellite known as Joe's Pizza. The crew there made a doughy delight that was popular in this part of the galaxy, which featured sausage and mushrooms. We orbited outside until a tech in PPE gear signaled us for pickup.

Landing back at Jen's Space Station, we plated our fare and settled back in the rec room to watch "Cat's Meow", a William Randolph Hearst tale set on his boat.

Midway through the viewing, Jen decided there should be a zero-countdown rocket launch. Let's just say we obliterated the launch pad and a nearby satellite. Later, I was called into service again, this time to help color Jen's hair, a space program first for me. I donned latex gloves while she mixed the topical solution, then I went into action, administering liberal strokes of goopy gel to her long strands, which had suffered the adverse effects of mortality combined with our often toxic air quality.

I returned to my regularly scheduled programming while she then applied a green face shield. With her hair askew and the alien visage, she was quite the interplanetary marvel. Some folding of vestiges followed before we retired to her cabin quarters for a slumber that seemed weightless and cosmic, as star dust danced through our heads.

News: Global coronavirus cases surged by another 100K+ cases, to well over 5.6 million, with nearly 349K deaths, 2.4 million recoveries. The U.S. had 1,709,388 cases, with 99,909 deaths, 465K+ recoveries. New York state had 372,494 cases and 29,310 deaths. Apparently, the secret to living a long life was having two cherries in your Manhattan cocktail, according to a 100-year-old woman — virus be damned.

May 27. I was floating in the most peculiar way, out of communication with ground control, in a radio blackout on the dark side of the Moon, cruising through the cosmos, Earth below, drifting, falling, weightless... Then, some crackling, radio chatter... or was that birds? A mourning dove? The parachute deployed. I emerged from the clouds. They had me in view. My parachute deployed. I was right on target. Sploosh! The underside of the capsule smacked the water and we went under for a moment, our bearings unsure. But then we bobbed up, and settled, and it was morning, and I was awake, and I was refreshed, and I was lying next to an angel who was curled up like a fetus, but not a fetus, but a glorious giver of pleasure and song and beauty... who just wanted to sleep a little longer... so I scrolled on my phone.

USA Today took a cue from the NYT and created its own front page with the photos of 100 of the now more than 100,000 Americans that had been struck down by the coronavirus.

Mother Nature continued to be a brat, sacking *northern* India this time, with a heat wave delivering brain-baking temps of around 115F degrees, according to BBC News. It compounded the difficulties in an area struggling with rising Covid-19 infections and swarms of locusts ravaging crops.

"MN" was putting the American West in the frying pan, too, punishing that region with record scorching heat: afternoon highs in the 100s and 110s from Northern California to the desert Southwest. I alerted Dad by text to this forecast, given that he and Dave were still out there. Dad replied, "Definitely in the nineties yesterday, today and tomorrow, but we're mostly at 6,000' in the high desert. Very arid, like 21% humidity, so that helps, too. Drinking lots of water. And the occasional beer!"

Let's throw an avalanche into the mix. An avalanche of evictions, that is, bearing down on America's renters, according to the NYT, targeting millions of lower-income families and hourly workers whose jobs had been cut during this pandemic and whose government relief payments and legal protections had run out, leaving them with little financial cushion and few choices when looking for new housing. "I think we will enter into a severe renter crisis and very quickly," a Columbia Law School professor tracking eviction policies said. These people would face displacement at a time when people were still being urged to stay at home and keep themselves and their communities safe.

These folks were probably not good prospects to buy QB Tom Brady's customized 2018 Becker ESV Cadillac Escalade, which the six-time Super Bowl champ had put up for sale with a $300K price tag. "From day one, it became my sanctuary from the outside noise," he said about the vehicle, being marketed as a "mobile office" with a 32-inch HD LCD screen TV, a rear 12-inch screen and a savant-controlled A/V system. It was stretched to an additional 20 inches, with the rear doors extended by 10 inches. The ride was $350K brand new and had 13,000 miles on it.

On the opposite end of MN's bag of tricks was a tropical depression, called Bertha, that she rendered on Miami, dropping six inches of rain in two hours. It had since moved due north, eventually soaking Ohio and western Pennsylvania and causing flash flooding.

Jen's eyes started to flutter open. My little China Girl. I hear her heart beating, loud as thunder, my little China Girl. She reached over to her bedside table and grasped a small plastic container of honey-colored oil and asked me to rub her feet, which I happily did, though my hands still ached from weekend yard work. But I knew that her podiatric sensations had the power of sending telegraph messages to "other" zones, which was an overarching plus. And it was not at all unpleasant to run my thumbs along the contours of her pretty feet and toes.

The rubbing concluded, Jen then grabbed a sonic vibrator — not for a nether region application but for facial stimulation, to counter the tugging downward pull of gravity, moving the faintly buzzing unit in circles around her face.

The rubbing and the circling and the oil and the vibrating and the energy of the morning had the collective effect of setting up another launch. "All systems are go!" declared Control. Stabilizers up, running perfect, we're now in orbit, thrusters on, across the stratosphere, rockets full, driving deep, penetrating the void, kaleidoscopic flashes, and then an incredible deafening implosion accompanied by a scream that cannot be heard in this starry biosphere.

Houston cheered our achievement, we slipped back into autopilot mode and Jen pulled a hand-typed page of scrawl from her side table. It was a message she wanted to read on camera about an upcoming virtual student concert she was producing. She read the passage once, then again. I reacted and blessed it. Related to her pupils, it was the perfect sum-up to what had been a most unusual semester of piano instruction. We made a plan to record it back at the site by the Inn where we had strolled last night and, on that note, showered and re-fueled our jets with java.

From Jen's bright, glass enclosed dining space, I gazed out on the patio, watching two chipmunks chasing each other, then two squirrels following suit. It seemed the local fauna and we humans had the same ideas this morning.

Jen atom-smashed the reverie, bursting into the room like a shooting star to "fix her face", check email and simultaneously serve us up a fine nibble of toast with butter, a white cheddar cheese, and Lucien organic strawberry preserves, along with de-shelled hard boiled eggs flavored "Asian-style" with white pepper and soy sauce.

Jen had a quick FaceTime call with her dad, too, who was home in Malaysia. He was watching international news on TV, sharing a story from our Minneapolis of the case of alleged police brutality wherein a white officer knelt on a black suspect's neck to bring him under control, which apparently resulted in the man expiring.

In my experience, police didn't go around applying that kind of tactic unless a suspect wasn't following their commands and instruction. I thought that might be the case here but did not know the events leading up to the confrontation. So, I self-informed.

"Officers were advised that the suspect was sitting on top of a blue car and appeared to be under the influence," an official police statement reported. "Two officers arrived and located the suspect, a male believed to be in his 40s, in his car. He was ordered to step from his car." The report continued, "After he got out, he physically resisted officers. Officers were able to get the suspect into handcuffs and noted he appeared to be suffering medical distress. Officers called for an ambulance." The man died soon after, the statement noted, adding, "At no time were weapons of any type used by anyone involved in this incident." Also, "Body-worn cameras were on and activated during this incident."

Of course, objectors of this alleged police brutality cried, "This abusive, excessive and inhumane use of force cost the life of a man who was being detained by the police for questioning about a non-violent charge." Yes, it was a non-violent charge but the suspect resisted and was belligerent. And now there was a protest mob gathering and press feeding off the frenzy like sharks smelling blood in the water. It seemed to be the worst of America on show.

It came time to do Jen's production. Because skies were cloudy, we nix'ed the Inn site, favoring an indoor setting of her standing by her piano. What could be more appropriate, right? With my iPhone in one hand and holding her typed message in the other, so that she wouldn't have to memorize it and could look straight into the camera more or less, we did a couple of takes. This was the introduction to the concert. We did a second short version, on her patio, which was the invitation to tune in. As we concluded the session, her quartet of cleaning ladies appeared, entering her house one by one after spraying the bottom of their shoes with an anti-bacterial solution.

I took the Post Road back to Fairfield, noticing that Lions Paw & Co's retail space in Downtown Fairfield was empty. It was a weird contrast to see a large "FOR LEASE" banner splashed across the front of the store, behind an iconic bronze statue of Mark Twain relaxing on a bench. The statue was a town fixture that many had posed with from time to time, sitting next to Twain or otherwise interacting with him. No doubt someone had slipped a face mask on him as people had done with many other local iconic statues.

Another sign, in front of the Shell Station in Ring's End Plaza, advertised, "Fireworks Sold Here", in advance of the Fourth of July no doubt. We would all be making our own fireworks show this year in the absence of a town-sponsored one.

Like a forceful weed, a new Prestige Dollar Store had popped up in the shopping complex anchored by Bob's Stores. It was no doubt on a short-term lease filling a space vacated by another more substantial business, though I didn't recall what was there. A shoe store? Exercise center?

Bob's Stores itself had a huge yellow banner with red-and-black letters screaming "25% Off Your Entire Purchase". I was guessing they were hurting for business and potentially on their last spindly legs, judging from the mostly empty adjacent parking lot.

Midday was spent working and doing email and social media catch-up. The global virus case stats continued to mount, surging to over 5.7 million, with nearly 354K deaths and over 2.4 million recoveries. The U.S. had 1,731,291 cases and, now, over 100K deaths (100,866), with over 480K recoveries. New York had 373,622 cases, 29,451 deaths.

Early afternoon, Phil announced that he was going to clean out and re-organize the shed. I think he was concerned about his motorcycle getting scratched since you had to reach over it and navigate around it to get to things like tools and chairs and what not. So he pulled everything out into the yard and started to re-plan what was going to go back in and how.

I tuned in to Gov. Cuomo for a few minutes. He was speaking from the National Press Club in Wash., D.C. Numbers continued trending down, including deaths yesterday to 74, which boded well for further re-opening in New York State, though mostly upstate.

About 4pm, I tuned in to CBS and a live look at the launch pad at the Kennedy Space Center in Cape Canaveral, Florida. Scheduled for 4:33pm was the blastoff of a spacecraft comprised of NASA's Crew Dragon capsule atop a 230-foot SpaceX Falcon 9 rocket. The capsule, as we knew, carried two astronauts, Bob Behnken and Doug Hurley, who were going to jet up to the International Space Station, for a stay lasting up to 110 days. It had been nearly nine years since NASA astronauts traveled in an American spacecraft from American soil. And over all that time, NASA and private company SpaceX had been collaborating to make this very day happen. Notably, this was also SpaceX's first-ever crewed mission in the company's 18-year history.

There were all sorts of threats to this mission. No, not of the terror sort, but Covid-19 to start. NASA had taken serious precautions to ensure the well-being of the crew, including testing them several times. Spectators were also encouraged to stay at and watch from home, so they were not arriving and hanging out en masse in the area.

Another major threat was weather. There had been a brief tornado warning in Brevard County, where the Center was located. And a thunderhead had been hanging around. The latter had moved on but been replaced by an all-consuming gray fog. Currently the mission was on "red" or no-go, with the weather considered too severe to permit liftoff. But if it cleared, it could still be doable.

While I waited for further developments, I read about some cargo that had been put aboard. One piece was art made of gold, brass and aluminum, meant to signify how far the space program had come and how far humanity had come and how far humanity *still* had to go in exploring the cosmos. The second item was a mosaic of more than 100K photos of 2020 graduates from all over the world.

I learned that President Trump, First Lady Melania and VP Mike Pence had even flown in for the occasion, flying by the launch pad before landing at the Space Center in Air Force One. You *knew* the President wanted this one badly.

At 4:22pm, just 11 minutes before launch, word came that the event had been postponed, as the weather had not improved. "Stormy weather has forced today's SpaceX launch to be scrubbed. Weather conditions violated several safety rules," confirmed the announcer. The next window was Sat. May 30, at 3:21pm. What a letdown. I had whipped myself into an excited froth akin to the feeling of watching Apollo missions in the early 1970s and then the Space Shuttle missions all through the 1980s, 1990s and 2000s, right up to July 2011, when Atlantis went up and back.

While I was watching this event, which became a non-event, Phil was loading back into the shed what we had decided to hold onto, finding an efficient place for every item. Several things got thrown out; other items got put out at the front tree with a FREE sign on them. The latter included bocce balls, a croquet set, step ladder, paddleball racquets, golf clubs and the like. Mostly stuff we had used when the boys were little but that had just gathered dust since. It was bittersweet to discard these but I hoped someone else would pick them up and get use from them.

I was fading and needed to perk up, so hopped in the truck and swung by our local Dairy Queen for a mini Oreo cookie Blizzard, my favorite. There were about six people in line, each standing six feet apart and all but I was masked. I figured that the separation and being outdoors was compliant enough without having to wear a mask, too. I shuttled my treat to Sasco Beach, straddling with my truck two handicapped spaces not far from the entry. That vantage point gave me a look at the whole beach and the sun, which was slowly making its way to bed.

A "special" cop wandered over wondering why I had parked like I had. He thought I didn't see the signs. I explained myself and said I would move if a handicapped motorist showed up, but didn't expect any to visit. He let me stay on and we struck up a chat. It turned out we knew many of the same people on the force, because of my periodic interactions with them of a positive celebratory nature. He was in his mid-70s and thought the reaction to the pandemic had been too extreme. He wasn't a fan of all the shutdowns and felt bad, in particular, for the high school seniors that couldn't celebrate their accomplishments in grand style this year.

I popped over to Penfield Beach as well during my outing, just for a look-see. There were some teens playing Spikeball in one direction, circles of friends ahead and kids splashing in the water to the right. All normal looking until you saw someone in a surgical mask performing some routine activity, eg. strolling by the water's edge. Another of those "oh yeah we're in a pandemic" moments.

I got on email when I arrived back home. Seeing the sky so clear above the beaches here, it was disheartening to learn, through Nat Geo that, as economic activity resumed in China, the amount of air pollutant nitrogen dioxide was rising above that nation to traditional levels for this time of year. I had *expected* that man's memory and appreciation of clean skies wouldn't last long — I just didn't expect that memory loss to take place so *quickly*. For all our technology, humans were not very smart, particularly when it came to taking care of Mother Earth.

A thought-provoking email came from FitBit, my exercise tracker maker. I thought it was my weekly performance stats coming through but it was encouragement to FitBit owners who had had or still had Covid-19 to sign up to be monitored as data from their FitBits could create an algorithm that could detect Covid-19 before symptoms even started.

Late evening, my eyelids came crashing down and, before shutting my eyes completely for the night, I connected with Jen via FaceTime. She had just showered and was wrapped in a towel, which was tucked up under her armpits. I tried my best to be a mentalist — David Aluminumfield (my take on David Copperfield) — and will her towel to drop... or to have a wardrobe malfunction à la Janet Jackson in the famous Super Bowl halftime show that would later be referred to as "Nipplegate" for the apparently unintentional reveal of her breast by co-performer Justin Timberlake. But Jen was having none of it. I got, instead, a pajama modeling session and goodnight wish.

News: Global coronavirus cases passed the 5.8 million mark, with nearly 358K deaths, over 2.5 million recoveries. The U.S. had 1,746,311 cases and 102,116 deaths, with over 490K recoveries. New York had 374,672 cases and 29,553 deaths.

May 28. I treated myself to extra morning sleep and did *not* start scrolling through my phone as a first activity of the day. Instead, I enjoyed an indulgent shower and a shave, brewed a pot of coffee and circled the property, absorbing the coolness and dampness of this Thursday. Blech was in the forecast — misty rain and fog transitioning to grayness, with 100% tropical humidity, temps stepping towards 70, and full-on rain from dinnertime on through the overnight. The precip was the outer edge of what had become Post-Tropical Cyclone Bertha.

Timed well, Travel & Leisure spotlighted two sets of folks of considerable wealth to talk about how they had been quarantining. "I'll allow it", as Simon Cowell might say on "America's Got Talent", as I delved into this story, though I usually couldn't give a rat's ass on this type of literary pulp.

Sooo, how *had* "poor" shoe icon Manolo Blahnik been managing in this pandemic, anyhow?! He said his "time in quarantine has been peaceful yet productive" self-isolating in Bath, England and engaging in pursuits like watching his favorite classic movies, developing some new cooking skills, wandering in his garden, dreaming of the Mediterranean, padding around in a 45-year-old pair of moccasins and sketching all the time — and not just shoes but the environment around him, eg. views from his window.

The other spotlight was on Lord and Lady Carnarvon of Highclere Castle, the real-life estate portrayed in the "Downton Abbey" television series. The castle would normally be crowded with visitors but had been shut off to travelers for the past two months due to the pandemic. So the couple had been inviting friends over for "Cocktails at the Castle", live filming the sessions while offering a virtual look, room by highlighted room, at their posh digs. A centerpiece of these cocktail sessions was their proprietary Highclere Castle Gin, born in the Victorian era when the Lord's ancestors built the castle and entertained guests with "dashing house parties with dancing, music and gin cocktails."

On the subject of cocktails, a group in San Diego, CA launched Quarantine Vodka "to elevate at-home cocktail creations during and long after lock down lifts", according to Beer Connoisseur. The U.S.-made, ultra-premium crystalline vodka crafted using the purest water in San Diego and distilled six times "is a spirit forged in hard times, but will be here for good". And in the spirit of sharing, for each bottle of the vodka sold via beverage service Flaviar, a bottle of antibacterial soap would be donated to those in need.

In a like spirit, Blood x Sweat x Tears Vodka of Eugene, Oregon announced plans to make hand sanitizer and donate it to local grocery workers.

Dad's adopted state of North Carolina was taking a smart approach to getting back to business and attracting visitors. It was offering safety and sanitation training and certifications for restaurants, hotels and attractions. The program, called "Count on Me NC", enabled visitors to easily identify businesses that had volunteered for the training, which covered everything from employee health checks to how to clean high-touch surfaces. More than 670 businesses had signed up to participate. The group's research indicated the public was eager to begin traveling and dining out again, but had very high expectations for cleaning and social distancing protocols.

Just what was it about wearing a mask that was such a problem for some people? That's what Los Angeles magazine wanted to know. And the aversion had actually erupted in violence in several instances: a Michigan dollar store guard was shot to death after refusing entry to a customer not wearing a mask; another store customer wiped his nose and mouth on a store employee who asked him to put on a mask while shopping; and other such clashes at retail across the country. Psychiatrists said "stigma" was one reason for avoidance — people thinking that their mask wearing indicated to others that they were sick or that they were afraid or weak. Others underestimated the seriousness of the pandemic or didn't fully understand this element of prevention. Another possibility was someone wanting to commit an intentional act of rebellion, an attempt to feel some sense of power amid a complicated global situation. Finally, there was a refusal to admit mask-wearing as a new normal.

Would we get our pre-coronavirus bodies back? Half of Americans feared they wouldn't, according to FOX News. Stressed out and anxious amid the pandemic, folks had been turning to junk food, alcohol and more carbohydrates while most gyms still remained closed nationwide. A survey showed that the average American had put on five pounds since the crisis began, while almost two-thirds said Covid-19 had messed up their plans for a healthy lifestyle in 2020. Now, with warmer weather here, people had invested in gym equipment, were trying to get out more to walk and were participating in streamed online fitness classes.

So, how was the Market going? Pretty swimmingly all things considered, according to CFA Michael Gayed. "After dropping to the March 23 lows at jaw breaking speed, the market has already rallied over 32% to May 22 close and counting," he said, adding a cautionary note, "This can change quickly. One indicator I have been watching is how steep the yield curve is getting. While the Fed can contain the short end of the curve, it has been proven relatively fruitless when trying to control the long end of the curve."

Jen was in the area late morning running errands and, with her mask on, swung by with an almost drive-by drop-off of a Key Lime pie from The Pantry. On the box top, she had written "Lion - Enjoy". The leonine assignation was my nickname between us. Hers had been "Mouse" when we first met five years ago; it had evolved to Lioness, as every Lion needed a partner.

NY Gov. Cuomo piped up from Brooklyn as the noon hour neared. Numbers were down again, with the exception of 74 more deaths yesterday, still "relatively positive" news.

Early afternoon, someone put a tiger in our tank, a burst of high-grade, premium unleaded with extra going power and gas economy, driving Phil and I to tackle a clean-out of the basement: another pandemic, stay-at-home, scrutinize-your-property activity. We hauled no-longer-wanted stuff out and added it to the growing FREE collection by the roadside. The unwanted or no-good-to-anyone stuff we put by our garbage cans. Camping gear got put in a pile to sort through. My vintage jukebox and 1918 tea trolley moved from the workshop to the guest room. Then Phil set in to removing loose paint and mortar from the intersecting walls in one corner of the workshop. The goal was to break it all up, leaving a space that was barely alive, then rebuild it. We had the technology. We had the capability to make the world's first beatific basement. Our basement would be that basement. Better than it was before. Better, stronger, faster. Or something like that. And it wouldn't cost six million dollars!

I needed to expel some cobwebs from my cranial cavity so threw a saddle on the Ranger and headed eastbound into the wilds of Bridgeport. As in previous ventures there, I noticed again that absolutely everyone I saw walking, standing or sitting around on the street was wearing a face mask, which was completely the opposite of Fairfield. It brought the reality of the pandemic back to the forefront. At the same time, I noted Bpt was doing its best to clean up. It had painted over graffiti in the downtown area and was, as I noted before, razing old structures to make way for new. How the pandemic would affect those plans, I wasn't sure.

Back home and online, I got stunning news on FB that a landmark live music club, The Acoustic, was shutting its doors for good. The owners cited the "cost of overhead and the uncertainty of what business will look like for us" as the reasons for closing. They planned two final livestream shows this weekend as a last toot of the horn. So many memories, so many years, so many great music acts, another victim of the pandemic.

Phil was on dinner duty tonight — another plus to having a son home from school. Aligned with it being National Hamburger Day, he made us some tasty California-style beef, avocado and onion burgers. With a slice of the Key Lime pie Jen dropped off this afternoon, the meal was perfection.

On FB early evening, I saw a post from a cabaret entertainer friend who was thanking friends for extending birthday wishes to her. She added a message about the future, "I hope when we get out of this quarantine, we will be able to parade down Fifth Ave leaving 2020 behind us, break social distancing rules with joy and tears in our eyes, embrace each other with genuine smiles and no masks, and realize how much we need each other. Stay healthy and stay focused."

I saw another post from a friend who said her elderly dad's microwave stopped working... and it just so happened that I had one to offer... AND it helped me get stuff out of the basement. We scheduled her for a pick-up tomorrow. Helping each other in hard times — and all the time actually, but certainly in hard times — that's what it was all about, right?

An email rolled in from Uncubed Intel about Ford motor company and how it was helping the NYPD disinfect vehicles during the coronavirus. It had created software that burned germs by raising interior vehicle temperatures to 133F.

Middle of the evening and as pre-agreed to, I traveled over to Jen's, taking the Post Road route. Restaurants like Quattro Pazzi, Aurora's and Tequila Revolucion were all lit up and had handfuls of patrons enjoying a drink and bite on their patios; Tengda in Westport was the same. It was heartwarming to see these flickers of life. An exclamation point on that feeling was a sign at the turn for Compo Road, "Westport We've Got This!" That was one of many inspirational messages posted around town, apparently by the same person as they were in the same black hand-written block lettering on white foamboard.

Jen was seated at her teaching piano working off her laptop on an invitation to her student concert tomorrow afternoon, to be facilitated through Zoom. I helped her edit it while being my distracting usual self nibbling on her shoulder. I left her to put finishing touches on it and went and showered, bedding down. But to scroll, of course, through some news items.

One item was about an eruption in Minneapolis. No, this was no volcano blowing its top, though I wouldn't put it past Mother Nature in 2020. This was people erupting, demonstrators, protestors, mobsters, opportunists. These were folks upset about the alleged brutality committed by the police there against George Floyd. Last night, they attacked the department's 3rd Precinct station in a move reminiscent of the 1976 film "Assault on Precinct 13", wherein a few cops and civilians defend a precinct house in Detroit being phased out from a mob trying to get in and kill them. In this modern-day scenario, officers evacuated the building as a safety measure, giving the mob the ripe opportunity to breach a door and enter the station to smash equipment and set fires, while other demonstrators outside set fires as well and shot off fireworks, chanting with megaphones the robotic, trite mob-popular phrase "No Justice, No Peace". The fires, including the torching of a liquor store across the street and barricades in front, set off the building's sprinkler system, which rained water down on desks and chairs and soaked the facility. The group outside also tried to used barricades to batter open the station's windows, which were covered with plywood.

In St. Paul, a Napa auto parts store was set on fire after being looted and vandalized. Also in St. Paul, police had to barricade the front entrance of a Target after dozens of people stormed it and tried to take merchandise without paying. Nearby, the windows of a Verizon store and vitamin shop had been shattered. Business owners rushed to board up their stores and hang signs reading "black-owned business" or "community-owned business". Other owners armed themselves and stood guard at their stores.

At the heart of the "uprising" were Black Lives Matter activists, who said they were aligning with Martin Luther King Jr.'s teachings — and, yet, King's methods were peaceful, and these were anything but. Said one leader, "That man is gone forever because some cop felt like he had the right to take his life. A lot of folks are tired of that. They're not going to take it anymore. That's why Minneapolis is burning." Of course, there was no discussion in any of this of the belligerent and drunken and resistant behavior of Floyd. He was apparently an innocent victim in the eyes of the mob.

Other reported incidents included shots being fired near Minnesota's Capitol, a police officer's car being smashed, police firing rubber bullets into and tear gassing crowds, and a driver plowing into a crowd of protestors, allegedly even accelerating and chasing one crowd member down.

In response to and to try and quell the aggression, Minnesota Gov. Tim Walz activated 500 members of the state's National Guard, to put down violent clashes, help prevent more properties being damaged, and to try and stop widespread looting, all of which was your typical side effect of these mob gatherings. Those who would take advantage, coming out of the woodwork, backing up pickup trucks and loading them up with stolen TVs, stereos, furniture and whatever else they could pilfer. The ironic thing, as ever, was that these acts were all being done in the communities in which these people lived, and to business owners that were from these communities, who attended its churches and whose children attended local schools. It was community members destroying *other* community members' businesses. The mayor, Melvin Carter, called for peace, noting, "Destroying places we rely on for jobs, food and medicine won't help us prevent it from happening again."

Like the governor, certain transportation groups and administrators took safety measures as tensions rose. The main transportation operator in the Twin Cities suspended its bus and light rail service, and lawmakers, state court staff and judges evacuated.

Of course, the Minnesota scene sparked other people in urban areas to hit the streets in solidarity. Reports came in of protestors gathered en masse on a corner in Chicago, and more than 70 arrests were made in Manhattan's Union Square area after protests and violence there. Charges included throwing a garbage can and striking an officer in the head, trying to remove the gun from a captain's holster and carrying a knife. Shots were also fired near the capitol building in Denver, Colorado.

A New York Post story, meanwhile, carried the story of another planned uprising — that of a couple promoting a "Post Pandemic Pan-Philadelphia Orgy", which was being advertised with Avengers-themed flyers posted around South Philly. The pair — he was a lighting guy and she was a sex therapist — had only begun dating in December but decided to quarantine together when the pandemic hit. They found themselves to be "quite compatible, and grateful to not be among the sexless masses." The orgy idea was birthed on the idea that "humanity is currently in the middle of the largest dry spell in all of history". The flyer noted, "Open Call. Space is limited. Submit inquiries via email. All applicants are subject to screening. Refreshments will be served."

Jen eventually joined me after having a FaceTime call with a school friend in Austin who was going to be her emcee for the Zoom showing tomorrow. We drifted off after our usual mattress acrobatics.

News: A 103-year-old woman survived her battle with the coronavirus and cracked open a Bud Light beer to celebrate. Global coronavirus cases advanced by another 100K in the past 24 hours, to 5.9 million, with nearly 362K deaths. The U.S. had 1,768,461 cases with over 103K deaths, nearly 499K recoveries. New York had 376,309 cases and 29,653 deaths. NY Gov. Cuomo issued an order that allowed NY businesses to deny entry to anyone not wearing a face covering.

May 29. Fri-yay. Yay. Woo hoo. I arose about six and, knowing I had much to accomplish, took my leave and rolled back along the Post Road (my Love Highway I had decided) to home.

A large dose of morning brew and I was barreling through email and social media, getting these activities crossed off my agenda early. I was amazed to see a Travel & Leisure item that said Cyprus would cover all costs for travelers should they test positive for coronavirus while visiting the country. Patients would only have to pay for their taxi ride to the airport and flight back home.

I was glad to put my new Ford Ranger to another test, that of carrying a load of debris to the dump. I laid down a thick tarp in the truck bed and loaded in household trash, bags of recyclable items, the old basement door, the broken-down TV unit and its drawers, some concrete, shed items and more. It held everything very well and I was to the dump and back within five minutes. Never had a run been so easy. The clerk there who received me at first said she admired my truck and asked if I had sprinkled salt in it yet to ward off evil. She said that was an Italian tradition and shared that she was half-Italian and half-Polish. A good egg that one.

I measured out and calculated what I would need for the doorway from the basement outgoing to the yard and then set off with face mask and gloves to Home Depot. With a department manager, I walked around and plucked up what I needed to get my job done — a new door, door jamb set, lock kit, insulating foam and shims — and loaded up the Ranger as I had the debris. The door and door jamb was slightly longer than the truck's bed so I covered the tailgate with a tarp and leaned those pieces against it. That worked like a charm and Phil helped me unload when I got back home.

Over a sandwich, I checked email and social media. Things were getting worse in Minnesota and sparking more trouble elsewhere across the nation, prompting Pres. Trump to tweet, "I can't stand back & watch this happen to a great American City, Minneapolis. A total lack of leadership. Either the very weak Radical Left Mayor, Jacob Frey, better get his act together and bring the City under control, or I will send in the National Guard & get the job done right...."

In Columbus, Ohio, protests turned chaotic as crowds surged up the steps of the State Capitol and broke windows. Elsewhere in that city, officers used pepper spray on large crowds of demonstrators downtown after a few protesters tossed smoke bombs and water bottles at lines of patrolmen. In Phoenix, hundreds of protestors marched toward the State Capitol and got into tense face-offs with and threw stones at police. In Louisville, KY, seven people were struck by gunfire as a mob surrounded a police vehicle. Rioters there also damaged property. KY's governor said the protests "reflected a city still affected by the legacy of slavery and Jim Crow", and added that protesters' anger underscored distress over the coronavirus pandemic, which had disproportionately affected black people.

The term "streeteries" had been birthed, referring to the trend of city and downtown nightlife districts closing off streets to cars so that restaurants could expand into the roadways and allow for more open-air dining and safe physically distant pedestrian walking in light of pandemic spread precautions.

CT Gov. Lamont checked in early afternoon, from our state capitol. He said our "numbers" were "75% off the peak now" and that the "metrics were headed in the right direction". He offered reminders to continue safe social distancing: outside is safer than inside, younger people are likely to be less compromised health-wise than older, small gatherings are better than large, an inside gathering should be limited to 10 people, an outside gathering should be limited to 25 people. And he spoke of our state's casinos, which were going to open back up tomorrow, which was in advance of neighboring states. They would follow guidelines such as no one out of state to stay at hotels, no smoking, keep masks on, dining outside only at least through June 20 and cautioning seniors and people that were health compromised to stay home.

Speaking of seniors, a neighborhood bulletin turned up in the mailbox, with lifestyle tips for older Americans amid Covid-19. It advised embracing technology to counter isolation, walking several times a day to help release endorphins and ensure ample Vitamin D, keeping the brain active through journaling and drawing, getting proper sleep, finding new hobbies, and rediscovering old hobbies.

Mid-afternoon, I worked on cementing the wall in the workshop, where Phil had scraped away loose concrete and flaking paint. It was very enjoyable work for me. My Grandad Lauterborn was a masonry contractor as a young man — I figured the work must be in my DNA.

I had to pop out to the local hardware store for more Quikrete cement mix. The going was slower than in past days now that many retailers had re-opened, joining restaurants that had *already* been open for outdoor dining. In other words, downtown Fairfield was thick with traffic and cars were piled up at every light. There were packs of kids on bikes, too, weaving in and out of cars and going from sidewalk to street. While I was glad to see the energy, I wasn't happy for the traffic's return. But I made it to the hardware joint and did my purchase through the window, with the shopkeeper passing my Quikrete through a partially opened front door.

At 4pm, I tuned in to Jen's Intermediate level students performing their songs in Jen's studio's Zoom-based Spring Concert. There were about 30 viewers at any given time and each student was introduced with a title card and a brief word about their school and background, with regard to piano experience. It was very pleasant and I could continue to work at my computer while catching it.

One big news item was that the officer who used his knee to pin down the now infamous martyr George Floyd had been arrested and charged with third-degree murder and manslaughter. The charge seemed to be a middle ground punishment — not *too* severe and not a let-off, though the officer's career was still ended, his reputation destroyed and his family shamed into hiding. Would the masses be quelled? Floyd's family said they wanted a first-degree murder charge, according to their lawyer. Time would tell. As an advance measure, Minnesota Gov. Walz put Minneapolis under curfew for the night and the National Guard in place to patrol the streets. Further, he implored residents to see the troops as a peacekeeping force meant to keep "anarchists" from taking over and destroying more of the city.

An Atlantic magazine article suggested fitness may never be the same, as people learned during quarantine that it can happen anywhere, in any form, anytime. Meaning, why bother to go back to the gym, particularly when it was going to be a completely different experience — a total hassle, really. Just imagine the hoops you would likely have to jump through: Pre-reserving a time slot a week in advance, getting your temp taken at reception, receiving a wristband that confirmed your timeslot to staff so you wouldn't overstay, replenishing your water bottle at a touchless filling station, dodging the maintenance workers spraying down equipment with clinging antiseptics, working out with latex gloves and a face mask, doing yoga in a class where you were six feet apart from anyone else, then leaving sweaty as you were no longer allowed to shower or have access to gym flip flops. Ugh. Totally devoid of any pleasure, comfort, relaxation or social connection. Why bother, right?!

A Washington Post article declared what many of us were feeling: "The pandemic isn't over. But we sure seem over it." Writer Dan Zak explained: "We're over it. The masks, the kids, the Lysol. Over it. The tragic hair, the diminished hygiene, the endless construction next door, the Zoom meetings from hell, the mind games from the unemployment office, the celibacy, the short tempers and long evenings, the looking forward to the mail, the feeling guilty about the mail carrier working double time, the corporate compassion pushing products we didn't need even *before* the world went funky and febrile. The now-more-than-everness, the president-said-whatness. Over it. Does 99.1 count as a fever? Over it. Some of us have reached the outskirts of Netflix, and we're over it. Some of us can't make rent; over it. And so we are deciding to have a summer after all, it seems. A summer of playing freely, of living dangerously. One hundred thousand dead, 40.8 million jobless claims. Not past it, but over it." And not only were we saying it but our leaders were saying it, too. "We can't keep fighting the virus from our living room," said Georgia Gov. Brian Kemp. "There is a pent-up demand to resume normal life," said President Trump. But what if the coronavirus surged back, because we were all over it and having a summer, and we *did* die from this? A Jacksonville, FL realtor addressed that question: "I have God in my heart, so God could take me out any day. He can take me out in any way he wants to. And if it's my time to go, it's my time to go. I don't think anyone I know is personally concerned. None of us are afraid, because we have God in our souls and God in our hearts."

Bull work. That's what they call it when you really go to town on a project, put your back into it, work up a sweat, grunt like a bull, give it your all, go whole hog. And that's what I did in the late afternoon until sundown, circular sawing, marking, measuring, Sawzall-ing, chiseling, fastening, hammering, prying, sweeping and just generally bulling my way through making a straight doorway, door frame and door happen for basement egress.

One of the most satisfying showers followed; some editing for Jen of a thank you note to her students, their families and friends that tuned in today from five or six different states; and making a catch-all salad with whatever I could find in the refrigerator and cabinet.

Pig work. Very disturbing pig work. That was the discovery I made scrolling through news to stumble headlong into a story about pigs that were roasted alive in a pandemic-induced oversupply extermination. Iowa Select Farms workers were caught on camera using a disturbing ventilation fan shutdown, wherein they close off airways to the hogs and pump hot steam into their barns overnight to slaughter them, boiling them alive essentially. Footage revealed the animals' heartbreaking cries as they succumbed to death at temperatures of more than 120F.

Can you repair your sense of horror with music? After that story, I tried, with Music for Youth's Digital Friday Night Cafe. This week featured Violinist Cedar Newman in a long burgundy red colored satin dress playing Eduardo Lalo's Symphonie Espagnole, and 16-year-old Fairfield Ludlowe High School alto saxophonist Bobby Master playing "Unchain My Heart" by Ray Charles. Brilliant stuff and a great distraction.

I realized that in watching this Friday feature and Jen's earlier concert that I was one of the consumers being referred to in Forbes' report on "3 Ways the Pandemic Has Permanently Changed the Minds of Consumers". One way was how the collective "we" were feeling about live entertainment in the "age of coronavirus". It noted that people were not so eager to go back to venues and were perfectly happy sourcing entertainment online, from concerts and movies to sports events and theater productions. We were also digging contactless payment, which I think spelled the end of cash as we knew it. And we had made a full swing over to telemedicine as a very satisfying experience.

Miracles do happen. And the proof is the arrival of Amadalyn Rose to my friends Becky and Kwong, at 134 hours and 52 minutes after checking into the hospital. "Yes, a long induction process but once she wanted to come, only 57 minutes of true labor," posted a proud mom to Facebook.

South Korea had been powering along so well with its reopening until… they just had the biggest spike in coronavirus cases (79) in two months. The jump forced more than 200 schools to close down again, just days after reopening. Most of the cases derived from a distribution center outside Seoul, but who was to say how many cases sprang from there and headed elsewhere? America was watching countries like this, to see if the same might happen to us.

News: Fairfield First Selectwoman Kupchick gave a briefing, noting 583 residents had tested positive, 120 people had passed and 256 had recovered, to date. Ninety percent of those deaths were residents in one of the town's seven assisted living facilities. Overall, CT had 41,559 positive cases to date and 3,826 deaths. Of that, Fairfield County had 15,353 cases and 1,246 deaths. She let us know that the restrooms at the beach pavilions were going to be reopening now and that the town libraries could do curbside transactions. Global coronavirus cases passed 6 million, with nearly 367K deaths and 2.659 million recoveries. The U.S. had 1,793,530 cases and 104,542 deaths, with nearly 520K recoveries. New York had 377,714 cases and 29,751 deaths.

May 30. I was up at dawn. Stormy came to join me, to sit on the sill of a window I had opened during the night when it began feeling muggy. It was *still* muggy, with 97% humidity and temps expected to hit 80F by late afternoon. Of course, it would be much hotter (about 20 degrees higher) for my Dad and Dave, who were at the tail end of their trip out West.

Dad had been sending me pics every day by email, essentially summing up their experiences. It was a lot of red rocks, beer being hoisted, their off-road truck tackling moonscapes, and many big sunrises and sunsets. His latest email, received this morning, carried photos of "dawn at Mesa Arch", a popular destination in the Sky district of Canyonlands National Park in Moab, Utah. The scenes looked more like Mars-scapes than Moab-scapes. D&D were among the first handful of people to tour the Park after its official post-Covid-19 opening yesterday. All the arrivals wanted to see the sunrise, so it turned into a mini "Indy 500, with Dave in the lead!" as Dad described it. "No rangers in the park, no other traffic possible since it's been closed for two months? Dave booked it, and the five or six cars waiting with us tried to keep up. When we hit the parking lot, people burst out of their cars and sprinted up the rocky hill. We made it with a couple of minutes to spare!"

Dad also reported getting to drive their Toyota Tacoma, which Dave had commandeered until that point. "I drove a few miles on a 'technical' 4WD trail, which means it's impassable to vehicles unless they have a transmission with low as well as high 4WD, big rugged tires, and extra high clearance. Our Toyota Tacoma also had a steel plate underneath to protect the engine. I was apprehensive — the road looked to me impossible to drive in any case — but it turned out to be fun, a real challenge, and I'm going to do it again tomorrow!" Fun? Yes, dustbins full.

I was envious of the time they were having, particularly in the midst of a worldwide pandemic, but happy to be pushing the limits of my own Ford Ranger truck with dump and Home Depot runs AND enjoying our own astronomical events, like Manhattanhenge actually. According to Travel + Leisure, the event "occurs every year before and after the summer solstice, when the sun aligns perfectly with New York City's street grid. Folks in Manhattan can stand in the middle of any east-west numbered street and watch the sun low on the horizon between buildings. There are four sunsets and four sunrises, and two of each take place on successive evenings and mornings. The rectangular Manhattan street grid, which is responsible for the alignment, was originally designed in 1811, after the population of the city nearly tripled in just 20 years." The first sunset occurred at 8:13pm last night. Another was set to take place at 8:12pm tonight, and promised to be even more captivating. As I was not yet ready to breach NYC in person (if I was even permitted to), I hoped to catch the event online in a livestream.

About NYC, the natives were restless again last night — protesters continuing to make trouble over the George Floyd case. Hundreds of people fanned out around Lower Manhattan and Brooklyn, clashing with police. One crowd tried to breach Brooklyn's 88th Precinct house, threw objects at police and burned a police vehicle in the Fort Greene area. The scene was the same in Atlanta, where large crowds gathered at the CNN Center, spraying graffiti on the giant red letters outside the headquarters, while others smashed windows and threw rocks at the building before police pushed them down the street. As the crowds moved along, they set fire to a police vehicle. The mayor there, Keisha Lance, implored people to "go home" and said, "This is not a protest. This is not in the spirit of Martin Luther King, Jr. This is chaos." In Minneapolis, Minnesota, despite a curfew being set, protesters were in the streets vandalizing businesses and setting fires, including a blaze at a gas station that threatened nearby homes. The crowds clashed with police, who fired tear gas at them. Protesters also tried to breach the 5th Precinct house there, which police had to defend with concrete barricades, fencing, tear gas, flash bangs and green-and-white smoke grenades. In nearby St. Paul, looters roamed the streets, spray painted "kill cops" and "justice for George" on walls, and had barbecues right on the street near already ransacked businesses. Pres. Trump put active-duty military police, from installations in North Carolina to Kansas, on alert for possible deployment to Minnesota. Same scene in Louisville, KY, with demonstrators riled up not only about GF but also Breonna Taylor, whom police shot in her apartment back in March. The crowd bundled the events into a consolidated anti-police stance. Police shot tear gas at the protestors, who carried "Black Lives Matter" and "I Can't Breathe" signs, as they spray painted buildings and tried to break windows. Ditto for Cincinnati, where protesters blocked the interstate, marched to police headquarters and the courthouse, broke windows and took down flagpoles.

Meanwhile, at the Kennedy Space Center, NASA and SpaceX were looking at making another launch attempt this Saturday afternoon. As of Friday morning, there was reportedly just a 50% chance of the event happening, though predictions could change considerably over the course of just a few hours, according to the launch weather operator.

I *so* needed a ride around in my truck before settling in to tackle the basement job again, and headed out going eastbound, by The Acoustic Cafe in its last death throes; the apparently breathing and surviving Redline Restorations classic car restorer and gallery; the shuttered Rampage Skate Shop and its adjacent graffitied walls; a stone mason's yard with gravestones and statues including one of Mother Mary and Jesus; Captain's Cove Seaport; Black Rock businesses like Eugene's Green Garage, the Barber & Beauty shop and Taco Loco Mexican restaurant; and Pho Nha Trang Vietnamese eatery. It was a great and much needed tour. Taking the community pulse, as usual.

Back on home turf, I mowed the lawn, shearing it to even green stubs. I recalled my Danbury friend's comment when he saw my grass — "Do you hand pick the weeds out?" It was a remark coming from a perspective of being impressed. Again, there was no excuse *not* to be caring so attentively to the lawn with being home so much, right?

Just before noon, NY Gov. Cuomo checked in from a community center in The Bronx, on "Day 91" of the pandemic. "This is a hard day, a day of light, a day of darkness", he started, and I thought bad news was coming. But he continued to say the numbers were "all good news", with the exception of deaths — 67 more yesterday, though overall that was "tremendous progress". He congratulated the state's residents — "WE accomplished what many said was impossible." And now NYC was looking to open up on June 8, which seemed a tall order since the "hottest" spots in the state were in NYC's buroughs. I was safely going to bet that the re-opening date was going to get pushed back.

Jen had sent out an email first thing in the morning that I only got to open midday. It was a genuine, from-the-heart message to a tight circle of contacts confirming that her spring semester had concluded and was celebrated with a Zoom concert, her son was headed to Georgetown this fall and that he had been seeing a girl for two years now, she had shelved her summer travel plans due to the pandemic, and she had enjoyed everyone's humor and memes during this dark period. She signed it "Rain drops, love and smiles, Jenny."

Early afternoon, there was a beeping and a clatter — another neighborhood celebration, of a little boy's birthday down the block. It was marked by a ten-car drive-by — families carrying signs and cars decorated, everyone beeping and hollering. What a great team effort.

And talk about team efforts... With great hope and anticipation, at 3pm, I tuned into PBS' live coverage of the historic launch of the collaborative NASA/SpaceX Falcon 9 rocket and Crew Dragon capsule carrying Astronauts Bob Behnken and Doug Hurley. Would this mission go today? Would the weather cooperate? Would all equipment function properly? Would two guys who coincidentally shared the same first names as Bob and Doug McKenzie, the fictional Canadian brothers (played by Rick Moranis and Dave Thomas) who hosted the "Great White North" sketch on SCTV, go into the record books? It was a go. And, Phil, who had been out for a ride on his motorcycle and returned with six minutes to spare, was on hand to witness it with me, in the same way I had joined my Dad and Mom in July 1969 for the televised landing of Apollo 11 on the Moon.

"10... 9... 8... 7... 6... 5... 4... 3... 2... 1... 0... Ignition. Liftoff of the Falcon 9 and Crew Dragon! Go NASA! Go SpaceX! Godspeed Bob and Doug!" was the initial cry. "America has launched, and so rises a new era of American spaceflight and with it the ambitions of a new generation continuing the dream." We watched this incredible rocket rip into the atmosphere, straight and true, all systems go. "Vehicle is supersonic!" was the callout as the rocket passed Mach 1, pulling 2.3 G's in just a minute and a half. And we have MECO (Main Engine Cutoff), Stage 1 separation, beginning its flight back. Yes, *flight back*, the rocket stage guided by computers to return to and land on a drone ship, incidentally called, "Of Course, I Still Love You". Stage 2 propulsion engaged. Five minutes in, the rocket was traveling at over 5,600mph. Nine minutes in, SECO (Second Engine Cutoff); Falcon 9 return to drone ship confirmed almost simultaneously. At about 12 minutes, the rocket was traveling about 16,000mph. 12:13: Crew

Dragon separation from booster rocket confirmed, leaving it to make its way unaccompanied to the ISS.

Ground: "Dragon SpaceX we've got separation call. We have a few words for you from our Falcon 9 team." Capsule: "Standing by." Ground: "Dragon, Chief Engineer on Dragon to Ground. Bob, Doug, on behalf of the entire Launch team, thanks for flying with Falcon 9 today. We hope you enjoyed the ride and wish you a great mission." Capsule: "Thanks Bob. Congratulations to you and the F-9 team for the first human ride for Falcon 9, and it was incredible. Appreciate all the hard work. Thanks for the great ride to space." Ground: "Copy all." Capsule: "Proud of you guys and the rest of the team. Thank you so much for what you've done for us today, putting America back into lower orbit from the Florida coast." Ground: "Copy all. Good luck and godspeed."

I was tingling. My heart was palpitating. And I even teared up. This was such a moment. Such a *long* awaited moment. And such a fantastic moment to achieve when there was so much misery, death, sickness, hurt and hate here on Earth. I looked forward to the next great moment in the mission, the link up, at about 10:27am tomorrow morning, of the Dragon capsule with the ISS. Go America! #goamerica

I reached out to Marlene to see if she had watched the launch from her high-rise perch in Miami, but she had forgotten to tune in. And she had *had* binoculars all ready to go, too. She would just catch a recorded version of it later, she said.

Meanwhile, America's urban areas were preparing for a fifth straight night of protests and violence in regard to the GF case. Officials were expecting it to be the most explosive yet. Attorney General William P. Barr warned protesters and said "groups of outside radicals" were exploiting the situation for their own agenda. Barr also reminded, "It is a federal crime to cross state lines or to use interstate facilities to incite or participate in violent rioting. We will enforce these laws." President Trump urged Minnesota leaders, in particular, to "get tougher" and offered the support of the military. Minnesota Gov. Walz declined the offer of militia but activated all of the state's National Guardsmen, a force of up to 13,200. Nevertheless, the U.S. Northern Command had put several military police units on four-hour readiness status.

Our state's own urban areas, Bridgeport and Hartford, had gotten caught up in the protests, too, with hundreds of people gathering in downtown Bridgeport, then blocking lanes of travel on north-south running Route 8, which closed at 3:40pm between exits 2 and 4. The demonstrators included members of a group called the Justice for Jayson organization, formed in the aftermath of the fatal shooting of 15-year-old Jayson Negron by a Bridgeport police officer. That group said that authorities were threatening to tear gas the people on the highway. Bridgeport police apparently condoned the protest activities, Tweeting that it commended the city community "for hosting a peaceful and meaningful protest." But Phil showed me Snapchat captures of the highway situation and there were idiots on motorcycles doing burnouts and showing off, certainly not conducting any sort of thoughtful gathering. Personally, I was thinking that I would be boiling mad if I had to get somewhere on Route 8 and couldn't. The police should have been clearing the blockage, not condoning it, in my opinion. But, of course, their hands were tied. If they went against the crowd, the crowd would cry abuse and get ugly. It was unnerving, really, to be sitting here in our peaceful community knowing that five to ten minutes away these events were happening. Phil commented, "If the coronavirus didn't make people buy guns, this will." And it would be both the good guys and bad guys buying them — the good for self-defense and the bad to go loot and cause violence. It was *truly* scary to think about.

Even the White House was in harm's way. Last night, protesters gathered outside the fences, and the building went into lockdown mode. President Trump praised the Secret Service for protecting the property and warned that any protesters who breached the fence would have been met by "vicious dogs" and "ominous weapons". The president was in residence at the time and said about the Secret Service, "I watched every move, and couldn't have felt more safe. They let the 'protesters' scream and rant as much as they wanted, but whenever someone got too frisky or out of line, they would quickly come down on them, hard — didn't know what hit them. The front line was replaced by fresh agents, like magic. Big crowd, professionally organized, but nobody came close to breaching the fence."

And not only were U.S. cities in an uproar, but international urban areas, too. I read over dinner — grilled food and fat fries on the patio, with Phil — that, in London, protesters marched through the streets of Peckham, a neighborhood known for being home to generations of African and Caribbean immigrants. The crowd carried "Black Lives Matter" signs. In Toronto, up to 4,000 people protested racism, with a reference to a black woman who fell from her high-rise apartment balcony this past week while being questioned by police. In Germany, people gathered in front of the American embassy to chant "black lives matter".

The crazy thing about these riots — and it rang true every time — was that people in the protesters' communities were the ones that ended up getting punished most. Like a disabled black woman in Minneapolis whose neighborhood was destroyed, leaving her with no refuge and no way of getting away. "I have nowhere to go now. I have no way to get there because the buses aren't running. People did this for no reason. It's not going to bring George back here. George is in a better place than we are. Last night, I'm going to be honest, I wish I was where George was — because this is ridiculous. These people are tearing up my livelihood."

Amid all this domestic chaos, the CDC Director Gao Fu said no viruses were detected in animal samples in the Wuhan, China region. They were found only in environmental samples, including sewage. "At first, we assumed the seafood market might have the virus, but now the market is more like a victim," he said. The Daily Mail called his admission "stunning", for *he* was the one to unequivocally point the finger of blame at Wuhan's market where wild animals were sold. He also said that "the novel coronavirus had existed long before". A study helped nudge the reversal — it found only 27 of the first 41 confirmed cases were 'exposed' to the market — and only one of the four initial cases in the first two weeks of December. Another study suggested the disease was taken into the market by someone already infected. That same study said the virus had already pre-adapted to human transmission, versus being something new that had to evolve... The plot thickened and became more confusing.

Since I wasn't going to be able to catch tonight's Manhattanhenge, I thought I would catch "Sascohenge" instead. This was where the sun dropped on the horizon at our Sasco Beach in such a way as to appear to be sitting between two trees. Of course, I was making all of this up, but it seemed plausible. And the sunset was indeed spectacular and *did* seem to fall between two scrubby trees as I looked down the length of the beach from my parking spot. There seemed to be much joy here — families dining, people taking sunset photos with their camera phones, a guy fishing, other people sitting on top of their trucks and in their truck beds, teens doing cartwheels, folks strolling. There was joy in town, too, with all the restaurant patios busting at the seams with people — Martel's, Aurora's, Old Post Tavern, Molto. And I think I only saw two face masks in the whole lot, other than restaurant servers who were required to wear them. It felt like we were our old selves, in our fairly sheltered hamlet of Fairfield anyhow.

We wondered if, by looking up into the night sky, if we could see the ISS and Crew Dragon pass over, or if we were even in their orbital path. We looked online and found a site called n2yo which tracked their current positions, with icons representing the crafts and the specific ground area they were passing over. Nearing 10pm, we could see that they were over the northeastern Pacific Ocean approaching the western end of Canada. With the Crew Dragon ahead of the Station, they would soar east over the length of Canada and then steer southeast directly over Boston (two hours to our east) and down over the Atlantic Ocean rounding the southern tip of Africa and arcing back northeast to pass over Australia. Their altitude was approximately 260 miles with an orbital speed of over 17,000mph. I grabbed the highest magnification binoculars we had and darted out into the back yard to have a look at the approximate overpass time — and I swear I saw a very high quick-moving object streak across the sky in the general direction of Boston. I'm not sure which craft it was but I was fairly certain it was one of them. A short time after, friends from the area confirmed the sighting on their Facebook pages. "We just saw the ISS fly over our house", one posted, adding, "It was so cool!" A snarky post, apparently from Andy Milonakis, stated, "Congratulations to the Astronauts that left Earth today. Good choice." Yet another posted, "We're sending people to outer space? That's what I call social distancing!"

About 10pm, Jen FT'ed me wondering if I was coming over to watch Saturday Night Live — it was a ritual with us. I replied that I hadn't received an invite and she said it was in the mail. We *did* have fun with each other. So over I went, taking the Post Road the length of the way to Westport and seeing more signs of revived life at other eateries with patios. As we sat down in her TV room to watch the program, which was a throwback rerun to maybe December, the broadcast was interrupted by a news bulletin. We actually thought it was part of the show but it was NYC

Mayor de Blasio, and he was saying essentially that he was proud of all but a few New Yorkers for keeping things peaceful and basically applauded them for taking a stand. Though, as he spoke, NBC was showing footage of a police vehicle in flames with firefighters struggling to put it out, and protesters shouting and throwing things and clashing with police trying to protect themselves with shields. I wondered which city he was talking about because it sure didn't seem to be *his*. The interruption drove us to retire early, though we never really retire, wink, wink.

News: Global coronavirus cases increased another 100K, to over 6.1 million, with nearly 370K deaths and just under half -- over 2.7 million -- recovered. The U.S. had 1,814,578 cases with 105,514 deaths, 528,342 recoveries. New York, still hardest hit, had 378,931 cases and 29,827 deaths.

May 31. We were up at six, awaking to a perfectly spectacular day for a change. Bright blue skies, a light breeze, temps in the low to mid-60s. Jen knew it was the kind of day that spurred me to want to go, and she was right and, yet, she still had a magical way of getting me to stay a little longer.

My route back home was the Post Road as before, and I noted various pop-up signs like "Proud Family of 2020 Staples High School Graduate", "Thank You First Responders" and "Thank U to the Frontline". There was the Tasty Yolk food truck parked near Fairfield Downtown, but not yet fired up and ready to serve. I b-lined to the little garden at the end of Beach Road, parked and walk up the ramp to take a peek at the beach — Jennings to my left, the Fairfield Beach Club and Penfield Beach to my right. The sand had just been groomed by a tractor towing a wide rake, so it looked pristine. A staffer at the Club was setting up seating and prepping for the day's visitors. I circled through the lot at Penfield Beach — same story there, getting ready for the day. As I made my final approach home, I popped into Bud's Deli but the counterwoman was busy with a customer's $100 request for a wide variety of lottery cards and was redeeming others for him. I didn't have the patience to wait, though I really was fixed on having their bacon, egg & cheese sandwich. I wished lottery services were transacted at one dedicated place rather than made a part of retail establishments, though I knew that the places that sold winning tickets got a cut of the payout, so there was an incentive. Still…

On the subject of "home approaches", the gumdrop-shaped Crew Dragon capsule (dubbed Demo-2) was making its own, to the International

Space Station, which would be home to the two astronauts aboard for a few months. I checked in on their current flight path at just after 9am. They were east of New Zealand, heading southeast over the Pacific Ocean but soon would be arcing Northeast to fly over the southern tip of South America (passing through the middle of Argentina and right over Rio de Janeiro in Brazil, which was suffering with over 500K coronavirus cases) and then northwestern Africa (Mauritania, Algeria), over eastern Europe and across Kazakhstan.

The link-up between Crew Dragon and the ISS was adjusted to approximately 10:30am EDT. "We're looking forward to rendezvousing with the space station today," Doug Hurley radioed SpaceX's mission operations team in Hawthorne, CA, according to the website Space. SpaceX woke up the astronauts with wake-up music at 4:45am EDT. It was the first time astronauts received a musical wake-up since the final shuttle mission in July 2011. The tune? "Planet Caravan" by Black Sabbath, appealing to the crew's rock music tastes apparently. Interesting choice!

The way the docking was going to play out was as follows: the tip of the capsule would open to reveal the docking mechanics, and the vehicle itself would dock autonomously, though the astronauts could override that if needed. The astronauts would then remain aboard for two hours, until 12:45pm, before they opened the hatch and joined NASA colleague Chris Cassidy and Russian cosmonauts Anatoly Ivanishin and Ivan Vagner, who had been in orbit since April. The soon-to-be five-person crew would hold a welcoming ceremony at 1:05pm. Behnken and Hurley would then spend the next one to four months at work in the orbiting laboratory. The duration would be determined mostly by the readiness of the next SpaceX Crew Dragon capsule, all according to Space.

All these spacemen were in a much better place today than all of us Earthlings. Worldwide, coronavirus cases were about to tick over 6.2 million with nearly 372K deaths. The U.S. remained hardest hit, with over 1.8 million cases and nearly 106K deaths. New York still had the most cases, at nearly 379K and nearly 30K deaths, but other states were now considered the hot spots, like Georgia, Virginia, Iowa and Missouri.

And if the virus battle wasn't enough, there were all the battles still raging, now pretty much everywhere, between protesters and police, with the Floyd case the spark of the conflict. In Downtown Miami, for instance, people marched near the Torch of Friendship then made their way onto I-95 to block traffic in both directions. They threw objects and set cars on fire as they went. Police fired tear gas and pepper spray into the crowds; at least 38 people were arrested. The city set curfews and shut down public transit services.

In California, the governor declared a state of emergency and deployed the National Guard to Los Angeles to help enforce a citywide curfew. In Indianapolis, one person was fatally shot. In Detroit, a man in a car was shot dead after someone opened fire toward a protesting crowd. NYC was described as a war zone, with nearly two dozen police vehicles torched. In Philadelphia, demonstrators broke into a store near city hall and attempted to tear down the statue of a former mayor. Besides the places named, the Guard had been activated in Georgia, Kentucky, Wisconsin, Colorado, Ohio, Tennessee, Utah and Washington.

I thought more about the Minneapolis officer, Derek Chauvin, at the heart of this, whose career was now over. Whether he was going to be found guilty of the charges of 3rd degree murder and manslaughter or not, he could never return to law enforcement. And, likely, he *would* be found guilty because demonstrators everywhere would not accept a *not guilty* decision. If you were of the opinion that the riots were bad at present, a not guilty decision would be like a worldwide incendiary device going off. So he *would* go to jail in all likelihood and *would* need to be isolated as he *would* be Target #1 in *any* prison. And when he eventually got out, he *would* need to go into a federal protection program as he *would* again be Target #1 on the street. And *now*, his wife of 10 years, apparently "aghast" at the incident and taking the side of the demonstrators versus supporting her husband, announced that she was divorcing him, probably the ultimate blow for him. The wife, Kellie, was about Jen's age, born in Laos in 1974, according to an article on Your Tango. Her country was ripped apart by war in those years and her family fled to Thailand where they lived in a refugee camp for three years. They eventually were given the ok to emigrate to the U.S. and settled in Wisconsin. Kellie said she never felt fully safe there. "We didn't know English. My parents didn't want us leaving the house because they didn't trust the world," she said. She trained in radiology and met Derek through the Medical Center where she worked. A looker, she was also crowned USOA Mrs. Minnesota in 2018. Her impression of Derek was that he was a "softie" and "a gentleman" and chivalrous. She was apparently married once before him, at 17, to a man who was abusive but with whom she had two children. That background had led to dedicating her spare time to helping other women who had been abused. Learning all of this, it seemed to me that because of her volunteer work, there was *no way* she could stay with Derek now, with the specter of this allegedly abusive action pinned to him. What future could they have anyhow, whether he was found guilty or not? Was she going to be shut up in some federally hidden home in some East Bumfuck? No way, she was bailing while the going was good and her looks were going to carry her to her next liason. She was no dummy.

With great excitement, at 10am, I tuned in to NASA TV to catch the aforementioned docking. Super exciting. I watched the Crew Dragon gumdrop make its approach, flip back its hatch and steer into place, first making a soft capture, then locking down latches to make a hard capture, connecting umbilicals. "Dragon SpaceX, docking sequence is complete," confirmed Control.

"It's been a real honor to be part of this nine-year endeavor," said the astronauts. From inside the ISS, Chris Cassidy welcomed the arriving capsule. Houston also chimed in to make note of this historic mission. Finally, SpaceX congratulated the astronauts on "ushering in this new era of human spaceflight."

My Dad and brother Dave were in a good, almost unearthly place today, too, in Utah, but mounting up to fly back east to Dulles Airport, concluding their weeklong trip out there in the rocky desert lands.

I had my own adventure to wrap up, that of my basement doorway project, which was getting into a nitty gritty stage with measuring, marking, cutting, measuring again, marking again and cutting again. I needed a new aluminum level to get ahead and zipped out to Hemlock to get it, transacting as before by calling in my product request, holding up my credit card to the window and collecting my purchase through a crack in the door. While onsite, I spotted two cool cars — it was the right kind of nice day to bring them out. One was a late 60s vintage Corvette Stingray convertible; the other was a Mercedes German military vehicle that had been converted into a family SUV. Circling back through the neighborhood, I passed Geronimo Southwest Grill and saw that their outdoor dining area was humming. I spotted a waitress in a very medical-looking mask and latex gloves taking an order from a couple. I imagined she introduced herself something like this: "Hi, I'm Amy, I'll be your surgeon… er, waitress, this evening."

Back home, when I got the frame and door set up in the basement doorway, I knocked off and headed out for two stops. The first was Home Depot, which took me on a path behind two motorcyclists, both driven by guys, and each with a girl on the back. They were riding side by side, and the girl on the bike on the left kept looking back at me each time the bike stopped at at stop sign. Was I too close? Was she digging my truck? Was she digging me? Did she want to see if I was looking at her? Did I know her? Did she know me? Was I supposed to recognize her? At a fork, they went right, I went left, so we would never know.

Home Depot was the usual madhouse, with the parking lot full again. I parked as far away as I could to lessen the chance that my truck might get scratched. I just needed some rough, pressure treated, gap filling wood to fit between the door frame and brick foundation on one side. I also needed a new chisel set to help do the work of carving out spots for the door hinges and door lock. Masked staffers were helpful in steering me to what I needed, the payment process with a masked cashier behind plexiglass was easy, and I was out and on to my next errand, Stop & Shop.

To this point, I would normally say the "dreaded" Stop & Shop, but they had gotten better and better at getting stuff in and shelves restocked. My shopping journey was quick and efficient and the only things I wasn't able to find were paper towels and disinfectant wipes. Both had been longtime absent mostly. New on the scene there were barrels of different-sized hand sanitizer. Toilet paper, for a change, was also very plentiful, with stacks of it on display, like a t.p. dam had broken somewhere and all the rolls came pouring out. Near to the registers, on a long table, were trays of pods and a big hand-scrawled sign, "Take A Free Seed Starter Kit". Though it looked like a "homegrown" effort judging from the sign, which seemed like a kid's work, it was actually endorsed by the store. I grabbed a pod — a two-inch high biodegradable "pot" with a cardboard wrap with Stop & Shop's logo on it, the phrase "Grow & Learn" and an encouragement to download the app of the same name, scan a package marker and "unlock your digital garden!" Inside the "pot" was a little pressed tablet, like an Alka-Seltzer and a marker that identified the seeds as "Beet". It was an internationally created item — a product of the Netherlands and England, packed in Poland, imported by TCC Retail Marketing in Westport, presented by the Stop & Shop Supermarket Company LLC of Quincy, MA and distributed through our store here in Fairfield.

Bravo, S&S, though I wondered how this was a smart marketing move? I applied my 35 years of accumulated marketing experience to the presentation and thought for a moment. Great diversion during an anxious time, particularly for children toward which this was aimed. Great way to remind people of the S&S brand. Positively reflective on the store as a provider of education and supporter of kids. Great way to give mom and dad a break while they are homebound, by keeping kids busy with this project. Good way to get a new generation stoked about vegetables, which would make them want to desire them as shoppers. The only disconnect was it also encouraged people to grow their *own* vegetables. And once you successfully grow your own vegetables, experience how satisfying it is to do that, realize there's a great difference in taste than the huge farm "processed" cookie-cutter output, recognize the cost savings, disconnect from the dependency on store-vended food and realize peace-of-mind with regard to knowing your food is safe and not tainted with something like e-coli bacteria, which has certainly happened time and time again in the past, you might never go back to store food. And, yet, people are busy. Families are busy. You need to have the land, the constant drive, attention and dedication to grow your own food. That said, S&S was not jeopardizing their business in my opinion, and only securing their brand. So, again, bravo S&S.

This particular grocery store visit was my first in the Ranger and I was happy everything tucked in nicely on and around the second row and passenger seats. And the wood and chisel set went in the truck bed. One truck. Multiple errands. Diverse haul. Happy me.

Unpack was easy, mixed salad followed and then news checks. The dominating topic was the rioting. In his daily briefing, NYC Gov. Cuomo said, "Last night was a long and ugly night all across this nation", that he had "seen a lot of disturbing video" and that he had deployed more state police and had National Guardsmen standing by. In San Francisco, dozens of businesses were looted. In Minneapolis, a large truck going full speed drove through a crowd of protesters; the driver was arrested. In our own CT, protesters walked out onto Interstate 84 in Waterbury, effectively shutting it down in both directions. A Twitter post that ended up being taken down showed a man dragging to a bus stop an ATM machine he had stolen, expecting to get on a city bus with it. PIX11 News showed a photo of St. Patrick's Cathedral in NYC that had been vandalized with graffiti during anti-police protests. In Jacksonville, FL, an officer had his neck slashed and was reportedly fighting for his life after a violent attack on police last night. That same crowd also vandalized several police cars, smashing their windows and attempting to light them on fire. In Chicago, protesters knocked officers down and dragged them through the streets. They also threw bottles of water, fireworks, bottles, gasoline and containers of urine at them. Crowd members also used pipes, hammers and other objects to damage property and break into and loot shops.

A new FB friend posted the words of Martin Luther King, Jr. and it was the most sensible thing — and yet least heeded — that I had read. The quote was from his book, "Strength to Love", first published in 1963: "Returning hate for hate multiplies hate, adding deeper darkness to a night already devoid of stars. Darkness cannot drive out darkness; only light can do that. Hate cannot drive out hate; only love can do that. Hate multiplies hate, violence multiplies violence, and toughness multiplies toughness in a descending spiral of destruction."

The word "antifa" was a new one to me, dropped in an NBC post that said President Trump will designate antifa as a terrorist organization after officials pointed to extremist groups and out-of-town demonstrators as responsible for the violent episodes at protests in major cities across America. Antifa was defined online as a political protest movement comprising autonomous groups affiliated by their militant opposition to fascism and other forms of extreme right-wing ideology. Attorney General Barr put the country's network of 56 regional FBI Joint Terrorism Task Forces on call. "Preventing reconciliation and driving us apart is the goal of these radical groups, and we cannot let them succeed," Barr said, then added, "The violence instigated and carried out by antifa and other similar groups in connection with the rioting is domestic terrorism and will be treated accordingly."

Congress had been debating a bill that would send a second round of economic stimulus payments to the American people. This was being issued as part of the HEROES Act and would be distributed as paper checks, which many had raised objections about. "Physical currency is increasingly becoming a relic of the past — a trend which the Covid-19 pandemic has seemed to accelerate," according to John Wu, president at Ava Labs.

June 1. My Mom would have been proud of me this morning. I got up with the sun and the first thing I thought of was my shorts. Yes, not a traditional go-to, but I had torn my favorite pair that I had practically been living in over the last few days as I did project work. They were just *so* comfortable. The tear was six inches along an inseam. An iron-on patch just wouldn't do the trick. So I pulled out my Mom's sewing kit, a beautiful wooden box with a gold latch and Chinese characters printed on the lid that spelled out the place, Lóngquán, where the box was handcrafted in China. That town is also known for making green jade porcelain used mostly by aristocratic and royal families. Mom had left me the box as a keepsake, and I now I hoped to honor the gesture by using its contents. That said, I located a good needle and spool of thread, threaded the needle (after 20 tries), pulled an ample amount of thread (a little longer than the tear), turned my shorts inside out, pulled the material together at the tear and off I went. Needle in, through, around. Needle in, through, around. Needle in, through, around. Sixty, seventy times maybe. It seemed like that anyhow. Then I tied off the end. I had remembered all she taught me for a sewing job like this. And when I turned my shorts right side out, they looked great. I had ended up saving a pair of shorts that others might not have bothered with and would have thrown out instead. And I had achieved this feat during a pandemic when we were all fearful that a second wave of the coronavirus might visit us. I was quite chuffed with myself, in fact, as Mom might have said.

The morning was a chilly one, at only 54F for the start of a month that was considered the kickoff to summer. In fact, I had to put on my pullover to head outside to water, still fostering the growth of some grass patches I had seeded and generally just keeping the lawn green. It really looked spectacular — one of the best looking lawns I had maintained in years. And they really *are* comparable. Last year, for instance, was a train wreck. In mid-summer, when Phil and I went to North Carolina for a week to visit my Dad, the lawn burned out when temps rose to around 100 and stayed that way all the time we were away. I had to pull up the charred grass especially in the back yard, in an area measuring a good 25 feet by 10 feet, re-seed it, lay straw down to hold the seed and water it faithfully so it would come back, which it did by fall.

Mike Lauterborn

Watering the plants and grass was such a relaxing, meditative endeavor. It was head clearing. And a way to focus on the day ahead, and make a mental to-do list. But for that moment as I tended to my garden, I felt like my grandfathers before me. My Mom's dad and his Victory garden. My Dad's dad and the tomatoes of which he was always so proud.

It was gladdening to leaf through an album of photos that Cable News Network posted of the SpaceX launch Saturday. There was a view of hundreds of spectators watching from a bridge in Titusville, FL, though there was absolutely no physical distancing going on and almost no mask wearing at all. President Trump speaking to a crowd at the Kennedy Space Center after the launch. SpaceX Founder Elon Musk with his arms stretched up in the air celebrating the successful launch. Second Lady Karen Pence, VP Mike Pence and Pres. Trump watching the rocket go up. A group of young people in bathing suits looking up at the launch from a beach in Cape Canaveral. Flight control personnel watching monitors at the KSC. The actual liftoff at 3:21pm. Astronaut Doug Hurley looking choked up as he said goodbye to his wife and son before the launch. Hurley and Behnken suited up and walking out of the Neil Armstrong Operations and Checkout Building at KSC.

I was without a fresh batch of paper towels due to the outage at Stop & Shop, but I thought I might go on Safari to find them, later in the day perhaps. A Paper Towel Safari, it was just what I needed. I would have to adopt my Australian big game hunter accent of course, and say stuff like, "'Ere we ah, in the outback of Fairfield, prowling for the beasts they called Paper Towels. Elusive, and sparse in these parts since March. A fluke of nature, really. Once in abundance, they'd been hunted nearly to extinction. And those that happened to lasso them, have kept them corralled and on their own homesteads. But the beasts were out there if you looked hard. Massive and white, often two-ply, and sporting absorbent properties. They're a chore to wrangle but a serious trophy if you can land them, particularly a pack. Greater value, that." The outing was on my to-do list.

Mid-morning, Phil wanted to pull his car off the street and park it in our driveway, which required me to move the Ranger which was parked at the end of the drive. Rather than just pull out and pull back in, I went on drive-about to see what I could see, sticking to our Beach Area. Not three blocks from my doorstep, I came across Joanie, all of 82 years, sweeping

364

her driveway. I had heard that her husband, Steve, had passed. As a retiree, he had been buying up used bikes, repairing and refurbishing them and reselling them from his property, along with wagons, sport strollers and other wheeled craft. In the past, I had bought two kids bikes, an adult woman's bike and a little red fire engine pedal car from him. I stopped to chat with Joanie and shared about those purchases while expressing my sympathies about Steve's passing. She said he was 87 or 84, she couldn't remember, and that he had a short bout with kidney cancer. "He had a big lump right here," she said, holding her side. He was diagnosed in February and started to do chemo, but he didn't like it and chose to let fate play out. He was gone by April 11, "at 10pm", said Joanie. The family buried him at a local cemetery, Gates of Heaven, and a family friend bought up all the bikes, as apparently pre-arranged. I mentioned that I was a writer and Joanie said her granddaughter was, too, a recent graduate of Housatonic Community College and now working at a Norwalk company, Forrester Network, a financial data company. I offered Joanie my help should she need anything at all and suggested her granddaughter get in touch, too. Writers should be friends with other writers, right?

I continued my local tour, by the Seagrape beach bar, which had an American flag affixed to the face of one section of steel fence that marked the boundary of its unofficial outdoor dining space. The fence sections were weighted down with white sandbags imprinted with the Seagrape's logo.

I popped into the Penfield Beach parking lot and strolled out onto the sand for a moment. The view was beautiful, with a remarkable cloud pattern in the sky, but it was too chilly to sit out, though there were three small groups braving it — a mom and her two small children, who were racing across the sand and chasing seagulls; a couple enjoying the serenity; and three already deeply tanned retirees who live for going to the beach, who were tucked up near the pavilion out of the wind's direct path. As I exited, I said to the kid wearing a face mask at the entrance shack, "You must hate wearing that all day." He replied, "I do, and it's up, down, up, down, all day."

Through the tall chain link fencing that surrounded the Fairfield Beach Club, I could see people swatting balls on the three or four tennis courts there. I didn't know tennis had been permitted again, though this was a private establishment so I figured it went by different rules... and, no doubt, club members sign liability waivers with regard to the coronavirus or any harm in general that might befall them while on the premises.

I wanted to have an up-close and personal look at the Club and pulled into their lot, chatting with the kid at the entrance shack. He steered me to the manager and I had a prowl, admiring the Club interior, grand fireplace, a table setting for lunch, the rows of cabanas each with their own shower, the in-ground pool, beach bar, outdoor tables and canvas sun shields... and the tennis courts, of course, which were in action with instruction and play.

Back home again, I did some more prowling, in the yard this time, trimming back and tying up seagrasses and other plants, and pulling a few weeds as I went. A couple passing with a dog noticed the sign above my front porch, "Seas The Day" and called out, "We love that!" I replied, "Carpe diem! You *have* to seize the day!"

Talking about seizing the day, Dad and I did that very thing on this date three years ago: a grand hike on foot from the near-top of Manhattan to the very bottom, which had been in the planning since 2015. There had always been much talk about it but no window of opportunity... until Wednesday, May 31st, the mid-point of my Dad's visit to my place in Fairfield. In a couple of hours the day before we set off, we mapped out our route -- not really the whole length of the Big Apple but a good stretch of it, from W. 125th in Harlem southeast to E. 7th Street in the ABC Street neighborhood of the East Village on the lower east side.

The morning of our trek arrived... and it was drizzling... not a promising start but I was confident there was brighter weather waiting to greet us in the hours ahead. And so we padded from my Beach Area setting to Fairfield Train Station... and promptly and just narrowly missed the train we were shooting to board. Not a dozen minutes later though, another came along and down the tracks we went, to Metro North's 125th Street, Harlem.

A few short blocks walk and we arrived at Sylvia's, founded by the legendary "Queen of Soul Food", Sylvia Wood. "Sylvia", of course, also happened to be my Mom's name. Mom had passed almost precisely four years before. It seemed a fitting place to start.

With home fries, corned beef hash, eggs, biscuits and good coffee in our bellies, we sidestepped puddles down to E. 103 Street and Fifth Avenue, on the east side of Central Park, to the Museum of the City of New York. This was traditionally a great place to visit at the start of *any* NYC adventure as you could better appreciate your environment with regard to its history, evolution and forward direction.

Continuing down Fifth, our next stop was the Guggenheim Museum at E. 88th Street. The spiral-shaped venue contained works by some of the most famous painters and sculptors in history -- Picasso, Modigliani, Calder, Renoir, etc. to name a few -- and we gaped at them all.

With a hankering for lunch, we paced down Madison Avenue for a bit before deciding the "pay-to-play" was too steep for our liking. We downshifted over to 3rd Avenue and stumbled on Neil's Coffee Shop, made to order for a nosh of BLT and hot Reuben on Rye sandwiches.

Of course, some liquid dessert was then on order, a pang satisfied by advertising world haunt P.J. Clarke's, which did us right with a Kolsch and Brooklyn Lager.

We picked up the march down Third to Hofbrau Bierhaus to honor our German heritage with some half liters of beer and a bratwurst platter with real German potato salad and sauerkraut on the side.

Reflecting back on a moment of personal history -- NYC's great 1977 Blackout, during which we were visiting the city and staying at the Hotel Tudor on E. 42nd Street -- we revisited the building, discovering it had become the Woodstock Tower private apartments.

We really stretched ourselves then, ambling all the way down to E. 7th. We made two stops along that passage, to NoRelation Vintage Clothing and Matchmaker Amy Van Doran's Modern Love Club and art gallery, both big recommends. A few zig-zags later and we had arrived at one of Dad's old haunts, McSorley's Old Ale House. We found the trademark sawdust on the floor and their sole two kinds of beer available: light and dark. And while tossing our beer back, we befriended a couple from Lyon, France -- Francois and Camille -- a friendly pair that countered the gruff, unsociable nature of the bartender whose poor attitude spurred our hasty departure.

From there, it was a short hop east along 7th to Zum Schneider, which had been promoted to me as THE place to go for a German experience, for yet another nod to our heritage. Sitting at a people-watching outdoor corner table, we enjoyed a couple rounds of beer, wonderful white asparagus (spargel) wrapped in ham with potatoes and hollandaise sauce, and apfelküchle pastry with vanilla ice cream for dessert. (Sadly, Zum closed earlier this spring.)

As pre-arranged, our final stop was the New York Comedy Club, back up northwards at E. 24th Street, where we took in the 9pm show and about seven comics' routines, which were a howl.

The home stretch -- in Manhattan leastways -- was from the Club to Grand Central Station, a 35-block push, then the 12:07am train back to our Fairfield home base.

150+ blocks. Over 16 miles. Several beers. Much German food. Lots of laughs and memories. And a few new friends. Mission accomplished. Bucket list scratch-off!

I read in Fairfield Ludlowe High School's Facebook forum page a note from the yearbook production coordinator. She stated that the printing plant that produces the FLHS book was one of two that remained open during the quarantine but, that, in order to continue production, they had to follow all the CDC safety protocols (which included social distancing guidelines that minimized staff from 400 to 100), which had delayed printing and distribution. She had just learned that the yearbooks were still on the assembly line and there was no definitive shipping or delivery date given.

Early afternoon, NY Gov. Cuomo got on the blower for his daily briefing, saying, with regard to numbers, "We're doing better than we've ever done before" and that the state is "testing more per capita than any country on the globe". Just yesterday, in fact, the state conducted 50,000 tests, and less than 1,000 people tested positive (a 2% rate). Still, there were 54 deaths yesterday, though that was the lowest daily death rate yet since the pandemic started. As to reopenings, five regions upstate entered Phase 2, western NY would join them tomorrow, and the Capitol district the day after that. All good, right? Then he addressed the rioting. "Now we're seeing these mass gatherings over the past several nights that could, in fact, exacerbate the Covid-19 spread. We spent all this time closed down, locked down, masks, socially distanced, and then you turn on the TV and you see these mass gatherings that could potentially be affecting hundreds and hundreds of people, after everything we have done. We have to take a minute and ask ourselves, 'What are we doing here? What are we trying to accomplish?'"

Immediately afterwards, White House Press Secretary Kayleigh McEnany gave a briefing about the very same topic, the nationwide rioting. "The First Amendment guarantees the right of people to peaceably assemble. What we saw last night in D.C. and across the country was *not* that. Seventeen thousand National Guard are deployed in 24 states but only two states have deployed more than 1,000 troops… For the lawlessness we have seen, far *more* needs to be done. Governors across the country *must* act, deploy the National Guard as it's fit, and protect American communities."

Meanwhile, "No justice, no peace, no justice, no peace" and "I can't breathe" and "No racist PO-lice" were the robotic cries of what looked like hundreds of "Black Lives Matter" sign-carrying people marching through Keney Park in Hartford, CT, being captured in video being broadcast by WFSB Channel 3. As irritated as *they* were, *I* was becoming equally agitated, having these protests fall on top of the months-long trying pandemic. And, on a related note, *why* weren't all the looters, lawbreakers, thieves, vandals and arsonists being arrested and duly prosecuted? Already there was billions of dollars in property damage, and sure to be more, and *this* was honoring the memory of GF? And, of course, there was the whole potential infection spread to consider. I did *not* want to go back to square one. *We* could not lock back down again.

And this virus wasn't kidding around. Worldometer showed that global coronavirus cases had grown by another 100K since yesterday, to over 6.3 million with over 376K deaths, nearly 2.9 million recoveries. The U.S. had 1,846,123 cases, 106,504 deaths and over 607K recoveries. NY had 380,752 cases and 29,969 deaths.

Late afternoon, I dropped down to the basement, cleared out the workshop and tackled the job of painting the walls — the cement patched area and all. The process had a calming effect. Painting always does. And the cellar was a quiet retreat from the noise of the world. The only interruption, in fact, was my Dad calling in through FaceTime, and that was anything *but* a disruption. He was back from Utah, at Dave's in West Virginia, and thinking of driving to my house tomorrow. He asked what it was like here with respect to the virus and I told him things had more or less picked up and resumed some normalcy. We would be able to pick up beer as needed, dine on a restaurant patio, sit on the beach, hike a trail, visit a park, grill in and enjoy the back yard, take a drive, etc. The bigger concern than the virus now was the rioting. Just in the last couple of hours, I heard of a planned demonstration on our own Fairfield Town Green that was set for tomorrow; dump trucks being used in Bridgeport to block protesters from accessing certain areas; crowds blocking traffic on I-95 in Norwalk; and a march this afternoon that went to and from Jesup Green. I feared that my Dad might get stuck at one of these blockages and, immobilized, might be swarmed and attacked. Really, this year was *sucking* left, right and center. To have to worry about the virus *AND* having your house burned down or your parent hurt? This had gotten ridiculous, *really*. The astronauts had the right idea getting the hell away from Earth.

I knocked off the work for the day, made a jumbo salad and cracked a beer. It was good to catch my breath for a bit finally.

Early evening, President Trump opened a can of whoop-ass. Speaking from the White House, he said, "My fellow Americans, my first and highest duty as president is to defend our great country and the American people, and that is *exactly* what I will do… The biggest victims of the rioting are peace-loving citizens in our poorest communities, and as their president, I will fight to keep them safe. I will fight to protect you. I am your president of law and order and an ally of all peaceful protesters. But in recent days, our nation has been gripped by professional anarchists, violent mobs, arsonists, looters, criminals, rioters, antifa and others. A number of state and local governments have failed to take necessary action to safeguard their residents. Innocent people have been savagely beaten… Small business owners have seen their dreams utterly destroyed. New York's Finest have been hit in the face with bricks. Brave nurses, who have battled the virus, are afraid to leave their homes. A police precinct has been overrun. Here in the nation's capital, the Lincoln Memorial and the World War II Memorial have been vandalized. One of our most historic churches was set ablaze. A federal officer in California — an African American enforcement hero — was shot and killed. These are not acts of peaceful protest. These are acts of domestic terror. The destruction of innocent life and the spilling of innocent blood is an offense to humanity and a crime against God. America needs creation not destruction, cooperation not contempt, security not anarchy, healing not hatred, justice not chaos. This is our mission and we will succeed, 100%, we will succeed. Our country always wins. That's why I am taking immediate presidential action to stop the violence and restore security and safety in America. I am mobilizing all available Federal resources — civilian and military — to stop the rioting and looting, to end the destruction and arson, and to protect the rights of law-abiding Americans, including your 2nd Amendment rights. Therefore, the following measures are going into effect immediately. First, we are ending the riots and lawlessness that has spread throughout our country. We will end it now. Today, I have strongly recommended to every governor to deploy the National Guard in sufficient numbers that we dominate the streets. Mayors and governors must establish an overwhelming law enforcement presence until the violence has been quelled. If a city or state refuses to take the actions that are necessary to defend the life and property of their residents, then I will deploy the United States military and quickly solve the problem for them. I am also taking swift and decisive action to protect our great capital, Washington, D.C. What happened in this city last night was a total disgrace. As we speak, I am dispatching thousands and thousands of heavily armed soldiers, military personnel and law enforcement officers to stop the rioting, looting, vandalism, assaults, and the wanton destruction of property. We are putting everybody on warning: our 7pm curfew will be strictly enforced. Those who threaten innocent life and property will be arrested, detained and prosecuted to the fullest extent of the law. I want the organizers of this terror to be on notice that you will face severe criminal penalties and lengthy sentences in jail. This includes antifa and others who are leading instigators of this violence. One law and order, and that's what it is... And once that is restored, and fully restored, we will help you, we help your business and we will help your family. America is founded upon the rule of law. It is the foundation of our prosperity, our freedom and our very way of life, but where there is no law, there is no opportunity. Where there is no justice, there is no liberty. Where there is no safety, there is no future. We must never give in to anger or hatred. If malice or violence reigns, then none of us is free. I take these actions today with firm resolve and with a true and passionate love for our country. By far, our greatest days lie ahead."

Late in the evening, I FaceTimed with Jen. She had enjoyed a leisurely day for a change, now that her spring semester was over, strolling Westport's Compo Beach and her neighborhood. She was mostly relaxing but also thinking about her house and if she should sell it. And if she did, how would I accommodate her stuff if she chose to come live with me? And how would all of that work with Phil, and then Evan, here later in the summer? We also spoke of the rioting and Trump's announcement to use powerful force to suppress it and she said that was how China rolled, like in Hong Kong when people protest there. No messing around. Right for the jugular.

"Boobs out." That's what Chrissy Teigen announced on Instagram. She had had breast implants since she was 20 and had now decided to have surgery to get them removed. "They've been great to me for many years but I'm just over it," she wrote. She was pretty candid about the whole thing, saying, "I'll still have boobs, they'll just be pure fat. Which is all a tit is in the first place. A dumb, miraculous bag of fat." Bless her heart, as folks in the South might say. And, oh, by the way, what a different orbit she was circling in than the rest of us on Planet Earth. What virus? What riots?

I saw that NYC was being locked down citywide, with a curfew going into effect at 11pm tonight through 5am tomorrow. It seemed to me like 7 or 8pm would have been a better start time. Why wait until it was dark when bad people can gather more easily and do bad stuff, and disappear into the darkness more easily? The police there had also been put on 12-hour shifts for max presence at potential riot hot spots. Yes, *riot* hot spots. Not *virus* hot spots. That was yesterday's news. Now we were full-on riots 24/7.

And, really, it was dominating *all* of our headlines and much of social media, where I saw a post from a Facebook friend that shared, "My car was vandalized by the crazy zealots. Smashed up with a crowbar or baseball bat, not sure which, but physically feeling sick after the experience and can't get out of bed. Just feeling awful." Just the day before, she had shared an IG post from ANTIFA America, which read: "ALERT. Tonight's the night, Comrades. Tonight we say "F— The City" and we move into the residential areas... the white hoods... and we take what's ours." The post was highlighted with a black fist, a fire and an extended middle finger.

June 2. I was up with the sun... *again*... and realized I had even *more* on my plate to do than usual with my Dad likely arriving today. The sunrise was photo worthy, creating a rainbow palette of colors above the treetops to the east. Unfortunately, its fiery nature immediately reminded me of the looting going on everywhere and all the fires being set.

A Guardian article, in fact, was headlined, "Widespread curfews fail to stop fresh wave of protests across U.S." In Philly, the mayor announced last minute a 6pm curfew, with an alert going out to residents' cellphones. But demonstrators were undeterred and chanted, "Whose streets? Our streets", clashed with police and blocked a highway. In D.C., military helicopters and pepper spray were used to disperse crowds. Confounding matters, residents in one area opened their homes to protesters who were illegally out after the new curfew and hid them inside when police corralled a group of them. In Oakland, police launched a barrage of teargas at a crowd of about 500 people to make them scatter. In St. Louis, four officers were wounded by gunfire. In Buffalo, NY, two officers were injured when a car driving full speed rammed into a line of police. Shootings were reported in Las Vegas. In Chicago, two people were killed in the suburb of Cicero. New York was an absolute war zone, with looters destroying businesses and setting fires everywhere. Fifth Avenue was particularly hard hit, with store after store broken into and ransacked. Hundreds of people broke through boards and streamed into Macy's flagship store in Herald Square to loot it. Ironically, GF's brother, Terence, rebuked protest troublemakers for "messing up my community", according to BBC News.

At the same time all this was going on, two sets of autopsy results came back on GF. Both concluded his death was a homicide but they diverged on what caused it. An independent autopsy said he died of "asphyxiation from sustained pressure" on his neck and back. The medical examiner's autopsy said the cause of death was "cardiopulmonary arrest", with no mention of asphyxiation as a contributor. Further, the M.E. determined Floyd had heart disease and that there was fentanyl and methamphetamine in his system. If anything, the combination of the restraint, underlying condition and drug usage contributed to his death. The charges against Officer Chauvin suggested that the restraint he employed *could have* or *might have* caused death. But, put yourself in the position of the officer, struggling with a drug-addled, combative, resistant, strong man who was not obeying commands to sit still — you *must* get his attention, put him down, immobilize him, no? There was little time or opportunity to consider the consequences. And why would Chauvin want to *kill* Floyd? He didn't *know* Floyd. There was *no* possible motive for him to willfully do harm to the man. You *must* listen to police, *immediately* heed their warnings. *They* are as much afraid of you as *you* are of them. A confrontation is always an anxious, emotional moment. And when one party is not cooperating, the anxiety level and opportunity for things to go south becomes immediately elevated. I understood the controversy, but Chauvin seemed to have been tried and condemned before *any* evidence had even been presented, and that was *not* justice as I understood it. And certainly justice wasn't going to be gained by *looting*. The looters were only opportunists taking advantage of the situation. And the anarchists were interested only in causing chaos, having more and more people follow their lead and then to command these rebel masses to do their bidding for their own gain.

I was getting so fed up with all of this happening, and growing more and more anxious about the possibility that these protester actions were not only going to cause a virus spike, but that trouble was going to come right to the doorstep of our own neighborhoods, like the Antifa America post threatened. On top of that, the economy was only going to worsen and stock market dive. The torch bearers were leading us all to ruin.

But you couldn't let these thoughts and actions paralyze you, because then you were done. So I forged ahead with my to-do list, stripping and washing bed sheets and clothes, cleaning the shower, changing the bath mat and towels, watering the lawn, making coffee, putting away dishes, planning dinner, vacuuming, promoting the free stuff on the lawn, answering emails, etc. All the things a productive, contributing, tax-paying member of society *should* be doing instead of being out on the street being stupid.

I was eager to find some positive news, *any* positive news at all, and found just one little nugget, about a Florida high school holding its graduation ceremony on jet skis. Organizers shared, "Unique times call for unique measures."

Late morning, I stepped out to Home Depot, mostly to get supplies to shore up the corner of my back porch which had been attacked by termites and lunched on. I pulled out and Sawzall-ed out all I could of the masticated mess, measured out and figured what I needed, and reported to HD for the round-up. In addition to wood and cement for a post hole, I picked up trash bags, a new toilet seat and lid, and… wait for it… tiki torch fuel and wicks, because *who* didn't need those ingredients in a pandemic?

On the way home, I got snarled up in a demonstration centered in our downtown, at Sherman Green and our Fairfield Beach Area. Some 300 people, all dressed in black, walked through our neighborhood, in rows 20-people wide across the road, halting traffic, carrying signs, raising fists, chanting chants, but otherwise doing no other harm and kept under wraps by our town's police, who were posted at every corner of the "parade". I couldn't get back to my house because of the throng so I parked across from our police station and walked near the route to just see what I could see. There were definitely many people *not* from the area, mixed in with teens that had nowhere better to be on this overcast on-and-off rainy day, and some little family pods.

As the group migrated en masse to Sherman Green, for more chants and some unity songs (it appeared from some video I later reviewed), I unloaded my gear and set about installing the new toilet seat in our upstairs bathroom. Nothing like having a nice sit-upon, and you can take that as you may!

Late afternoon, it was time to roll out again, to meet friends for a drink or two or seven in South Norwalk. It was my first time visiting that city since the pandemic started and was a surprisingly painless process. My route to SoNo took me past Sherman Green, where some 50 people remained (some three hours after the march) to stand by the roadside and encourage passing motorists to beep their horns if they agreed with their signage messaging.

I-95 had more cars on it than the last time I had ridden it, but it was still a speedway. The trucks were particularly aggressive, bearing down on you from behind and boxing you in left, right and center.

In Norwalk, I passed the SoNo Collection mall, which had apparently re-opened, and several eateries — Calle Arepas, Evaritos — noticing their sidewalk corrals. I spotted my friends Linda and Julie at a hi-top sidewalk table in front of Public Wine Bar on the main drag, Washington Street. They whooped about the truck, which I went and parked around the corner, walking through an alleyway to get back to them.

It was good to see familiar faces and be with other people after being locked away so long. Kind of like being paroled and having that first public encounter, and a pour of a favorite beverage you missed. That was wine in this case, two bottles worth, which we made quick work of, along with arancini in vodka tomato sauce, while remarking how good it was to see each other in the flesh, how we had been initially jolted by the pandemic, how we had reinvented how we work, and how much life had changed while some things remained the same — the desire to feel the sun on our skin, to be surrounded by laughter, to clink glasses, to hug and joke and be human without reservation. Linda said there were just a couple of people she really wanted to see when she emerged from the pandemic, and I was one of them. That was really something to say.

We moved down the street to Il Posto, where our trio grew to a quartet with the addition of second cello Kathy. She was feeling very musical and stoked about her self-applied hair coloring treatment. I told the ladies I had done Jen's for her — they laughed. "It's all about the roots!"

I was in a cocktail sampling mode, and sprawled out for one called "On the Porch" made with Bully Boy American whiskey. Then I tried an Old Fashioned, made with the same liquor, a favorite on premise it appeared. And as a group, we ordered several dishes to share including pizza with prosciutto, lobster Mac 'n cheese, a salad and calamari. As we munched and chatted, we took in the Daytona Beach-like scene, noticing other patios start to fill in, like Oishi, in front of which the lovely Trusha stood guard; passersby and their different mask types (we saw one with a Versace logo); souped-up cars with blaring radios, trick lights, custom rims and revving engines; pretty girls with bare midriffs all gussied up with nowhere to go swinging their bottoms from side to side as they walked down the avenue; and the sun starting to glow and light up the historical buildings we sat amongst. This was another version of Manhattanhenge… SoNohenge.

Kathy left us and we remaining three crossed the street to The Village, yet another eatery, enclosed by bright golden yellow partitions. Playful Natalie was our server and took care of me with a bourbon cocktail and our table with a bucket of mussels and some more calamari, which was nice and salty. It was Linda's birthday tomorrow, so we just had to give her a cheer, and pay the tab on her behalf.

We were done and done at that point, parting with thoughts about gathering at my home next week and wishes for good health and fun and continued good spirits until then.

I tried Jen to alert her that I would be stopping in but she must have been busy. I went ahead and stopped in anyhow. She received me but kept her distance, saying I had been out without any pre-discussion with her and that I could possibly have contracted the virus in Norwalk. At this point, I thought we were pretty safe and I felt I could vouch for Linda and Julie, too, but Jen was not having it. I actually tried chasing her around her kitchen counter to try and get a hug, to no avail. She had a sniffle, too, and didn't want to compromise herself. She wasn't going to budge, it was clear. I was done and done, and maybe for two weeks she suggested. Yep, she was quarantining me. Maybe all for the best with my Dad coming? We would have further discussion about this disturbance in the pandemic force.

I didn't last long at home. My eyelids closed like a double set of garage doors. I was done and done for the third time this night. Hasta la vista, baby.

News: Global coronavirus cases ticked up by another 100K to well over 6.4 million with nearly 380K deaths, over 2.945 million recoveries. The U.S. had 1,868,754 cases and 107,534 deaths, nearly 619K recoveries. New York had 381,861 cases and 30,044 deaths.

CHAPTER 7

TWO-WEEK RE-OPENING
MARK REACHED

June 3. Today marked two weeks since Connecticut's Phase I re-opening took place. Were infections up? It didn't seem noticeably so, if they were. Had the re-opening gone okay? It was like a new seed starting, just trying to break through the soil. Slow and uncertain. Were we on an upswing? The mood had seemed hopeful, until the new crisis — the protesting — started. That certainly seemed to kick us back two squares, with new hurt applied to the economy, new division between people, new levels of mistrust, new anger and frustration, new opportunity for virus spread. 2020 was just one multi-layered mud cake, each layer delivering another bitter mouthful of misery. Slice after slice, right down to the crumbs. Mind fuck after mind fuck. Literally bent over a fence and repeatedly violated. It was a year like no other.

Related to the protesting and in a slap in the face to law enforcement everywhere, so-called celebs John Legend, Natalie Portman and others called for defunding the police and using the money to increase spending in education, health care and programs for black communities. An open letter, created by Movement 4 Black Lives, a coalition of more than 100 organizations representing black communities, was circulating in conjunction with the Black Lives Matter movement and Blackout Tuesday, which centered on the music business suspending operations for the day yesterday. Regular folks adopted the sentiment by posting black squares on their social media pages, in an apparent show of solidarity amid alleged racial injustices in the U.S.

Pres. Trump had issued his own letter to his supporters, noting that in light of the "dangerous mobs of far-left groups running through our streets and causing absolute mayhem", he was calling for the designation of ANTIFA as a terrorist organization, to send a united message that law-abiding Americans would not stand for their radical actions any longer.

Meanwhile, NYC Mayor Bill Blah Blah Blah de Blasio announced that he was extending a citywide curfew through June 7 because of the destructive "looting and destruction" that had continued night after night across the city. Gov. Cuomo criticized the mayor and the NYPD for their handling — or lack thereof — of the protests, particularly last night. De Blasio had refused to deploy the National Guard or *any* armed forces as Pres. Trump had recommended. The Bronx was particularly bad, with a car mowing down and seriously injuring a police sergeant investigating break-ins. At least three suspected looters held down and beat an officer in the Fordham area. Fires and looting were rampant, leaving "a trail of broken storefronts and littered streets". NYPD Commissioner Dermot Shea said that the department had made over 700 arrests late Monday and early Tuesday for looting, attacks on officers and other offenses.

Ironically, health care workers turned out in large groups to show support for the protesters, though *they* were now going to have to work even harder at their jobs, treating not only virus patients but all the injured, wounded and burned from these widespread skirmishes. We had found ourselves in a world that had run off the tracks, had gone completely bat shit and left all reason and common sense behind. This had truly become distressing. And even more insane was that Cuomo was going forward with reopening NYC on June 8, entering Phase I. How could that be possible or practical given this new crisis eruption and the new cases of coronavirus that had likely been spread due to the complete lack of any physical distancing among protesters? The patients were running the asylum. There was no doubt about it.

A Fox Los Angeles story reported that 95% of over 400 individuals arrested this past weekend in Santa Monica *traveled* to the city. The charges against them included looting, assault with a deadly weapon, assault on a police officer and curfew violations. The outsiders "came with the intent of capitalizing on the large crowds and fragile state of the nation from the coronavirus pandemic for personal gain." News footage showed many people carrying merchandise and running out of stores that had been broken into.

The protests and rioting — depending on how you looked at it — were spurring all sorts of comments and insights on social media. A friend posted to Facebook, only half kidding, "After watching the news last night, I put on a horror film to cheer me up." Another friend posted a photo of himself lying in a hammock with sangria and the comment, "Holding my own peaceful protest of 1. I'll figure out what I'm angry about as soon as I'm done relaxing." Another: "When your family's safety is put in jeopardy by so called peaceful protesters, then you are now dealing with domestic terrorism." Another, accompanied by a photo of armed security: "ATTENTION Looters/Thugs - you ain't gonna get in Saks Fifth Avenue!! Boards, barbed wire, security and attack dogs!! You disgusting thugs should be shot for what you are doing to our city!!" A Twitter post: "Phase 1: reopen retail for curbside pickup. Phase 2: gather by the thousands to torch cities and loot businesses. Phase 3: reopen churches and gyms at 25% capacity." A FB post, with pennant graphic: "Marked Safe From Fuck Knows What Today". Another: "Dear 2019, I apologize for all the things I said about you... I MISS YOU!!! I would love if we can get back together."

A National Review article titled "The Suicide of the Cities" posited that "Regardless of whether Trump or Biden is elected in November, it's easy to envision the following happening: Americans will flee the cities as they did in the post-1968 era. Thirty years of great progress for cities will be undone by the events of one spring. People will move to suburbs and exurbs. A lot more families will buy guns. Gun owners vote heavily Republican. People in less densely populated areas vote Republican, too. Trust in the government to provide basic services was already shaky and will tumble further. People who don't trust the government to provide for them vote Republican. There will be an increase in homeschoolers. Homeschoolers vote Republican. The involuntary experiment for telecommuting, particularly among white-collar workers, has proven that workers can be relied upon to work from home. People don't trust the New York City subway anymore but those who don't need to come into the office can live anywhere. This is especially true of some of the most successful people — lawyers, people in finance. High-income people will be disproportionately among those leaving. The balance of cities, already hit by a fiscal hurricane because of the duration of the lockdown, will tip toward heavy consumers of government services and away from high earners. Cities will be forced to raise taxes. The taxes on high earners and corporations will seem punitive. Even more of them will flee as taxes go up. The things successful people like about cities, such as high-end restaurants and culture, will follow them out to the suburbs. Corporate office parks in the suburbs will see a resurgence. People who stop commuting into cities will lose interest in them and their institutions. They will lose interest in funding cities. This will worsen the fiscal problems for the cities. Cities will lose congressional seats. Federal funding will be steered away accordingly. Voters left behind in cities will be a combination of the indigent, immigrants working in low-end jobs, the young, and the woke. These people will vote for a hard-left agenda focusing on aid to the poor, forgiveness for criminals, hatred of the rich, and boutique woke issues such as global warming that will push the Democratic Party well to the left. In other words, the demonstrators and rioters are going to remake the cities in their own image. And it's going to be disastrous for those cities." I had to concur. I had no *current* interest, *near-future* interest or *long-term* interest in visiting NYC. Our long-time courtship was over. Down and beaten like a dead horse.

I had to nervously laugh, getting an email from Road Runner Sports wishing me a Happy Global Running Day! The first thought that popped in my mind was "Run for your life!", which you could embrace in a health benefit type of way or… really, *run* for your life, the torch-bearing mob is coming.

I wasn't surprised to get another email, from a company called Defenders, promoting security equipment to "PROTECT YOUR HOME". I wasn't surprised by a Twitter update, either, informing that protesters laid down in the road on I-84 in our state's capital, Hartford. Why were we allowing this? How was this a tribute to GF? How was this helping anyone? It only served to frustrate drivers, fan already anxious flames, and block the flow of goods, services and much needed medicines. Police were just standing by letting it all happen, too. Yes, sure, it was peaceful, but how much more of this so-called "peaceful" demonstrating did we need to tolerate? What was the end goal supposed to be? What would make the crowd happy? As Gov.

Cuomo commented yesterday, demonstrators were asking for an overnight shift in policies that had not changed for 30, 40, 50 years, despite all efforts.

Woo-hoo, folks could now get a haircut in Connecticut. Now they could look stylish running to CVS for disinfectant, or to meet friends out for a physically distant drink, or rock their protest outfit. Scottie, beam me off this planet. Did the ISS need another crew member? Where could I apply for astronaut training?

Talk about repurposing your business! SmartBrief shared, "If you're a die-hard baseball fan (or just up for what would be an epic night), you can now book an entire major league baseball stadium in Pensacola, FL on Airbnb for $1,500 per night. The clubhouse has been converted to a sleeping space."

CT Gov. Lamont gave his Covid-19 update yesterday, noting that trends were all headed "in the right direction", including just eight new deaths, hospitalizations down to 434, tests to date up to 268,572 and a topped-out number of positive cases to date hovering at 42,979. We seemed to have gotten a handle on the virus but, again, all these mass protest gatherings *had* to be raising the risk of a potential spike back up. I really hoped that wasn't the case, but it seemed inevitable.

So, how was the hotel industry doing? An email from Radisson affirmed its "global commitment to cleanliness and hygiene" and said that it had developed new safety protocol recommendations for its hotels, to ensure guests' safety and peace of mind from check-in to check-out. Obviously, they suspected concerns among potential visitors were high and they were doing all they could to shore up and lure people back. I was ready to give it a go. I don't think hotels had *ever* been clearer. If you didn't go now, when would you *ever* go?

Mother Nature continued to F with us. Yesterday, there were nine reported tornadoes from Colorado to Minnesota; and baseball-sized hail damaged cars and property in Nebraska.

In a historic move, our town's leaders unanimously approved the 2020-21 budget with a proposed *zero percent* tax increase over last year's budget. The majority leader noted, "The Democratic caucus felt it was important to limit taxes this year given the current economic circumstances and with great consideration for the suffering of our neighbors and small businesses as a result of the novel coronavirus pandemic. I'm proud of our bipartisan work. It's important to come together during these challenging times, to lean on each other, to trust each other, and to work toward the common goal of helping our town during these unprecedented times."

Got gas? Sure, America had it, but Americans weren't heading to the pumps for it... until about four weeks ago, that is, when demand started to tick back up. That was Michael Gayed CFA's view, anyhow, after a precipitous drop from average weekly consumption over the last five years of 9.12 million barrels to 5.08 million barrels by the second week of April, a 44% drop.

Mid-morning, I got a text from my Dad, whose visit we were anticipating. "I've decided to go home this morning, rather than come on up to you. I'm still a bit tired from the trip and I don't want to push my luck relative to the virus. I'd rather come visit later in the summer anyway when things have returned to whatever 'normal' will be when this is over. Thanks for the invitation. Wish me luck on the drive home."

In the What The Hell 2020 category, WKRC reported that a massive asteroid "taller than the Empire State Building" was headed towards Earth. Traveling at a speed of 11,200 miles per hour, the asteroid was expected to pass by us, though could graze our atmosphere.

Midday, I created a big pot of outstanding chili and left it on the stovetop as a go-to for the day, then I just had to break out of the cocoon— nothing wild, just needed fresh air after all the brain-pummeling social media and news. I motored to the dump, carrying grass clippings and plant snippings accumulated over the last couple of days. Then I rolled around to Penfield Beach, pulling right up to the beach edge. But not a minute after I got there, it started raining, so I zipped back home. I had to cover the FREE stuff sitting curbside in front of my house, so it wouldn't get wet. And as I was doing that, an itch overcame me. No, nothing medical, just an itch to chuck the whole damn lot... and my old, broken, stained living room couch at the same time.

Enter, the Ranger. Have I mentioned that "I love my truck?" The hauling capacity of this little beauty is phenomenal. So, I put down the tailgate and, with Phil's help, took out the couch, put it in the truck bed, and added to the load a cabinet, a folding table with a broken leg, nearly a dozen old pillows, a box containing the rotted wood from the porch corner, a slab of marble and miscellaneous bric-a-brac, ready to go to the dump tomorrow.

We then hauled a chair, that I had wanted to chuck, back into the house. It had sentimental value — I had typed up my first book sitting in it. And as we incorporated it, we switched around the furniture and decor and cleaner treated the wood floor. The White Tornado had struck again. As before, I was quite chuffed with myself. And Mom would have been proud.

Back to the doom-and-gloom news, led off by a Nat Geo passage that shared that rural hospitals were struggling *before* Covid-19 hit and were even worse off at present. "Now with many patients unwilling to go to a hospital for fear of infection, these medical centers have too few patients to stay afloat financially." Said a health services expert, "If you lose your hospital, you've pretty much lost your town." Death knell.

That same Nat Geo email talked about the rubber bullets that police have fired at looters and rioters. They were meant to be fired into a fleshy part of the body and sting like a paintball. But they often hit other areas and can cause fractures, blindness, nerve damage, deep skin lacerations and organ injury that leads to death. The remedy in my opinion: stay the hell home.

The heartbreak continued for Amanda Kloots, Broadway Actor Nick Cordero's wife. She had been told that chances were low that Nick would survive from his coronavirus-related complications. "I've been told a couple times that he won't make it. I've been told to say goodbye. I've been told it would take a miracle," she said.

I'm sorry, I wasn't getting this whole GF thing, reading that Paris, France had now dug in its heels, according to TIME. Literally thousands of people defied coronavirus precautions to take to the streets. Some set fires and looted and were pummeled with tear gas. Others took a knee and raised their fists. Electric scooters and construction barriers went up in flames. The chant "I can't breathe" rippled through the crowd. And Paris wasn't alone. Expressions of anger sprang up in the Dutch capital of The Hague, and in Tel Aviv, and Sweden, and Sydney. The world was on a bender.

I was actually inspired to set fires, too. I got out my lighter, hammered my tiki torches into the ground at each corner of my patio and lit 'em up, pounding my chest like Tom Hanks in "Castaway"… "I… have… made… fire!" It was actually good that I tested them out, as thunder, lightning and rain erupted mid-evening, which is when Jen and I connected, too. She had banished me to quarantine for my outing last night, but still wanted to play warden and check on the inmate. I showed her my redecorating efforts while she told me about her house and committing to listing it. We were both taking big steps forward. Attaching the parachute and jumping. The time was now. There was no better time. There would be no better opportunity.

Wow, I had to say 2020, you were really outdoing yourself. Mid-evening tonight, the USGS and Facebookers reported a magnitude 5.5 earthquake southeast of Los Angeles. No reports yet on damage as the event was too fresh. At the same time, Tropical Storm Amanda whipped El Salvador, killing 14 and displacing 25,000 families.

Some new news on Mr. GF. He had tested positive for Covid-19 on April 3, which was confirmed through a nasal swab upon his autopsy. It was also discovered he had other significant conditions such as arteriosclerotic and hypertensive heart disease, in addition to fentanyl intoxication and recent meth use. And why was this info not top headlines? Because people wanted to cover their eyes and paint him as a saint who could not *possibly* have done any wrong. Resisting, struggling, not listening to commands, knowingly infected, probably infecting the officers, high on drugs. This... was... no... saint.

And the resulting misery of the whole situation continued to rain down, like the awful news of a 29-year-old police officer, trying to control rioters in Las Vegas, who was shot at point-blank range in the back of the head and was now on life support.

Reports from UNESCO and the International Council of Museums said that one in eight museums worldwide may not open again after the extended quarantine and shelter-in-place orders. Many had tried to engage people in virtual tours, but that hadn't necessarily translated into much needed funds to stay afloat.

News: Global coronavirus cases ticked up more than 150K in the last 24 hours to over 6.55 million with over 386K deaths, over 3.1 million recoveries. The U.S. had nearly 1.9 million cases, with over 109K deaths, over 684K recoveries. New York had nearly 383K cases, over 30K deaths.

June 4. Ah, yes, it was another day for you and me in pandemic paradise. And a moist one it was at that, with a good amount of rain soaking the landscape last night. That included the contents of my truck bed, but all that was going to the dump anyway. It would just be slicker and heavier to handle.

In the news, more fuckery and antics, from the House of Pain that had become the world. Pack it up, pack in, let me begin… with this nugget from Fox News about looters captured on video piling in a Rolls-Royce Cullinan SUV worth at least $330,000 after ransacking a store in NYC. It was their getaway car, according to an NBC producer's Tweet, which added, "Looters are literally pulling up in nice cars and cleaning out stores in #Soho. What #curfew?" A NYC resident shared that, in general, "cars would drive up, let off the looters, unload power tools and suitcases, and then the cars would drive away. Then the cars would come back, pick them up and then drive off to the next spot. They seemed to know exactly where they were going."

The NYT said that the three other Minneapolis policemen who were with Officer Chauvin had been charged with aiding and abetting second-degree murder, and Chauvin faced an increased charge of second-degree murder. Reportedly, the announcement was applauded by protesters but was "not nearly enough. There need to be convictions. There needs to be systematic change" was the opinion. That sounded to me like we could expect the crowd to continue to "jump around, jump up, jump up and get down." Meanwhile, Chauvin's soon-to-be-ex-wife filed paperwork to have her last name changed back to her maiden name. She was planning to "get down", too, but in altogether different way as she gunned for a new man.

On the other side of the world, a school security guard at a kindergarten in southern China wounded at least 39 people in a morning knife attack — 37 of the wounded were children. The incident immediately conjured thoughts of the horrific shootings committed in Dec. 2012 at Sandy Hook Elementary School in which 26 people died, including 20 children between six and seven years old.

D.C. had actually become a war zone, according to Popular Mechanics: overflights by military helicopters, the use of an ambulance helicopter to disperse crowds, a Blackhawk carrying elite FBI hostage rescue team members dressed in camo and wearing night vision goggles, hundreds of U.S. Army troops including a battalion of paratroopers flown in on huge transport planes to bases across the Beltway region — all meant to secure the area from unrest. The operation even had a name: Themis, after the Titan goddess of divine law and order.

More fallout: Rioters in Memphis stole a puppy from a nearby shelter, abused it on live TV and later strangled it to death, leaving it on the street.

In Richmond, rioters set fire to an occupied multi-family residence with a child inside and repeatedly blocked firefighters' access to the scene; the child, fortunately, was saved. A Dodge dealership in San Leandro, CA was targeted by looters who stole 50 high-performance cars — including every one of the venue's Dodge Challenger Hellcats worth $100K apiece — right off the lot. "Gone In Sixty Minutes" in real life. The Center City area of Philadelphia was pretty much destroyed judging from photos posted online: a helicopter flying above dense black smoke rising from several police vehicles set on fire in front of City Hall, a Dilworth Park Starbucks ablaze, statues defaced, expletives spray painted on the outside of City Hall, young people with their arms full of stolen clothing, high-end sneakers and electronics, and trash and debris littering sidewalks.

On an up-note, our CT Gov. said state schools could hold in-person graduations starting July 6, though no one seemed clear on how that was going to work.

Another up-note: the listing agent for the house next door said an offer was accepted and the closing would happen end of June. On a related note, there had been no interest yet in the room I had for rent, which she broadcast through a realtor's forum.

The *best* up-note, though, was a friend's FB post: "Good morning my lovelies. May the world be kind and assholes be scarce."

I had to bust out of my quaran-coon again. The news was getting to me, but I also had junk to deliver to the Transfer Station, or "the dump" as we locals call it. What an easy process. Bing, bang, boom... and I picked up two old steamer trunks, too, that were being trashed by Bridgeport's Black Rock Galleries. Did I *need* two steamer trunks? Probably not, but they appealed to me and it was hard to see decades-old artifacts being put to waste. I thought I might refurbish and sell them if I didn't end up embracing them myself.

As I was already out, I did a loop-around to see what was what. There were paddle boarders leaving Penfield Beach, crossing the road to their cars. Swimmers wading in from Long Island Sound, peeling off wet suits. Joggers everywhere. Cars rushing west on the Post Road. Masked technicians reporting for duty at the Premier Dental office. A family enjoying coffee al fresco at Shearwater Coffee. Lacy panties and bras hanging in the windows at In the Mood Intimates, waiting for torsos to fill them. We had a wonderful town, there was no doubting it, and we all hoped it would stay that way through these very uncertain times.

One thing that *would* be very different this year was the absence of the Faxon Law Fairfield Road Races, a two-day running event that attracted thousands of people to our beach area, that was to have been held this coming weekend. Because of the Covid-19 outbreak, it was pushed to late September. If they were lucky, organizers hopefully wouldn't have to scratch it for the year. The lack of social distancing at these huge unauthorized protests certainly put our future in jeopardy and made many question why *anyone* had to listen to guidelines if the rules weren't being applied to protesters. There was definitely a double standard and that double standard threatened us all.

I dropped into the basement late morning, to pick up on one of the multiple pandemic projects I had going on. This was the refurbish-and-organize-the-workshop effort, which required today some wall paint touch-up and some more wall cement work. While I was at it, I Rustoleum spray-painted a metal shelving unit. Because the basement was mostly underground, it was very cool down there, maybe 25 degrees cooler than the main floor above. But you tended to forget that when you were in the work zone. So it was a shocker when I came up out of the pit for lunch and hit the main floor air: oofa. Phil was studying at the dining room table and had opened all the windows wide — letting the air circulate, on one hand, but the heat get in, too. All 80+ degrees of it. Yes, full-on summer decided to visit us today. I had made the right choice in pursuing subterranean missions.

A great email rolled in from my financial go-to Michael Gayed CFA, stating that "The Great Acceleration" was happening. As he explained it, that was the concept "that previously existing socioeconomic developments have been pushed into overdrive. Tele-commuting, the dominance of high-tech, and the shift to online learning have all taken multi-year jumps forward in the space of just months." Post-secondary education models were also permanently shifting.

I made another run out, doing a drive by Penfield Pavilion's parking lot, where a dozen bikes were resting in a row against the rock seawall. And I parked for a spell at Sasco Beach, too, seeing groups of "Sun Sippers" lounging and wading in the water. A woman sat under a colorful green, blue and yellow sun umbrella wearing a big floppy hat and reading a book. I popped to South Pine Creek Beach as well and looked up and down — again, pockets of people sunning and socializing. A mailbox up the road had a heart, globe and peace sign painted on it, which I translated to Love & World Peace. To see all of this happiness, serenity and frolicking, you couldn't imagine there was a pandemic and rioting going on. But then you went home and got on social media and within a minute, there were live streams of thousands of angry people walking across the Brooklyn Bridge, or some politician announcing Covid numbers for the day, and it all came rushing right back.

I did more of the same work in the basement in a fourth corner before retiring from the project for the day and kicking back with a citrusy IPA and All-In Man-Sized Salad. Darkness crept around the house and the mild air took on a slight chill. It was hard to sit still, so I ventured out yet *again*, this time just to Penfield Beach. There, the evening light was a mysterious blue, perhaps reflecting the water, and most folks were organized into circles of sports chairs or communities of beach towels side by side and end to end. Others sat at picnic tables, in groups or solo. Again, it was easy to forget there was world chaos... and, again, a reminder was never far off... like the 200 or so people that I saw on the loop going back home, gathered on the lawn at First Church Congregational to hear a preacher tell them the media was lying to them and the police were lying to them and "the man" was lying to them. A state police car and town police car idled nearby keeping an eye on things. Though the gathering grossly violated the state's restriction on gatherings of no more than 25 people, it was given an apparent pass and exception. If it had been a neighborhood party though, it would have been broken up and the hosts likely fined. Again, there was an interesting double standard at work here.

My eyelids were like wet tarps, drooping, drooping, drooping. I was in bed by 9:30pm.

News: Our Fairfield First Selectwoman reported that, for the town, 613 residents to date had tested positive for the virus and 129 residents had passed. Ninety-two percent of those deaths were at nursing homes. Two-hundred and sixty-four of the 613 had recovered. CT overall had 43,091 cases, 3,989 deaths and 406 hospitalizations. Globally, coronavirus cases had surged over 6.6 million, with nearly 389K deaths, over 3.19 million recoveries. The U.S. had

1,903,783 cases with over 109K deaths, nearly 689K recoveries. New York had 382,837 cases and 30,164 deaths.

June 5. Of course I had gone to sleep too early, and so it was that I popped awake at about 2am. Jen had tried to return a FaceTime attempt I had made before going to sleep, but I had silenced my phone so didn't catch it. I texted her to acknowledge her attempt, and say I was now up, probably stirred by the rain. My text must have pinged her phone as she texted back, "It's raining? Rest... you are not up. Go back to sleep." But I was up and probably for the duration, so I FaceTimed her. We couldn't see each other as neither of us had turned on our lights, but our voices comforted one another. She said she had spent part of the day packing yesterday — all her sheet music and related books in her teaching room, as a prep to move if she decided to sign the broker contract and move ahead on selling her house. She had fixed the price in her head, which included the broker's commission. I told her about my neighbor's house selling, in a day, evidence of a hot market. She was further encouraged. She said she planned to take the sales income and re-invest it, in a condo or small house, and perhaps rent it, versus putting the money in the bank or in stocks, which she thought were still volatile. An attractive property in a good area that would retain and grow value was a good approach. She still hadn't given me a thumbs-up on moving into my place — I expected her hand would be forced one way or the other if she sold her house quickly. I really believed we could do it; I think *she* was only *half* sure.

I tired again and we signed off, but I was back up again at 4, and just went and showered to start the day. Dad was up early, too, texting me to say that, on the return home from Dave's West Virginia home, he had managed to turn "a 300-mile, five-hour trip into a 450-mile, ten-hour trip, first by getting lost in the horse country farmlands of Northern Virginia (my GPS went haywire) and then by deciding to drive the length of the Skyline Drive through the Shenandoah National Park followed by the Blue Ridge Parkway right down the crest of the Appalachian Mountains all the way to Roanoke! Such incredibly beautiful valleys, completely different from the canyons we'd just been bouncing through in Utah. Looooong drive, but I did it. Not sorry."

Before shouldering the day's news, I thought I would cruise over to Penfield Beach and catch the 5:21 sunrise — or whatever trace of it I could perceive given misty, drizzly, overcast conditions. It was the right move. It was just me, the sand, the serene water and a muted though beautiful horizon glow. And though I was alone, the evidence of other humans was everywhere. Yesterday had been a warm weather day, of course, and warm weather means Beach Day, and Beach Day means humans, and humans mean drinking vessels, apparel and sand toys, and all those things mean a percentage of them are going to get left behind on the beach, sometimes forgetfully but mostly thoughtlessly. And so it was that there were dozens of paper soda cups, and plastic bottles, plastic sand toys, hair scrunchies, t-shirts, shoes and more, all littering the beach, from Penfield to Jennings. And this was with the beachgoer capacity at *only 50%*, which continued to be the restriction at the parking lots. It was hard to be proud of being human some days. What remarkable creatures we are but what selfish, savage beasts we can be, too.

Amidst the splashes of litter, I noticed a horseshoe crab on its back, far up the beach, no doubt deposited there by choppy storm waters and surge. I assumed it was dead and picked it up by its lance-like pointy tail to check. But it squirmed. So I decided to be its savior and trekked it down to and into the water, and off it happily swam. I scanned the beach for others, noting two more. Same discovery, same end run. Then another two. And another two. I ended up saving seven of eight. The eighth had already expired and was limp and would soon be seagull breakfast. I wondered if anyone from the adjacent beachfront homes had seen my numerous rescue runs as I walked back to the truck to return home, my good deeds done.

Now I was ready for the news, which I hoped contained some, *any*, positivity.

A glimmer of hope on the rioting front: Residents of cities and towns across the country were taking back the streets and preventing attacks from looters, like in northwestern Idaho, where scores of natives armed themselves to guard their neighborhoods from a rumored arrival of ANTIFA agitators. The same was happening in Italian areas of The Bronx, and in Philly, San Antonio and other places.

And while global coronavirus cases were up another 100K from yesterday, to over 6.7 million worldwide, with over 393K deaths… and the U.S. had 1,923,189 of those cases to date with 110,179 deaths… and New York had 383,899 of those cases to date, with 30,281 deaths, the virus had pretty much been tamed according to many, despite continuing spikes here and there.

Even Jen was infected with positivity. I caught her ear for a moment while she was driving to Home Depot to pick up some sheetrock. She had a contractor at the house doing some touch-up painting and repair, ready to market the house. She said, "Even if I don't sell it, I have a place that makes me happy." So she would be content any way the ball bounced.

And on that happy note, I got an even happier communication, from the great optimist himself, President Trump. Nothing could deter him. Through all the attacks, all the mud slinging, all the attempts to derail him, he had stood firm, he had stuck to his plan, he had not wavered from the mission he set out to achieve when he took office. In a live press conference spurred by newly released very positive jobs data, he called today "a very big day for our country, an affirmation of all the work we've been doing. We had the greatest economy in the history of the world... and that strength let us get through this pandemic, largely through... Vaccines, we're doing incredibly well with that... Therapeutics, likewise, we're doing extremely well. Cures, we're doing well... We have ready-to-go two million vaccines if they check out for safety... If you look at so many different places that have opened up... the ones most energetic about opening, they are doing tremendous business... You have to remember... many of our states are closed... New York, New Jersey... They're starting to get open. And I hope they also use our National Guard. Call me. We'll be ready for them so fast, their heads will spin. We did it in Minneapolis... They were ripping that place apart... The National Guard went in and, in one night, it was over. You don't see a problem there anymore, not even a little... When we had our tremendous numbers (jobs), just prior to the China plague that floated in... we had the most people working in the history of our country, almost 160 million people... We're going to be back there. I think we're going to be actually back higher than ever before. And the only thing that can stop us is bad policy... What we've been doing is right. And the reason it's been — and is — so good is because the body was strong. We could actually close our country, save millions of lives, stop people very early on from China... We did a lot of things, then we ended up with empty cupboards. We went into a ventilator period the likes of which nobody's seen since the second world war. We mobilized... and then we did tests. We're over 20 million tests, more than anybody in the world... And when you do more testing, you have more cases. We have more cases than anybody because we do more testing than anybody. But this is outstanding, what's happened today. They thought the number would be a loss of nine million jobs, and it was a gain of almost three million jobs... This leads us on to a long period of growth. We'll go back to having the greatest economy anywhere in the world, nothing close... And I think we're going to have a very good upcoming few months. I think you're going to have a very good August, a very good July, maybe a spectacular September, but a spectacular October, November, December, and next year's going to be one of the best years we've ever had economically... Now we're opening and we're opening with a bang. And we've been talking about the V. This is better than a V. This is a rocket ship... Somebody told me yesterday, 'Sir, this is like a hurricane... You're back in business in one day, two days, three days, and it's devastating and it's hard, and this was a hurricane, and it's going to get better fast, because a lot of the numbers you see, they're early numbers. They're not even from this last month. And by the way... you had the greatest 50-day rally in the history of our exchanges... and we have a lot of protesters, and we have a pandemic... and we've made tremendous progress on both... but the people are now starting to return to work... We're a positive force and the key to the world in a sense. The fact that we're doing well, I see already that they're starting to do much better in other parts of the world... I'd like to just say that Renewal, Restoration and Recovery of the most vulnerable areas of America is going to be my focus... We're going to work together. It will all work out. Some governors may need a little help yet, but I think for the most part they're in good shape."

Adding to this positivity, he addressed the root of the problem that had spurred all the demonstrations and frustration across the country, demanding equal justice for all, perhaps something that had fallen by the wayside, had gotten rusty, principles that needed to be freshened. GF was not an exemplary individual but the police that confronted him may have overstepped boundaries for controlling him. These are not precise, predictable encounters. But, to be fair, all people should receive equal justice, about which the President said, "Equal justice under the law must mean that every American receive equal treatment in every encounter with law enforcement regardless of race, color, gender or creed... It's what our Constitution requires and it's what our country is all about."

"I just want to finish by saying to save the economy, we passed several pieces of critical legislation, totaling $3 trillion. We're set up to do more. I think we should because we are dominant... China was going to catch us in 2019 and become the dominant economy... I want them to have a great year, but we're going to have *better* years than they ever had. We have a much better system... We made Americans sure of themselves and we took care of families. We gave benefits and we sent $1,200 to every individual making less than $75K and $4,000 almost dollars to every family of four earning less than $150K... The job surge that we're seeing right now is widespread. Leisure and hospitality added 1.2 million jobs. Construction jobs are up 464K. Education and Health Services rose 424K. Retail Trade is up 368K. And Manufacturing rose to 225K. Everything you've seen this morning is unexpected. We also smashed expectations on the unemployment rate. The prediction was that the unemployment rate would rise to over 20% and, instead, it dropped to around, a little more than 13%... Today, if you think about it, is probably the greatest comeback in American history. But it's not going to stop here. It's going to keep going, because so many places are closed... they haven't even opened yet. We're going to be stronger than we were when we were riding high. And our stock market is almost — it's just short — of an all-time high."

And now *I* was high. High with excitement about the future, for a change. Sure, our summer might be muted. And we might continue to be saddled by masks. And be physically distant from each other for a while longer. And debate across the aisles. And life might be forever changed in so many ways at so many levels. But we still had our hope, and resilience, and roll-up-our-sleeves-can-do gumption, and we would get to the other side of this dark cloud, in some semblance of intactness, though some would be more intact than others. And we would rally like never before, and with a full-blown Strawberry Moon penumbral eclipse happening overhead. Of course. Because this was 2020, the most chaotic year in recent memory, when nothing was normal, nothing predictable, everything askew, even laughable in all its ridiculousness. And we were going to survive it one way or another. Is it New Year's Eve yet?

ABOUT THE AUTHOR

A 24-year resident of Fairfield, CT, Mike Lauterborn has been the Editor of Fairfield HamletHub online news service since Nov. 2011, serving Fairfield County, Connecticut. As a lad through high school, Mike was a dedicated journal keeper and graduated from college with a degree focused on creative writing. For the next 20+ years, Mike worked in corporate marketing, promotion and advertising leadership roles before transitioning to journalism, contracting with regional magazines, newspapers and online news services.

Mike has documented over four decades of American culture, including all of his past travels. One of the most significant of these was in Fall 2003, when Mike set off by van to follow in the path that acclaimed author John Steinbeck had taken in 1960 driving counter-clockwise around the perimeter of the United States to write "Travels with Charley". Mike used Steinbeck's book as his map for a similar journey that became "Chasing Charley".

In this *new* non-fiction book, Mike has taken on another adventure, an unplanned one that didn't take him much farther than his own community over several months as he witnessed how the Covid-19 disease set its aggressive hooks into the meat of the world, and thrashed it, and tore it apart, threatening the very existence of mankind. He recorded the pandemic's impact at the international and national levels, and observed its effects very first-hand in his own coastal community and amongst its citizens and leaders. He captured every aspect of the attack of this "invisible enemy" to create a detailed, insightful record of these times and road map for future generations to see how we handled the crisis and to learn how to face similar challenges as they arise, to perhaps avoid the "pandemonium" that took us all by surprise.

Printed in the United States
By Bookmasters